SPORTS IN HIGHER EDUCATION

Issues and Controversies in College Athletics

Edited by

GARY SAILES

San Diego, CA

Bassim Hamadeh, CEO and Publisher

Michael Simpson, Vice President of Acquisitions

Jamie Giganti, Managing Editor

Jess Busch, Graphic Design Supervisor

Brian Fahey, Licensing Associate

Kate McKellar, Interior Designer

First published in the United States of America in 2014 by Cognella, Inc.

Trademark Notice: Product or corporate names may be trademarks or registered trademarks, and are used only for identification and explanation without intent to infringe.

Cover image copyright© 2008 by iStockphoto.com / Trawick-Images
Cover image copyright© by Shutterstock Images / maxstockphoto
Cover image copyright© by Shutterstock Images / fengzheng
Cover image copyright© by Shutterstock Images / cozyta
Cover image copyright© by Shutterstock Images / Pierre E. Debbas
Cover image copyright© by Shutterstock Images / Mark Herreid

Printed in the United States of America

ISBN: 978-1-60927-486-3 (pbk) / 978-1-60927-487-0 (br)

www.cognella.com   800.200.3908

Contents

American college sports have reached a period of tremendous growth and wealth since their early days in 1906. Today, the NCAA boasts participation of more than 430,000 student-athletes in sports at more than 1,000 public and private colleges and universities on nearly 18,000 teams within its three divisions (I, II, and III). The NCAA receives annual revenues in excess of $500 million, derived chiefly from media, sponsorships, and ticket programs tied to its men's basketball national championship tournament. NCAA Division I athletic programs, which typically house the association's largest schools, has received the brunt of attention and criticism from scholars and the American media.

American college sports scandals have dominated the news in the American media landscape the past year. News of coaching sex scandals, huge monetary payments to student-athletes, inflated coaches' salaries, and student-athletes both breaking the rules leading to suspensions and declaring for the professional draft in football and basketball prior to graduation have caused the major controlling interests in college sports, namely the National Collegiate Athletic Association (NCAA), to scurry and clamor into damage-control mode. The criticisms aimed at the NCAA for its lack of institution control over its member schools, coaches, and student-athletes have been the target of the media and academic scholars for decades. Consequently, in no period in college sports history have the scandals been so serious and numerous as they have been in the 2011–12 school year. The demand and outcry for

INTRODUCTION

reform has been wide and clear. University presidents have extended their control over their respective athletic departments and collectively developed stiffer penalties for coaches, athletes, and teams that break the rules. Further scrutiny has been established to ensure that schools and programs are in compliance with NCAA rules and regulations.

Despite the recent major negative developments in American college sports, alumni loyalty and fan interest in college sports competition and its rivalries are at an all-time high. The contract the NCAA has with CBS and other affiliates to televise every game in the men's national basketball championship and Division I bowl football games is unprecedented. The Big Ten Network, ESPNU, and other developing college sports media entities are a testament to the interest and growth in Division I athletic competition. Fan attendance is at an all-time high as are the revenue streams generated by fan and alumni interest. College sports are fun, entertaining, and a venue for preferred programming among sports fans across the globe.

The popularity of college sports has been seen to bolster freshman admission applications and enrollments—e.g., the Flutie Factor (more on this later)—on a university or college campus when their men's or women's basketball or football teams receive national attention as they make a run for or compete in a national NCAA Division I championship. The increased interest in college sports has extended to the classroom where courses focusing on American college sports are taught at colleges and universities nationwide. Sport Management and Sport Sociology faculty members teach this course to enrolled students in classes that have extensive wait-lists of non-enrolled students looking to get into these popular classes. At Indiana University, interest in the class was so extensive that extra sections of the course and the recruitment of instructors became necessary.

This book is the outgrowth of a project I initiated to fill a gap in the academic topic of sports in higher education. I teach undergraduate and graduate classes on college sports at Indiana University and was surprised to learn there was no comprehensive textbook on college sports that I could use as the main textbook in my classes. Consequently, in the development of my courses I contacted colleagues who are members and scholars in the North American Society for the Sociology of Sport (NASSS) and who teach courses in college sports. I requested that they provide me with sample course materials and titles of the textbooks they used, and assumed someone would provide me with the title of a comprehensive text on sports in higher education. What I learned was that everyone who replied to my request also found no adequate comprehensive textbook and had to construct a reader (as I was forced to do) for their respective classes. Moving on, I surveyed faculty members who taught courses in college sports at their respective universities and inquired about what topics they covered and what should be included in a comprehensive textbook for such a course. This textbook is the outgrowth of that survey.

This anthology contains nine comprehensive chapters, each written by scholars with strong expertise and research experience in their respective topic areas within college sports. The chapters in this book are History, Governance, Commercialism, Student-Athlete Experience, Gender, Deviance, Race and Ethnicity, Coaching and Administration, and Reform. The authors for each chapter are members of NASSS and have a scholarly interest in college sports. This collaboration would not have been possible without their interest, experience, dedication, and research knowledge.

I believe readers will find this anthology complete and intellectually stimulating. It was my intent to take the reader on an extensive inside view of college sports to evoke thought and dialogue. I also believe faculty members and students will find the material indulging yet challenging. Interest in college sports goes far beyond box scores, national championships, and school spirit. There are dozens of issues that will ultimately stimulate dialogue in any class and add to the interest and success of such a course. Also, faculty members who adopt this textbook for their classes will receive ancillary materials, which include a sample course syllabus, PowerPoint lecture notes, and sample test questions.

Today, sports, especially college athletics, seem to occupy every facet of American society. College athletics have been the topic of discussion recently in many of our prominent social spheres—judicial, legislative, and educational systems to name a few. Sport scholar George Sage (1990) noted, "The person who studies sport without studying its history will never truly understand any given state of sport or the forces operating to change it" (p. 7). Therefore, to better understand how we have arrived at our current state of sports, this chapter will present a brief history of college athletics in the United States.

The chapter will follow the progression of college athletics from competitions that were student-led to the current administrative structure. The material presented will focus on (1) early student-led sporting experiences, (2) movement to faculty- and administrator-controlled sport, (3) creation of the National Collegiate Athletic Association (NCAA), (4) early reform issues, (5) early college sporting experiences for women, (6) further calls for reform, and (7) our current state. This should not be mistaken as a complete history of college athletics as such a feat could not fit within the confines of one book, let alone one chapter. Thus, the material included should lay a foundation for the chapters that follow.

The goal of this chapter is to show the threads woven through time that link the beginnings of student-led sporting experiences with the current reality of college athletics in the United States. The college sporting structure in the United States is unlike any other in the world and this chapter will highlight the cultural contexts from which such a system grew and flourished.

1

A HISTORY OF COLLEGE ATHLETICS

BOBBI KNAPP

EARLY STUDENT-LED SPORTING EXPERIENCES

During the early to mid-nineteenth century opportunities for postsecondary education were limited. College enrollment was often limited to white, upper-class males. The few institutions that existed were small liberal arts institutions that emphasized classical studies such as Greek and Latin. Of these, Harvard and Yale sat at the top of the hierarchy with other schools often viewed as inferior. Nearly all of the colleges had strong religious connections, as seen in the preponderance of clergymen in the role of college presidencies. These presidents maintained paternalistic policies that mandated rigid class schedules and control over student life that extended into the extracurricular.

In an attempt to distract themselves from the rigors of their strict college lives, many students created their own extracurricular activities. Literary societies, which provided the students with a place to discuss current literature not found within the rigid structure of the college curriculum, were some of the first student-led organizations. It was not uncommon by the late 1800s for colleges to include speech, debate, and musical groups. It was out of this oppressive classical educational environment that college sport developed and soon came to dominate students' extracurricular lives. Sport competition became a common distraction from the normal college life, which was often seen as repressive during this time. In fact, some faculty members and administrators also came to back sport as they believed it to be a positive force in maintaining student discipline and limiting students' demonstrations.

Early on, student-led sport began as very informal and impromptu games. As far as sports were concerned, there was very little organization at the time. Students scrapped together equipment, such as bats and balls, and held their competitions on vacant fields. Games were enjoyed more as opportunities for recreation and exercise than as competitions. For the most part, faculty members' attitudes toward extracurricular student-led sporting activities were tolerant unless the participants were seen as being rowdy or placing lives or college property at danger, in which case sanctions would be made to cease such activities.

Early colleges were often isolated due to the lack of developed communication and transportation systems, so the growing desire for competition had to be met within the institutional system itself. Thus, interclass struggles came to dominate the extracurricular in the nineteenth century and often continued into the twentieth century. These interclass competitions, also referred to as scraps or rushes, often pitted underclassmen against upperclassmen. These contests were often viewed as initiation rites for the incoming freshmen. In 1827, on the first Monday of the fall term, sophomores at Harvard were pitted against the freshmen in what some have termed a medieval-like football competition. What came to be known as Bloody Monday was a soccer-like contest called football between two teams of nearly one hundred people each. Bloody Monday-type competitions soon became a tradition at Harvard and similar contests spread to other institutions including Yale in the 1840s. These competitions were not limited to Bloody Monday and took various forms throughout the year depending on the college. Lacking any strict policy on interclass competitions, college officials often only intervened in times of crisis.

Soon student-led sports became more organized, and at the center of that organization was the team captain. Captains were often elected to their positions based upon their playing abilities as well as their leadership qualities. While other students were involved with the scheduling of games and maintenance of team finances, the team captain determined who played and in what position. The captain also set the training regimen for the team, organized practices, and formulated plays and team strategies. The captain was instrumental in providing stability to the organization from one year to the next. Given the growing popularity of sports on campus, and their central role to the team, the captain was often an esteemed position and was looked upon as the key leader in the campus community.

The movement to more organized student-led sports took several forms including dedicated sporting spaces and increased competitive spirit, which in turn spurred movements toward recruiting and higher sporting costs. Harvard is believed to be the first college to establish a gymnasium in one of its dining halls, in 1826. In the same year Yale began the process of clearing ground for an outdoor gymnasium. As was often the case, these two schools set the precedence for others to follow, and follow they did. Just a year later, gymnasiums sprung up at Amherst, Brown, and Williams. By the mid-1800s, a high degree of competitive spirit began to imbibe the college sporting culture. As a result, as early as the 1870s and 1880s many athletic teams were engaged in recruiting talented students from the surrounding preparatory and high schools. It often fell upon the shoulders of the captain to search out such talent. In addition to recruiting, the higher emphasis on beating one's opponent pushed many clubs to start training tables (specially prepared food for improved athletic performance), improve their means of travel, and to purchase more expensive equipment. These rising costs meant that many athletic teams were often in debt, leaving many faculty members embarrassed by the student-led teams' inability to maintain fiscal responsibility.

The rule of student-led sport was relatively short-lived and was soon replaced by faculty and administrative control. The popularity of student-led sports in many ways contributed to administrative takeover. The move to decentralize students' control was based on several factors including increased costs, inability to control athletic growth, and an awakened understanding of the potential role of sport in promoting colleges. As noted earlier, the financial irresponsibility of

student-led teams was seen as an embarrassment to many faculty members. Also, with the increased focus on winning came the push—and increased costs—to recruit better players and to hire professional coaches, both of which contributed to outside forces taking over formerly student-controlled sports.

University administrators soon came to understand that people could more easily relate to their institutions through their athletic programs rather than through other academic or extracurricular activities. In many people's minds, the determination of whether one was a viable institution rested on one's performance not in the classroom but on the athletic field. As such, college presidents began to use athletics to promote their institutions and in so doing often took over both athletic costs and the control of athletics. Shortly after the varsity crew team's win at the 1875 Saratoga regatta, noting the publicity received from the win, Cornell President Andrew D. White absorbed the team's $1,100 debt and charged it to the college's advertising fund. It was his belief that the victory did more to promote Cornell than if the board of trustees had spent $100,000 to attempt to do the same.

EARLY INTERCOLLEGIATE ATHLETIC SPORTS PROGRAMS

Student-led sports rapidly expanded from unorganized, thrown-together games on the college green, to widely ritualized interclass skirmishes, to full-blown intercollegiate competitions. Much of this early structure of college sport was based upon the system in place in England, most notably at Oxford and Cambridge. Yet, the process of transformation was unique for each sport and soon deterred from the precedent set by their English cousins.

Crew—The First Intercollegiate Competition

Taking cues from students at Oxford and Cambridge, who founded boat clubs in the 1810s and 1820s, students at Yale and Harvard had formed boating clubs on their campuses by 1844. As Rader (2009) noted, the Harvard oarsmen first used their boats mainly as a means of transporting members across the inlet to enjoy drinks in Boston establishments. The Harvard crew also competed in Boston-area regattas against a number of noncollegiate clubs before engaging in the first American intercollegiate sporting event.

In the summer of 1852, a member of the Yale crew was approached by the superintendent of the Boston, Concord, and Montreal Railroad, James N. Elkins, about being part of a regatta that would be used to promote a new railroad line into the heart of New Hampshire's White Mountains resort area. The site of the proposed race was the tranquil Winnipesaukee River as it entered Lake Winnipesaukee, which, conveniently, could be viewed from one of Elkin's observation trains. Superintendent Elkins offered to pay all expenses if the Yale crew member put together a regatta on the lake between Yale and Harvard. Seeing it as an opportunity for an all-expense-paid vacation, members of the Yale and Harvard crews quickly agreed to the regatta. With little dedicated training, the teams took to the water in front of an estimated one thousand spectators and completed the first intercollegiate athletic competition in roughly fourteen minutes, with the Harvard crew earning the victory.

Although the Yale faculty banned the competition for the next two years, the seed of intercollegiate athletics had been planted and it didn't take long for it to flourish. Within three years, Harvard and Yale were back at it, and in 1858 the College Union Regatta Association was formed with Harvard, Yale, Brown, and Trinity as the founding members. The association held regattas near Worcester, MA, in 1859 and 1860, both drawing between fifteen thousand and twenty thousand spectators. The 1859 event, which Harvard again won, made front-page news in the *New York Herald*. The 1860 regatta is perhaps more

Oxford–Harvard boat race, London, 1869

notable due to the events after the race. Harvard fans celebrated their team's victory by collecting items to burn in a huge bonfire, resulting in some physical altercations with the local police.

In an attempt to improve its competitive odds, Yale constructed a new boathouse through funds raised by undergraduates, alumni support, and a promissory note from two Yale professors. Yale also hired a professional coach, its first, to train the men for competition. The changes apparently worked, as Yale soon after captured its first win against Harvard in a dual meet. But it would be Harvard, in 1869, that would go on to compete in the first international intercollegiate competition when its crew went up against Oxford in London.

Amherst–Dartmouth baseball game, Hanover, NH, 1890

Baseball—A National Pastime

Baseball soon followed crew as an intercollegiate sport. In 1859, Williams played Amherst, ending in a 73–32 victory for Amherst. After its trouncing, the Williams team accused Amherst of recruiting its pitcher from a local blacksmith shop (Reiss, 1997). The Civil War temporarily disrupted the growth of college baseball, but by the late 1860s and early 1870s most colleges fielded baseball teams.

Throughout most of the nineteenth century, baseball was the most widely played sport on college campuses. During the later part of the century, the Harvard Base Ball Club, formed in 1862, dominated intercollegiate competition with a seven-year undefeated streak. In search for competition, it was not uncommon for college teams to play local high schools. Some of the better college teams even competed against professional baseball teams. From 1868–1874, 60 percent of Yale's games were played against professional teams (Reiss, 1997). During the summer, many of the college players, often under aliases, traveled with these same professional teams. It was these connections to the professional game that would become the focus of many reformers' criticisms in the early twentieth century.

Track and Field—Taking the Prize

In the 1860s many colleges participated in field days, which were devoted to intramural-type contests of running, jumping, and throwing (similar to the field days still popular in many American grade schools). The first intercollegiate track and field competition took place in 1873 when, as part of the Saratoga regatta, James Gordon Bennett Jr., publisher of the *New York Herald*, provided a silver challenge cup valued at $500 for the winner of a two-mile race. Three men, one each from

Amherst, Cornell, and McGill (Canada), competed in the event. The runner from McGill earned the cup and thus an international player became the first winner of a United States intercollegiate track competition.

The popularity of track and field continued to grow after this initial competition. The next year the Saratoga competition became more organized with the creation of the Intercollegiate Association of Amateur Athletics of America (IC4A), which remains the oldest college association in the United States still in existence.

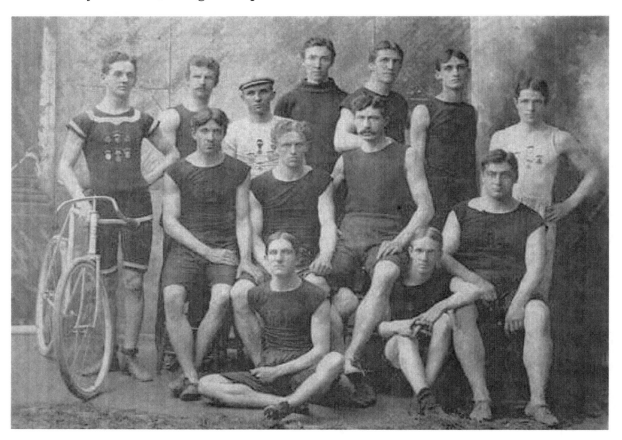

Washington & Jefferson College Track and Field Team, 1895

expanded to five events—the 100-yard dash, 120-yard high hurdles, mile run, three-mile run, and a seven-mile walk. It was common for track and field athletes to compete for valuable prizes such as challenge cups or even cash. In 1876, college track and field

Football—The Great Spectacle

Baseball may have been considered the national pastime, but football soon came to dominate intercollegiate athletics. The development of football in the United States was a bit more complicated than crew or baseball, as it took several forms. After being defeated by Princeton in baseball, the Rutgers Varsity Football Club challenged Princeton to a game. This game, held in 1869, is considered the first intercollegiate football match, which Rutgers won 6–4. The game played was more the soccer-type game that developed out of the Eton School in England, called association football. By 1870, most of the eastern schools were playing soccer football, including Columbia, Princeton, Rutgers, and Yale.

In England, another form of football had developed at the Rugby School, referred to as rugby football. Legend has it that during an 1823 game, William Webb-Ellis, a Rugby student, mistakenly picked up the ball and ran with it. This "mistake" ushered in a competing code of football, rugby football, which revolved around the running game. Back in America, Harvard refused to join the other eastern schools in soccer football, instead choosing to develop its own type of football called the Boston game. The Boston game had more in common with rugby than with soccer. In 1874, McGill University in Canada traveled to Cambridge to play Harvard in two games—the first was under the rules of the Boston game, which Harvard won, and the second game was under rugby rules, which produced a tie. The Harvard squad found the rugby game enjoyable and never returned to its Boston-style game after beating McGill in a rugby football match the following fall. The first intercollegiate rugby football game between colleges in the United States occurred in the spring of 1875 between Harvard and Tufts College.

It was a game scheduled the next year, between Harvard and Yale, that really set the stage for football as we now know it. The two influential schools agreed to play under modified rules in New Haven in the fall of 1876.

Yale would go on to defeat Harvard in this initial matchup (foreshadowing a similar outcome for years to come). Following the game, Princeton and Columbia, along with Harvard and Yale, formed the Intercollegiate Football Association (IFA). The IFA adopted modified rugby rules and created a season-ending championship game. The first championship game played between Yale and Princeton (won by Yale) began the tradition of the "big game" played on Thanksgiving Day.

Americanizing the Game

Major modifications to the game throughout the 1880s helped mold it into the Americanized version of football with which we are now familiar. No person figured more prominently in those changes than Walter Camp, the "Father of American Football," who played for Yale from 1875–1882, first as an undergraduate and then as a medical student.

Walter Camp, pictured as Yale's captain, 1878–79

Camp continued his involvement with Yale football until his death in 1925.

During his tenure with the [Yale] Bulldogs, Camp, as well as other football rules committee members from Princeton and Harvard, was instrumental in instituting several game-changing modifications to the sport. Some of the more notable changes included the institution of blockers, a new method of putting the ball into play, required progression on the field, methods of scoring, and forms of tackling. In rugby-style football, players could not run interference for the ball carrier. In the new modified rugby football game (referred to as simply football from now on), teams from Yale and Princeton created plays that foreshadowed modern blocking routes. The teams developed a method of protecting the ball carrier by mobilizing players to each side of the runner.

Another major modification was the introduction of a line of scrimmage that effectively separated the offense and defense while the ball was put into play by the snapper-back, who originally snapped the ball back with his foot. This position, renamed the center, was later allowed to use his hands to pass the ball back to his team's quarterback. An unanticipated consequence of the new style of play was that unless the team in possession of the ball fumbled, kicked, or scored, they remained in possession of the ball. Some teams used this to their advantage, maintaining possession of the ball for an entire half without relinquishing the ball or scoring, making for some very boring games. To amend this oversight, the rules committee implemented the down-yardage rule, which required teams to gain five yards in three attempts or lose possession of the ball. This rule was also the reason for the "gridiron" pattern on the

football field as chalk lines were laid down every five yards.

Other changes included different methods of scoring and new ways of tackling. Methods of scoring changed several times from the 1880s to 1910s, as the style of the game itself changed from a kicking game to more of a running one. In 1883, teams received two points for touchdowns and one point for a safety. Points for touchdowns would change to four points in the late 1880s, five points by the late 1890s, and finally to six points in 1912 (Reiss, 1997). The implementation of the low tackle in 1888 helped further distinguish this game from rugby, which did not allow tackling below the waist. It was also this modification that would contribute to the football crisis of the early twentieth century.

Growing Popularity

Before football would reach its crisis point, it would first see an incredible spike in its popularity on campuses across the country. It is hard to imagine now, but up until the mid-1880s football routinely attracted just a few hundred students and alumni to games. But by the late 1890s, football on many college campuses was replacing baseball as the most popular sport. Although there were most likely several factors at play in this transformation, the instigation of the "big game" on Thanksgiving Day—pitting rival schools against each other—and the ensuing media frenzy probably had the biggest effect.

The Thanksgiving Day game became a spectacle of pageantry and sport. The New York games especially became huge social events. Streets were crammed with people decked out in their team's colors. Writing of the spectacle, Richard Harding Davis noted:

Everything on four wheels and that will hold twenty men on its top … goes up Fifth Avenue on Thursday morning. It is like a circus procession many miles long. It begins at ten in the morning, four hours before the game. … There is everything, from the newest English brake to omnibuses. … All blanketed in the true colors … every coach carries twenty shouting men and exciting young women smothered in furs; and the flags, as they … fill the air with color … and the coaches themselves toss like ships in a heavy sea, rocking

Thanksgiving Day game played in New York netted $5,432.50, and just two years later the gate receipts jumped to $14,425.10 (Oriard, 1993).

The Football Crisis

Part of the football spectacle was what many at the time considered the sheer brutality of the game, which often resulted in serious injury. The move to allow tackling below the waist is often referenced as the cause of the increased brutality and injuries on the football field. With this change in defensive style, there was a resulting movement to "mass momentum" offensive plays. As indicated by the

1914 Yale–Harvard highly attended football game

from side to side … as the men on top jump up and down in time to the rhythm of the rival cheers. (Reiss, 1997, p. 117)

The battle to sell more newspapers led many papers, such as the *New York Herald*, *World*, and *Journal*, to expand their sporting coverage, and the Thanksgiving Day game drew their attention to football (Rader, 2009). The expanded coverage helped draw even more spectators to the games. The Thanksgiving Day game played by Yale and Princeton in 1879 provided each team with $238.76 in gate receipts. By 1889, a

name, these plays amassed a large number of players aimed at a particular point in the defense. Although a number of mass plays existed, the flying wedge, invented in Harvard in 1892, was probably the most infamous. The play involved about nine players falling back and then when signaled coming together at a point directly in front of the ball carrier (Moore, 1967). The play amassed a number of victims and was abolished within two years, but other forms of mass momentum plays continued.

Mass momentum plays, lack of proper safety equipment, and an American spirit that often encouraged winning at all costs

An image from 1909 University of Washington yearbook providing a comical take on the dangers of football

propelled football into crisis mode at the turn of the twentieth century. In 1902, a dozen deaths were attributed to football (numbers refer to all football levels unless otherwise indicated). Just two years later twenty-one players were killed and more than two hundred were said to have been injured. By this time a number of universities had abolished football, often due to the real or perceived brutality of the sport. Institutions such as Indiana, Columbia, Marquette, Northwestern, Stanford, and California dropped the sport; others, such as West Point and Annapolis, limited play to their campuses. The 1905 season is often seen as the turning point in college football brutality, a point precipitated by two

noteworthy incidents. In a late season game, Bob Maxwell, a lineman on the Swarthmore team, was left bloody and mangled after receiving a continuous pounding from the Penn players during the execution of their 11–4 victory. Although Maxwell would go on to play professionally for a number of years, Harold P. Moore of Union College would not be so lucky. Moore died of injuries suffered in a late-season game against New York University. These incidents, as well as numerous other injuries and deaths attributed to football, would be the catalyst for momentous changes in intercollegiate athletics.

Basketball—A Slow But Steady Contender

By the late nineteenth century, baseball and football were deeply entrenched in American college life. Unlike the specialization we see in today's athletic world, during this time the all-around athlete was more common and more revered. In an attempt to fill male athletes' time between the end of football and the beginning of the baseball season, Luther Gulick, the head of the Physical Training Department at the Springfield YMCA Training School, challenged his instructors to come up with a game that would engage natural body movements and could be played inside during the harsh winter months. In the fall of 1891, James Naismith, an instructor at the school, introduced the world to the game of basketball.

The game of basketball is unique in that it was created in the United States, and also because it was a game quickly taken up by women college students across the country. In the decades immediately preceding Naismith's creation, there was an increase in the number of women enrolled in colleges.

Dr. James Naismith

Senda Berenson, founder of women's basketball, 1892

In large part, this increase was due to the creation of more women's colleges and the expansion of coeducational opportunities spurred by the Morrill Land Grant Act of 1862, which provided states with land to support new colleges and universities.

In 1892, just a year after Naismith invented the game, Senda Berenson, a physical education instructor at Smith College, modified the rules to make the game more socially acceptable for women to play. At this time popular opinion, which was often supported by the medical establishment, thought women to be inherently weak and unable to engage in strenuous physical activity. Seeing the potential benefits of basketball for women's physical and mental health, Berenson modified the game, dividing the court into three parts with players assigned to specific areas. This modified version afforded less opportunity to run and dribble the ball. In the first intercollegiate game, played in 1896 at the Page Street

Armory in San Francisco, Stanford defeated the University of California–Berkeley team, 2–1. It would not be until eleven years later that Cal would play its first men's intercollegiate basketball game.

Some have suggested, interestingly, that the popularity of the sport with women may have originally stunted the growth of men's basketball. Again, at this time women were generally seen as inferior to men. Also, in a rapidly changing world spurred by urbanization, industrialization, and the diminishing frontier space, many males turned to sports to prove their masculinity, and a sport played by women limited men's opportunity to do this. Due to the uniforms, the weather-sheltered courts, and the fact that girls played the game, many football fans of the time referred to basketball as a "sissy" game. Although the sport did not rise to a spectator-centered sport until the mid-1930s, it too would have

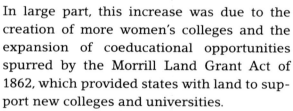

a powerful impact on the creation of college athletics as we know it.

CREATION OF THE NCAA

A revolutionary development in the history of intercollegiate athletics was the creation of a multi-institutional organization that formed in response to the football crisis of the early twentieth century, as well as to questions of morality and sportsmanship. As noted earlier, the 1905 football season claimed a number of victims and the level of brutality and number of injuries drew the attention of those in positions of power. President Theodore Roosevelt convened a meeting with representatives from the big three—Harvard, Yale, and Princeton. Coaches, faculty members, and alumni who were invited to the White House Conference on Football left agreeing to conduct themselves and their teams based on the written and unwritten rules of the game. The involvement of the president suggests the seriousness of the issue.

Real reform efforts, however, came from Henry McCracken, who was chancellor of New York University in 1905 when Union College football player Harold P. Moore was killed in a football matchup between the two schools. McCracken pushed for reform and called a meeting with nearby college presidents. This gathering culminated in a nationwide invitation for colleges to convene at the end of the month to create a new football rules committee. Delegates from more than sixty colleges attended the meeting in New York and quickly agreed on formation of the Intercollegiate Athletic Association (IAA). The purpose of the IAA was to set the standards of conduct for the member colleges. By 1906 the IAA's rules committee

had already implemented new regulations intended to reduce the level of brutality. Yet, the 1909 football season saw an uptick in fatalities, prompting members of the rules committee to implement new rules formed especially to abolish mass momentum plays. In the following year, the IAA was renamed the National Collegiate Athletic Association, which it remains today. For nearly its first half century, the NCAA set the rules for various sports and organized a number of national tournaments, but it was left up to the colleges to self-discipline.

Early Reform Issues

Relatively early in the formation of men's intercollegiate athletics, issues arose and with them came cries for reform. Although preceded by a number of smaller attempts, the Carnegie Report of 1929 is probably the best known and the most comprehensive early reform document. After fielding similar requests without pursuing them, the trustees of the Carnegie Foundation in January 1926 authorized the inquiry of college athletics with the goal of shedding light on the state of athletics, both good and bad, and based on that to provide suggested points of improvement. The researchers took careful steps in the organization, deployment, and analysis for this project. Input from eighty-three experts was requested in selecting the areas of college athletics that needed further scrutiny. It was decided early on by the researchers that simply sending out questionnaires and evaluating the responses would not be enough to really get to the heart of the issues that plagued athletics at that time. Instead, five researchers set out to conduct site visits with 130 colleges and universities (the final number included in the report was 112) and talk with hundreds of coaches, faculty members, students, alumni, and others connected to the institutions to provide more meaningful findings. Two years later, in 1928, nearly all of the data collection was complete and work began on putting together the report. In 1929, the report, totaling more than three hundred fifty pages, was released and its contents remain relevant today. The report focused on commercialization, recruiting and subsidization, professional coaches, abandonment of amateurism, diminishing educational values, and lack of student involvement in decision making as some of the most damaging aspects of college athletics. To those writing the report, it came down to the twin evils of commercialism and professionalism (Benford, 2007). As Clotfelter noted in 2009, despite numerous changes in college athletics since the report was published, it still provides an amazingly accurate depiction of college athletics today.

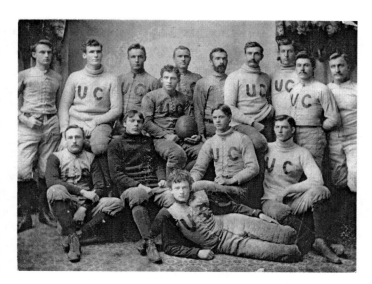

University of Chicago Football Team, 1892—Stagg is in center holding the football

Commercialization

The Carnegie Report defined commercialism as "the placing of a higher value upon monetary and material returns, whether direct or indirect, from any athletic activity than is placed upon its returns in recreation, health, and physical and moral well-being" (Savage, Bentley, McGovern, & Smiley, 1929, p. 11). Commercialism was an overarching term that encompassed a plethora of issues such as gate receipts, press coverage, dishonesty, gambling, recruiting, subsidizing, athletic costs, and disconnect from the academic mission. Football, with its increasing public interest, press coverage, alumni involvement, gate receipts, and questionable recruiting practices, often became the focus of discussions of commercialism—and the Thanksgiving Day Big Game was held up as the prime example.

Many of the issues enveloped in the term *commercialization* are interrelated. The increased emphasis on winning pushed programs to amp up their recruiting efforts, which in turn increased athletic costs due to traveling, equipment, and facilities, and this in turn put a higher emphasis on collecting more gate receipts—and all worked together to further separate the athletic program from the academic mission of the college. The importance of winning is evident in the example of the University of Chicago and its president, William Rainey Harper. Upon being hired as president of the newly formed university, Harper quickly set out to produce winning teams as a means of publicizing the institution. In 1892, Harper hired former Yale standout Amos Alonzo Stagg as football coach for the university, making Stagg the first professional coach in college football.

Issues of recruiting and subsidizing followed the increased emphasis on winning in college programs across the nation. The Carnegie Report noted the use of aggressive recruiting tactics and the use of—and often alumni-sponsored—"slush funds" to subsidize athletes. The 1929 Iowa football scandal exemplified this issue. Five months before the release of the Carnegie Report, the Big Ten Conference (the oldest currently existing conference, formed in 1895) took preemptive action by suspending the University of Iowa from the conference for recruiting violations (some scholars have suggested this was an attempt to deflect attention from other conference schools). Upon taking on leadership of the Big Ten as commissioner in 1922, Major John L. Griffith quickly endeavored to reform athletic programs within the conference. In 1927, the conference adopted regulations dealing with recruiting and alumni involvement in athletics, which stated that athletes should not receive any financial awards (scholarships, loans, or remission of tuition) based on their athletic skills. Further, the granting of any money by alumni was deemed unethical (Schmidt, 2007). In a conference meeting in May 1929, leaders in the conference officially suspended athletic relations with the university based on evidence of alumni-driven recruiting and subsidizing violations. Evidence presented showed that an alumni slush fund was maintained with university knowledge to subsidize athletes (especially football). Some athletes were allowed to take out promissory notes that were never repaid. Others collected money for jobs they didn't work or at which they put in minimal hours. Standout football players such as Tom Stidham were offered monthly fees to play football for the Hawkeyes. A self-investigation uncovered additional violations

not presented by the conference committee. Yet when the Carnegie Report was released it indicated that evidence of subsidization was found at all but two schools in the Big Ten—Illinois and Chicago—thus adding to the fodder that Iowa was used as a scapegoat.

Another result of the increased focus on winning was inflating costs of athletic programs. The Carnegie Report noted that since 1906 the costs of intercollegiate athletics had "mounted amazingly" (Savage, Bentley, McGovern, & Smiley, 1929, p. 32). In fact, by the end of World War I, an NCAA survey found that one hundred fifty colleges were spending a combined total of more than $1 million on their athletic programs every year. This amount is unimaginable in today's intercollegiate athletics where some programs alone are spending more than $100 million a year, but the amount needs to be understood within the context of the time, when $1 million was a sizable amount even when it was divided among the lot.

Paralleling the rising costs was the push to attract more gate receipts. By 1903 universities such as Harvard were starting to build reinforced concrete stadiums that could hold tens of thousands of spectators. Not long after, Yale completed its sixty-seven thousand-seat capacity stadium, with similar structures popping up throughout the country in the 1920s. This early example of our current day "arms race" in intercollegiate athletics was all in an attempt to cash in on football's growing popularity.

This movement from student-centered to spectator-centered sport often brought with it an increasing disconnect between athletics and the academic mission of the institutions. The Carnegie Report noted the emphasis on sports often came at the expense of the educational program at the institutions under review. As the spectacle of intercollegiate athletics increased, it demanded more time from the athletes. Athletes had to dedicate more time to practice in an attempt to create and maintain successful teams—with success being measured in wins. More games were necessary to appease the growing appetite of the fans and to garner more gate receipts. Also, the time spent in traveling increased as colleges and universities scheduled games with institutions across the country.

Another cause of academic disconnect was the move for many institutions to recruit athletes who were not necessarily students. In the 1860s and 1870s some colleges in the Northeast hired professional rowers to spur the crew on to victory. Similarly, the "tramp athlete" was a well-known secret of early intercollegiate athletics. These guys would travel the country getting paid to play football for different colleges, sometimes within the same season and almost always under a new assumed name. Any attempt to engage such athletes in the academic rigor of higher education rarely had positive outcomes. Indeed, some athletes were quite clear about their intentions. In the late 1870s, Princeton President James McCosh was told by a student that he was there to play football not to study (Ingham, 1978). Inconsistency with the academic mission can be further seen in some of the actions taken by coaches to keep players on the field. It is said that Coach Stagg at the University of Chicago would take it upon himself to talk with a professor in support of maintaining a player's eligibility (Reiss, 1997). Such revelations caused many to be concerned about the influence college athletics was having on the educational mission.

Professionalism

Commercialism went hand in hand with issues of professionalism. The paid coach symbolized for many at this time all that was wrong with intercollegiate athletics. As further proof of the increasing disconnect between athletics and academics, one just has to examine the salaries of coaches and professors. When Harvard hired its first professional football coach in 1905, the athletic committee agreed to pay William Reid $3,500, which was slightly less than the average salary for a full professor. Yet in addition to his base salary Reid received additional funding from Harvard's alumni, which catapulted his salary closer to what the president of the university received at the time (Ingham, 1978). It was not uncommon for some of the bigger-name coaches such as Reid and Fielding Yost at the University of Michigan to receive compensation that superseded what full professors at the same institution were being paid. This imbalance in salary structure put into question the academic integrity of the institutions, as professional coaches often pushed the limits of academic integrity to ensure wins, and thus keep their jobs. As noted earlier, this increased focus on winning in college athletics had a number of significant ramifications.

EARLY COLLEGE SPORTING EXPERIENCES FOR WOMEN

At this same time, women's sporting opportunities at the college level were beginning to develop. As noted earlier, modified basketball for women was developed by Senda Berenson in 1892. Not long after, in 1901, Constance Applebee introduced field hockey to college women in America. Applebee had been heavily involved with the development of the game in England before coming to the United States. A few decades later, Applebee helped in the development of lacrosse for women college athletes. Perhaps surprising to some, at the turn of the century it was not uncommon for women in colleges outside the Northeast to have opportunities to participate in varsity athletics.

Oregon Agricultural College (Oregon State) women's basketball team, 1900

Constance Applebee, field hockey, circa 1903

Such opportunities for women were soon limited by popular notions, often instigated by medical professionals, that any vigorous physical activity might damage women's reproductive systems. In her book, *The Eternally Wounded Woman*, Vertinsky (1994) detailed the many arguments put forth during this time that were meant to limit women's physical activity, arguments such as vital force theory (the belief that we were all

born with a finite amount of energy and that women should conserve theirs for childbirth and rearing) and menstrual disability (general belief that all women's ailments connect back to their reproductive systems). These medically supported beliefs, as well as other cultural gender norms of the time, had a profound effect on the development of women's intercollegiate athletics.

The 1920s were a liberating time for U.S. women in many ways. To open the decade, women's hard-fought battle for the right to vote was won in 1920 when the Nineteenth Amendment was ratified. Opportunities for women in sport were also awakening as women increasingly sought out physical activity and sport. On an international scale, more events such as swimming and diving were being added to the Olympic program for women (1920). On a national level, associations such as the U.S. Field Hockey Association (1922) and the National Women's Athletic Association (1921) were formed, helping to enhance opportunities for women. During this decade the Amateur Athletic

Union (AAU) offered track and field competitions and basketball tournaments for women. In 1926, the AAU sponsored a basketball tournament for women using men's rules (though the women's modified rules would continue to be used for decades later, and in some instances, at the high school level, into the 1990s). In 1926, Gertrude Ederle came home to a ticker-tape parade in New York after successfully swimming the English Channel in 14 hours and 39 minutes, beating the fastest men's time, which was 16 hours and 33 minutes. The close of the decade saw the Tuskegee Institute offering track and field scholarship to female athletes. Overall, the progressive governmental and societal reforms of the 1920s provided women with a few more sporting opportunities than experienced by previous generations.

Not everyone was happy with the strides women were making in sport. As Cahn (1998) noted, these women "stood on the borderline between new feminine ideals and customary notions of manly sports, symbolizing both the possibilities and the dangers of the New Woman's daring disregard for traditional gender arrangements" (p. 10). As social discord mounted, once again in disfavor of women's involvement in competitive athletics, women's physical educators took strict control of the development of women's athletics at the college level. The development of sport that resulted was motivated by educational objectives, social mores, medical opinions, and the negative examples in men's intercollegiate athletics (as outlined in the Carnegie reports and earlier reform documents).

The educational objectives of the women physical educators in charge of women's athletics often emphasized broad opportunities rather than elite varsity athletics, which were more apt to encourage higher levels of skill and competition. The Committee on Women's Athletics (CWA) formed in 1917 as an extension of the American Physical Education Association. The CWA was charged with making and revising rules through its subcommittees for basketball, field hockey, soccer, swimming, and track and field. The materials put out by the CWA encouraged intra-institutional sports (Gerber, 1975). When outside forces such as the AAU pushed for higher levels of competition for females, the women's physical educators recoiled and formed a women's division of the National Amateur Athletic Federation led by Lou Henry Hoover (Mrs. Herbert Hoover). Thus, while men's college athletics often developed outside the educational umbrella, women's college athletic experiences were directed by leaders within the physical education departments on campuses.

The slogan "a sport for every girl and a girl for every sport" encompassed the philosophy of the women physical educators (Gerber, 1975). It stemmed from this philosophy, and the increasing push for some level of competition, that several sporting competitions arose—play days, telegraphic meets, and sports days. A survey conducted in 1936 showed that of the responding schools, 74 percent engaged in telegraphic meets, 70 percent in play days, and 41 percent in sports days (Rader, 2009). Telegraphic meets were competitions in which the women competed in an activity at their own school and then telegraphed the results, thus there was no face-to-face competition involved. Play days were often organized as more social affairs than competitions. To further ensure such an environment, women from different schools were picked to play on a team to further reduce any competitive desires. The sports day was the least popular (at least from the organizers' standpoint), as indicated in the 1936 survey, and involved women playing on teams that represented their colleges but often with modified rules that stemmed the competitive spirit and with a refusal by organizers to announce winners. It would take several decades before women's intercollegiate athletics would truly embrace the idea of inter-institutional competition, and even then it would continue its connection to academic departments on campuses until the early 1980s.

The height of women's administration of women's intercollegiate athletics came in the 1970s and early 1980s with formation of the Association for Intercollegiate Athletics for Women (AIAW). The AIAW was founded in 1971, one year before the gender equity legislation, Title IX, was passed. Similar to earlier women's associations governing women's college sports, the AIAW's philosophy was in line with the academic mission of higher education. The founding philosophy was simple: athletic programs should exist for the enrichment of athletes' lives. The goals and objectives reflected this—women should have power over their sporting lives, women should be provided opportunities to coach and administer, women should have opportunities in many sports and at different levels, women should have opportunities for competition, promote athletic programs as educational and developmental, and most notably create a central focus on athletes' rights.

The main motivation behind the creation of the AIAW was to administer championships and increase opportunities in women's college athletics. By nearly all standards, the AIAW was successful in this mission. The AIAW championship structure was markedly different than the NCAA's. In the AIAW an institution has the opportunity to play its way to the national championship, with all members able to compete in state championships. Those successful at the state level would move on to the regional competitions (the United States was divided into nine regions) and then on to the national championship. At its height, the AIAW administered forty-one national championships in nineteen sports (in three divisions), as well as 460 state and regional tournaments. Its membership made it the largest intercollegiate athletic association of its time, but it lacked the money and influence of the NCAA.

Some have suggested that the AIAW's success and the success of Title IX may have been the downfall for the association. Many members of the NCAA funded what they referred to as a war chest to fight the passage of Title IX, and after its passage supported amendments that would exclude athletics or at least football and men's basketball from the legislation. When all this failed to come to pass, athletic directors such as Ralph Floyd at Indiana University made it clear that their intentions were to take over women's sports in order, in their minds, to save the men's programs. In 1981 the NCAA voted to sponsor championships for women's basketball. This was appealing to many coaches of women's athletics for a number of reasons—the two most prominent being the NCAA's ability to pay teams to travel to their tournaments, and the cultural standing of the NCAA as the institution governing intercollegiate athletics. In 1982, the AIAW closed its doors and for many its history remains forgotten.

INCREASING POWER OF THE NCAA AND FURTHER CALLS FOR REFORM

Although the Carnegie Report (1929) influenced the development of women's sport in terms of providing an example of what not to do, it had very little effect on men's intercollegiate athletics and the further development of commercialism and professionalism within the programs. Indeed, *The New York Times* reported that two-thirds of the colleges cited in the report had no plans to change their programs (Branch, 2011). It would not be until 1941 that the NCAA was given some power to police member institutions. Until that point, the organization existed mainly to set rules for various sports, host tournaments, and to assert amateurism. In the 1941 organizational meeting, the members approved a measure that would allow by a two-thirds vote the expulsion of members who violated the association's rules. Despite this measure, institutions still violated the rules with little or no punishment, and no school was expelled from the institution.

The end of the decade saw a decided shift in NCAA policy. In an attempt to better regulate the condition of sports at that time, the association decided to break away from a major tenet of amateur athletics—the ideal that athletes should not receive monetary reward for playing. The "sanity code," which was adopted in 1948, permitted the extension of scholarships and jobs to athletes, but only on the basis of financial need. For many, this restriction justified maintenance of the amateur status.

The athletic world would be rocked by a number of major scandals in the 1950s that would result in further strengthening the regulatory powers of the NCAA. In 1950, the United States Military Academy admitted

that all but two members of its varsity football team had been dismissed for cheating on examinations. Even more damaging to the reputation of college athletics was the uncovering of a large gambling ring involving college basketball. The New York District Attorney's Office indicted thirty-three players from seven colleges for "point-shaving." Players were being paid by gamblers to keep the margin of points between teams within a certain range.

The scandal also revealed illegal recruitment and subsidization of players, and made many in the public question the lengths that schools would go to for national renown on the athletic courts and fields. With little faith in members' ability or willingness to self-monitor, and with members unwilling to vote out offending schools, in 1952 the NCAA

Sherman White, a Long Island University basketball player indicted in the point-shaving scandal of 1951

membership moved to allow the organization to impose sanctions on institutions that violated the association's regulations. The 1952 convention also approved the naming of Walter Byers as the first full-time executive director of the NCAA, legislation governing postseason bowls, and the establishment of a national headquarters in Kansas City, MO (now located in Indianapolis, IN).

Additional power was bestowed upon the NCAA in a very different form—television. As noted in the earlier discussion on football, early media played a large role in the increased popularity of intercollegiate athletics. This symbiotic relationship would reach new dimensions with the introduction of television sets into nearly every American household. Initially, each college negotiated its own television contract, resulting in a virtual flooding of football games telecast throughout the country. The alarming decrease in game-day attendance, a drop of 1,403,000 in just two years, resulted in the pushing through of a measure allowing the NCAA to control television deals. NCAA officials allowed the telecast of only seven regular season games in each region and negotiated a football telecast package with the Westinghouse Broadcasting Company. The move resulted in increased game-day attendance, inflated television ratings, and an influx of money to the NCAA and its members.

The television dollars were—and continue to be—a main source of money for the NCAA and also its main source of power. In 1952, NBC signed a one-year deal with the NCAA to show a restricted number of football games for $1.14 million. In 1969, ABC paid $6 million, which it increased to $29 million by 1979. The combined ABC–CBS contract in 1981 provided $65.7 million to be distributed to the NCAA, the participating schools, their conferences, and the member schools of the NCAA. Although it took college basketball longer to develop a television following, in 2011 CBS and Turner Broadcasting paid the NCAA $771 million to broadcast the men's basketball tournament. The influx of television dollars and increased pressure to win on a national scale have worsened many of the issues (as can be seen in the Knight Commission reports of the 1990s and 2000s), including those of commercialism, recruiting and subsidizing of athletes, professional coaches, abandonment of principles of amateurism, lack of students' rights, soaring costs, and disconnect from the academic mission.

Commercialism

The commercialism of intercollegiate athletics has reached a scale unfathomable to people in the 1920s. Rader (2009) referred to big-time football and basketball programs as being commercial enterprises. This full-scale commercialization of athletic programs is most directly linked to their relationships with the media. Some reformers admonishingly refer to this as the "edutainment" business, a business that continues to grow and envelope college athletics (Benford, 2007). Sports such as volleyball have undergone major rule changes to better accommodate television restrictions and draw and keep the attention of the television audience. Media time-outs are now routine in sports. To appease television viewers, games are scheduled most every day of the week, often causing campuses to shut down due to the diminished learning environment and to accommodate the crowds (Branch, 2011). A more recent development has been the creation of networks dedicated to one school's athletic teams, such as the Longhorn Network, showcasing University of

Texas athletics, which premiered August 26, 2011.

Commercialization can also be seen in the corporate sponsorships and advertising plastered throughout sporting venues. Sponsorships often intensify the entertainment aspect of college athletics. Many colleges are turning to outside businesses such as IMG College in an attempt to increase their advertising monies. And most schools now have clothing contracts. Nike's contract with the University of Oregon was recently extended and on a yearly basis provides for a $500,000 cash payment to the athletic department, $1,950,000 in gear for the athletic teams, and up to an additional $150,000 in extra gear if so requested by the athletic department. With current trends, there is no end in sight as to how far commercialism in college sports will reach.

Recruiting and Subsidizing Athletes

Commercialization of college athletics is an overarching issue that influences other areas such as recruiting and subsidization of student-athletes. The intensified recruitment of athletes can be seen in the hiring of coaches specifically for recruiting and the expanding regulations put forth by the NCAA to control such practices. In 1975 the NCAA bylaws included a forty-five hundred-word section on recruiting, which has expanded over the years as new technologies have been introduced.

Unlike professional sports, there is no draft to enter college athletics so the recruiting of star athletes gets very competitive. In fact, an entire industry around recruiting services has developed to help provide coaches—and the public—with information about potential college athletes. In February 2012, the NCAA investigated Oregon over alleged recruiting violations based on the use of recruiting services and the number of coaches recruiting. A number of other alleged violations made headlines in 2011. The NCAA said a number of violations were committed by the University of North Carolina football team, including the alleged payment of star players, agents, and alumni. A larger scandal was brewing in Miami, when a Hurricanes' booster admitted to paying out hundred of thousands of dollars and other incentives to seventy-two former Miami University players. Recruiting violations and slush funds are not new in intercollegiate athletics, but the increased demands placed on winning may have heightened the risks some programs are willing to take.

Professional Coaches

One of the main reasons for the increase in the win-at-all-costs mentality is skyrocketing coaches' salaries. The universities are paying the coaches to win; a losing season can result in a short tenure. In 2006 the average pay of major college coaches was $950,000; this jumped nearly 55 percent to $1.47 million in 2011. In 2011–12, the contracts for the top paid men's basketball coaches exceeded $5 million plus bonus incentives that could reach over a half-million dollars. Contracts for the top paid football coaches also exceeded $5 million but many of their bonuses surpassed $1 million. This trickles down through the ranks, as also in 2011–12 the top paid assistant football coach received $1.3 million with others pushing the $1 million mark. Some suggest that these exorbitant salaries tell the story of skewed priorities and further disconnect from the academic mission of the institutions.

Academic Disconnect

Calls for reform in regard to academic integrity have been made again more recently, further intensified by a number of academic scandals that have made headline news. Institutions such as Florida State, Purdue, Kansas, LSU, and Ohio State, to name a few, have had their institutions associated with athletic cheating scandals including writing papers for players, taking exams for players, and helping players take online exams or complete correspondence courses. An example of a larger-scale violation occurred at the University of Minnesota where a tutor admitted writing four hundred papers in the 1990s for members of the men's basketball team. A former tutor at the University of North Carolina was found to have written papers for two football players, both later deemed ineligible. Administrators such as James Duderstadt, former president of the University of Michigan, note that such scandals harm the integrity of the universities.

Yet the cries of academic disconnect extend beyond the academic scandals found in some athletic programs. Other factors include the amount of time athletes are expected to put into their sport, questionable education achievement of some student athletes, and sacrifices made by the general student population. Although NCAA regulations mandate that athletes put in no more than twenty hours a week into activities with an athletic purpose, studies show that many football players are putting in nearly forty-five hours a week and that most other athletes are devoting at least thirty-five hours weekly. The time required to participate in intercollegiate athletics as well as the travel demands further distance athletes in big-time programs from the academic mission of higher education. Also, the education that some athletes receive has been scrutinized due to such issues as clustering and accusations of athletic academic support services pushing athletes to "major in eligibility." Clustering is the disproportionate grouping of athletes into particular classes and particular majors, often seen as "easier." In 2008, clustering was found most often in social science, interdisciplinary, communication, sport-related, and business majors. The clustering phenomenon raises questions about certain professors who may give preferential treatment to athletes. Of more importance, clustering may have a detrimental effect on students' academic achievement, as students tend to do better academically when they are engaged in classes they see as meaningful to their future careers. Those interested in reform have suggested that increased transparency at the institutions would help alleviate this issue.

An additional concern is the effect the focus on athletics has on the majority of the student body. About $1.4 million is collected from student fees for schools in the more lucrative FBS division (football bowl series). But schools in the FCS division (football championship series), which bring in less money from ticket sales and television contracts, have seen skyrocketing athletic budgets with higher amounts coming from student fees. From 2005 to 2009, spending for athletics in the FCS increased by 42 percent (nearly twice as fast as academic spending). Southern Illinois University in Carbondale was one of the top four colleges that saw the biggest increase in athletic spending during this five-year period. The SIU athletic budget for the 2005–06 academic year was $10.5 million. For 2009–10 the athletic budget increased to $23.2 million. At SIU student fees are a major source of funding for the athletic department. In the 2009–10 academic year,

40.8 percent of athletic revenue came from student fees, an additional 14.7 percent from direct institutional support, and 5.3 percent from indirect facilities and administrative support from the university. This was during a time of deep cuts for higher education throughout Illinois. Probably the most visible allocation of student fees directed toward athletics can be seen in the development of the Saluki Way project for which student fees are slated to cover more than half of the $76 million in construction costs, which include a new football stadium, renovations to the basketball arena, a new track, and an academic services building for athletes. Those concerned with academic reform of college athletics see such spending as skewed priorities that support enhancing the athletic infrastructure while making sacrifices to the academic experiences of all students.

More recently the administrators in the NCAA have acknowledged the need for further academic reform. At a retreat for university presidents called by NCAA President Mark Emmert in August 2011, a number of rules emerged that are meant to improve academic quality in athletics. A number of changes related to scholarships include the ability for institutions to award multiyear scholarships, provide financial aid to former athletes who are no longer eligible to compete, and to award additional scholarship money (up to $2,000) to fill the gap between full athletic scholarships and the actual cost of attending college. It should be noted that a number of these rules were challenged by the NCAA membership, and depending on voting outcomes may soon be off the table. Additional changes were made raising the minimum Academic Progress Rate to 930, which indicates that half the athletes on a given team are on track to graduate. Eligibility requirements for incoming freshmen were raised from a 2.0 to 2.3 grade point average in addition to the required standardized test scores mapped out in the NCAA's sliding scale. It is yet to be determined the outcomes of these measures.

CONCLUSION

The state of today's intercollegiate athletics is strongly connected to its past. The issues brought forward by the Carnegie Report in 1929 remain prevalent in our present day sporting environment. The history of college sports in the United States is almost repetitive in its cycles of scandal and reform. The study of intercollegiate athletics does more than educate us about the institution, it also helps us to better understand our culture. The symbiotic relationship between sport and culture means sport influences our culture and that our culture influences sport. If we wish to understand the issues that arise in sport, we need to do so with an eye to the cultural context in which they occur. As noted in the beginning of this chapter, the structure of intercollegiate athletics in the United States is distinctive. This chapter and those that follow should help you better understand the factors that continue to influence this uniquely American institution.

REFERENCES

Benford, R.D. (2007). The college sports reform movement: Reframing the "edutainment" industry. *The Sociological Quarterly* 48, 1–28.

Branch, T. (2011, October). The shame of college sports. *The Atlantic*. Retrieved from http://www.theatlantic.

com/magazine/archive/2011/10/
the-shame-of-college-sports/8643/

Cahn, S.K. (1998). *Coming on strong: Gender and sexuality in twentieth-century women's sports.* Harvard University Press.

Clotfelter, C. (2009, Oct 27) Big-Time College Athletics 80 Years Later. *Duke Today*. Retrieved from http://today.duke.edu/2009/10/clotfelter_oped.html

Coakley, J. (2001). *Sport in Society: Issues and Controversies.* Boston: McGrawHill.

Gerber, E. (1975). The controlled development of collegiate sport for women, 1923–1936. *Journal of Sport History 2*(1), 1–28.

Ingham, A.G. (1978). *American sport in transition: The maturation of industrial capitalism and its impact upon sport.* University of Massachusetts.

Moore, J.H. (1967). Football's ugly decades, 1893–1913. *Smithsonian Journal of History* 11, (Fall 1967), 49–68.

Oriard, M. (1993). *Reading football: How the popular press created an American spectacle.* Chapel Hill: The University of North Carolina Press.

Rader, B.G. (2009). *American sports: From the age of folk games to the age of televised sports. 6th ed.* Upper Saddle River, NJ: Pearson Prentice Hall.

Reiss, S.A. (Ed.), (1997). *Major problems in American sport history: Documents and essay.* Boston: Houghton Mifflin Company.

Sage, G.H. (1990). *Power and ideology in American sport: A critical perspective.* Champaign, IL: Human Kinetics.

Sander, L., and Fuller, A. (2011, June 26). In athletics, ambitions compete with costs. *The Chronicle of Higher Education.* Retrieved from http://chronicle.com

Savage, H.J., H.W. Bentley, J.T. McGovern, and D.F.M.D. Smiley. (1929) *American College Athletics.* New York: Carnegie Foundation for the Advancement of Teaching.

Schmidt, R. (2007). The 1929 Iowa football scandal: Paying tribute to the Carnegie Report? *Journal of Sport History* 34(3), 343–351.

Vertinsky, P.A. (1994). *The eternally wounded woman: Women, doctors, and exercise in the late nineteenth century.* Urbana: University of Illinois Press.

Intercollegiate athletics have been a part of higher education and university life since the early eighteenth century, when athletics were made part of the curriculum at the Rugby School of England. Intercollegiate athletic competition in the United States, albeit primarily unsanctioned, is traced back as early as the 1820s to crew competitions, football, and rugby games between Ivy League schools such as Harvard, Yale, and Princeton (Falla, 1981; Howard-Hamilton & Watt, 2001; Zimbalist, 1999). Besides the Princeton vs. Rutgers football game (won by Rutgers, 6–4) the generally accepted first organized intercollegiate athletic contest was a rowing regatta between Harvard and Yale, complete with more than one hundred thousand fans lined on the banks on Boston's St. Charles River. Among those taking in the event were future U.S. President Franklin Pierce and, ironically, officials of the Boston, Concord and Montreal Railroad, the first corporate sponsor of college sports (Falla; Funk, 1991; Howard-Hamilton & Watt; Staurowsky & Abney, 2010).

Today, thousands of college students compete in intercollegiate athletics on varsity and subvarsity sports teams sponsored by the National Collegiate Athletic Association (NCAA) or other national governing bodies such as the National Association of Intercollegiate Athletics (NAIA) and the National Junior College Athletic Association (NJCAA), to name a few. Almost from the day that Rutgers and Princeton played the first

2

THE ADMINISTRATION AND GOVERNANCE OF INTERCOLLEGIATE ATHLETICS

DAVID RIDPATH

official intercollegiate football game in 1869, the faculties of the two schools canceled the following year's contest because they feared an overemphasis on the game over academics and studying. One of the reasons faculty members and others feared this new vocation was the lack of organization and governance, specifically concerning rules of the game and academic integrity. By 1883, the now famous Harvard and Yale football game had been played several times. To the disgust of both institutional faculties, representatives of athletic interests (boosters) from both schools were trying to use this very popular contest to raise funds to acquire property to build their own football fields. The 1883 game, played at the Polo

Grounds in New York City, drew more than ten thousand fans and generated the money for the boosters to pay for the new fields. For the first time, intercollegiate sport began to dictate university policy—and conflict with academia and the subject of how to control this ever-growing aspect of American higher education became paramount (Falla; Zimbalist).

Values in intercollegiate athletics have changed dramatically over the years. In the late 1800s, after intercollegiate athletics took a stronger foothold on campuses across the nation, college sports were played for fun and leisure. The faculties and administrators in early higher education never planned for anything as frivolous as athletics; the concentration was solely on academics. Still, students gravitated toward recreational activities that college authorities saw as an avenue for students to release pent-up energies. In the 1920s, the importance of physical education in higher education was emphasized by nearly all institutions having a requirement in physical education. This, combined with an increased emphasis on intercollegiate athletics, made physical education a big business on campuses of higher learning.

As early as the 1890s prominent universities were determined to win in intercollegiate sports at any cost. While football was the main focus of colleges and universities, other sports were also starting to supersede academic requirements to get athletes on the field. Professional baseball pitchers were becoming campus stars playing college baseball under pseudonyms. Coaches were even inserting themselves and non-students into football games in the quest to win (Falla).

AN ATTEMPT AT GOVERNANCE AND THE START OF THE NCAA

Such events made it clear that some type of national organizing body was needed to regulate intercollegiate athletics. The bedrock of all attempts at governance was the principle of amateurism. Even today all NCAA rules, regulations, policies, and procedures are developed with amateurism as the core principle. By definition, amateurism is defined in NCAA bylaw 2.9 as *"student-athletes shall be amateurs in an intercollegiate sport, and their participation should be motivated primarily by education and by the physical, mental and social benefits to be derived. Student participation in intercollegiate athletics is an avocation, and student-athletes should be protected from exploitation by professional and commercial enterprises"* (p. 4). Regardless of debate on whether amateurism exists in its truest form, it is still the concept that the NCAA operates by and expects its member institutions to operate under. Therein lies the problem: a focus on winning and revenue generation, which arguably exists today, can be interpreted as going against the concept of amateurism. The interesting part of this debate is that the argument is not new. Intercollegiate athletics has struggled with its place within the educational system literally since its inception.

At the beginning of the twentieth century, several attempts at organizing an intercollegiate athletics governing body were made before the official formation in 1910 of the NCAA, the primary and most well-known intercollegiate athletic governing body. On January 11, 1895, there was an historic meeting of the Intercollegiate Conference of Faculty Representatives, which later became known as the Big Ten Conference. This is the first intercollegiate conference on record that made regulations regarding athletes' academic eligibility and participation. Eligibility and participation rules began to resonate across the country on other college campuses, but many abuses of campus academic requirements still existed and more needed to be done to govern this growing enterprise. There were many pockets of compliance, but abuses of academic standards by intercollegiate athletics needed to be addressed collectively by all higher education institutions at a national level.

It was in 1905 that a nationwide call for college football reform led to a more formal approach of a national governing body and rules for intercollegiate athletics. Collaboration among institutions was not started initially for academic or booster abuses, but for regulating the sport of college football on the field of play. The call for reform in the rules of the game came from President Teddy Roosevelt himself. In the eyes of many, college football, with its mass momentum formations and anything goes philosophy, had reached an unacceptable level of violent play and resulted in several serious on-field injuries and even fatalities. President Roosevelt used the prestige of his office to try to calm the fears of much of the public about the growing sense of lawlessness surrounding college football, including the abuse of institutional academic requirements within the whole of intercollegiate athletics. Many colleges and universities, fearing the overemphasis of football and seeing the dangers of the game, suspended football, including Columbia and Northwestern. Harvard President Charles Eliot threatened to totally abolish the game on his campus (Funk, 1991; Sack & Staurowsky).

There was a sense that something needed to be done at the highest levels to regulate and control intercollegiate athletics as society clamored for the college game to adopt stricter rules on and off the field. The response to this public outcry led to the initial meeting in 1906 that was the forerunner of the NCAA and the Intercollegiate Athletic Association of the United States (IAAUS). Although most of the concerns with college athletics focused on excessive violence, questions regarding the relationship of academics and athletics received nearly as much attention at this first meeting and this attention manifested itself throughout subsequent years (Funk; Sack & Staurowsky). From this historic 1906 meeting and several meetings later, the IAAUS was born. Four years later, in 1910, this association of colleges and universities officially became known as the National Collegiate Athletic Association (NCAA). The most well-known and largest intercollegiate athletics governing body is the NCAA. In this chapter, the focus will largely be on NCAA governance and compliance, but there will be a discussion of other governing bodies in intercollegiate athletics and what role they have in the governance of college athletics.

In the words of Captain Palmer Pierce of the United States Military Academy at West Point, one of the founding fathers of the NCAA and later its first president, the association would be forever known as "the voice of college sports" (Crowley, 2010; Falla).

During the 1920s intercollegiate athletic competition continued to grow exponentially across the nation. Colleges and universities were adding sports and building formidable athletic programs in the process. The NCAA membership held its first championship in the sport of track and field in 1921. The post-World War II era brought forth the first significant rules and regulations adopted by the membership as a whole. The post-war NCAA returned to the business of restoring and maintaining integrity in intercollegiate athletics. The first NCAA "convention" was actually called the "Conference of Conferences" in July 1946. The participants in this conference drafted a statement called "Principles for the Conduct of Intercollegiate Athletics" (Brown, 1999; Sack & Staurowsky). The principles concerned adhering to the definition of amateurism and not allowing professional athletes to compete, holding student-athletes to the same sound academic standards as the student body, awarding financial aid without consideration for an athlete's ability, and developing a policy of recruiting that basically prohibited a coach or anyone representing a member school from recruiting any prospective student athlete with the offer of financial aid or any equivalent inducement. These principles collectively became known as the Sanity Code, or Article III of the NCAA Constitution when it was first presented in 1947. This code was initially developed to help colleges and universities deal with the growing levels of abuse and violations in intercollegiate athletics, specifically football and men's basketball. The code was a tortured, yet in some ways a brilliant, effort to reconcile a number of disparate interests and athletic philosophies concerning intercollegiate athletics (Falla; Sack & Staurowsky).

Overemphasis on athletics has led to an inevitable clash of academic integrity versus athletic success at institutions that sponsor intercollegiate athletics. In simple terms, an athlete must remain academically eligible in order to compete, and it has been this way in theory for most of the history of governing intercollegiate athletics. If one is not academically eligible and not making satisfactory progress toward a degree, competition for that individual is prohibited.

Thus, many people including students, boosters, academicians, alumni, and coaches have tried to beat the system—and in many cases have succeeded. Both the effort and business of superseding academic requirements to gain athletic success have been around since the beginning of intercollegiate athletics itself and have had a significant influence on how intercollegiate athletics is governed today. Nevertheless, during the development of the Sanity Code values in intercollegiate athletics remained skewed toward winning and athletic success, rather than academic achievement and graduation. Even when the Sanity Code was established, the penalty for noncompliance was banishment from the NCAA. Several schools led by the University of Virginia revolted and the Sanity Code itself was short-lived as NCAA policy, but it established the template for future efforts at governing the NCAA (Crowley; Falla).

CURRENT GOVERNANCE STRUCTURE IN INTERCOLLEGIATE ATHLETICS

Intercollegiate athletics is made up of very different and distinct educational institutions yet the governance structure in many ways is very similar. Intercollegiate athletics has come a long way from the days when students ran their own practices, devised their own training programs, and scheduled their own contests. The nature of intercollegiate athletics quickly changed from being social occasions to becoming highly competitive events and complex governance structures. As mentioned previously, by 1905 football competitions had become so intense that some people advocated reform or elimination of the sport. One way of implementing reform was to establish associations to govern intercollegiate athletics (Abney & Staurowsky; Ridpath & Abney). Today, intercollegiate athletic programs are regulated by national governing bodies and conferences.

Intercollegiate athletics in the United States is governed by several organizations. The primary governing bodies of intercollegiate sport in America are the National Collegiate Athletic Association (NCAA), National Association of Intercollegiate Athletics (NAIA), National Junior College Athletic Association (NJCAA), National Small School Athletic Association (NSCAA), and the National Christian College Athletic Association (NCCAA). It is also important to note that while intercollegiate athletics is primarily an American phenomenon, it also exists in other countries but under different models. For example, in Canada, like other countries that support some type of intercollegiate competition, athletic scholarships are not offered (unlike the awarding of scholarships at many schools in the United States).

The NCAA is the largest and most influential governing body in intercollegiate athletics. Current membership in its three divisions counts nearly thirteen hundred institutions. In all divisions, the NCAA governance structure includes voluntary membership by its member institutions and affiliated individuals such as presidents and chancellors, faculty members, coaches, athletic department personnel, athletic conference personnel, and of course the athletes. All work in conjunction with a national office staff of more than three hundred (the current national office is based in Indianapolis, IN) to carry out the mission and functions of each division and of the NCAA as a whole. Many NCAA rules and policies are set by one or more of the one hundred twenty NCAA committees that include about one thousand representatives from member institutions. The NCAA Executive Committee, consisting of college presidents and chancellors from each of the three divisions, is the overarching NCAA governance body. Its responsibilities include dealing with key association-wide issues (including all legal issues) and strategic plans, ensuring that each division is meeting its mission and the general mission of the NCAA, and overseeing the association's budget (www.education.stateuniversity.com).

NCAA membership is separated into three competitive divisions known as Division I, II, and III. Division III is the largest as it is comprised of nearly 40 percent of the members. Football-playing institutions in Division I, formerly referred to as Division I-A and I-AA subdivisions, are referred to as the Football Bowl Subdivision (FBS) and the Football Championship Subdivision (FCS). The main criteria used to establish an institution's divisional classification are size, number of sports offered, financial base and sport-sponsorship minimums, focus of programming, football and basketball scheduling requirements, and availability of athletic grants-in-aid (Staurowsky & Abney). Currently, NCAA Division I teams must sponsor a minimum of fourteen sports (at least six male and eight female sports, or a seven-seven split) and meet a minimum threshold for financial aid. Division I is made up of 66 percent public institutions. Division II teams must sponsor a minimum of ten sports with at least five male and five female sports, or six female and four male teams. Division II programs must also meet a minimum threshold for financial aid and 53 percent are public institutions. Division III is made up of non-scholarship teams and represents primarily private institutions (80 percent). Division III programs must also sponsor ten sports, at least five female and five male teams, or six female and four male teams (Abney & Parks, 1998; Hums & McLean, 2009; Ridpath & Abney; Staurowsky & Abney).

The need to govern intercollegiate athletic programs effectively is crucial, since an athletic program is often viewed as the main window in which institutions are perceived by the general public. And it's through an athletic program that the public may form an opinion of the university at large. This phenomenon is often referred to as the "Front Porch Theory" (Suggs, 2003). Some university administrators believe that successful athletic programs can generate additional revenue and marketing potential for the institution at large, including enhancing academics and research (Gerdy, 2006; Suggs). Governing a multimillion-dollar enterprise can be complex, but is often grounded in a typical business model. A simple way to look at intercollegiate athletic programs is to view it as a business operation. Although there is not a traditional business constructed with the areas of profit and loss, shareholders, public trading of stock etc., it is still attempting to operate as a more for-profit business model within a nonprofit educational enterprise (A. Zimbalist, personal communication). At the larger and more commercially noticed universities, such as those in NCAA Division I, there are many forces at work such as sponsorship and television money that make intercollegiate athletics more big business. Even smaller athletic departments, however, are managed in a similar fashion, albeit on a much smaller scale.

INTERCOLLEGIATE ATHLETIC CONFERENCES

Before formation of the NCAA, intercollegiate athletic programs (or what served as an attempt to have such a program) at some institutions were loosely federated within athletic conferences. As mentioned previously, in 1895 one of the first attempts at regulating intercollegiate athletics occurred at the "Conference of Conferences," which later became the Big 10 Conference (Falla). The topics discussed at this meeting included how to prevent athletes for hire (those who were not full-time students) and restricting athletic eligibility to bona fide enrolled full-time students who were not delinquent in their studies (*Big Ten History*, 2009; Staurowsky & Abney, 2007).

The role of athletic conferences in the governance of intercollegiate athletics has remained relatively unchanged throughout the more than one hundred years of intercollegiate athletics. The basic functions of a conference include establishing rules and regulations that support and sustain a level playing field for member institutions while creating in-season and postseason competitive opportunities (Staurowsky & Abney). Conferences whose members are part of the NCAA must follow baseline NCAA rules and regulations; they can make their own rules and regulations that are stricter than NCAA requirements but they cannot be less or they would be in violation of NCAA mandates. Conversely, individual institutions may have stricter requirements with regard to such areas as recruiting, eligibility, and financial aid, but their standards cannot be less than the affiliated conference, or if applicable the NCAA. Many conferences and institutions have stricter initial eligibility requirements than the NCAA, and conversely some institutions have lowered overall admission standards to NCAA levels to aid in recruiting better athletes who may not meet original admission requirements.

Intercollegiate athletic conferences today, specifically those in the highest level of NCAA Division I-A, are centered around negotiating television contracts (since Division I football is not controlled by the NCAA, but by a group of six conferences and Notre Dame university, commonly known as the Bowl Championship Series) and distributing the revenue and proceeds that conference members agreed to share (Grant, Leadley, & Zygmont, 2008).

Conferences are unofficially separated into major, mid-major, and small college categories. The general consensus is a major conference is one that is able to compete in Bowl Championship Series (BCS) and have a chance to play for a national championship. Conferences such as the Southeastern Conference (SEC) and Atlantic Coast Conference (ACC) fit in the major category, while conferences that are not deemed a BCS conference such at Conference USA and the Mountain West Conference are usually referred to as the "mid-majors." It is important, however, to note that the main decision-making power within the NCAA governance structure is within the hands of the major conferences. Within the previously discussed NCAA committee structure, representatives of each of the six BCS conferences with automatic BCS bids have guaranteed seats on the Division I Board of Directors (made up of university presidents). Of the twenty available seats, only seven seats are available for the mid-major conferences. So not only does the power of the BCS come from controlling the massive revenues of football, these conferences also control much of the governance of the NCAA itself. (Staurowsky & Abney).

THE ATHLETIC DEPARTMENT

In basic terms, most intercollegiate athletic programs at any level are separated by ***internal and external divisions***. Internal divisions (or internal operations) are defined as those functions that deal with the inside functions of a department or business, or what is commonly called operations management. According to *Management and Control of Production and Operation* (2012), operations management involves all operations within the organization, or managing the functions internally of the organization. Internal-related activities in a standard business may include managing purchases, inventory control, quality control, storage, logistics, and evaluations. A great deal of focus is on efficiency and effectiveness of processes. Therefore, operations management often includes substantial measurement and analysis of internal processes (Ridpath & Abney).

Internal operations in intercollegiate athletics can be viewed in a similar organizational and operational structure, with the emphasis on managing organizational processes within the business. Internal operations in intercollegiate athletics may include (but need not be limited to) the following:

- Business and Finance
- Clerical/Administrative Support
- Human Resource Management
- **Regulatory Compliance/Legal** (For the purposes of this chapter we will focus on this area)
- Ticketing and Box Office Operations/ Revenue Control
- Sport Team Management and Supervision

- Executive Team Management (usually headed by an athletic director and several associates or assistants)
- Facility and Event Management
- Academic Support Systems
- Food Service
- Computing
- Equipment Room (uniforms and sport implements/specific equipment)
- Video and Scouting Services
- Policies and Procedures
- Sports Medicine/Athletic Training Operations
- Strength and Conditioning
- Capital Improvements/Deferred Maintenance Issues

External operations can be defined in simple terms as interacting with business and functional environments that traditionally occur away from the organization but are still essential components of an organization. Since intercollegiate athletics depend on major sources of revenue from outside sources such as ticket sales, sponsorship agreements, special events, and private donations, external operations are often looked at as the most important and vital entity of a department. Some athletic departments generate their entire operating budget themselves from these external functions and do not rely on a student-fee model and/or institutional subsidies (Ridpath & Abney, 2012; Ridpath, Chapman & Denhart, 2011; Vedder, Villwock & Denhart, 2010). Typical functions of external operations in intercollegiate athletics, but not an inclusive list are:

- Development/Fund-Raising
- Marketing
- Ticket Office-External Functions with Development, Marketing, and Special Events
- Broadcast Operations (television, radio, Internet)
- Media/Public Relations
- Sports Properties Rights Holders (includes outsourced sponsorship operations such as IMG College, Learfield Sports, Nelligan Sports Marketing)
- Licensing
- Special Events/Marketing

SUPERVISORY POSITIONS WITHIN A TYPICAL INTERCOLLEGIATE ATHLETIC DEPARTMENT

Most athletic departments are headed by a director of athletics. At the NCAA Division I level, this is almost always the case. Also mandated is a senior position reserved for the highest-ranking female in the department or senior women's administrator (SWA). Specific roles for the SWA vary widely among institutions. Internal and external departments are headed by associate or deputy athletic directors, and they are supported by assistant athletic or program directors who lead each component. The AD acts as the CEO and focuses primarily on revenue generation, while the associates and assistants run the department on a day-to-day basis (Ridpath & Abney).

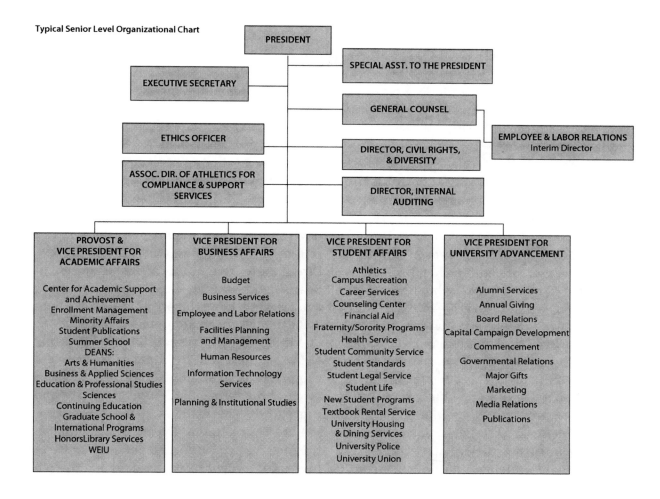

Typical Senior Level Organizational Chart

PRESIDENT

SPECIAL ASST. TO THE PRESIDENT

EXECUTIVE SECRETARY

GENERAL COUNSEL

ETHICS OFFICER

EMPLOYEE & LABOR RELATIONS
Interim Director

DIRECTOR, CIVIL RIGHTS, & DIVERSITY

ASSOC. DIR. OF ATHLETICS FOR COMPLIANCE & SUPPORT SERVICES

DIRECTOR, INTERNAL AUDITING

PROVOST & VICE PRESIDENT FOR ACADEMIC AFFAIRS

Center for Academic Support and Achievement
Enrollment Management
Minority Affairs
Student Publications
Summer School
DEANS:
Arts & Humanities
Business & Applied Sciences
Education & Professional Studies
Sciences
Continuing Education
Graduate School & International Programs
HonorsLibrary Services
WEIU

VICE PRESIDENT FOR BUSINESS AFFAIRS

Budget
Business Services
Employee and Labor Relations
Facilities Planning and Management
Human Resources
Information Technology Services
Planning & Institutional Studies

VICE PRESIDENT FOR STUDENT AFFAIRS

Athletics
Campus Recreation
Career Services
Counseling Center
Financial Aid
Fraternity/Sorority Programs
Health Service
Student Community Service
Student Standards
Student Legal Service
Student Life
New Student Programs
Textbook Rental Service
University Housing & Dining Services
University Police
University Union

VICE PRESIDENT FOR UNIVERSITY ADVANCEMENT

Alumni Services
Annual Giving
Board Relations
Capital Campaign Development
Commencement
Governmental Relations
Major Gifts
Marketing
Media Relations
Publications

UNIVERSITY ADMINISTRATION IN INTERCOLLEGIATE ATHLETIC GOVERNANCE

An athletic department may operate as a university auxiliary such as housing and/or dining services. This means that a department must generate its entire operating budget through revenue generated from its own products and services. There are only a few athletic departments able to do this. Most athletic departments generate substantial revenue in addition to receiving university subsidies, so they cannot be considered a true auxiliary (Ridpath, Chapman & Denhart, 2011; Vedder, Villwock & Denhart, 2010). Many athletic departments are heavily subsidized by the university usually via a student activity fee that varies from institution to institution. In 2010, *USA TODAY* conducted a study that determined only seven NCAA Division I athletic departments were self-supporting (Gillum, 2010). Since athletics is a very public and popular entity at the university, this phenomenon makes governance of intercollegiate athletics vitally important to an institution and many levels of supervision and control are involved.

PRESIDENTS AND CHANCELLORS— THE CEOS OF THE INSTITUTION

By most intercollegiate athletic governing body standards, the university president/chancellor is ultimately responsible for the conduct of the intercollegiate athletic program. The popularity of college sports has essentially dictated presidential control as the enterprise was one that had exhibited little presidential leadership and control prior to the late eighties. The Knight Commission on Intercollegiate Athletics proposed in 1989 a new concept of presidential control in its "One Plus Three" model, which was outlined in its groundbreaking initial report, "Keeping Faith with the Student Athlete." The One Plus Three model consists of the "One" being presidential control, and the "Three" referring to academic integrity, fiscal integrity, and enhancing the athletic certification program. This report generated such widespread acclaim that the NCAA moved to integrate presidential control of intercollegiate athletics into its rules compliance mandates, along with changing its governance approach and focus on this new model of intercollegiate athletic governance. While some may argue that little progress has been made, it is difficult to argue that these changes and the report did not have a significant influence on the current governance procedures of intercollegiate athletics. There have been two follow-up reports by the Knight Commission, "A Call to Action" in 2001 and "Restoring the Balance: Dollars, Values, and the Future of College Sports" in 2010. All of the reports have had a significant influence on intercollegiate athletic governance that likely will continue in the future.

INSTITUTIONAL ATHLETIC BOARDS

Most universities have an Intercollegiate Athletics Committee as a mechanism to assist in maintaining institutional control, although it is not required by the NCAA or any other governing body. NCAA Bylaw 6.1.2 states that having an oversight board is not a requirement for membership, but if one is used Bylaw 6.1.2.1 governs what the composition of the board must be and that it should have broad-based campus participation. The role of this committee varies by institution. Often these committees exist as oversight boards for athletic department decisions and serving more of an advisory capacity, even though there are detailed descriptions of athletic board responsibilities at many NCAA institutions. The intent of an oversight committee is to scrutinize budgets, approve hires, and approve and enforce policies and procedures. The makeup of most ICA committees is broad and diverse, with members ranging from faculty members, administrative staff, athletic staff, students, and even community members (Institutional Control, 2011; Ridpath & Abney).

For example, according to Rutgers University Policy 50.1.14, Governance of Intercollegiate Athletics (April 15, 2010), the athletic board's responsibility falls under the direction of the board of governors. In its oversight role, the Committee on Intercollegiate Athletics has areas of responsibility that include reviewing and endorsing the university president's goals with regard to the conduct of the athletic program; reviewing the athletic budgets, capital expenditures, and any future debt-service commitments; reviewing the athletics mission statement to ensure it is consistent with the university's mission, core principles, and educational values; promoting the full integration of intercollegiate athletics in the administrative and academic structure of the university; reviewing governance policies related to intercollegiate athletics; consulting with the university president on the hiring of high-level athletics personnel; and recommending approval of contracts above $300,000 (Rutgers University Policy, 2010).

While Rutgers' ICA committee appears to wield great authority and influence, Ohio University's ICA committee serves in primarily an advisory/informational capacity, with the director of athletics governing the direction of most of the proceedings:

> General policies concerning athletics at Ohio University are determined by the President and Board of Trustees in consultation with the Director of Athletics. The Intercollegiate Athletics Committee assists the President, Provost, Director of Athletics, and the NCAA Faculty Athletics Representatives in the interpretation and implementation of athletic policies. The ICA is an advisory group reporting to the President; it works closely with the Director of Athletics and the Athletic Department. On an on-going basis, most of the Committee's work will be in direct consultation with the Director of Athletics and other staff in the Athletics Department. As a means of keeping the President informed, minutes of meetings will be sent to the President on a regular basis (Ohio University, March 1, 2011).

In its advisory role, athletic boards do many things and have duties that are generally similar across different universities. Some of these duties include reviewing gender equity plans; strategic planning efforts; self-study reviews; periodic review of governance policies involving such issues as student athlete eligibility processes, disciplinary practices, and student absences from campus for athletic participation; representation on search committees for head coaches and/or senior staff; and responding to requests from the president and/or director of athletics as needed (Ohio University, March 1, 2011; Ridpath & Abney; Rutgers University Policy, 2010).

FACULTY ATHLETIC REPRESENTATIVE

Unlike an athletics oversight board, the position of faculty athletic representative (FAR) is a requirement of NCAA membership. According the NCAA Bylaw 6.1.3, an NCAA-member institution shall appoint a faculty athletics representative who must hold faculty rank but his or her duties are to be determined by the institution, and often the duties vary. The Faculty Athletic Representatives Association (FARA) has attempted to standardize the job description and duties of the FAR. According to the FARA website: *A FAR is a member of the faculty at an NCAA-member institution. He or she has been designated by the university or college to serve as a liaison between the institution and the athletics department, and also as a representative of the institution in conference and NCAA affairs. Each institution determines the role of the FAR at that particular university or college* (www.farawebsite.org). According to one of FARA's Guiding Principles, the role of the FAR is: ... *to ensure that the academic institution establishes and maintains the appropriate balance between academics and intercollegiate athletics*" (www.farawebsite.org). The FAR is also one of only five institutional representatives authorized to request an NCAA legislative interpretation on behalf of the institution. This includes only the chief executive officer, director of athletics, senior woman administrator, and compliance coordinator (or their designate). In addition, the FAR usually serves as the chair or as a permanent member, by position, of the intercollegiate athletics committee (Ridpath & Abney).

UNIVERSITY GOVERNING BOARDS

University governing boards, often called trustees, governors, regents, or visitors, play an important role in setting policy and aligning intercollegiate athletics with the educational mission of the institution at large. The overall mission of these oversight boards is to ensure accountability and adherence to the mission of the institution. Often its duties include duties such as monitoring the effectiveness of teaching, research, service, fiscal responsibility, and fulfilling all legal obligations. The university president reports to the board on these issues and usually serves at the pleasure of the board.

According to the Association of Governing Boards' (AGB) 2007 Revised Statement on Board Responsibilities for Intercollegiate Athletics, AGB recognizes that intercollegiate athletics can attract, generate, or lose large sums of money and often is the institution's most visible component, compelling institutional leaders to pay close attention. Consequently, boards should exercise appropriate oversight while avoiding micromanagement and viewing athletics with a dispassionate perspective. Central to board

oversight is to call for the athletics department to embody the proper tone, direction, and values consistent with the academic mission of the institution (AGB statement, 2007; Ridpath & Abney).

Specifically:

> Boards should be confident that the institution's chief executive, academic, and athletic leaders have set appropriate standards of accountability and benchmarks against which to evaluate the success of the intercollegiate athletics program. These standards and benchmarks should encompass such areas as finances, admissions, student-athlete welfare, academic advising, graduation rates, facilities, capital expenditures and conflict-of-interest policies. In addition, Boards should be informed about the impact of intercollegiate athletics on the campus culture in all areas, including admissions, social life, academic values, student body composition, and fan conduct and atmosphere at campus events (AGB statement, 2007).

State legislatures are critical in that they are the ones controlling the money to higher education for public institutions. Many states are restrictive on public and/or instructional funds used for athletic purposes. In addition, the recession and current economic climate have reduced state funding for athletics even more (Knight Commission, 2010). Along with little public money being provided for athletics and capital improvements, universities are constantly challenged with finding other revenue streams to fund departments. The dichotomy is that many state legislators demand athletic success from institutions they follow and/or attended. Many legislators also serve on boards of trustees/governors and have influence on decisions in intercollegiate athletics by virtue of their political position.

ATHLETIC BOOSTERS

The athletic booster club and university foundation are an important resource for intercollegiate athletic programs, owing mainly to dwindling resources from public

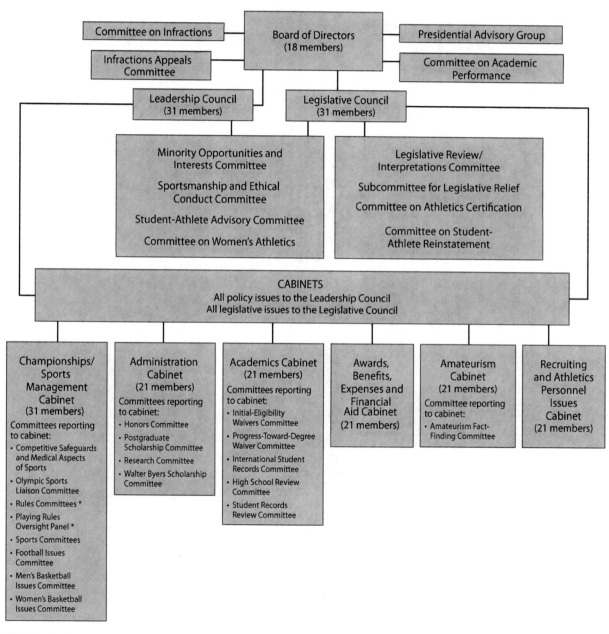

* For Information Purposes

EXECUTIVE COMMITTEE

Responsibilities
A. Approval/oversight of budget.
B. Appointment/evaluation of Association's president.
C. Strategic planning for Association.
D. Identification of Association's core issues.
E. To resolve issues/litigation.
F. To convene joint meeting of the three presidential bodies.
G. To convene same-site meeting of Division I Legislative Council and Division II and Division III Management Councils.
H. Authority to call for constitutional votes.
I. Authority to call for vote of entire membership when division action is contrary to Association's basic principles.
J. Authority to call Special/Annual Conventions.

Members
A. Eight FBS members from Division I Board of Directors.
B. Two FCS members from Division I Board of Directors.
C. Two Division I members from Division I Board of Directors.
D. Two members from Division II Presidents Council.
E. Two members from Division III Presidents Council.
F. Ex officio/nonvoting—President.[1]
G. Ex officio/nonvoting—Chairs of Division I Leadership Council and Division II and Division III Management Councils.

[1] May vote in case of tie.

ASSOCIATION-WIDE COMMITTEES

A. Committee on Competitive Safeguards and Medical Aspects of Sports.
B. Honors Committee.
C. Minority Opportunities and Interests Committee.
D. Olympic Sports Liaison Committee.
E. Postgraduate Scholarship Committee.
F. Research Committee.
G. Committee on Sportsmanship and Ethical Conduct.
H. Walter Byers Scholarship Committee.
I. Committee on Women's Athletics.
J. International Student Records (Divisions I and II).
K. NCAA Committees that have playing rules responsibilities.

DIVISION III PRESIDENTS COUNCIL

Responsibilities
A. Set policy and direction of division.
B. Delegate responsibilities to Management Council.

Members
A. Institutional Presidents or Chancellors.

DIVISION III MANAGEMENT COUNCIL

Responsibilities
A. Recommendations to primary governing body.
B. Handle responsibilities delegated by primary governing body.

Members
A. Presidents or Chancellors.
B. Athletics administrators.
C. Faculty athletics representatives.
D. Student-athletes.

DIVISION II PRESIDENTS COUNCIL

Responsibilities
A. Set policy and direction of division.
B. Delegate responsibilities to Management Council.

Members
A. Institutional Presidents or Chancellors.

DIVISION II MANAGEMENT COUNCIL

Responsibilities
A. Recommendations to primary governing body.
B. Handle responsibilities delegated by primary governing body.

Members
A. Athletics administrators.
B. Faculty athletics representatives.

DIVISION I BOARD OF DIRECTORS

Responsibilities
A. Set policy and direction of the division.
B. Consider legislation at its discretion.
C. Delegate responsibilities to Leadership and Legislative Councils.

Members
A. Institutional Presidents or Chancellors.

DIVISION I LEGISLATIVE COUNCIL

Responsibilities
A. Recommendations to primary governing body.
B. Handle responsibilities delegated by primary governing body.
C. Adopt legislation for the division.

Members
A. Athletics administrators.
B. Faculty athletics representatives.

DIVISION I LEADERSHIP COUNCIL

Responsibilities
A. Recommendations to primary governing body.
B. Handle responsibilities delegated by primary governing body.
C. Help manage the governance substructure.

Members
A. Athletics administrators.
B. Faculty athletics representatives.

funds. Private funding has become critical. Most athletic foundations/booster clubs exist as a 501c3 nonprofit organization by IRS standards, with the clubs' primary mission focused on raising money for athletic scholarships. This enables donors to take up to an 80 percent tax deduction for funds donated to an athletic department. These foundations also provide salary augmentation to coaches and staff members, funding for capital improvements and other needs such as travel expenses. For many departments this is one of the main, if not the primary, source of funds. While typically not a formalized position in the governance structure, the clubs' influence, because of the funding provided, needs to be acknowledged as these organizations, which might be completely private, influence tremendous authority over the direction of intercollegiate athletics (Ridpath & Abney).

RECRUITING, ACADEMIC ELIGIBILITY, FINANCIAL AID AND EXTRA BENEFITS

Rules Compliance

Issues and controversies within NCAA intercollegiate athletics typically fall into the four categories of recruiting, academic eligibility, financial aid, and the enforcement and infractions process. NCAA rules and regulations focus on amateurism, recruiting, eligibility, playing and practice seasons, athletically related financial aid, championships, and enforcement (2010–2011 NCAA Division I Manual). While there are many other rules and regulations within the nearly six hundred-page 2012 NCAA Manual, the current regulation of NCAA Division I athletics revolves around the core issues of getting

the athlete to campus, maintaining academic eligibility, providing permissible financial assistance, and having a pseudo-judicial system to enforce the rules that the membership set forth. The mechanisms in place to try to manage all of these areas and ensure that the institution is operating within NCAA, conference, and institutional guidelines usually falls to an internal part of an athletic department—the compliance office. An athletic compliance office structure varies by institution, and the size and emphasis is usually dictated by the size of the athletic department and/or if the department has run afoul of NCAA regulations. The office is usually headed by an associate or assistant athletic director of compliance, and the office may have a primary or dual reporting line to offices outside of athletics to demonstrate institutional control of the athletic department. Staffing can vary from a few generalists who have expertise in many NCAA areas or specialized individuals who concentrate on academic eligibility, financial aid, recruiting, and other areas of NCAA rules and regulations. Many schools have increased their compliance staffs exponentially in response to NCAA sanctions (J. Foley, personal communication).

Rules compliance has become important to institutions due to the intense media spotlight and popularity of intercollegiate athletic programs, specifically in the NCAA. Even the smallest violation can become local—and even national—news due to the technology and social media outlets available today. Institutions strive to keep negative compliance news out of the media, and the growth of compliance as a profession in intercollegiate athletics has been a direct result of the desire of an institution to stay out of the papers. Just as positive athletic news can be a public relations boon to a university, conversely the same is true with negative news. Due to the complexities and high stress environment of athletic compliance offices, the turnover in these positions is high. In addition, those who work in compliance are now becoming better trained and many have legal and advanced degrees.

The concept of rules compliance has technically been with intercollegiate athletics since its inception, as there have always been rules to follow. Rules compliance as an obligation of the membership is currently covered by NCAA Bylaw 2.8. While many schools followed the rules, many did not and NCAA institutions made more rules and regulations in an attempt to keep competitive equity as level as possible for all institutions in all sports. The NCAA manual grew from a mere two hundred pages in 1984–85 to nearly six hundred pages today. The growth and matriculation of NCAA rules virtually mandated that institutions adopt a pseudo internal affairs department similar to what might be found in corporate America. The purpose of this department was to self-detect and self-report NCAA violations to their conference office and the NCAA. In addition, the institution would develop corrective measures to ensure that the violation did not occur again. If the violation was determined to be major by the NCAA, there typically would be an investigation and potential adjudication and sanctioning of the offending institution and individuals. Another impetus for putting individuals in these positions was largely driven by the NCAA "death penalty" case against Southern Methodist University, which resulted in their storied football program being suspended for two years. Other universities took notice, and compliance offices to help manage and deal with NCAA rules violations were essentially born.

In the mid-1980s to the end of that decade, when compliance offices were being formed across the NCAA, institutions realized the heightened scrutiny and the desire to avoid NCAA violations but still often shortchanged the importance by assigning compliance oversight to an assistant coach, lower-level staff member, or even to administrative support personnel. Several benchmarks in the areas of eligibility, recruiting, and financial aid in the 1990s would force institutions to place a higher importance on rules compliance along with providing more resources and a higher budget to avoid breaking NCAA rules.

IMPORTANT AREAS OF ICA COMPLIANCE

Academic Eligibility

One area that often falls under the purview of the athletic compliance office or at least works very closely with it is academic support. Due to the multitude of academic eligibility rules and the demands that an athletic schedule can have on an individual athlete academically, it is critical that the institution provide a level of specialized academic support services for the athletic population. A typical academic support services office for athletics is made up of a director and several assistants/counselors. Other than the compliance office, an academic support office is a conduit to the greater university at large and must have great relationships with the academic division, deans, and faculty members. Similar to the compliance office, oftentimes this entity will report directly to someone outside the athletic department, such as the provost, to eliminate any potential conflict of interest charges or undue pressure from the athletic department.

Historically, many institutions have been accused of "looking the other way" when an athlete begins to fail academically (Wyatt, 1999). Viewing the benefits of intercollegiate athletics in a more practical sense, athletics has given a large number of student athletes the opportunity to attend colleges and universities that they otherwise might have not attended (Blackburn & Nyikos, 1974: Vedder, Villwock & Denhart 2010). Intercollegiate athletics has become a dichotomy; it can be good or bad for the participants, dependent primarily on the goals and motivation of the institution. Arguably many believe that college athletics today has become dehumanizing and shows less respect for fun and fair play, and the research suggests the reason lies in the fact that sports today are organized around the needs of frustrated adults (Zimbalist, 1999), the commercialization of the games, and the emphasis on revenue and winning rather than on the values of the sandlot, high school, and college participants (Alley 1974; Tunis, 1958). Thus, the need for greater oversight and rules compliance has become paramount

The abuse of academic requirements spread to the primary and secondary levels of education, where outstanding athletic prospects existed. College and university personnel began to influence the education—or lack thereof—of prospective student athletes by bending the rules, primarily by falsifying transcripts and standardized admission test scores, to gain admission of the prospect to the institution. Academic abuse at the base of higher education denied some individuals the chance to be successful in college, or admitted many who just were simply not prepared or skilled enough to attend college. If a prospective student athlete was not prepared academically for the rigors of college-level work, graduation could be an unattainable goal. Up until the mid-1980s, a high proportion of incoming freshman student athletes fit this category (Chu, Seagrave, & Becker, 1985).

Hanford (1974) reaffirmed this predicament when he stated in a groundbreaking American College of Education (ACE) report that "the problems of intercollegiate athletics will be solved only when its relationship to the education process is finally defined" (p. 336). Some will argue that this relationship today is still extremely complicated and has not yet been defined despite repeated attempts by the existing governing structures.

Initial Eligibility

The NCAA's first attempt to enact a national standard of athletic eligibility dependent on academic performance was the 1.600 grade point average rule, enacted in 1965. This translated to all NCAA athletes needing at least a C- academic average to compete on the playing fields. In 1973 this rule was modified to a more standard 2.0 GPA requirement. This basic standard held for more than a decade although there were numerous stories of athletes being shepherded through easy courses—if at all—to ensure that a 2.0 GPA was maintained (Ridpath, 2002). It became clear that ensuring that prospective athletes were indeed ready for college-level academic work was imperative to guarantee academic primacy and a level playing field academically.

In 1986, the NCAA enacted NCAA Bylaw 5-1-(j), later known as NCAA Bylaw 14.3, or what is more commonly called Proposition 48 (NCAA 1986, 2000). This remains probably one of the more significant attempts at defining the relationship that Hanford spoke of in 1974 and is still being debated today. Proposition 48 enacted a national initial eligibility standard with requirements for prospective student athletes to be completed prior to initial college enrollment (Howard-Hamilton & Watt, 2001; NCAA, 1986). The requirements consisted of passing a specific number of college preparatory classes, achieving a certain grade point average in those college preparatory classes, and obtaining a corresponding ACT or SAT correlated on a sliding scale to a specific GPA. These standards were enacted to curtail potential academic abuses, increase the chances for a student athlete to be able to perform college-level work, and improve chances for graduation (Benson, 1991, 1994, 1997).

Proposition 48 and its later iteration, Proposition 16, were not without controversy in that they likely disadvantaged those from lower socioeconomic backgrounds and minorities as the tests were culturally biased. Although research demonstrated that college preparatory test scores and a core college prep curriculum are the best predictors of college success, the NCAA did the right thing by adopting the "partial qualifier" measure, which enabled those with lower test scores and high GPAs—and vice versa—the ability to earn a scholarship and practice in the initial year of enrollment (Ridpath, 2002).

There have been changes to initial eligibility standards over the years to include an adoption of a full sliding scale, an increase in successful completion of college preparatory courses from fourteen to sixteen, eliminating the partial qualifier provisions, along with provisions to assist those who have certified learning disabilities in obtaining initial eligibility (NCAA, 2010–11). An example the NCAA uses on its website (www.ncaa.org) in describing the current sliding scale for initial

eligibility is that the former partial qualifier standard has been fully expanded. For example, if a prospective athlete earns a 3.0 grade point average in sixteen core courses, that individual must score at least 620 on the SAT or 52 on the ACT. As the GPA increases, the required test score decreases, and vice versa. These measures were taken to decrease any perception that initial eligibility was culturally biased and unfair.

Continuing Eligibility

Once prospective NCAA athletes are cleared to compete, they must continue to meet academic standards to maintain eligibility. These often are referred to as "continuing eligibility" or "progress toward degree" rules. Satisfactory progress and continuing eligibility are largely the purview of the institution, but several NCAA requirements have to be met, including being enrolled in a full-time program of studies and making progress toward a degree by completing 40 percent of the coursework required for a degree by the end of their second year, 60 percent by the end of their third year, and 80 percent by the end of their fourth year. The purpose of these rules is for all athletes to continually be on track to earn their degrees within a maximum of five years of full-time enrollment, as an NCAA athlete is only able to earn five years of athletically related financial aid (www.ncaa.org).

Academic Progress Rate

A new wrinkle with regard to academics and athletic eligibility is the Academic Progress Rate for NCAA Division I institutions. While most eligibility rules were geared toward the individual and team, the APR is intended to ensure institutional accountability. According to the NCAA website, the APR is a metric developed to track the academic achievement of teams each academic term.

In simple terms, each athlete receiving athletically related financial aid earns one retention point for staying in school and one eligibility point for being academically eligible. A team's total points are divided by points possible and then multiplied by one thousand to equal the team's Academic Progress Rate score. The NCAA calculates the rate as a rolling, four-year figure that takes into account all the points student athletes could earn for remaining in school and remaining academically eligible during that period. Teams that do not earn an APR above 925 out of a possible 1,000 face penalties ranging from scholarship reductions to more severe sanctions. Teams that fall below 900 can face even more severe sanctions to include postseason bans and restricted association membership (www.ncaa.org).

Financial Aid

Another critical area of NCAA compliance is managing athletic support and other financial aid for athletes. Financial aid is governed by NCAA Bylaw 15 and includes all types of financial assistance available to those who compete. The most common form of athletic financial aid is the athletic scholarship. A full or complete athletic scholarship consists of tuition, books, course-related fees, room, and board. Some scholarships can be a portion of a full scholarship for certain teams classified as equivalency sports. Other teams, such as football and men's and women's basketball, are considered head-count sports and all receiving athletic aid must receive a full ride. Teams are restricted by team limitations such as eighty-five total scholarships for football, and thirteen and fifteen scholarships for

men's and women's basketball, respectively. All teams have different team and individual limits (detailed in NCAA Bylaw 15).

One of the more confusing areas of financial aid for athletes, and one of the more challenging for compliance offices, is determining permissible financial aid outside of the scholarship. These nuances often require an athletic department to employ one or several athletic financial aid counselors to monitor this fast-changing environment. Every dollar an athlete earns will get scrutiny and this includes employment, academic scholarships, government grants, loans, and even money from family members and friends, etc. All are subject to a compliance audit and are potential violations. Since this area includes money, it is important to have strict monitoring of this area to ensure NCAA rules on financial aid and amateurism are not broken (NCAA, 2010–11).

Recruiting

Another key area of NCAA compliance, and also one of extreme scrutiny and potential public embarrassment, involves athlete recruitment. The challenge for compliance offices is that the bulk of recruiting takes place off-campus and away from the direct eyes of the compliance staff. Like financial aid, this is an area that requires multiple levels of oversight, but in the end it is largely based on the compliance rules education given to the coaches who are on the front line recruiting those athletes.

Athlete recruitment at many schools is also a very public undertaking that has intense public interest as fans from the high school and interested colleges wait and watch where a key prospect may go, and with it raising hopes that the gaining institution may increase its fortunes through the playing field. With the advent of Internet sites that follow every recruiting move, competition for the best players by competitive coaches, and the advent of social media, the chances of a violation occurring exponentially increase.

NCAA Bylaw 13, which covers recruiting, consists of fifty-two pages and several hundred sub-bylaws. It is a broad bylaw that addresses such issues as what specific coaches are allowed to recruit, how many can recruit, how many phone calls are allowed and when, how many in-person contacts are allowed, and how many in-person evaluations are allowed. And these are just a few of the issues covered in the recruiting bylaws. Indeed, the complex rules present a challenge to compliance offices on a daily basis (NCAA, 2010–11).

NCAA Enforcement and Infractions

Arguably the main power invested in the membership and the NCAA National Office rests within its enforcement and infractions division. Colleges and universities place huge resources via their aforementioned compliance and academic support services in an attempt to avoid major NCAA sanctions, which can have a detrimental effect on the competitiveness of an athletic program.

The uniqueness of the current NCAA enforcement and infractions process is grounded in self-policing by the institutions along with self-reporting violations to the NCAA enforcement staff to adjudicate the violations. The uniqueness of the process is based upon a commitment to follow the rules and checks and balances by peers and peer institutions that try to promote a level playing field in an ultra-competitive revenue-driven environment. It can be argued that

institutions will try to operate on the fringes of the rules to get that competitive advantage over another school.

The specific guidelines for the NCAA enforcement and infractions process are found in NCAA Bylaws 19 and 32 (NCAA, 2010-2011). Bylaw 19 covers the internal national office-based enforcement staff. The mission of NCAA enforcement is:

> "It shall be the mission of the NCAA enforcement program to eliminate violations of NCAA rules and impose appropriate penalties should violations occur. The program is committed to fairness of procedures and the timely and equitable resolution of infractions cases. The achievement of these objectives is essential to the conduct of a viable and effective enforcement program. Further, an important consideration in imposing penalties is to provide fairness to uninvolved student-athletes, coaches, administrators, competitors and other institutions." (Bylaw 19.01.1, NCAA, 2011, p.319).

It is an obligation of the institution as a condition of membership to self-report to the conference and NCAA any violations of NCAA regulations and to cooperate fully in any and all NCAA and conference inquiries. Not cooperating or even the perception of non-cooperation is a violation of NCAA rules and can have serious repercussions for an institution, such as occurred with Georgia Tech and the University of Central Florida who were cited by the NCAA in 2011 for non-cooperation and outright misleading NCAA investigators by certain staff members. The NCAA made clear that but for these actions, the penalties would have been less severe ("NCAA Places," 2011; "NCAA Alleges," 2011). Institutional staff members have a heightened obligation to abide by NCAA rules as they could find themselves under a show cause order, which would effectively limit their ability to work at an NCAA-member institution. Also, the school that employed that person could be subject to NCAA penalties itself. Due to the availability of many qualified individuals to serve in coaching and administrative positions, institutions will almost always stay away from individuals who are sanctioned in this manner, lest they be subject to sanctions themselves.

Currently, NCAA rule violations are classified as secondary and major. There have been some recent moves by the NCAA enforcement staff and Committee on Infractions to modify the penalty structure ("NCAA Enforcement," 2011), but as of this textbook printing the traditional level of violations remain in force.

Secondary violations (commonly called minor violations) are classified in the 2010–11 NCAA Manual, Bylaw 19.02.2.1, as *a violation that is isolated or inadvertent in nature, provides or is intended to provide only a minimal recruiting, competitive or other advantage and does not include any significant recruiting inducement or extra benefit. Multiple secondary violations by a member institution may collectively be considered as a major violation.* Institutions will typically report ten to twenty secondary violations per year. A strong system of self-reporting is, ironically, demonstrative of a well-run compliance program and lends to an athletic department that is doing the auditing and follow-up needed to ensure the school is abiding by NCAA rules. Conversely, a program that does not have a history of self-detecting and self-reporting is often viewed with skepticism.

NCAA major violations are those that are typically headline-grabbing and something that institutions strive to avoid through strong compliance programs, avoidance, or in extreme cases simply hoping they do not get caught, as the competitive desire to win might overwhelm the desire to do the right thing as an NCAA member. NCAA Bylaw 19.02.2.2 stipulates that *all violations other than secondary violations are major violations, specifically including those that provide an extensive recruiting or competitive advantage.*

Bylaw 19 also details presumptive penalties for secondary and major allegations along with the makeup of the Committee on Infractions (COI), which is the adjudicating body that determines sanctions, if any, using information provided by the institution, conference, and NCAA investigators. This is usually done in a one-day administrative hearing in which certain people must appear to answer questions and discuss the case. Allegations of NCAA major violations will typically trigger an on-campus investigation by the affiliated conference and NCAA enforcement investigators.

Bylaw 19 also covers the appeal rights of an institution and potential eligibility ramifications for the athlete, but the procedures of an enforcement investigation and the procedures of a COI hearing are covered in NCAA Bylaw 32. Once the NCAA has received information from the institution or other sources that it deems potentially credible, it will typically send a Notice of Allegations to the institutional president or CEO informing him or her that the NCAA is beginning an investigation of these allegations. It does not mean the institution or involved individuals are responsible, just that there is information the NCAA must confirm or refute. If the information is found to be not credible, the enforcement staff will terminate the investigation and inform the president via official letter.

No two NCAA investigations are alike but there are specific procedures that NCAA investigators and involved individuals must follow. Individual interviews must be recorded and the tape provided to the interviewee. Individuals interviewed or alleged to have violated NCAA rules have the right to be represented by counsel at all times during the investigation. The NCAA has no subpoena power but if a person refuses to talk to the NCAA and is an athletically related employee it could be deemed a failure to cooperate.

If the information is found more likely than not to be credible, the NCAA under Bylaw 32.6.1 will send the institutional president a Notice of Allegations. This is *"when the enforcement staff determines that there is sufficient information to warrant, it shall issue a cover letter and notice of allegations to the chancellor or president of the institution involved with copies to the faculty athletics representative and the athletics director and to the executive officer (usually a commissioner) of the conference of which the institution is a member"* (p. 407). This notice also includes notice to specific individuals and steps that the institution must take during this phase of the investigatory process to ensure integrity. Typically this means that there will probably be a COI hearing within six to eighteen months after receipt of the notice for the institution to have final disposition of the case. There are opportunities for a summary disposition process and expedited hearing if the institution, involved individuals, and the enforcement staff agree on the findings of fact and proposed penalties, if any. This

agreement must still be approved by the COI, but it is a much quicker way to end what can be a very painful process for an institution (See Chart Path of an NCAA Investigation).

A COI hearing is an extremely structured process. The COI is made up mostly of peers from NCAA institutions including athletic directors, conference commissioners, and faculty athletic representatives. These are voluntary positions but require a large volume of work that includes numerous conference calls and at least six meetings per year lasting three to four days each, during which there are several hearings and administrative business to attend to. A full-time staff member at the NCAA is designated as the administrator for the COI to assist in managing the day-to-day operations. In response to a congressional-mandated review of the enforcement and infractions process conducted by former Solicitor General Rex Lee in 1991, the NCAA added two outside nonaffiliated members to the COI to give a better appearance of fairness and impartiality (House Subcommittee on the Constitution, 2006). These individuals are typically lawyers and/ or retired judges.

Before the hearing there will be a prehearing conference, sometimes conducted in person but it could also be via conference call. The purpose of this meeting is to discuss and clarify any remaining issues, what the staff still believes are violations, and identify what the institution wants to challenge the severity of or dispute before the COI. Once the prehearing is finished final documents are submitted by both parties to the COI in advance of the hearing. Procedurally, the hearing will consist of opening statements from the institution, enforcement staff, and potentially involved individuals. Once the initial introductions and statements have

NCAA Division I Legislative Process

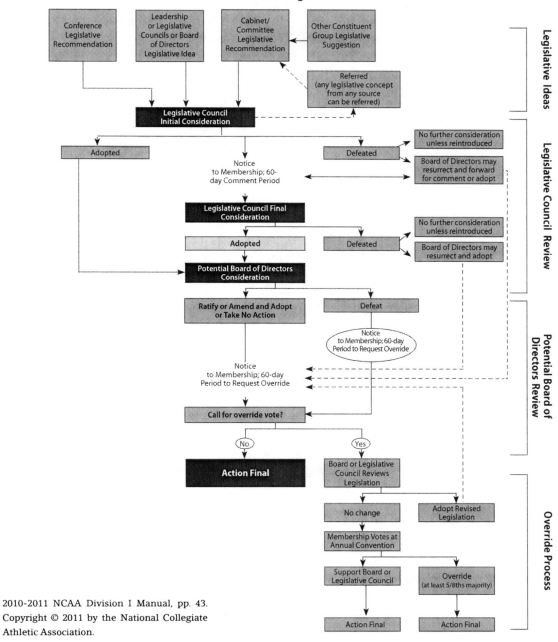

been made the enforcement staff will state what allegations it believes are violations. The institutional party will follow that with its perception and reasons as to why it should not be considered a violation or if they substantially agree. Even if there is substantial agreement, the COI will ask questions as it assists them in assessing which penalties, if any, to apply to a certain allegation. The COI will ask questions of both parties until it feels satisfied that it has enough information to analyze and assess penalties. This can go on for hours depending on how many allegations are involved. Some hearings have lasted nearly sixteen hours or have gone over several days. Some take only a few hours. It all depends on the volume of allegations.

After the hearing the COI will analyze and adjudicate the information for about six to eight weeks before issuing a public infractions report detailing findings and sanctions. If the institution disagrees with the findings, which can include probation, restrictions on postseason play, scholarship losses, and adverse employment actions, it can file a Notice of Appeal within fifteen days. The appeal is heard by a separate committee (also recommended by the Lee Commission in 1991) called the Infractions Appeals Committee. Having standing to appeal findings by the COI is very narrow. According to Bylaw 32.10.4, *"a penalty determined by the Committee on Infractions shall not be set aside on appeal except on a showing by the appealing party that the penalty is excessive such that it constitutes an abuse of discretion"* (p. 413). Bylaw 32.10.4.2 follows by stating *"findings of violations made by the Committee on Infractions shall not be set aside on appeal, except on a showing by the appealing party that a finding is clearly contrary to the evidence presented to the Committee on Infractions; the facts found by the Committee on Infractions do not constitute a violation of the Association's rules or there was a procedural error and but for the error, the Committee on Infractions would not have made the finding of violation"* (p. 413). Appeals hearings are conducted in a similar fashion as a COI hearing, and even though the standards for appeal are narrow

the IAC has changed several findings by the COI over the years and has made the process fairer to all involved.

Changes are probably coming to the NCAA enforcement and infractions process as the NCAA itself is undergoing radical changes in the era of large television contracts and conference realignment. Recently, NCAA Vice President for Enforcement Julie Roe Lach and NCAA President Mark Emmert discussed membership-driven recommendations in 2012 that would focus enforcement on more serious cases and de-emphasize time spent on minor or secondary violations. This can include a complete revision of the NCAA rulebook, staffing, and even changes to the COI. As of this textbook printing many issues were still being discussed, but what is clear is that the NCAA is evolving with the business of intercollegiate athletics while attempting to maintain the amateur model and keep college sports part of the overall educational process. It will be interesting to see what changes will be made to NCAA compliance and rules enforcement in the future, as well as with intercollegiate athletics as a whole as the constant evolution continues.

REFERENCES

Websites:

http://www.farawebsite.org

http://naia.cstv.com/

http://www.ohio.edu/facultysenate/standing-comm/ICA-Committee-page.cfm

http://www.icmrindia.org/courseware/Management%20Control%20Systems/MCS11.htm

http://www.theciaa.com/information/about_ciaa/index

http://naia.cstv.com/member-services/about/

http://www.thenccaa.org/history.html

http://www.nirsa.org/Content/NavigationMenu/AboutUs/NIRSAGovernanceCommission/governance.htm

www.bluefishjobs.com

www.education.stateuniversity.com/pages/1851/College-Athletics-NATIONAL-COLLEGIATE-ATHLETIC-ASSOCIATION.html

http://www.eiu.edu/ncaa/docs/Recertification_Report_Attachments.pdf

1983 NCAA Division I Manual (1st ed.). (1983). Mission, KN: National Collegiate Athletic Association.

1991 NCAA Division I Manual (1st ed.). (1996)1. Overland Park, KN: National Collegiate Athletic Association.

1996 NCAA Division I Manual (1st ed.). (1996). Overland Park, KN: National Collegiate Athletic Association.

1999 NCAA Division I Manual (1st ed). (1999). Overland Park, KN: National Collegiate Athletic Association.

2000 NCAA Division I Manual (1st ed.). (2000). Indianapolis, IN: National Collegiate Athletic Association.

2009–2010 NCAA Division II Manual. (2010). Indianapolis, IN: National Collegiate Athletic Association.

2009–2010 NCAA Division III Manual. (2010). Indianapolis, IN: National Collegiate Athletic Association.

2010–2011 NCAA Division I Manual. (2010). Indianapolis, IN: National Collegiate Athletic Association.

"About the NCCAA," (n.d.), Retrieved March 5, 2011, from http://www.thenccaa.org/history.html

"About the NAIA," (2011), Retrieved March 4, 2011, from http://naia.cstv.com/

Abney, R. and J.B. Parks. (1998). Intercollegiate athletics. In J.B. Parks, B.R.K. Zanger, and J. Quarterman, eds. *Contemporary sport management* pp. 119–138). Champaign, IL: Human Kinetics.

"AGB statement on board responsibilities for intercollegiate athletics," (2007, November 16), Retrieved March 1, 2011, from http://www.agb.org/news/2010-08/agb-statement-board-responsibilities-intercollegiate-athletics

Benson, M., ed. (1991). *A graphic display of initial eligibility rules applied to 1984 and 1985 freshman student-athletes (NCAA Research Report 91–04)*. Overland Park, KN: National Collegiate Athletic Association.

Benson, M., ed. (1994). *Executive Summary of Reports 91–01 to 91–06 (NCAA Research Report 91–07)*. Overland Park, KN: National Collegiate Athletic Association.

Benson, M., ed. (1997). *Characteristics of student-athlete data in the 1995–96 NCAA initial eligibility clearinghouse (NCAA Research Report 97–02)*. Overland Park, KN: National Collegiate Athletic Association.

Blackburn, R. and M. Nyikos. (1974). College football and Mr. Chips. *Phi Delta Kappan* 56, 110–113.

Brown, G. (1999, November 22). NCAA answers call to reform. *NCAA News* pp. A1–A4.

Chu, D., J. Seagrave, and B. Becker, eds. (1985). *Sport and higher education.* Human Kinetics Publishers, Inc.: Champaign, IL.

Crowley, J. (2006). *In the arena: The NCAA's first century.* Indianapolis, IN: NCAA.

Denhart, M., R. Villwock, and R. Vedder. (2010). *The academics-athletics trade off: Universities and intercollegiate athletics.* Washington, DC: Center for College Affordability and Productivity.

Falla, J (1981). *NCAA: The voice of college sports.* National Collegiate Athletic Association: Mission, KN.

Funk, G. (1991). *Major violation. The unbalanced priorities in athletics and academics.* Leisure Press: Champaign, IL.

Gerdy, J. (2006). *Air ball: American education's failed experiment with elite athletics.* Oxford: University of Mississippi Press.

Gillum, J. (2010, April 1). Schools raising fees to keep up with costs of college sports. *USA TODAY.* Retrieved on March 5, 2011, from http://www.usatoday.com/sports/college/2010-04-01-college-sports-subsidies_N.htm

Grant, R. R., J. Leadley, and Z. Zygmont. (2008). *The Economics of Intercollegiate Sports.* Hackensack, NJ: World Scientific.

Grimes, and Chressansiths (1994). Collegiate sports, NCAA sanctions, and alumni contributions to academics. *The American Journal of Economics and Sociology* 53, 27–38.

Howard-Hamilton, M., and S. Watt. (2001). Student services for athletes. *New Directions for Student Services 93*, 1–7.

Hums, M. A., and J.C. MacLean. (2009). *Governance and policy in sport organizations.* Scottsdale: Holcomb Hathaway.

Institutional control: Constitution, Article 6. 2010–2011 *NCAA Manual.* NCAA: Indianapolis, IN. p. 45–46. Retrieved March 3, 2011, from http://www.ncaapublications.com/product-downloads/D111.pdf

Knight Commission on Intercollegiate Athletics. (1991, 1993). *Reports of the Knight founda-tion commission on intercollegiate athletics.* Charlotte, NC: W.C. Friday.

Knight Commission on Intercollegiate Athletics (2001). *A call to action.* Charlotte, NC: W.C. Friday.

Knight Commission on Intercollegiate Athletics (2010). *Restoring the balance: Dollars, values, and the future of college sports.* Charlotte, NC: W.C. Friday.

Knight Commission on Intercollegiate Athletics. (2009, October). *Quantitative and qualitative research with football bowl subdivision university presidents on the costs and financing of intercollegiate athletics. Report of findings and implications.* Art and Science Group, LLC: Carrboro, NC. Retrieved March 1, 2011, from http://www.knightcommissionmedia.org/images/President_Survey_FINAL.pdf

Naughton, J. (1996). Report finds lagging graduation rates among basketball players. *The Chronicle of Higher Education.* Retrieved on September 22, 1999, from http://www.chronicle.com.

"NAIA legislative services," (2011), Retrieved March 4, 2011, from http://naia.cstv.com/member-services/

NCAA, (n.d.), "Composition & sport sponsorship of the NCAA," Retrieved December 10, 2010, from http://www.ncaa.org/wps/portal/ncaahome?WCM_GLOBAL_CONTEXT=/ncaa/NCAA/About+The+NCAA/Membership/membership_breakdown.html

(n.a.), "NCAA alleges violations at UCF," (2011, November 10), Retrieved March 31, 2012, from http://espn.go.com/college-sports/story/_/id/7212871/ucf-knights-accused-recruiting-violations-ad-resigns-men-basketball-coach-suspended (n.a.), "NCAA places Georgia Tech on probation," (2011, July 18), Retrieved March 31, 2012, from http://espn.go.com/college-sports/story/_/id/6769894/ncaa-places-georgia-tech-yellow-jackets-four-years-probation

"NJCAA National News," (2009), National Junior College Athletic Association, Retrieved October 25, 2010, from: http://www.njcaa.org/newsArticle.cfm?articleId=8880

Ohio University, (2011), "Ohio University: Faculty Senate: Standing Committees: ICA Committee page," Retrieved March 1, 2011, from http://www.ohio.edu/facultysenate/standingcomm/ICA-Committee-page.cfm

Ridpath, B. (2002). *NCAA student athlete characteristics as indicators of academic achievement and graduation from college.* Ann Arbor, MI: UMI Dissertation Services, Pro Quest.Ridpath, B. (2002).

Ridpath, B., and R. Abney. (2012). Governance in Intercollegiate Athletics. In King, C., D. McClellan, and G. Rockey, eds. *Handbook of college athletics and recreation Administration (1st ed.).* Hoboken, NJ: Jossey Bass.

Ridpath, B., M. Chapman, and M. Denhart. (2011). *An examination of increased NCAA Division I athletic department budgets: A case study of student perceptions of fee allocations for athletics.* Paper presented at the College Sports Research Institute Annual Conference, Chapel Hill, NC.

"Rutgers University Policy number 50.1.14 Governance of Intercollegiate Athletics," (2010, April 15), Retrieved March 1, 2011, from http://policies.rutgers.edu/PDF/Section50/50.1.14-current.pdf

Staurowsky, E. J., and R. Abney. (2010). Intercollegiate athletics. In P. Pedersen, J.B. Parks, B.R.K. Zanger, and J. Quarterman, eds. *Contemporary sport management* (4th ed., pp. 142–163). Champaign, IL: Human Kinetics.

"Today's NJCAA," (2011), Retrieved March 2, 2011, from http://www.njcaa.org/todaysNJCAA.cfm

Sack, A., and E. Staurowsky. (1998). *College athletes for hire. The evolution and legacy of the NCAA's amateur myth.* Westport, CT: Praeger Publishers.

Suggs, W.,(2003, May 2), "Sports as the university's 'front porch'? The public is skeptical," Retrieved January, 3 2011, from http://chronicle.com/article/Sports-as-the-University-s/11599

"Today's NJCAA," (2011), Retrieved March 2, 2011, from http://www.njcaa.org/todaysNJCAA.cfm

Tunis, J. (1958). *The American way in sports.* New York: Duell, Sloan, and Pierce. Underwood, C. (1984). *The student athlete: eligibility and academic integrity.* East Lansing, MI: Michigan State University Press.

Wyatt, J (1999). Our moral duty to clean up college athletics. *The Chronicle of Higher Education* 45, A56.

Zimbalist, A. (1999). *Unpaid professionals: Commercialism and conflict in big time sports.* Princeton, N.J.: Princeton University Press.

This chapter touches on several themes that concern the commercialization of college sports. These include the changes in college sports fueled by commercialization, the structure of an athletic department's budget, the differences between college sports divisions and the overseeing organizations, the relationship between college sports and the media, and the ethical considerations that arise because of commercialization. In addition, the chapter is enriched with challenging case studies that focus on such topics as the financial well-being of athletic departments, the relationship between the NCAA and the media, and whether college athletes should get paid.

The changes in college sports that came about through commercialization are mostly seen in the sports that produce the lion's share of revenues and expenses, namely men's football and basketball. The conditions that enable the commercialization of college athletics are identified. These conditions then serve as the basis for changes in college sports. Coakley (2009) and Clotfelter (2011) both identify important conditions and the changes fueled by these conditions. These conditions can be traced back to material rewards, the purchasing power of spectators,

3

COMMERCIALISM IN COLLEGE SPORTS

Christian Gilde, Mike Maleg, & Gary Sailes

This Graphic was designed by Kathy and Rebecca Samley

and a distinct lifestyle that commercial sports perpetuate and fans live (Coakley, 2009). The changes that can result from such conditions are that college sports turn more and more into a consumer good, assume an increased entertainment function in the collegiate realm, work as an instrument to attract and manage powerful sponsors, and bring the campus community closer together (Clotfelter, 2011).

The structure of an athletic department's budget can be sizeable and complex. Revenues and expenditures are the main sources of information that one must understand to make sense of an athletic department's budget. Thus, this part of the chapter examines one particular school's budget to make the budgetary dynamics more accessible. On the revenue side, sponsorship monies, media revenues, and ticket incomes stand out. On the expenditure side, staff salaries and financial aid for athletes make up the main share of all expenses.

The different divisions that emerge in college sports and that are defined by organizations such as the NCAA are clearly distinct entities based on their membership, resources, and power. The NCAA distinguishes among three divisions and two subdivisions. A disturbing development among these divisions is the increasing resource disparity between Division I and Divisions II and III. In addition, this part looks at how the NCAA was able to develop its (financial and regulatory) power over time.

The relationship college sports have with the media is special and mutually beneficial. Through this tight and mutually dependent relationship the media can and do exert unprecedented power over college sports. Naturally, media provide filtered information that can influence society. Media can elect what to present to their audience and how they present it. This gives rise to the question of how much the media are part of the commercialization of college sports. Even more interesting and complex is what role regulatory agencies such as the NCAA play in this triangular relationship among the school, media, and NCAA.

The last part of this chapter discusses ethical considerations regarding the commercialization of college sports. In this context interesting questions, such as should college athletes receive professional salaries or how does money in college sports agree with the academic mission of the university, arise. Other issues that point to ethical concerns are the influence of sports money on the campus culture and the payment of substantial head coach salaries. At the end of this chapter, college sports experts and innovative thinkers provide suggestions on what needs to be done to improve the moral fabric of university athletics.

All these points are very important to understand the commercial nature of college sports; these points are addressed in this chapter and supported with interesting case studies, discussions, exercises, and research activities.

INTRODUCTION

In his recent book "Big-Time Sports in American Universities," Charles Clotfelter notes that between 1985 and 2010, average salaries at public universities rose 32 percent for full professors, 90 percent for presidents, and 650 percent for football coaches. Clotfelter as cited in Pappano (2012).

This development begs the question: Are college sports commercialized? Or, might it be better to rephrase the question and ask: Why shouldn't college sports be commercialized? Because of scholastic ideals and the academic mission? Think about the following facts for a moment: First, the higher education price index has increased between three to six percent per year over the last two decades

(Commonfund Institute, U.S. Department of Labor, 2006), which is an increase at a faster rate than the comparable inflation rate; and second, more and more students see themselves as consumers with rights rather than knowledge-seekers who are privileged. By reflecting on these developments one cannot help but realize that higher education is located in an economic market and run like a business. So why should this be different with college sports?

Well, it is not different for college sports. Despite all of the high standards and glossy promises, college sports is a commercial enterprise that serves at least three functions: to generate a (emotional/intangible) profit by operating according to a business model; to create a brand and recognition; and to provide entertainment. The first function has been the center of many discussions, because only twenty-two NCAA Division I schools in 2009–2010 have had more money coming in than going out (Berkowitz & Upton, 2011). Having said that, more often than not brand strength and brand recognition make up for the financial losses in some of the schools that lost money, or perhaps broke even. Who has not heard about college sport powerhouses such as Ohio State, the University of Michigan, Michigan State, and UCLA? Many students want to attend schools such as these simply because of their outstanding sport teams. These schools are already well known for their high levels of academic quality and rigor.

This brings us to the third function that also offsets many of the financial losses incurred by sports programs. The entertainment that college sports provide for many universities is considerable. On football Saturdays, many campuses come to a grinding halt; if

a television network calls, the school reorganizes the academic calendar. These things are justified because they supposedly create community, bring alumni back, and provide the institution with a well-recognized name. If this behavior is surprising, one just has to think about what schools such as Michigan State and Ohio State are best known for, next to their academics: it is sports. And even if the latter two benefits are hard to measure, they are nonetheless visible and considerable.

Thus, college sports follow the trail of money. As Rod Tidwell said in the 1996 film, *Jerry Maguire*, "Show me the money!" To follow the money trail, here is a random selection of college athletic highlights that made the headlines recently:

Table 1. Sample of Profit-Generating College Sports Programs:

School	Generated Revenue	Total Expenses	Difference
Oregon	$119,709,341	$77,856,232	$41,853,109
Alabama	$125,562,153	$98,961,214	$26,600,939
Penn State	$106,614,724	$88,041,921	$18,572,803
Michigan	$106,640,861	$89,133,850	$17,507,011

(Berkowitz and Upton 2011)

1. Following is a table showing a sample of profit-generating college sport programs (2009–2010).
2. NCAA Agrees to $10.8-Billion Deal (over 14 years) to Broadcast Its Men's Basketball Tournament *(Source: Wolverton, 2010)*
3. Median total team revenues by football subdivision I (119 teams) in 2006 were

$35,400,000. (Fulks 2008, Lederman 2008 as cited in Coakley 2009)

4. Highest-Paid Coaches (2010–2011):
   Men's Basketball
   Rick Pitino (Louisville): $7,531,378
   Mike Krzyzewski (Duke): $4,195,519
   Football
   Mack Brown (Texas): $5,193,500
   Nick Saban (Alabama): $4,833,333

(Wieberg 2011)

5. "Salaries for coaches in men's college sports have more than doubled since 2003; last year the average Division I-A head football coach took home nearly $1.5 million, and at BCS schools that figured surpassed $2.1 million. Commissioners of the top five BCS conferences averaged more than $1.1 million in '09, while nine bowl executives currently make more than $350,000." (Wolff 2012)

These considerable figures show that the commercial world is part of college sports. Academic scholars often proclaim that there is a division between the learning world and the athletic world. This division, however, often exists until game day; then many faculty members, students, and administrators are interested in how their team performs. A lot of them even attend the game. Angell (1928) so eloquently remarked: "Intercollegiate athletics are the feature of our universities best known to the American public" (p. 119). And students, administrators, and alumni are not about to change this reality. Unless a student attends Harvard, Yale, Princeton, or Stanford, it is the sports team that will associate the student with a well-recognized school. Clotfelter (2011) so bluntly concedes that "in no other large country in the world is commercialized

athletic competition so closely tied to institutions of higher education" (p. 6).

Besides fulfilling these functions, college athletics that enjoy commercial support often grow and change. This is addressed in the next section.

CHANGES AND GROWTH INFLICTED BY COMMERCIALISM

"The real perpetrators of exploitation [of athletes] are the owners of the professional teams and the university administrators whose chief concern are profits. ..."

Gary Sailes (1986)

By reflecting on Sailes' statement, it is possible to explain what the commercialization of college sports means: if college sports are organized around and played for profit and the commercial needs supersede the academic needs, then college sports are commercialized. When we think of commercialized college sport, we think mainly of men's football and men's basketball played at the Division I level of the NCAA. These are the only sports that generate sufficient revenue to enable them to be considered commercial (Clotfelter, 2011). Although other college sports may raise modest amounts of income, none comes close to these two economic giants on college campuses. How did these two sports grow and become commercialized, while others did not?

The growth of collegiate sports in recent history has been fuelled by increased spectator interest, the abandoning of professional sports due to too much focus on material values, powerful organizations such as the NCAA, sponsorship by companies, and increased media coverage. Other reasons for the recent growth of collegiate sports are the fact that college sports have adopted more commercial values and their operations have been corporatized, a development that triggered, indirectly, increased interest in profit and revenue generation.

Allen Guttmann (1978) has argued that modern sport, in part because of its emphasis on commercialism, has become a phenomenon far removed from the notion of play and from our conception of amateur sport as a somewhat pristine environment in which athletes challenge each other and themselves. "The tendency to transform human behavior into transactions of the marketplace has made sports into a matter of profit and loss" (Guttmann, 1978, p. 62). Is his criticism valid? Has sport changed over the last forty years in the extent to which business considerations affect modern sport?

The commercialization of college sports leads to changes in the fabric and goals of college sports; these changes shift a school's and athletic department's fabric and goals more toward an approach that favors fiscal rigor. It also changes the rules applied to collegiate sports; it might even relax these rules and neglect to consider the academic mission of schools. It turns an area that should emphasize education into an area that focuses on edutainment (this means focusing more on entertainment of the student body than on its education). This edutainment provides a total entertainment experience for the consuming audience. It turns college athletes into entertainers and even uberhuman heroes that are put on pedestals.

When looking at the commercial nature of college athletics, it is interesting to see under which conditions the business of college sports thrives. The next few paragraphs touch on this topic.

Conditions Under Which the Business of College Sports Thrives

Sports at universities and colleges have experienced considerable growth over the last century. Competition in college sports is the major growth factor that fuels media coverage and encourages schools to operate by keeping an eye on the bottom line (Woods, 2011); however, compared with the United States where membership on college sports teams enjoys considerable support, in most other countries university-level sports are supported and sponsored either by local athletic clubs or private and public sources (Hyland, 2008). Consider how one might describe the prevalence of athletics in American higher education to someone from another country in which college sports are, at the most, a by-product of the academic landscape. Years ago, Pritchett (1929) wrote that a visitor from a European university would entertain two questions after seeing American sports:

> What has this astonishing athletic display to do with the work of an intellectual agency like a university? … How do students, devoted to study, find either the time or the money to stage so costly a performance? (p. vi)

To answer these questions one has to focus on two important dimensions of college sports. For one, college sports generate recognition and create a brand. The more recognizable an institution, the more students and funds it will be able to attract; therefore, it will capture much needed intellectual and monetary resources to enable operation of the university. For the other, on U.S. college campuses sports is one of the major factors that create and sustain community; thus, sports are deemed to be worth the time and money spent. This prominent status that college sports enjoy in higher education in the United States allows them to grow and prosper.

But besides the benefits of generating attention and creating community there are several costs associated with the business of university sports. College sports are often not profitable and have to be subsidized by big donations, student fees, and endowment funds. College sports also often require a university to lower its admission standards for athletes so that they can be admitted to a school.

Coakley (2009) identifies five social and economic conditions under which commercial sports prosper, conditions that might be extended to college sports:

- Material rewards have to be offered.
- Commercial sports flourish mostly in populated areas.
- The economic conditions have to be such that spectators can afford the entertainment offered.
- Commercial sports require a lot of money.
- Commercial sports are good at emphasizing a lifestyle based on consumption.

One or more of these conditions are most likely in place when college sports become commercialized and grow into important societal influencers. These changes are discussed in the upcoming section.

Commercialization Produces Change in College Sports

When taking a stroll across many college campuses, for example Boston College, one cannot pardon the feeling of experiencing next to a strong academic presence, a strong athletic presence. Without a doubt Boston College is the biggest college sports show in Boston. This is especially true in college football, basketball, and ice hockey. Signs of this athletic presence include the college football stadium that seats in excess of forty thousand fans; the basketball arena that can seat about eight thousand fans; the college football coach whose salary far exceeds that of any professor; the sports museum that displays the school's proud football heritage; and various Frozen Four championships of the men's ice hockey team. This presents a world that is in a sense commercial and part of an entertainment industry that thrives on brand recognition, fan buy-in, and media coverage.

With the increased commercialization of the college realm, branding has become a standard practice in college sports. Schools brand their name, prized sports stars, and events. UCLA, Alabama, and Penn State are brands that are worth millions of dollars and allow fans to identify with these college sports powerhouses. An example in the realm of prized sports stars that make a school's front page are Heisman Trophy winners in college football. In the case of branded events, the Rose Bowl and the NCAA basketball tournament (March Madness) come to mind.

College sports have, to a certain extent, a social identity that is created by society itself and changes as society changes. The powers that control society also influence college sports. These influential powers are mostly corporate sponsors, company managers, media personnel, advertisers, coaches, school administrators, and NCAA officials. In a survival-of-the-fittest fashion, college teams that are top-level command the greatest power and money, with lower-division teams wheeling less power and money. One influential power, the sponsors, is examined a bit closer in the next part.

Sports as a Business Operation

One can experience the commercial power of college athletics when football and basketball events dominate the event calendar of the school. What other area in higher education can literally bring all university operations to a standstill when it stages an event: parking is hard to find, classes are cut, academic offices are closed, and students, staff, and faculty members are encouraged to attend and support the athletic event.

To justify these operations and big-time college sports, Clotfelter (2011) offers the following reasons:

1. Following the Greek philosophy of education, athletics is seen as a valuable part of a complete education.
2. Monetary rewards can be reaped from big-time college sports operations.
3. Athletic fame draws the attention of the public for the academic mission of an institution and provides heightened visibility.
4. Mass allegiance can have the ability to build communal bonds on campus.

Another reason why schools engage in big-time and commercialized college sports, even though they are mostly deficit-bearing, is the entertainment function (Clotfelter, 2011). Ask people on the street what a certain university is best known for and the answer of most people: it's the football or basketball team. "Recognizing this entertainment function and the conflicts that come with it [big-time commercial college sports] helps to explain some otherwise curious aspects of American higher education. Not only does it explain the outsized attention given to sports in big-time sports universities, the high salaries paid to coaches, and the rampant commercialism, it also helps to explain the value of the NCAA cartel and the reluctance of universities to acknowledge the importance of athletics to their overall missions" (Clotfelter, 2011, p. 21). Thus, how big of a role do athletics play in the overall operation of a school? This is relative and depends on many factors that will be addressed throughout this chapter.

In this context, Clotfelter (2011, p.15) identifies four main roles that must be examined to understand big-time (commercial) athletic operations:

1. Sports are a consumer good that have a market.
2. College sports are a business enterprise that follows a business model.
3. Universities use college sports as a tool to create and maintain support from powerful constituencies.
4. Athletic programs can strengthen campus community.

To enable this lavish and entertaining college sport spectacle, schools have to seek sponsorship from different sources, such as alumni, companies, and public entities. Following are some advantages and disadvantages of college sport sponsorship:

Advantages:
- Increased revenue for athletics
- More exposure for brands
- Increased merchandising sales
- Makes the sports program more appealing
- Enables the payment of competitive coach salaries

Disadvantages:

- Turning college athletics into a business
- A sponsor's social irresponsible conduct might reflect badly on the school
- Misrepresentation and exploitation of athletes
- Where do the loyalties of coaches lie?

Corporate sponsors seek to support college sports because these sports have fans that have high disposable income and are loyal and well-educated. Next to pursuing this attractive fan base, sponsors also support college-level sports because of the following:

- Maximum exposure
- Brand awareness
- Association with winning products
- Cross-product marketing
- Return on investment

But who are the sponsors/corporate partners that want to be part of a daring enterprise such as college sports? Following is a list of some major corporate partners for 2011 that support the NCAA:

Table 2. Company Industry Sector

Allstate	Insurance
AT&T	Telecommunications
Buick	Automobile
Capital One	Banking
Coca-Cola	Nonalcoholic beverages
Enterprise Rent-A-Car	Car rental
Infiniti	Automobile
LG	Electronics
Lowe's	Home improvement

Northwestern Mutual	Mutual Funds
Reese's	Candy
Unilever	Consumer products
UPS	Parcel delivery
Wheat Thins	Consumer Products

Source: National Collegiate Athletic Association.

Sponsors often contribute considerable sums of money to the budgets of a governing organization (e.g., NCAA) as well as a college athletic department. These budget matters will be discussed in the upcoming paragraphs.

A COLLEGE ATHLETIC DEPARTMENT'S BUDGET

A school's athletic budget is a complex being. It takes some patience and insight to understand the dynamics of such a budget. The truth of the matter, however, is that according to Fulks (2009) there are about nineteen hundred intercollegiate sports programs in the United States, and less than twenty-five of them consistently make more money than they spend (Coakley, 2009). Thus, it is a misconception that college sports are a big money-maker for a school and are self-supporting. Often, these losses are offset by special fund-raising campaigns, corporate sponsorship, increased student fees, public monies, and monetary infusions from a school's endowment. Orszag and Orszag (2005) dispelled another misconception: despite previous claims, the amount of money spent on big-time college sports has no effect on the academic quality of incoming students.

Following is a table (Coakley 2009, p. 493) that presents the median revenues and expenditures of an athletic department by Division I subdivisions:

To see the bigger picture, in the following table Clotfelter (2011, pp.18–20) lists the annual expenditures of selected athletic departments.

Table 3.4. Top 100 Universities by Expenditures on Athletics, in Millions of Dollars, Fiscal Year 2009

Rank	University	Expenses ($ M)
1	University of Texas, Austin	112.9
2	Ohio State University	102.1
3	University of Florida	101.5
4	Louisiana State University	94.0
5	University of Tennessee	92.5
...		
50	Oregon State University	50.2
51	Northwestern University	48.6
52	Baylor University	48.5
53	University of Colorado, Boulder	48.2
54	Georgia Tech	48.1
...		

96	Florida International University	21.3
97	Western Kentucky University	21.0
98	Tulane University	20.8
99	Boise State University	20.5
100	Marshall University	20.0

Source: U.S. Department of Education. www.ope.ed.gov/athletics. Copyright in the Public Domain.

The commercial and financial management of a university and its athletic department can be quite complicated. Schools have to plan, finance, and schedule all the sports activities and put contingency plans in place in case financial losses are incurred. Often, the contingency plans to offset financial losses are tipping into the school's endowment, increasing advertising revenues, seeking more sponsorship monies, and diverting money from tuition income.

The next section presents an example of one school's athletic budget, namely that of Indiana University at Bloomington.

An Example: Indiana University at Bloomington

To make the financial dynamics of an athletic department's budget more accessible, a case

Table 3. Median Revenues and Expenditures by Division I Subdivisions, 2006

	Median Total Revenues	Median Generated Revenues	Median Total Expenses	Median Net Revenue (or Deficit)
Football Bowl Subdivision (N=119)	$35,400,000	$26,342,000	$35,756,000	-$7,265,000
Football Championship Subdivision (N=(118)	$9,642,00	$2,345,000	$9,485,000	-$7,121,000
Division I–NO Football (N=94)	$8,771,000	$1,828,000	$8,918,000	-$6,607,000

Source: National Collegiate Athletic Association

study will be used. The athletic budget gives the university a tool to strategically plan and control the financial well-being of the athletic department and make decisions based on this information. It shows in detail the approximate expenditures and receipts for a fiscal year. The athletic budget can also provide the school and its administrators with a means of monitoring and evaluating the financial performance of its sports, and their different sources of expense and revenue over time. Possible inconsistencies in the budget can point out possible problems and red flags to the school as far as its athletic department's financial performance is concerned.

This part will take a closer look at the annual athletic budget of one university, Indiana University at Bloomington. Starting with the expenditures, which were $65,796,415 for the 2009–2010 fiscal year (Berkowitz, Upton, & Gillum, 2010), one can see that support staff and coaching salaries and benefits of $22,780,182 consume the lion's share of this athletic department's budget (34 percent of the total expenses); salaries for the coach, training staff, and athletic support personnel have to be covered. Financial aid for student-athletes of $10,254,216 (15 percent of the total expenses) is the second-largest item on this department's expense sheet (Berkowitz, Upton, & Gillum, 2010). Other large positions on the expense sheet are $8,927,557 (13 percent) for direct facility maintenance and rental, and $3,439,674 (5 percent) for team travel (Berkowitz, Upton, & Gillum, 2010). In conclusion, coach and staff salaries represent the biggest expense on an athletics department expense sheet— and here in particular, the football coach received an annual salary of $1,260,000 in 2010 (Wieberg, 2011). Following is a chart that shows the institution's expense distribution.

Following the expenses are the revenue streams of Indiana University at Bloomington, which were $69,287,811 for the 2009–2010 fiscal year (Berkowitz, Upton, & Gillum, 2010). Here, NCAA conference distributions with $24,179,840 (35 percent), contributions with $18,475,498 (27 percent), ticket sales with $13,346,437 (19 percent), and royalties and contracts with $5,015,808 (7 percent) are the major sources of income (Berkowitz, Upton, & Gillum, 2010). This shows that next to fans, media and sponsors have a considerable stake in the activities of an athletic department. The two main sports that generate most of the revenue at Indiana are men's basketball and football (Schoettle, 2010). Not surprisingly, these two sports are also the two major expense lines in the budget. The figure that follows presents this institution's sources of income.

Finally, when subtracting expenses from revenues one can see that for fiscal year 2009–2010 Indiana University at Bloomington generated a profit of $3,491,369. This places the university among the twenty-two NCAA Division I schools that were profitable in 2009–2010. When browsing through the Indiana budget and databases that report the financial details of college sports programs (such as the *USA TODAY* database), one will realize that many institutional budgets of Division I schools have a similar makeup and can be understood and interpreted in a comparable fashion.

The overall financial state of Bloomington is satisfactory, for now. The university's profitability is marginal, the ability to generate NCAA income and royalties from sponsorship contracts seemed good, and the ability to produce revenue through ticket sales promising. The future of Bloomington seems to be encouraging to remain among the small number of NCAA teams that break even in college sports.

Limitations of a financial analysis of any sort become apparent when different methods of compiling data are used and financial relations expressed in statements, and in form of ratios and other financial indicators are taken too literal or out of context.

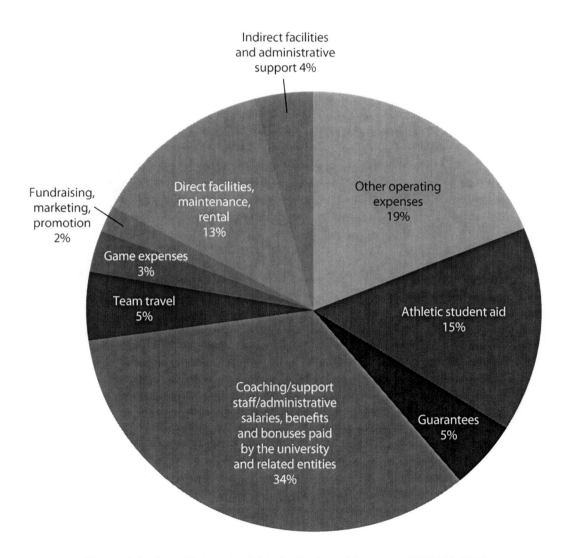

Figure 1. Indiana University Athletics Budgeted Expenses FY 2009-2010

Source: Indiana University Athletic Department.

MOST BIG-TIME SCHOOLS WINNING THE PROFIT GAME

In 2009–10, athletics programs at 22 of the 228 Division I public schools generated enough money from media rights contracts, ticket sales, donations and other sources (not including allocated revenue from institutional or government support or student fees) to cover their expenses. See chart on page 67.

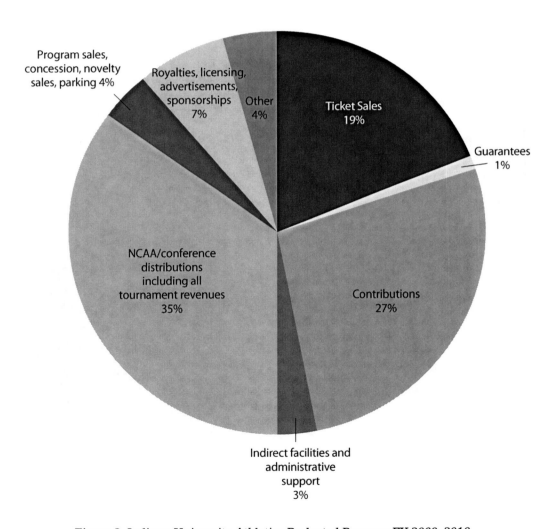

Figure 2. Indiana University Athletics Budgeted Revenue FY 2009–2010

Source: Indiana University Athletic Department.

CASE STUDY: ATHLETIC DEPARTMENTS SEE SURGE FINANCIALLY IN DOWN ECONOMY

More than $470 million in new money poured into major college athletics programs last year, boosting spending on sports even as many of the parent universities struggled with funding reductions during tough economic times, a *USA TODAY* analysis has found.

Much of the rise in athletics revenue came from an escalation in money generated through multi-media rights deals, donations and ticket receipts, but schools also continued increasing their subsidies from student fees and institutional funds.

Altogether in 2010, about $2 billion in subsidies went to athletics programs at the 218 public schools that have been in the NCAA's top-level Division I over the past five years. Those subsidies grew by an inflation-adjusted 3% in 2010. They have grown by 28% since 2006 and account for $1 of every $3 spent on athletics.

Even with 2010's more modest growth rate, these increases run counter to the national trend of declining state support for public colleges, many of which have imposed layoffs, salary freezes, cuts in course offerings and substantial tuition and fee hikes. While about a third of the 218 Division I schools trimmed athletics budgets last year, about a third either increased their spending faster than money came in, or spending cuts didn't keep up with losses.

"Athletics apparently has no oversight," says Ken Struckmeyer, an associate professor at Washington State who co-chairs the Coalition on Intercollegiate Athletics, a faculty group that advocates for athletics reform. "They generate (money), then they spend whatever they bring in—and if that's not enough, the board of regents provides a subsidy to help them win. ... Apparently the measure of success of universities now is wins by the football team or the basketball team."

USA TODAY, through open-records requests, has compiled a database of financial reports schools send annually to the NCAA. All told, nearly $6.2 billion was spent last year on athletics at the 218 schools. That means athletics spending grew by 3% in 2010. Total revenue grew by 5.5% in 2010.

With revenue growing faster than expenses, there has been an increase in the number of schools whose revenue generated by the athletics department activities exceeds the department's total expenses—the NCAA's benchmark for whether an athletics program is financially self-sufficient. There were 22 such schools in 2010, up from 14 in 2009; there were 25 such schools in 2008.

Five of the 22 self-sufficient programs reduced spending in 2010—Georgia, Michigan State, Kansas State, Texas A&M, Virginia Tech.

The financial figures underscore the widening gap between the financially solid programs and the rest of the pack.

The NCAA, in an annual report on Division I finances released Wednesday, noted that the median net surplus for the 22 self-sufficient programs was about $7.4 million, and the median net deficit for the other 98 major programs was about $11.3 million. The gap of nearly $19 million is up from $15.6 million in 2009. The NCAA report includes information from private schools.

Questions:

1. The article reports that "much of the rise in athletics revenue came from an escalation in money generated through multi-media rights deals, donations and ticket receipts, but schools also continued increasing their subsidies from student fees and institutional funds" (Berkowitz & Upton, 2011). Do you believe it is appropriate that budget short-falls of sports programs should be offset by subsidies from student fees and institutional funds? What could be some other sources of revenue that could help programs to balance these annual financial shortfalls?

2. Try to list ten top-ranking athletic pro-grams in the United Sates. After listing the programs, compare the programs on your list with the table presented above. Are some institutions you wrote down on both lists? Do you believe the revenues generated in these programs and benefits reaped from their existence justify their operations? Why or why not?

DIFFERENCES AMONG COLLEGE SPORT DIVISIONS

Although there are several bodies that gov-ern college sports in the United States (and recently some schools in Canada), the most powerful by far is the National Collegiate Athletic Association (NCAA). Other govern-ing bodies are the National Association of Intercollegiate Athletics and the National Junior College Athletic Association. The 1,281-member institutions of the NCAA are further divided into three divisions, depending on level of competition and the size of their program (National Collegiate Athletic Association, 2012). For football, Division I is further divided into the Football Bowl Subdivision (FBS), which has about 125 teams, the Football Championship Subdivision (FCS) which includes about 120 schools, and the Non-Football Subdivision (NFS), which consists of those schools that do not support football but do have Division I basketball teams. NCAA Divisions II and III encompass about 300 and 450 schools, respectively (National Collegiate Athletic Association, 2012). Division II schools award fewer athletic scholarships than Division I institutions, and Division III schools award no scholarships at all.

In sum, the differences among the NCAA Division I, II, and III can be found in the num-ber of sports an institution sponsors and the number of athletic scholarships an institution can award. FBS schools also must meet a minimum attendance figure for their games.

The average NCAA school sponsors about seventeen teams, eight for men and nine for women (Woods, 2011). But there is a noticeable financial disparity between NCAA Division I schools and those in Division II or III. This will be discussed in the next section.

Differences between Division I, II, and III Sports Culture Based on Financial Considerations

Not only is there a gap in the number of sports supported and scholarships awarded among the divisions, but there is also a wid-ening financial gap between the divisions. NCAA data on revenues and expenses from the 2009–2010 fiscal year show a widening gap between schools with self-sufficient ath-letics programs and schools that rely on in-stitutional subsidies to balance their athletics

School	Total revenue	Generated revenue	Allocated revenue	Total expenses	Difference
Oregon	$122,394,483	$119,709,341	$2,685,142	$77,856,232	$41,853,109*
Alabama	$130,542,153	$125,562,153	$4,980,000	$98,961,214	$26,600,939
Penn State	$106,614,724	$106,614,724	$0	$88,041,921	$18,572,803
Michigan	$106,874,031	$106,640,861	$233,170	$89,133,850	$17,507,011
Oklahoma State	$106,362,128	$100,708,922	$5,653,206	$83,748,207	$16,960,715
Iowa	$88,735,093	$88,209,386	$525,707	$74,438,196	$13,771,190
Texas	$143,555,354	$143,555,354	$0	$130,436,534	$13,118,820
Oklahoma	$98,512,287	$98,512,287	$0	$87,678,199	$10,834,088
Georgia	$89,735,934	$86,533,389	$3,202,545	$77,250,831	$9,282,558
LSU	$111,030,795	$111,030,795	$0	$102,326,769	$8,704,026
Kansas State	$53,436,790	$50,201,682	$3,235,108	$42,337,682	$7,864,000
Florida	$117,104,407	$112,693,506	$4,410,901	$105,824,376	$6,869,130
Texas A&M	$82,774,133	$82,774,133	$0	$75,941,926	$6,832,207
Arkansas	$78,072,620	$76,377,647	$1,694,973	$71,801,905	$4,575,742
Purdue	$61,653,561	$61,653,561	$0	$58,365,143	$3,288,418
Michigan State	$83,545,892	$83,545,892	$3,348,785	$78,162,447	$2,034,660
Nebraska	$73,483,733	$73,483,733	$0	$71,738,068	$1,745,665
West Virginia	$62,030,104	$57,774,867	$4,255,237	$56,607,917	$1,166,950
Indiana	$69,287,811	$66,905,296	$2,382,515	$65,796,415	$1,108,881
Virginia Tech	$63,613,464	$56,706,913	$6,906,551	$55,738,633	$968,280
Ohio State	$123,174,176	$123,174,176	$0	$122,739,754	$434,422
Washington	$64,034,410	$61,851,895	$2,182,515	$61,640,598	$211,297

*School says unusual surplus is due to non-cash gift of John E. Jaqua Academic Center for Student Athletes. Note: Amounts not adjusted for inflation.

Steve Berkowitz and Jodi Upton, "Athletic Departments See Surge Financially in Down Economy," *USA Today*, June 16, 2011. Copyright © 2011 by USA Today. Reprinted with permission.

budgets (Brown, 2011). The following excerpt from an NCAA presentation reveals that only twenty-two Football Bowl Subdivision teams make more money than they spend:

The median net surplus at those 22 institutions was about $7.4 million (ranging from $211,000 to $41.9 million), compared with the median net deficit for the remaining Football Bowl Subdivision schools of about $11.3 million. (Brown, 2011)

NCAA President Emmert says that, as far as divisions are concerned, the "gap in revenue, either from self-generated or institutionally allocated sources, is significant. Indeed, it is coming to redefine what we mean by competitive equity" (Brown, 2011).

Other highlights (Brown, 2011):

- The revenues and expenses report shows the "real cost" of athletics is about $9 million for Division I schools. That figure, which has fluctuated between $8 [million] and $10 million over the past three years, represents the median institutional subsidy necessary to balance the athletics budget.
- As in the past, ticket sales, alumni/booster contributions, and NCAA/conference distributions make up more than 50 percent of total generated revenues.
- Football continues to drive the revenue train. In the FBS, 58 percent of football programs showed revenues that exceeded expenses by about $9 million. Although 56 percent of men's basketball programs generate revenues over expenses, the net gain is much less than in football—approximately $3.7 million.
- The percentage of total revenues that come from either direct or indirect institutional support, or student fees (that is, "allocated revenue"), is 26 percent in the FBS, 73 percent in the FCS and 80 percent for institutions without football.

Source: "Report shows widening financial gap in Division I," by Brown, G., 2011. Copyright 2011 by the National Collegiate Athletic Association.

The previously mentioned disparity and competition for financial resources between NCAA schools begs the question as to how the NCAA was able to develop this financial power over time. This point is addressed in the next section.

The National Collegiate Athletic Association (NCAA)

The National Collegiate Athletic Association (NCAA) originated from talks in the White House organized by President Theodore Roosevelt in the early days of the twentieth century in order to prevent further injuries or endangerments of college athletes. In a follow-up meeting in 1906, sixty-two institutions formed the Intercollegiate Athletic Association of the United States (IAAUS), which officially renamed itself the National Collegiate Athletic Association in 1910 (NCAA History, 2010).

The contemporary NCAA began in 1951 with the arrival of Walter Byers as executive director. Byers made this organization into what it is today—the most powerful regulatory body in collegiate sports that has oversight and influence.

By the 1980s college football had become a considerable source of revenue for the NCAA and its respective football schools (National Collegiate Athletic Association, 2012). In 1981, Jim Host of Host Communications approached the NCAA's Executive Director Walter Byers about starting a sponsorship program. Byer's response to this idea was along the lines of "over my dead body" (Lee, 2004). In 1983, however, Byers changed his mind and contacted Host to help him start the program. The NCAA Corporate Partner Sponsorship Program was launched in 1985 and had the following arrangement:

- The deal began by offering Gillette Corporation the rights to every NCAA Championship event.
- The primary event for exposure was the NCAA Basketball Tournament, but companies slowly began to take advantage of other events.
- As other sports grew in popularity, sponsorship packages originally valued at $500,000 grew to $1 million.

While the program grew to an all-time high of nineteen corporate partners, Host felt the program needed to change to experience further growth. Host's idea was to combine marketing rights with television ad buys and other media exposure. For the NCAA, this meant the bundling of marketing and media rights and approaching major television networks about becoming the primary sponsor for the program. Initial negotiations between the NCAA and CBS broke down. Hence, the NCAA began negotiations with Fox, ABC, and ESPN to locate another main sponsor.

But after further talks with CBS, the NCAA signed an eleven-year, $6 billion contract (Lee, 2004) to broadcast the NCAA basketball tournament. The NCAA-CBS contract began on September 1, 2002, and included the following rights to all sponsorship: television, marketing, licensing, publishing, and special event rights. The contract allowed CBS to subcontract out rights to other companies (Lee, 2004). Through these contracts, the NCAA 2010–2011income of $845.9 million was somewhat restructured and can be broken down into the following major areas (National Collegiate Athletic Association, 2012):

- Television and marketing rights fees (81 percent)
- Championships (11 percent)
- Investments (4 percent)
- NIT, LLC Eligibility Center, LLC College Football Arbiter eOfficials (2 percent)
- Sales and services (1 percent)
- Contributions: facilities/other (1 percent)

Source: National Collegiate Athletic Association (2012). Finances, Revenue 2010–2011.

Next to revenue, the NCAA also has considerable expenses, which were $778 million for the 2010–2011 season (National Collegiate Athletic Association, 2012). Following the revenue is a breakdown of the NCAA expenses in 2010–2011.

In 2010 the NCAA signed a new fourteen-year, $10.8 billion contract with CBS and Turner Broadcasting for rights to its men's basketball tournament. The deal brings about $740 million annually to the NCAA; the sum constitutes the majority of the annual NCAA revenue (Wolverton, 2010).

The NCAA has media contracts with ESPN, ESPN Plus, CBS Sports, CBS College Sports, and Turner Sports for all 89 championships (NCAA, Broadcast and Media Services, 2012). CBS and Turner Sports jointly own the multimedia rights to the Division I Men's Basketball Championship. ESPN has the multimedia rights to 24 of the 89 NCAA championships (NCAA, Broadcast and Media Services, 2012). Turner Sports has the rights to 67 of the 89 NCAA championships (NCAA, Broadcast and Media Services, 2012). The most prominent of these are the NCAA Men's

Division I Basketball tournament (CBS and Turner Sports) and several men's football divisions (ESPN).

The NCAA awards eighty-nine national championships in the three membership divisions annually (NCAA Championships History, 2012). The annual football champion is decided by the Bowl Champion Series (an association made up of the conferences and independent schools that compete in Division I FBS and four bowl games).

One faithful ally and partner of the NCAA and schools over the years that allowed the NCAA and its schools to fortify their power are the media. The relationship the NCAA and schools have established with the media is addressed in the next section.

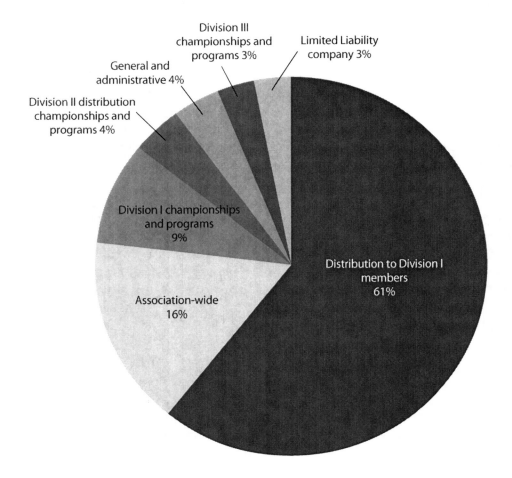

Figure 3. NCAA Expenses Breakdown 2010–2011

MEDIA AND COLLEGE SPORTS: A MUTUALLY BENEFICIAL (COMMERCIAL) RELATIONSHIP

It's not just the game you're watching. It's soap opera, complete with story line and plots and plot twists. And good guys and villains, heroes and underdogs. And all this gets scripted into cliffhanger morality plays.

—Temple (1992)

To understand the realm of college sports today, one has to understand that most of the college sports we experience and consume are mediated. The media are an important conduit between those who perform the service of sports entertainment and the spectators.

Not everyone can enjoy sports live. Therefore, media function as a channel that delivers sports to people in a filtered manner and, to a certain extent, socially creates the sport experience. Whether this is an objective way to receive information that keeps the educational mission of these events in mind is questionable. The media provide economically, socially, and politically modified and reinterpreted information (Coakley, 2009), and those people who are in power of the media serve as a filter for the information presented to their audience (Coakley, 2009). College sports are more and more affected by the timetables media set for their programming. In sports, those who control media can influence what events are covered and what information is passed on to the consumers (Andrews & Jackson, 2001; Brookes, 2002; Bruce, 2007; Dempsey, 2006; Martzke & Cherner, 2004; Rowe, 2004; Whannel, 2002).

Today, there are different media that cover different kinds of sport. Broadcasting media, such as television and radio, usually cover college football and college basketball. Other less profitable college sports, such as baseball, soccer, and track and field, have to avail of alternative media. Newspapers, publicity campaigns, and the Internet are often used to make these sports accessible and allow them to share some of the limelight.

The relationship between college sports and the media has become an important means of existence for universities and college sports. Sponsorship contracts, TV broadcasts, and political power bear witness to this development. This owes to the fact that both college sports and the media have become an influential and integral part of our contemporary, everyday social fabric that fulfills an entertainment function in society. For instance, Penn State's beloved football coach Joe Paterno had to resign in 2011 after a long and prosperous career following charges of sexual abuse brought against one of his former assistant coaches. Paterno was accused of not doing enough to stop this disturbing behavior (Armas, 2011). How much of a role media played in this story has yet to be determined.

What are some of the prevailing themes that have come out of college sports media of late? Controversy swirls around such topics as ethics, gender, and consumption. For example, allegations of student-athletes not living up to academic standards and being advantaged when it comes to grading have emerged recently. Women athletes and smaller collegiate sports have been neglected because they have less promotional appeal than men's football and basketball. All this, of course, goes against the academic mission of a school and what a holistic college experience represents. Consumption and considerable material inequities between big and small sports schools and the paying

CASE STUDY: NCAA AGREES TO $10.8-BILLION DEAL TO BROADCAST ITS MEN'S BASKETBALL TOURNAMENT

In a move expected to shore up the long-term financial health of college sports, the NCAA announced on Thursday that it had signed a 14-year, $10.8-billion contract with CBS and Turner Broadcasting to televise its men's basketball tournament. The deal will funnel at least $740-million annually to NCAA member colleges and will very likely include an expansion of the tournament field to 68 teams.

Athletics officials throughout college sports applauded the news, which comes as many programs have seen their own marketing agreements and budgets reduced.

"In this economy, think about how many things have gone backward," said Christine A. Plonsky, women's athletic director at the University of Texas at Austin. "The fact that this is a positive move forward is attributable to some really hard work at the negotiating table. ... And when you're talking about opportunities for young people, it's a blessing."

While the vast majority of those dollars will go to elite programs like those at Texas, many smaller athletics departments rely on their tournament distribution to support the day-to-day activities that keep their programs afloat.

"Clearly, it is not hundreds of thousands we're talking about, but it is very important that we receive some stability of funding," said Kent Weiser, athletic director at Emporia State University, a Division II program in Kansas. Emporia State has used its NCAA money to help pay for tutors, laptop computers, and buses to transport players to games. "These are things that Division I takes for granted but that make a lot of things possible for us," Mr. Weiser said.

The proposal to expand the tournament by three teams, which the NCAA's Division I Board of Directors will vote on next week, was one of several that the association's Division I Men's Basketball Committee considered. A separate proposal to increase the field to 96 teams was tabled, a move that drew praise from some observers. .

"Rejecting a proposed 96-team format should be applauded, as it appeared to create more conflicts and intrusions on the athletes' academic obligations," Amy P. Perko, executive director of the Knight Commission on Intercollegiate Athletics, said in an e-mail message. "That result was incompatible with the NCAA's operating principles for postseason competition."

Worries Over Dollars

More than 95 percent of the NCAA's revenue comes from its tournament contract, but in recent years association officials had expressed concerns that the next deal might not be as large.

The previous CBS contract—worth $6-billion, or about $500-million a year—was not set to expire until 2013. But association officials began renegotiating last summer with the hopes of avoiding a severe reduction in rights fees. (CBS was reportedly worried about losing money on the last deal, which was heavily backloaded.)

Under the new agreement, which includes Internet, wireless, and marketing rights, every game will be shown live on one of four national television networks.

CBS shares early-round coverage with TBS, TNT, and truTV, but isn't on the hook for the full $10.8-billion.

When television networks agree to pricey sports deals, they often cover their costs by adding commercial air time during games. But the NCAA prevented CBS and Turner from doing that, said Kevin O'Malley, a television consultant and a former CBS executive who helped the NCAA broker the new contract. Under the deal, no game can have more than four commercial breaks in each half—the same arrangement the NCAA had in its previous tournament contract.

While several people lauded the NCAA for the guaranteed money it brought in, others said the big payout could lead to a further escalation of coaches' salaries and unnecessary facilities growth. And one critic questioned the logic of signing such a long-term contract in an uncertain media environment.

"We don't know what the TV or digital-rights market might look like in 14 years— much less in five years," said Andrew Zimbalist, a professor of economics at Smith College who studies the finances of college sports. In other words, it's possible that the association could have left money on the table.

Soucre: Brad Wolverton, "NCAA Agrees to $10.8-Billion Deal to Broadcast Its Men's Basketball Tournament," *The Chronicle of Higher Education*; April 22, 2010. Copyright © 2010 by Chronicle of Higher Education. Reprinted with permission.

of student-athletes were issues that have recently topped the news as well.

The media-sports relationship and the mediated sports experience that this relationship produces change rapidly. Therefore, it is important that spectators and sport scholars adopt a critical stance regarding the information they receive, and are media literate in order to understand and judiciously process the information provided by the media (Kellner, 2003a, 2003b, 2004; Scherer, 2007).

Recently, a strong mutual dependency between the media and the commercial aspects of college sports has developed, and it is hard to imagine that one could exist without the other.

Questions:

1. The NCAA has signed a fourteen-year, $10.8 billion contract with CBS and Turner Broadcasting for the rights to its men's basketball tournament (Wolverton, 2011). Do you believe that this places too much power in the hands of two organizations, namely the NCAA and CBS Television? What could be some alternative ways of disbursing the power and providing different avenues of revenue generation?

2. While some people praise the NCAA for the money it brings in, others say the big payout could lead to a further escalation of coaches' salaries and unnecessary facilities growth (Wolverton, 2011). Which position do you support?

ETHICAL CONSIDERATIONS IN THE COMMERCE OF COLLEGE SPORTS

When talking about ethics, we talk about how people perceive what is right or wrong, good or bad. Ethics are used to assess and manage behavior in the college sports world. Ethics are usually formed around standards or norms for conduct (Encyclopædia Britannica, 2012) such as thriving for excellence and commitment to the game. As far as ethical behavior is concerned, avoiding misconduct and deviant behavior (Encyclopædia Britannica, 2012) are some of the foci in college sports. In this context, ethics often center around being the best and winning.

Take, for instance, the following situation: Allowing athletes to receive as much money as they can seems like a good idea, but it would require considerable oversight. Thus, advocates for college athletes embrace the notion that the market should decide what college athletes earn (Dohrmann, 2011). This presents a compensation approach opposed to the one that provides students with stipends under the auspice of the NCAA. Also, would it be ethical to allow college athletes to get as much money as the market demands? Wouldn't this attitude stifle the ethical values of the athletes and infringe upon the academic mission of the university?

Should we create a general code of ethics for student-athletes that addresses such issues as athletic misconduct, drug and substance abuse, and academic performance? To a certain extent we already have such a framework in place. It is important that unethical or borderline behavior never become acceptable or standardized. How might the schools, the NCAA, and sport fans prevent this type of behavior?

What remains a complex and neglected topic in codes of ethics is the status of college athletes. Are college athletes amateurs who must perform as semiprofessionals? This question is addressed next.

Amateur Athletes and Semiprofessionals

College sports and amateur sports do not have people or institutions (such as large corporations) that own them per se, but they are affected by institutional officials and corporate sponsors that influence the university and its sports operations. Amateur sports organizations are mostly interested in the athletic and not so much in the business performance of the organization (Coakley, 2009). Both professional and amateur athletes perform for the sports audience and, to a certain extent, entertain, while the amateur athletes' compensation is limited.

The legal status of college athletes is at best confusing and often ambiguous when viewed in the light of commercial considerations of college sports. For instance, even when individual college athletes generate a million dollars or more for their school, they are still not allowed to receive more than a yearly sports scholarship that is worth not more than the tuition, fees, and living stipend a school charges. The big question that arises here is whether this reward system makes sense and is fair? The next part focuses on how these rewards influence the sports culture on campus.

Campus, Culture and Money

Is it fair that a college football player is paid a scholarship worth about $40,000 a year, whereas his coach gets an annual salary of $4 million? How does this influence the sports culture of a campus?

Following are some reasons why college athletes do not get paid professional salaries:

- One has to decide who gets paid and how much.

- How can gender equity when paying student-athletes be assured?
- Most athletic departments operate in the red.
- Institutions would have to eliminate nonrevenue sports.
- Paying athletes as employees threatens the tax-exempt status of college sports.

This nonpayment of college athletes sparked an underground economy. Sack (1991) surveyed the college football population and reported that a relatively high percentage seemed to know athletes at their school who received illegal money, and many of them felt there was nothing wrong with accepting under-the-table money. Another important variable in this underground business is the involvement and knowledge of school officials and the stance a university as whole takes on this issue.

An example for how complicated the relationship between money and college sports culture is involves Southern Methodist University, which, with its board of governors being aware of this situation, paid its players in the 1980s. Some athletes received money upon signing with the school and others received payments on a monthly basis (Finley, Finley, & Fountain, 2008). As a result, the NCAA decided to punish the school with its death penalty, which prohibited the university from playing football for one entire season (Finley, Finley, & Fountain, 2008).

Not only can indiscretions of student-athletes be considered socially irresponsible, consider head coach salaries in college football and college basketball that can consume a sizable portion of a school's athletic budget. These considerable compensation packages can also influence the sports culture on campus as well as the social fabric of an entire state. By receiving these kinds of salaries, the head coaches command a sizable amount of power, respect, and influence in society. For instance, Duke basketball coach Mike Krzyzewski received $4,195,519 for the 2010–11 season (Wieberg, 2011). Duke University has on its campus a small lawn area called K-Ville (Krzyzewski-Ville) where hundreds of students camp out for weeks every year after January 1 to score tickets for the upcoming game in March against state rival the University of North Carolina, Chapel Hill. Another example is Alabama, "where it's less a joke than honest truth that the governor toils in the shadow of the flagship university's football coach" (Wieberg, 2011). This coach is Nick Saban who earned $4,833,333 for the 2011 football season (Wieberg, 2011). Following are two tables that present in more detail salary figures for the highest-earning college basketball and football coaches in the nation.

Table 5a. Highest-Paid Coaches: Top 10 in compensation for 2010–11 Division I men's basketball season (from teams that made the NCAA Tournament):

Coach (School), total pay
1. Rick Pitino (Louisville), $7,531,378
2. Mike Krzyzewski (Duke), $4,195,519
3. John Calipari (Kentucky), $3,917,000
4. Bill Self (Kansas), $3,615,656
5. Bill Donovan (Florida), $3,575,400
6. Tom Izzo (Michigan State), $3,565,000
7. Thad Matta (Ohio State), $2,649,000
8. Sean Miller (Arizona), $2,305,805
9. Jim Calhoun (Connecticut), $2,300,000
10. Rick Barnes (Texas), $2,200,000

Note: Reprinted from "Salaries escalate: NCAA coaches gain leverage," by S. Wieberg, 2011, *The Indianapolis Star.* Copyright 2011 by The Indianapolis Star.

Table 5b. Highest-Paid Coaches: Top 10 in compensation for 2011 Football Bowl Subdivision season (from about 100 public institutions among 120 FBS schools):

Coach (School), total pay
1. Mack Brown (Texas), $5,193,500
2. Nick Saban (Alabama), $4,833,333
3. Bob Stoops (Oklahoma), $4,075,000
4. Les Miles (LSU), $3,856,417
5. Kirk Ferentz (Iowa), $3,785,000
6. Bobby Petrino (Arkansas), $3,638,000
7. Gene Chizik (Auburn), $3,500,000
8. Brady Hoke (Michigan), $3,254,000
9. Will Muschamp (Florida), $3,221,000
10. Mark Richt (Georgia), $2,939,800

Note: Reprinted from "Salaries escalate: NCAA coaches gain leverage," by S. Wieberg, 2011, *The Indianapolis Star.* Copyright 2011 by The Indianapolis Star.

Commercialism and money influence and to a certain extent corrupt college sports. How schools can respond to this is covered in the upcoming paragraphs.

How Can Schools Handle College Sport Commercialism in the Near Future?

Various college sports experts and innovative thinkers, such as Andrew Zimbalist, Jay Coakley, and Michael Malec, have offered suggestions on how schools might better handle the commercialization of college sports in the near future. In a recent *Sports Illustrated* article (Wolf, 2012), Andrew Zimbalist, an economist, suggests the following to achieve a more equitable distribution in college sports pay:

- Place limitations on salaries that are unethically or far beyond industry standard.
- Disclose what money college sports really generate and lose (often they operate in the red).
- Reduce the number of football scholarships.
- Reduce spending on nonrevenue sports at FBS schools.
- Create an NCAA football playoff.

Sociologist Jay Coakley also has some misgivings about the pay structure in college athletics. Coakley, however, sees as the major problem the fact that schools have been turned into entertainment businesses and their goals and operating methods are mostly commercial and not in line with the academic mission of the university. Therefore, following the Drake Group reform proposals, Coakley (2009, pp. 503–504) makes the following recommendations in order to realign the college sports goals with academic rather than commercial goals:

- Disclose the average academic performance for college athletes.
- Resurrect the rule that makes freshmen ineligible to play on varsity teams.
- Reinstitute multiyear athletic scholarships (that are based on need).
- Refine college sports eligibility standards (e.g., student-athletes should maintain at least a 2.0 GPA).
- Require all athletic departments to use a uniform and transparent financial accounting/reporting system.

- Remove academic counseling/support services from athletic department control.
- Change number and timing of athletic events so that students do not have to miss classes or choose between education and sport.

Michael Malec (2007) decries the current commercialization and entertainment focus of college sports. He offers the following suggestions to reduce the excessive commercialization of college sports:

- Big-time athletic departments are run like for-profit corporations in many respects. To de-corporatize these operations, coaches' salaries need to be capped, sponsorship contracts need to be strictly regulated, and the fierce competition for every commercial dollar needs to be disengaged (Zimbalist, 1991).
- NCAA-endorsed professionalism becomes particularly vivid when taking a closer look at the recruitment packages for student-athletes. These recruitment agreements look like professional sports contracts for academic stakeholders who should not be considered as professionals.
- A vocabulary needs to be introduced to college athletics that does not evolve around marketing exposure, operational efficiency, and financial viability, but focuses on pride, achievement, and honor (Dunnavant, 2004).
- School administrators and NCAA officials need to ensure that graduation guidelines and regulations for college athletes are more strictly enforced.

- Students who are athletes need to be given greater opportunity to be students rather than athletes. The curriculum of athletes has to be more adequately structured to reflect the academic needs of these students and provide them with a chance to be more involved in their own lives.
- The athletic performance and other pressures put student-athletes and their coaches in an awkward position; they too often have to choose between performing well athletically or academically. In an environment primarily geared toward learning, the choice is clear: academics come first.
- It is no secret that only a miniscule proportion of those athletes playing college sports will make it to the professional level. Faculty members and staff have to communicate this to athletes. Schools have to put in place infrastructures that allow these students to embark on normal job careers after their athletic lives in college are over.
- More often than not coaches want their only benchmark of assessment to be their athletic performance; however, since academics should be and are the primary focus in a university setting, academic performance has to enter the equation when evaluating coaches.

The proposed points above overlap somewhat, and not all can be implemented easily or quickly. Still, these scholars argue that many of these steps can be realized. Which of these proposals do you favor, and why? Which do you oppose, and why?

1. "Let the market decide. That is the mantra of many pay-to-play advocates in college sports. Rather than allow schools to give stipends under the watchful eye of the NCAA, advocates believe athletes should be free to make as much money as they can on their own" (Dohrmann, 2011). Do you believe this would be a good economic system for college sports? What other economic systems could college sports consider?

2. "There's only one way to let the free market decide while maintaining some semblance of a level playing field: Have a clearinghouse for endorsement deals and payments from agents" (Dohrmann, 2011). Do you believe the organization that should run the clearinghouse should be the NCAA? Why or why not? What might be some other ways to oversee the clearinghouse or other solutions to this possible free market system?

3. "Because of Title IX, any benefit orchestrated by the university [or clearinghouse] would also have to be provided to female athletes" (Dohrmann, 2011). Do you believe there would be an equitable distribution of benefits between male and female athletes? At universities and colleges, should revenue-generating sports help the loss-generating sports?

DISCUSSIONS AND EXERCISES

1. One big part of college sports is tailgating. Which commercial efforts would you use to capture the tailgating crowd? Owing to the commercialization of this activity, however, some issues arise. How would you deal with such tailgating issues as student alcoholism (underage drinking), vandalism, and commercial exploitation by big companies?

2. Li and Burden (2002) report, "It is estimated that over half of NCAA Div. 1 athletic programs have outsourced some or all of their marketing operations and rights to nationally prominent marketing companies." Do you believe it is a good idea for schools to outsource their marketing operations and rights to professional marketing companies? Why or why not?

3. College sports seems to be more and more using the business model and more and more moving toward commercialization. Due to this movement, the NCAA and some schools are considering limiting the influence of the commercial in college sports even more. What might be some more stringent limitations for college sports that some schools and the NCAA might put in place over the next three to five years?

4. College sports have a rather broad fan base ranging from students, to alumni, to regular sports fans. What are some new fan segments that could be attracted? What type of marketing efforts would you use to approach/capture these segments? What markets would you avoid?

5. There seems to be a conflict between the commercial and academic missions of universities. Discuss the following issues in the light of the aforementioned conflict:

- Violating academic integrity
- Violating NCAA rules to win and to gain a competitive advantage
- Paying athletes as workers

CASE STUDY: PAYING COLLEGE ATHLETES: THE FREE MARKET PLAN

Allowing athletes to receive as much money as they can get sounds like a good idea, but it would require significant oversight. And that's where it gets tricky.

Let the market decide. That is the mantra of many pay-to-play advocates. Rather than allow schools to give stipends under the watchful eye of the NCAA, advocates believe athletes should be free to make as much money as they can on their own. Imagine football stars signing endorsement deals—"This is Andrew Luck for Toyota of Palo Alto"—or a top NBA prospect, like Kentucky freshman forward Anthony Davis, accepting whatever lucrative inducements an agent might offer in the hopes of landing him as a future client.

This model—call it the Free Market Plan—is sensible and popular with athletes and fans. It would also likely require something that many of its advocates would be loath to embrace: more oversight.

Much of the NCAA rule book has been written with one idea in mind: that one school should not, because of affluent boosters or rule-breaking coaches, have an unfair advantage over another. There is little doubt that the Free Market Plan would put an end to that notion. What would stop an alum with a car dealership from promising an SUV to every blue-chip recruit? Or a sports agent with ties to a university from taking care of all its players, even those without pro potential? Other programs would be at a competitive disadvantage unless they could offer similar inducements.

There's only one way to let the free market decide while maintaining some semblance of a level playing field: Have a clearinghouse for endorsement deals and payments from agents. That organization would review all benefits received by players similar to the way leagues review contracts to ensure that they comply with salary-cap rules. It would also make sure that no deals are made just to give a program a competitive advantage and that none of a player's compensation is being facilitated by the school. This matters because of Title IX; any benefit orchestrated by the university would also have to be provided to female athletes. And the penalties for those who don't work within this system would have to be severe to prevent abuses.

The organization best equipped to run that clearinghouse? The NCAA.

Source: George Dohrman, "The Free Market Plan?" *Sports Illustrated*; November 7, 2011. Copyright © 2011 by Time Inc. Reprinted with permission.

- Neglecting to demystify the myth of going professional
- Embracing business ethics in college athletic departments

6. Do you believe student-athletes should get paid? Why or why not? Once you have created an argument for or against paying student-athletes, think about the following suggestions:

- If a student-athlete signs a professional contract, his or her athletic scholarship turns into a loan.

- A school has an obligation to establish an adequate curriculum for college athletes.
- The cost of a college degree has economic value and is a type of compensation (e.g., tuition, fees, room and board, living stipend).
- An underground college sports economy has existed in college sports since the 1920s (Sack, 1991) (e.g., college athletes receiving money).

7. Looking at Table 2 in this chapter, one can see that college sports cost more money than they generate. Based on this information, would you propose changes to the current structure of college sports programs? If yes, what changes would you suggest? Frequently, college sports programs bring quite a few intangible benefits to a school such as media attention. Would this fact affect your argument?

8. Recently, *Sports Illustrated* reported on how UCLA basketball lost its way and game by deviating from moral and ethical standards set by John Wooden. The article mentioned, among other things, that some members of the team engaged in partying at the mansion of a wealthy UCLA fan and then were chauffeured to a West Hollywood club where they received VIP treatment (Dohrmann, 2012). Do you believe that these ethical and moral missteps could stem from the media and commercial attention the team received because of its Final Four appearances? If so, what could UCLA and other schools do to fix the problem?

ACTIVITIES

1. Get together in groups of two or three for the following activity. Use Tables 5.1, 5.2, and 5.3 for this project. The tables show the college football salaries for coaches employed at SEC teams. Type the data of these tables into an Excel spreadsheet and label the columns accordingly. Once you have inserted the data into the spreadsheet, do some statistical analysis. Produce a basic analysis of the data using descriptive measures such as mean, minimum, and maximum. Then take the data set and test whether an association exists between football coach salaries and team rankings for each year examined. Where possible, create graphs to demonstrate whether an association exists. Explain the data and your findings. Also, address questions such as: What do the statistical results mean? What do the graphs you generated tell you? What do the overall results you generated suggest for the SEC conference and college football in general? Following are the Tables 5.1, 5.2, and 5.3.

2. This project involves some observation research on your part. Visit some sports events of your school (e.g., basketball, football, volleyball, etc.). Observe what type of advertising is displayed at these events, such as commercial announcements over loudspeakers, billboards, banners, and signs. Also, see for what companies these advertisements are displayed. Classify these advertisements you observed according to the following criteria:

- This advertisement is for what product?
- This advertisement is of the following type: newspaper, magazine, radio, television, outdoor, Internet, other.

- This advertisement informs, persuades, or reminds its target audience about the product.
- How much of each type of advertisement does the company use?
- How many people can the company reach with this type of advertisement?

- How often is this advertisement aired/displayed during an event?
- How targeted is the audience for this advertisement?
- Is this advertisement paid for by some major sponsors of your school? Do you believe this advertisement is effective?

Table 6a. 2009 Data

RANK	SCHOOL	HEAD COACH	CONFERENCE	SCHOOL PAY	OTHER PAY	TOTAL PAY	MAX BONUS
2	Alabama	Nick Saban	SEC	$225,000	$3,675,000	$3,900,000	$700,000
20	Arkansas	Bobby Petrino	SEC	$1,900,000	$958,000	$2,858,000	$550,000
16	Auburn	Gene Chizik	SEC	$500,000	$1,550,000	$2,050,000	$1,300,000
4	Georgia	Urban Meyer	SEC	$250,000	$3,750,000	$4,000,000	N/A
21	Florida	Mark Richt	SEC	$809,340	$2,287,236	$3,096,576	$475,000
27	Kentucky	Rich Brooks	SEC	$400,000	$1,217,517	$1,617,517	$1,095,000
3	LSU	Les Miles	SEC	$300,000	$3,451,000	$3,751,000	$650,000
17	Mississippi	Houston Nutt	SEC	$200,000	$2,309,000	$2,509,000	$715,000
19	Mississippi State	Dan Mullen	SEC	$250,000	$950,000	$1,200,000	$100,000
13	South Carolina	Steve Spurrier	SEC	$507,500	$1,524,000	$2,031,500	$900,000
8	Tennessee	Lane Kiffin	SEC	$350,000	$1,650,000	$2,000,000	$540,000
72	Vanderbilt	Bobby Johnson	SEC	N/A	N/A	N/A	N/A

Table 6b. 2010 Data

RANK	SCHOOL	HEAD COACH	CONFERENCE	SCHOOL PAY	OTHER PAY	TOTAL PAY	MAX BONUS
4	Alabama	Nick Saban	SEC	$5,166,666	$830,683	$5,997,349	$700,000
35	Arkansas	Bobby Petrino	SEC	$2,700,000	$13,000	$2,713,000	$475,000
6	Auburn	Gene Chizik	SEC	$2,100,000	$3,500	$2,103,500	$1,500,000
21	Georgia	Urban Meyer	SEC	$4,010,000	$0	$4,010,000	$575,000
1	Florida	Mark Richt	SEC	$2,811,340	$126,400	$2,937,740	$600,000
46	Kentucky	Joker Phillips	SEC	$1,700,000	$6,600	$1,706,600	$1,105,000
7	LSU	Les Miles	SEC	$3,751,000	$154,000	$3,905,000	$400,000
15	Mississippi	Houston Nutt	SEC	$2,500,000	$9,000	$2,509,000	$0
38	Mississippi State	Dan Mullen	SEC	$1,200,000	$8,295	$1,208,295	$0
34	South Carolina	Steve Spurrier	SEC	$2,000,000	$32,500	$2,032,500	$1,000,000
16	Tennessee	Derek Dooley	SEC	$2,118,391	$3,000	$2,121,391	$475,000
54	Vanderbilt	Robbie Caldwell	SEC	N/A	N/A	N/A	N/A

Table 6c. 2011 Data

RANK	SCHOOL	HEAD COACH	CONFERENCE	SCHOOL PAY	OTHER PAY	TOTAL PAY	MAX BONUS
7	Alabama	Nick Saban	SEC	$4,683,333	$150,000	$4,833,333	$700,000
17	Arkansas	Bobby Petrino	SEC	$3,635,000	$3,000	$3,638,000	$650,000
2	Auburn	Gene Chizik	SEC	$3,500,000	$0	$3,500,000	$1,200,000
5	Georgia	Will Muschamp	SEC	$3,221,000	$0	$3,221,000	$450,000
26	Florida	Mark Richt	SEC	$2,811,400	$128,400	$2,939,800	$525,000
32	Kentucky	Joker Phillips	SEC	$1,701,339	$1,150	$1,702,489	$1,105,000
9	LSU	Les Miles	SEC	$3,751,000	$105,417	$3,856,417	$700,000
20	Mississippi	Houston Nutt	SEC	$2,756,250	$15,500	$2,771,750	$715,000
45	Mississippi State	Dan Mullen	SEC	$2,500,000	$0	$2,500,000	$650,000
12	South Carolina	Steve Spurrier	SEC	$2,800,000	$28,000	$2,828,000	$1,000,000
10	Tennessee	Derek Dooley	SEC	$2,293,391	$37,200	$2,330,591	$475,000
49	Vanderbilt	James Franklin	SEC	N/A	N/A	N/A	N/A

Note: The data on college coach salaries for tables 5.1, 5.2, and 5.3 are adapted from *College Football Coach salary database, 2006–2011,* by S. Berkowitz, et al, 2011, *USA TODAY.* Retrieved from http://www.usatoday.com/sports/college/football/story/2011-11-17/cover-college-football-coaches-salaries-rise/51242232/1. The data on college football team rankings for tables 5.1, 5.2, and 5.3 are adapted from *2010 5-Year Program Ranking,* by Scout.com, 2011, *College Football News.* Retrieved from http://cfn.scout.com/2/995246.html.

3. For this activity look at the athletic budgets of ten major universities in the *USA TODAY* database. Look at these budgets for five consecutive years. Find out and compare what are the major expenditures of these schools. Also, find out and compare what are the major revenues for these schools. Place the information in a table. What does this information tell you about these institutions? In addition, how many of the schools you selected are self-sufficient and have more money coming in than going out?

Following is the *USA TODAY* web link to the schools' athletic budgets: Berkowitz, S., Upton, J., Gillum, J. (2010, April 2). NCAA College athletics finance database. *USA TODAY.* Retrieved from http://www.usatoday.com/sports/college/ncaa-finances.htm

REFERENCES

Andrews, D. L., and S.J. Jackson. (2001). *Sports stars: The cultural politics of sporting celebrity.* London/New York: Routledge.

Angell, R.C. (1928). *The Campus.* New York/London: Appleton.

Armas, G.C. (2011). Paterno to retire after season amid scandal. *Associated Press.* Retrieved from http://nbcsports.msnbc.com/id/45186257/ns/sports-college_football/

Berkowitz, S. et al. (2011). College Football Coach salary database, 2006–2011. *USA TODAY.* Retrieved from http://www.usatoday.com/sports/college/football/story/2011-11-17/cover-college-football-coaches-salaries-rise/51242232/1.

Berkowitz, S., J. Upton, and J. Gillum. (2010, April 2). NCAA College athletics finance database. *USA TODAY*. Retrieved from http://www.usatoday.com/sports/college/ncaa-finances.htm

Berkowitz, S., and J. Upton. (2011, June 6). Athletic departments see surge financially in down economy. *USA TODAY*. Retrieved from http://www.usatoday.com/sports/college/2011-06-15 athletic-departments-increase-money_n.htm.

Brookes, R. (2002). *Representing Sport*. New York: Oxford University Press.

Brown, G, (2011),. "Report shows widening financial gap in Division I," Retrieved from http://www.ncaa. org/wps/wcm/connect/public/NCAA/Resources/Latest+News/2011/June/Report+shows+widening+financial+gap+in+Division+I.

Bruce, T. (2007). Media and Sport. In G. Ritzer, ed. *The Blackwell Encyclopedia of Sociology* (pp. 2,916–2,921). London: Blackwell Publishing.

[CBS classic logo]. Retrieved April 1, 2012, from http://commons.wikimedia.org/wiki/File:CBS_classic_logo.svg

College Football News (2011). 2010 5-Year Program Ranking. *Scout.com*. Retrieved, Dec 15, 2011, from http://cfn.scout.com/2/995246.html

National Collegiate Athletic Association, (2012), "NCAA Championships History," Retrieved from http://fs.ncaa.org/docs/stats/champs_records_book/ summaries/combined.pdf.

Clotfelter, C. T. (2011). *Big-Time Sports in American Universities*. Cambridge: Cambridge University Press.

Coakley, J. J. (2009). *Sports in Society: Issues and Controversies (10th ed.)*. McGraw-Hill Higher Education.

Commonfund (2011 Update). Higher Education Price Index (HEPI). *Commonfund Institute*. Retrieved from http://www.commonfund.org/CommonfundInstitute/HEPI/HEPI%20Documents/2011/CF_HEPI_2011_FINAL.pdf

Dempsey, J. M., ed. (2006). *Sports-Talk Radio in America: Its Context and Culture*. Binghamton, NY: Haworth Half-Court Press.

Dohrmann, G. (2012, March 5). Not the UCLA way. *Sports Illustrated* 56–63.

Dohrmann, G. (2011). Paying College Athletes: The Free Market Plan? *Sports Illustrated*. Retrieved from http://sportsillustrated.cnn.com/vault/article/magazine/MAG1191781/index.htm

Dunnavant, K. (2004). *The Fifty-Year Seduction*. New York: St. Martin's Press.

Ethics. (2012). In *Encyclopœdia Britannica online*. Retrieved from http://www.britannica.com.proxyserver.umwestern.edu/EBchecked/topic/194023/ethics

Finley, P. S., L.L. Finley, and J.J. Fountain. (2008). *Sports Scandals*. Westport, CT. Greenwood Press.

Fulks, D. L.,(2009), "2004–2008 NCAA Revenues and Expenses of Division I Intercollegiate Athletic Programs," Retrieved from http://www.ncaapublications.com/productdownloads/RE09.pdf

Guttmann, A. (1978). *From Ritual to Record*. New York: Columbia University Press.

Hyland, D.A. (2008). Paidia and Paideia: The Educational Power of Athletics. *Journal of Intercollegiate Sport* 1, 66–71.

Kellner, D. (2003a). Toward a critical theory of education. *Democracy and Nature* 9(1), 51–64.

Kellner, D. (2003b). *Media Spectacle*. Routledge, London.

Kellner, D. (2004). The sports spectacle, Michael Jordan, and Nike. In Miller, P., and D. Wiggins, ed. *Sport and the Color Line*. London: Routledge.

Lederman, D. (2008, May 16). A (money) losing proposition. *Inside Higher Ed*. Retrieved from: http://www.insidehighered.com/news/2008/05/16/ncaa

Lee, J. (2004). The value of the NCAA brand. *Sport Business Journal*. (March 8). Retrieved from http://www.sportsbusinessdaily.com/Journal/Issues/2004/03/20040308/SBJ-In-Depth/The-Value-Of-The-NCAA-Brand.aspx?hl=walter%20byer&sc=0

Li, M., and W. Burden. (2002). Outsourcing Sport Marketing Operations by NCAA Division I Athletic Programs: An Exploratory Study. *Sport Marketing Quarterly*.

Malec, M. (2007). College Sports. In C. Gilde, ed. *Higher Education: Open for Business, College Sports*. Landham, MD: Lexington Books.

Martzke, R., and R. Cherner. (2004, August 17). Channeling how to view sports. *USA TODAY* pp. 1C, 2C.

National Collegiate Athletic Association, (2012), "NCAA.Broadcast and Media Services," Retrieved from http://www.ncaa.com/media.

National Collegiate Athletic Association, (2012), "NCAA Corporate Champions and Corporate Partners," Retrieved from http://www.ncaa.org/wps/wcm/connect/corp_relations/CorpRel/Corporate+Relationships/Corporate+Alliances/partners.html

National Collegiate Athletic Association, (2010), "NCAA History," Retrieved from http://www.ncaa.org/wps/wcm/connect/public/NCAA/About+the+NCAA/who+we+are/About+the+NCAA+history.

[NCAA Logo]. Retrieved April 1, 2012, from http://commons.wikimedia.org/wiki/File:NCAA_logo.svg

National Collegiate Athletic Association, (2012), "Finances, Expenses 2010–2011," Retrieved Feb 7, 2012, from http://www.ncaa.org/wps/wcm/connect/public/NCAA/Finances/Finances+Expenses

National Collegiate Athletic Association, (2012), "Finances, Revenue 2010–2011," Retrieved Feb 7, 2012, from http://www.ncaa.org/wps/wcm/connect/public/NCAA/Finances/Revenue

Orszag, J. M., and P.R. Orszag. (2005). *The empirical effects of collegiate athletics: an update*. Indianapolis: National Collegiate Athletic Association. Retrieved from http://216.197.120.83/webdocs/90.pdf

Pappano, L. (2012, January 20). How Big Time Sports Ate College Life. *The New York Times*. Retrieved from http://www.nytimes.com/2012/01/22/education/edlife/how-big-time-sports-ate-college-life.html?_r=2&ref=edlife

Pritchett, H.S. (1929). Preface. In W. C. Ryan (Study), *The literature of American school and college athletics*. New York: The Carnegie Foundation for the Advancement of Teaching.

Rowe, D., ed. (2004). *Sport, culture and the media: Critical readings*. Maidenhead, Berkshire: Open University Press.

Sack, A.L. (1991). The underground economy of college football. *Sociology of Sport Journal* 8(1), 1–15.

Sailes. G. A. (1986). The exploitation of the black athlete: some alternative solutions. *Journal of Negro Education* 55(4), 439–442.

Scherer, J. (2007). Globalization, promotional culture and the production/consumption of online games: engaging Adidas's Beat Rugby campaign. *New Media and Society* 9, 125–146.

Schnaars, C., J. Upton, and K. DeRamus. (2011, November 17). *USA TODAY* College Football Coach salary database, 2006–2011. *USA TODAY*. Retrieved from http://www.usatoday.com/sports/college/football/story/2011-11-17/cover-college-football-coaches-salaries-rise/51242232/1

Schoettle, A. (2010). IU football gains ground as sports program nears financial crossroads. *Indiana Business Journal* (September 4). Retrieved from http://www.ibj.com/iu-football-gains-ground-as-sports-program-nears-financial-crossroads/PARAMS/article/22077

Temple, K. (1992). Brought to you by ... *Notre Dame Magazine* 21(2), 29.

Whannel, G. (2002). *Media sports stars: Masculinities and moralities.* London/New York: Routledge.

Wieberg, S. (2011). Salaries escalate: NCAA coaches gain leverage. *The Indianapolis Star.* Retrieved from http://www.indystar.com/article/20111229/SPORTS/ 112290351/Salaries-escalate-NCAA-coaches-gain-leverage

Wolverton, B. (2010, April 22). NCAA Agrees to $10.8-Billion Deal to Broadcast Its Men's Basketball Tournament. *The Chronicle of Higher Education.* Retrieved from http://chronicle.com/article/NCAA-Signs-108-Billion-De/65219/

Woods, R. B. (2011). *Social Issues in Sport (2nd ed.).* Champaign, IL: Human Kinetics Publishers.

Wolff, A. (2012, January 23). Scorecard: A Smart Way to Share. *Sports Illustrated* 13–14.

Zimbalist, A. (1991). *Unpaid Professionals.* Princeton, N.J.: Princeton University Press.

Regional and community interest in high school sports provides a rich pool of talent for sports at the intercollegiate level (Fondren, Gill, and Picou 2010). On most Division I campuses, where college football is king, sports programs tend to be well funded and highly competitive; they must be if programs are to attract top student-athletes. During the Renaissance, the "scholar-athlete" represented the "ideal Renaissance man," referring to someone who was "socially adept, sensitive to aesthetic values, skilled in weaponry, strong of body, and learned in letters" (Baker, 1988, p. 59). Interestingly, the scholar-athlete or to use today's terminology, that of student-athlete, is the only term that employs a hyphen to explain a student's role in an extracurricular activity. For example, colleges and universities do not term students who participate in band as "student-musicians" or debate team members "student-politicians." As such, student-athletes represent a unique population (Broughton, 2001). Given the emphasis placed on collegiate athletics today, how does participation in a collegiate sport influence the lives of female and male student-athletes, both on and off the field?

Individuals within and outside of collegiate sports would benefit from a greater understanding of the student-athlete experience. This experience represents a continuous journey between a student-athlete's primary status (i.e., academic, student, scholar) and extracurricular status (i.e., athlete). As a result, a student-athlete's college experience can be complicated as he or she balances responsibilities of this dual role. The student-athlete's environment includes both facilitators and inhibitors to his or her development

4
THE STUDENT-ATHLETE EXPERIENCE

EMMETT GILL
AND KRISTI FONDREN

and well-being. A person in the environment perspective is on approach for truly understanding the development of student-athletes. Given the foregoing paragraphs, we focus on five questions as we understand the student-athlete experience at the collegiate level:

- What is the current state of athletics and the culture surrounding sports on U.S. college and university campuses today?
- What is the recruiting process like, and what factors affect student-athletes' decisions on where to attend college?
- What challenges do student-athletes face when attempting to balance being both a student and an athlete, inside and outside of the classroom?
- What are relationships like between student-athletes, nonathletes, fans,

and faculty members? Among student-athletes and coaches?

- How do outcomes for student-athletes compare with those for nonathletes as they leave college (i.e., graduation rates, professional aspirations, beyond college)?

Using the above questions as a guide, this chapter highlights both qualitative and quantitative research studies that direct our attention to important issues in the study of sports in higher education and the student-athlete experience. As noted previously, a main goal in this chapter is to enhance our understanding of student-athletes by exploring how their environment influences their development. We acknowledge that it is difficult, if not impossible, to discuss all of the positive and negative developmental milestones and the trajectories by which they occur. Nonetheless, this chapter aims to provide individuals with a greater understanding and appreciation for the experiences associated with being a student-athlete at the collegiate level.

Some of the topics explored here include college and the sporting culture, the recruiting and admissions processes, balancing academic and athletic roles, socializing agents or the influence of significant others, use and influence of social media, and deviance among student-athletes. This chapter closes with a discussion of potential benefits and positive outcomes associated with intercollegiate sports participation.

Our exploration of the student-athlete experience begins with a discussion of the culture of sports at National Collegiate Athletic Association (NCAA)-member institutions. We turn to this topic first to situate student-athletes within the broader social milieu of college athletics.

COLLEGE AND THE SPORTING CULTURE

Sports: A New Tribal Religion.

More than any other activity, collegiate sports has a long and noteworthy place in the history of American universities beginning with the inaugural Princeton–Rutgers football game of 1869 (Fondren, Gill, and Picou 2012). In college towns across America today, game day is something close to magical, something sacred, for followers of this new tribal religion. The quasi-religious character of sports manifests itself through various rituals and traditions (homecomings, pilgrimage to home games, tailgating, face-painting, chants, cheers, game day events), totems (nicknames, mascots, heroes and legends we know about—coaches and players), and sacred places (stadiums, locker rooms, places in town, places on campus) associated with universities' sports teams ,which will be discussed in more detail below.

Since Missouri hosted the first homecoming for alumni in 1911, colleges and universities across the United States today have annual homecoming festivities (Pinto 2010). Today, each college town has its own set of game day traditions, totems, and sacred places that make sports participation unique. The pregame and postgame rituals of tailgating (i.e., eating, drinking, socializing) are a tradition, if not an art form (Fondren, Gill, and Picou 2012). Louisiana State University (LSU), named best tailgating scene in 1996 by ESPN, celebrates game day with a Cajun twist that includes crawfish, shrimp, and jambalaya. Ole Miss, often listed in the top five of college football traditions, has The Grove, a ten-acre site shaded by oak trees in the middle of the campus. When walking through The Grove on game day, it is not unusual to see white linen tablecloths held in place by silver candelabras amid a complete buffet of Southern cuisine. While Auburn and Alabama fire up the barbeque grills well before kickoff, a common scene at Clemson and South Carolina is the Low Country Boil—a combination of shrimp, potatoes, corn, crab, and sausage all cooked in one pot.

But, tailgating is not the only game day tradition surrounding collegiate football. Vaught-Hemingway Stadium is filled with the sound of Ole Miss fans yelling the "Hotty Toddy Cheer" while Tennessee fans sing along to "Rocky Top" as players battle between orange and white checkerboard end zones. When taking the field on game day, Clemson players touch Howard's Rock seconds before running down a grassy hill leading directly into Memorial Stadium. Although banned from use during conference games, it is not uncommon to see determined Mississippi State fans cheering on the Bulldogs with their favorite noise-making device—the cowbell. At South Carolina, fans cheer their team as they run onto the field to the soundtrack of *2001: A Space Odyssey* while onlookers at Georgia Tech watch as their team is lead onto the field by the Ramblin' Wreck, a restored 1930 Model A Ford sports coupe. Although George Edmundson retired in 1998, Florida's infamous "Mr. Two Bits" still returns, sign in hand, for special Florida games, such as those against Tennessee and Florida State. LSU's "Mike the Tiger" is housed north of Tiger Stadium in a glass-enclosed area with a pool where fans can view "Mike" on game day before the cat is placed in a cage and rolled outside the locker room of the opposing team. While Georgia has the most recognized mascot in all of college football, the English bulldog "UGA" (pronounced "Ugh-gah"), Florida State has

"Chief Osceola" and "Renegade" as part of their pregame highlights and traditions. Of course, when it comes to football traditions, we must not forget Oklahoma's "Sooner Schooner" or Notre Dame's "Touchdown Jesus" as Texas and Purdue battle over who has the largest bass drum on the field (Pinto, 2010).

Also, sports stadiums represent one of the most sacred places for students, fans, and alumni alike. Boise State's "Smurf Turf," so named because of the blue Astroturf, is home to one of the most recognized fields in college football today (Pinto, 2010). At Georgia teams face off "between the hedges," a reference to the English privet hedge surrounding the field at Sanford Stadium, one of the ten largest stadiums in college football (Fondren, Gill, and Picou 2010). Among the largest stadiums in college football with seating for more than one hundred thousand fans are "The Big House" at Michigan (107,501), Penn State's Beaver Stadium (107,282), Tennessee's Neyland Stadium (102,037), and Ohio State (101,568). While seating comes nowhere near that of college football stadia, Kentucky's Rupp Arena and Duke's Cameron Indoor Stadium rank among the most well-known sites in men's basketball. In a similar vein to Penn State's Paternoville, a tent city that emerges outside the stadium before home games (Pinto, 2010), students at Duke University (affectionately referred to as "Cameron's Crazies") set up camp at Krzyzewskiville (Pappano, 2012). While K-Ville is legendary, similar scenes play out at Oklahoma State, Texas A&M, North Carolina State, the University of Missouri, San Diego State, and Xavier University as students anticipate upcoming sports event. At the University of Kentucky, students do not wait for basketball season but begin a campout at the official start of basketball practice (Pappano, 2012).

In addition to stadiums, there are also other places viewed as sacred. For example, Auburn has "Toomer's Corner," the official gathering place after home football games for fans, students, players, and, at times, coaches. When celebrating a huge victory, it is not unusual for Toomer's Corner to be "rolled" with toilet paper, or similarly for students at Wake Forest to "roll" the Quad and students at John Brown University to "roll" the basketball court for the home opener. Fans at Clemson come together at the Esso Club, a converted gas station and one of the area's most popular game day attractions. Alabama is home to The Quad and Dreamland, both popular spots where generations of fans congregate before and after home games.

As may be inferred from above, big-time sports on college campuses influence student and fan behavior alike (Pappano, 2012). Fan identification is one of the most important factors in the role of sports teams (Fink, Trail, & Anderson, 2002) as fans tend to experience intense reactions to collegiate spectator sports and their teams' performance. Consider the mocking chants from Duke's "Cameron Crazies" during free-throw attempts, fans at Michigan and Cornell taunting hockey players, or students at the University of Maryland and their attempts to distract opponents by shaking newspapers (Marshall, 2011). Team identification suggests that as individuals identify with a university, or in this case a team, they feel a sense of oneness or belonging to the team and tend to define themselves in terms of the team and its players (Mael & Ashforth, 1992, p. 144). But despite the intimacy of fans and students with college athletic teams, data suggest that these individuals do not develop intimate relationships with student-athletes themselves (Carodine, Almond, & Gratto, 2001).

So have athletics now become the public face of colleges and universities as the above might suggest? Is the relationship between academics and athletics mutually beneficial? The material that follows focuses on these questions.

Dual Identity Institutions.

College sports, particularly big-time revenue-producing sports such as football and men's basketball, occupy a prominent place on college campuses across America. Is this positive or negative? Well, that depends on when, where, and who you ask. Nearly fifteen years ago, Toma (1998) found that athletics was not only viewed positively by those outside the university, but was viewed favorably by administrators, faculty, students, and staff alike. More specifically, Toma identified three ways athletics promoted institutional identity: (1) drawing people to campus, (2) creating dialogue about the institution, and (3) linking the institution to other well-known universities through competition with them (1998). Toma's research included eleven Division I universities (Arizona, BYU, Clemson, UConn, LSU, Michigan, Northwestern, Nebraska, Notre Dame, UNLV, and Texas A&M) across a range of conferences, all of which had similar emotional and financial investments in their respective universities' athletic programs.

Most studies regarding institutional identity primarily focus on Division I athletics (Fondren, 2010; Pappano, 2012; Toma, 1998, 1999), but a recent study examining the intersection between revenue-producing sports programs and institutional identity found that Division II and III universities are also using the reputation of their athletic programs to promote their respective universities (Feezell, 2009). So not only do collegiate athletics produce revenue for Division I, II, and III schools but athletic programs can also be used effectively to promote the institutional identity of the university and bring students, alumni, and members of the community together.

While it may appear the relationship between athletics and academics within dual identity institutions is mutually beneficial, Pappano, who coauthored *Playing with the Boys: Why Separate Is Not Equal in Sports* with Eileen McDonagh (2012), argues that promoting an athletic identity over academics undermines the integrity of the university. Today we live in an era where head coaches make more than university professors. According to a recent article in *The New York Times*, the average salary for a full professor increased 32 percent between 1985 and 2010 whereas the average salary for football coaches increased by 650 percent (Dozier, 2012). More specifically, the average salary for a head football coach at a Division I school was $1.36 million in 2009 (Wieberg, Upton, Perez, and Berkowitz, 2009), whereas basketball coaches whose teams made it to the NCAA tournament earned $1.4 million in 2010 (Upton, 2011). Division II schools, on the other hand, are competitive but generally have less funding compared with Division I colleges and universities. In Division III schools, academics are top priority and sports are viewed more as an extracurricular activity; they do not offer athletics scholarships or redshirt players. Some Division III sports may be viewed as competitive but this is generally not the case for big-time revenue-producing sports such as football or men's basketball. As expected, average salaries for Division II and III football coaches in 2010 were significantly

lower, at $82,500 (Moore, 2011) and $49,140, respectively (Wallace, 2011).

As explained above, on most Division I campuses, where football is king, sports programs tend to be well funded and highly competitive; they must be if programs are to offer athletic scholarships and attract top student-athletes. The recruiting and admissions process are discussed next.

GETTING THERE, GETTING IN: THE RECRUITING AND ADMISSIONS PROCESS

Recruiting Season.

The recruiting process for a student-athlete typically begins anywhere between the seventh and tenth grade. This is partly due to the advent of camps and recruiting services that give male and female student-athletes greater exposure at younger ages. In fact, several recent stories have surfaced indicating that college coaches have offered prospective student-athletes scholarships as early as the seventh grade, although this is not typical (Kruder, 2010).

The recruiting process can begin in a number of ways, as well as at different points in a person's athletic career, such as when a coach watches the student-athlete play in person or on film, or a student-athlete may receive a letter or a visit from a member of the coaching staff. Regardless, following the initial contact a student-athlete makes an official visit to the interested university. Prospective student-athletes are allowed five official and countless unofficial visits to college campuses. These visits, particularly official visits, allow a recruit to observe firsthand the workings of the athletic program, meet the coaching staff, and gather information about academic programs offered by the university. Throughout recruiting season, prospective student-athletes may receive scholarship offers by coaches representing interested sports programs. Once an offer is made, prospects may verbally commit at that time or officially commit on National Signing Day by signing a National Letter of Intent.

As the finale of the recruiting process for most sports, National Signing Day falls on the first Wednesday in February when college programs "officially" sign prospective student-athletes. It is not uncommon for prospects to verbally commit to a school after receiving an offer and then later de-commit before National Signing Day to accept an offer from another program. Once a National Letter of Intent is signed, however, the recruit is committed to that program. The only way a recruit can be released from his or her commitment at this time is for the university's sports program to release the student, meaning he or she loses one year of eligible playing time.

While National Signing Day is the first "official" day a recruit can sign a National Letter of Intent, prospective student-athletes can sign scholarship letters or offers over the months to come. Sports journalists have of late voiced concern over the issue of over-signing, particularly in Division I football programs. When a coach over-signs he offers more scholarships than the number available for the sport in a given year. Over-signing is a concern because some student-athletes are left without an athletic scholarship and are forced to walk-on or pursue options with other NCAA-member institutions.

Another concern with the recruiting process is the lack of involvement of student-athletes' parents in certain sports, particularly women's and men's basketball, as well as football (Losing to Win, 2011). When some student-athletes enter college they are still of minor age, and until they are eighteen years old (and even beyond) parents should stay involved with the development of their son or daughter. Parents are encouraged to attend recruiting visits when possible and should seek out evidence of supports and opportunities for student-athletes outside of athletics. Head coaches have great influence over student-athletes, but many have position and/or assistant coaches with whom the student-athlete may have more direct and frequent contact. Parents should utilize the accessibility of these coaches to stay abreast of their son's or daughter's coursework, progress toward graduation, and their social, physical, and emotional well-being.

A concern of athletic departments and the NCAA when it comes to recruiting are the outside influences of student-athletes' real-life networks, i.e., student-athletes' relationships with noncustodial parents, extended family, high school coaches, summer league coaches, recruiting services, agent runners, and runners. Athletic departments are concerned that the nature of some of these relationships may result in violations of NCAA bylaws such as impermissible or extra benefits to student-athletes. Related to this is the involvement of boosters, or wealthy alumni from universities, in the recruiting process. In the past the NCAA was more concerned with boosters rather than the social networks cited previously. Now, however, the NCAA has developed a very broad view of boosters and almost anyone who is not considered a close relative of a student-athlete, especially those who play in big-time revenue-producing sports, can be considered a booster.

The NCAA's rules governing booster contact are designed to protect the interest of student-athletes, but it can also be detrimental to some in that athletic department and NCAA anxieties may supersede the psychological and social needs of student-athletes. For student-athletes with few resources, the extended social network of aunts, uncles, coaches, and legal guardians are necessary for their development and well-being. In particular, student-athletes from inner city, rural, and single-parent environments depend on extended family members to overcome psychological, social, and financial challenges. As such, community leaders and role models—e.g., former coaches, teachers, distant relatives, neighbors, pastors, and others—play a meaningful role in the livelihood of student-athletes and should not be separated when they visit campus. While parents or significant others may be influential in the lives of student-athletes, including school-choice decisions, what other factors play a role in a student-athlete's decision regarding where to attend college and continue playing sports?

Decision Time.

One SCORES survey indicated that 95 percent of Division I student-athletes chose to attend their particular university to increase their chances of being drafted (NCAA, 2011). But the reality is that in men's basketball, for example, there is only a 0.03 percent chance of a professional career. As for women's basketball, only 32 women (2 percent) out of just over 127,000 high school senior players will eventually be drafted by the Women's National Basketball Association (WNBA). In football the odds are slightly better, with 0.08 percent or 250 of just over 317,000 high school senior players being drafted by a National Football League (NFL) team. In baseball, 4

percent of high school players will have a chance of playing professionally. Baseball drafts about 600 NCAA athletes from the 6,700 college seniors each year, a number that is far higher than any other professional sport and that represents a need to feed the sport's large farm system (NCAA, 2010).

While a majority of student-athletes believe their particular university will increase their chances of becoming a professional athlete, a majority of research conducted on athletic recruiting has focused on the perceived importance of attributes cited by prospective student-athletes when deciding where to attend college (Cooper, 1996; Doyle and Gaeth 1990). For example, Division I baseball and softball recruits indicated the following five attributes as most important to them in terms of school choice: (1) scholarship amount, (2) team reputation, (3) atmosphere, (4) school location, and (5) academic programs (Doyle and Gaeth, 1990). Similarly, basketball recruits ranked the importance of forty variables when making decisions concerning school choice (Cooper 1996). Among the most important attributes were relationships between players and coaches, coaches' commitment to the program, and the particular style of play adopted by the team. Continuing this line of research, Klenosky, Templin, and Troutman (2001) interviewed NCAA Division I football players and asked why similar attributes were important to them in terms of school choice.

In some cases, in sports such as basketball, there is cause for concern because Amateur Athletic Union (AAU) coaches can have a significant influence on the initial recruiting and transfer processes and decisions concerning school choice. Also, high-profile programs with top-rated basketball players typically have some association with shoe companies, and such an association can affect a school-choice decision made by a student-athlete because of a shoe company's relationship with a particular college and its athletic program. At the same time, family and economic compensations are often major deal makers or breakers for student-athletes whose families are struggling financially. As such, these compensations should not be disregarded as financial needs may trump other concerns for many student-athletes when making decisions on where to play college sports.

While we are able to learn more about the reasons behind school-choice decisions for student-athletes, we still know very little about the extent to which recruiting processes intersect with the identity of educational institutions (Fondren, 2010). Using the University of Mississippi (Ole Miss) as a case study, Fondren (2010) found that institutional identities can intersect with recruiting practices when coaches and others from competing institutions are vying for the same top athletes. For example, although the University of Mississippi has attempted to improve its image concerning race with the removal of "Colonel Rebel" and the Confederate battle flag from sporting events, rival universities and coaches are not above implementing negative recruiting tactics to sway black athletes from signing with Ole Miss (Barnhart, 2003; Feldman, 2007; Fondren, 2010; Greenburg, 1996). According to the Women's Sports Foundation (2008), negative recruiting is viewed as "an unethical recruitment strategy" that provides programs with "an unfair advantage based on perpetuating stereotypes, myths, and misconceptions" (p. 1). Negative recruiting strategies include, but are not limited to, misrepresenting the current state of race relations, discussing

the sexual orientation of current players or coaches, comments regarding the coaching style, or inaccurate information concerning coursework or academic rigor at a university.

Although it is discouraged, rumors of negative recruiting (i.e., "bad-mouthing" or pointing out the faults or weaknesses of a competing program rather than highlighting the strengths of one's own program) seem to appear in early February near National Signing Day as coaches become desperate for a talented signing class (Barnhart, 2003; Feldman, 2007; MacDonald, 2008). The negativity, or mud-flinging, typically begins when rivals perceive any given school as a threat. Is negative recruiting wrong? The answer is unclear among coaches and players and is nowhere to be found in the NCAA Division I Manual (The National Collegiate Athletic Association, 2006). According to a representative at the NCAA, the association is more concerned with what coaches "do" (e.g., economic compensation, contact violations, recruiting violations) rather than what coaches "say" to prospects (personal communication with NCAA representative, April 5, 2010).

While some coaches publicly deny any instance of negative recruiting, others privately acknowledge it exists; however, a fine line exists between what one coach considers negative recruiting and what another, such as former Clemson head coach Tommy Bowden, refers to as "comparative analysis" (MacDonald, 2008). It is acceptable for recruiting coaches to point out the strengths and weaknesses of competing programs, compare graduation rates of student-athletes, and offer pros and cons given the size of each community; however, it is argued that negative recruiting occurs when "facts or half-truths are selectively highlighted to create an unflattering narrative of the rival, turning some recruiting and political campaigns into plays on people's fears" (MacDonald, 2008, p. 1). Is negative recruiting an effective strategy? It depends. Prospective student-athletes who have the opportunity to take an official visit to an interested campus and athletic program are less likely to be influenced by negative recruiting strategies (Fondren, 2010).

At the end of the recruiting process, a student-athlete has to make a decision on where to attend college and play sports. Following this decision, he or she must be admitted to the university. We turn to the admissions process next.

Admissions.

When speaking of a student-athlete's initial entrée into higher education, an understanding of the admissions experience, access to admissions, initial eligibility, the NCAA clearinghouse, and special admissions is important. Recruited collegiate student-athletes typically access the admissions process via their sports coaching staff. Position coaches typically serve as initial intermediaries between a recruited student-athlete and the admissions department. Student-athletes must submit their high school transcripts and complete a college entrance examination just like nonathletes. Unlike nonathletes, however, athletic department officials may provide support to ensure that student-athletes complete all aspects of the admissions process such as the FAFSA, Pell grants, or in/out-of-state requirements.

Student-athletes must also be approved by the NCAA clearinghouse. The clearinghouse evaluates academic records to determine eligibility at a Division I or II college as a freshman student-athlete. Students who want to participate in college sports at the

Division I or II level during their first year of enrollment in college must register with the clearinghouse (NCAA Clearinghouse, 2008). There is a registration fee for domestic and international students.

Two controversial issues involving student-athlete admissions, and initial eligibility, are their standardized test scores and grade point averages (GPAs) when compared with nonathletes. A gap of 25 to 200 Scholastic Aptitude Test (SAT) points exists between select Division I student-athletes and nonathletes (Shulman & Bowen, 2001). With respect to the GPAs, one study found that the GPAs of Division I student-athletes fell well below those of nonathletes (Bowen & Levin, 2003). In 2008, the University of Texas at Austin had the biggest SAT gap between student-athletes and nonstudent-athletes attending schools affiliated with the Big 12 Conference (Knobler, 2008). At the University of Texas at Austin, the average SAT score for student-athletes was 1,037, and the average SAT score for nonathletes was 1,230. While the data are somewhat dated, there still is cause for concern regarding the academic preparation of some student-athletes.

Student-athletes with standardized tests scores and GPAs below the university minimum standards may be considered for special admission. Special admission for student-athletes is a delicate topic, although universities have special admissions for women and people of color. In special admissions cases, admissions officers typically evaluate the student-athlete's profile against the academic profile of the university, the student-athlete's contribution to his or her team, and the type of academic support resources available to help the student-athlete graduate (Nordeen, 2006). At the University of Oregon, between twelve and fifteen student-athletes receive special admissions per year and about two-thirds of those are football players (Baker, 2010). At the University of California, student-athletes who play football were forty-three times more likely to gain special admissions than their nonathlete peers (Zagier, 2009). Selective institutions tend to have the largest gap in academic qualifications between student-athletes and nonathletes. For instance, under Ivy League conference policies, each institution can grant thirty-five special admits for student-athletes who play football each year (Milberger, 2009).

At the beginning of the 2012 basketball season, three members of the St. John's University Red Storm men's basketball recruiting class—Jakarr Sampson, Norvel Pelle, and Amir Garrett—were ruled academically ineligible by the NCAA Clearinghouse (Darcey, 2012). The student-athletes' ratio of grades in core courses to SAT scores did not meet the minimum NCAA standard. A NCAA prospective student-athlete needs a certain average in the core classes and a corresponding GPA. For example, at the 2.0 cutline, which is approximately a C average, a prospective student-athlete needs a SAT score of 1,000 or above. Conversely, with a lower SAT score, higher grades are needed (NCAA Clearinghouse, 2008).

Given the above discussion, how prepared are student-athletes for college life, both academically and socially? The following material addresses ways in which student-athletes continuously negotiate their dual role as student and athlete, both on and off the field.

WHO AM I: STUDENT, ATHLETE, OR STUDENT-ATHLETE?

Preparation for and Adaptation to College Life.

Once student-athletes are admitted and arrive on campus the academic, athletic, and social acculturation begins. One SCORES survey item indicated that 90 percent of student-athletes felt academically underprepared upon entering the first year of undergraduate studies. Some student-athletes' feelings of preparation deficiency stem partly from their high school experience and initial experience at a larger university (NCAA, 2011). Student-athlete integration and adaptation also are dependent on when they arrive on campus, their preparation for and outlook on college, their role models or socializing agents, and the interaction effects between all of these factors.

Up until the 1970s, student-athletes were not eligible to compete as freshmen, which allowed them the time to adapt to the increased demands of their academic and athletic roles. As recent as 2011, individuals and organizations, such as the New America Foundation, proposed that the NCAA return to freshman ineligibility for all Division I football and men's basketball players (Yglesias, 2011). Proponents of freshman ineligibility believe that one year without the pressures of big-time collegiate athletics will (a) help student-athletes develop an academic identity and (b) decrease their athletic identification, particularly their focus on professional sport careers.

To help with adjustment to college life, some student-athletes arrive on campus earlier than others. They may graduate from high school a semester early and decide to matriculate one semester or summer session earlier than other student-athletes. The NCAA currently encourages the early or summer arrival of student-athletes who happen to be entering freshmen. Doing so allows them to earn up to six hours of college credit while at the same time provides them with a gradual adjustment to their dual role as student and athlete. When student-athletes arrive early they have the opportunity to matriculate in courses without the full demands of their athletic role (i.e., competitions, travel, community service, and media obligations).

Also, there is the practice of grayshirting student-athletes. Grayshirting occurs when an incoming freshman waits until the second semester to enroll as opposed to entering during the fall. A student-athlete who grayshirts may accept a scholarship offer, but may choose to enroll in a community college, prep school, or other educational institution until the second semester. Thus, grayshirted student-athletes are allowed five calendar years to compete in four seasons. When a student-athlete grayshirts he or she will play his or her last season of college sports six years after high school instead of five years. Opinions vary on the practices outlined above, but each alternative provides student-athletes with an opportunity to adjust to the expectations of being a collegiate student-athlete.

Balancing Athletics and Academics.

When student-athletes arrive on campus they already are optimistic about their potential to succeed academically, but that attitude can quickly turn to cynicism (Adler & Adler, 1989). A student-athlete's disparagement can be the result of many sources, both internal and external. For instance, time management can become a significant issue, especially for Division I football and men's basketball

where student-athletes can devote anywhere from thirty to sixty hours a week to their sport (Zimbalist, 1999). What people without direct knowledge of the thirty-six men's and women's collegiate sports fail to consider is the mental and physical time student-athletes need to recuperate from their athletic role. On average, student-athletes experience a meaningful number of injuries ranging from torn ligaments to concussions. These injuries add another "thing to do" for student-athletes and further complicate their daily routines as they are learning to manage their time as student-athletes. Among the responsibilities that student-athletes already must juggle are attending class, studying for classes, weight training, conditioning, practice, competitions, meetings, and film sessions.

The amount of time student-athletes spend on their athletic role far outweighs the time spent on academics. In 2010, the NCAA accused the University of Michigan football program of five major violations including conducting voluntary workouts that exceeded the NCAA time limits on workouts. Coaches used extra conditioning to discipline players for missing class and over the course of three months student-athletes were participating in two extra hours per week of football-related activities (Windsor, 2010). One SCORES survey item indicates that 83 percent of student-athletes only study enough to remain eligible and 59 percent complained of not having enough time to study. To avoid over-identity with sport, isolation, or cynicism, student-athletes should be encouraged and taught to schedule their unstructured time so that they can take advantage of the various programs, activities, organizations, and other campus resources. Rodney Rodgers, the former Hillside, Wake Forrest, and NBA star, once shared that during his time in college the famous writer Maya Angelou taught a class on campus. Rodgers shared that he was unable to take it or to hear her lecture during her entire year at the university (Loosing to Win, 2010).

As indicated above, time demands have the potential to isolate student-athletes from the rest of the campus environment outside of athletics (Adler & Adler, 1989; Davis, 1990; Sellers, 1993). Division I male student-athletes devote between 30.7 and 44.8 hours to their sport per week, and female student-athletes spend 29.3 to 37.1 hours per week to their respective sport (NCAA, 2011). Student-athletes in some sports engage in activities related to their sports for eleven months per year. Sometimes student-athletes fail to enhance their academic identity because key players in their immediate circle may not be interested in academics (Price, 2000). Another SCORES survey item indicated that 54 percent of student-athletes identify more as an athlete than as a student (NCAA, 2011).

Data suggest, then, that the importance, intensity, and frequency of sport-related interactions can contribute to student-athletes committing a great deal of time to their athletic identity. This suggests that there is an almost constant conflict between academic and athletic roles, which places the student-athlete at a disadvantage in the classroom (Hollis, 2001). Scholarship student-athletes are cognizant and frequently reminded that they are on an athletic as opposed to an academic scholarship. The conflict results in role strain where the obligation to one commitment detracts from the obligation to another (Simon & Van Rheenan, 2000). The conflict is further exacerbated when academic expectations for student-athletes are relaxed (Adler & Adler, 1989). Given that student-athletes must learn to negotiate their dual roles as student and

athlete, academic advisers, learning specialists, tutors, and faculty mentors are among the socializing agents who help student-athletes adjust, especially during their first semesters on campus.

ASCDUs and Academic Support.

Every Division I school is mandated to have an Academic Support and Career Development Unit (ASCDU), which includes athletic department academic advisers, learning specialists, and an assistant or associate athletic director, all of whom typically join the student-athlete admissions process by evaluating transcripts, tests scores, individual learning plans (ILPs), and any potential learning disabilities. While student-athletes are introduced to ASCDUs via the admissions process, the unit's primary role is to provide academic support and career development opportunities for student-athletes once they are on campus.

Some ASCDUs allow parents to remain involved in their son's or daughter's development after the student-athlete signs a release that allows academic advisers and other athletic department officials to discuss grades and other issues. Parents should meet or at least speak with ASCDU staff members to understand how they will try to ensure internships and experiences that will aid in the student-athlete's identity exploration. The parent, for instance, should ask, "What are you going to do to try to ensure my son or daughter's interests and major match?" Parents should also understand if concessions will be made for the sake of their son's or daughter's academic, social, and career development. Parents should share their commitment to their children's success with athletic departments so key personnel understand that parents are a resource and are involved.

ASCDU academic advisers help student-athletes improve the likelihood of academic success. The number of student-athlete advisers is dependent on the institutional resources, the reporting line for the ASCDU, and whether the student-athlete has selected a major. ASCDUs provide support in the form of study skills development, content tutoring, time-management strategies, academic advising, class scheduling, and career-development exploration (Meyer, 2005). ASCDU academic advisers also provide ancillary services including performing class checks, encouraging student-athletes to develop relationships with professors, and teaching study skills classes for student-athletes.

Academic advisers teach student-athletes the importance of preparation in academic success, the significance of a degree in achieving their post–athletic career goals, and how to navigate the various systems and processes across the university. ASCDU academic advisers, outside of coaches, typically become an important confidant for student-athletes. Academic advisers do not typically engage in content or other tutoring, but they still spend a meaningful amount of time counseling and sometimes consoling student-athletes. In addition to academic advisers, tutors and learning specialists also assist in socializing student-athletes. In particular, tutors almost always develop lengthy relationships with student-athletes, in part because of the amount of work invested in improving the likelihood of student-athletes' academic success.

In or around 2005, supervision of some ASCDUs was transferred from the department of athletics to the department of student affairs or the office of the provost (Heuser & Carty, 2008). The change in the reporting line reflected a need to ensure that athletic department policies regarding student-athlete development were consistent with those of nonathletes to avoid controversies regarding student-athlete admissions and to meet the developmental needs of a unique population.

Student-athletes can have up to two academic advisers—one in the athletic department and another in the department, college, or school. One advantage of having an academic adviser in the athletic department is that athletic advisers can help student-athletes cope with and adapt to their role as student-athletes within the larger university structure because of their understanding of the university's goals and the student-athletes' goals. A second advantage is that athletic academic advisers are familiar with how to help student-athletes craft their athletic schedule around their academic schedule so that they progress toward graduation. A disadvantage, however, is that athletic advisers may consciously or unconsciously cluster student-athletes into an academic major for a variety of reasons, including pressure from coaches. One cause for clustering is believed to be largely due to NCAA legislation (Lieber-Steeg, Upton, Bohn, & Berkowitz, 2008).

The most common majors for student-athletes playing football are business, communication, criminal justice, sociology, and sport management (Suggs, 2003). A closer look at the 2008–2009 Kansas State University's football team shows that 33 of 120 football student-athletes were seeking degrees in the social sciences. Even so, 40 percent of student-athletes have stated that college sports prevented them from taking the courses they wanted (Suggs, 2003), perhaps due to convenience and athletic scheduling. Another disadvantage of having academic advisers within the athletic department is that student-athletes can become overly reliant on athletic academic advisers for advising, time management, counseling, and mediation with faculty and coaches.

At some smaller Division I and Division II institutions academic advisers from the larger university community, as opposed to the athletic department, provide student-athletes with academic support. For example, at Norfolk State University (NSU) there are fifteen sports and 281 student-athletes, but only one athletic department staff member for student-athlete development. At NSU, a coordinator for academic support monitors student-athletes' academic success, progress, and performance. The coordinator supervises fifteen academic enhancement counselors (AECs) who primarily work as university advisers or in some academically related role. Their responsibilities include—but are not limited to—scheduling, classes, creating progress reports, and distributing travel letters. University allies include STARS and ACCESS, which provide tutors for athletes, and disability services and the library, which provide space for learning. An advantage for having academic advisers outside the athletic department is that student-athletes are often provided with intangibles for campus success, including access to university-wide mental health and career-development services. Regardless of where academic advising occurs or who provides the service, the overall goals of both academic and athletic department advisers should be to encourage student-athletes to identify their interests, utilize their strengths, maintain their continuing eligibility, and eventually graduate.

While there are pros and cons to having academic advisers both within and outside athletics departments, former student-athletes who turn professional and report being positively affected by the athletic department support services have displayed their gratitude by giving back to their universities. For example, in 1997 Steve Smith, a former Michigan State University basketball All-American and member of the 2003 NBA Champion San Antonio Spurs, donated $2.5 million toward construction of the Clara Bell Smith Student Athlete Academic Center. This donation, in memory of his mother, Clara Bell Smith, is the largest gift ever by a professional athlete to any college or university. This donation helped fund the construction of a comprehensive study center for student athletes (Michigan State University, 1998).

STUDENT-ATHLETES AND SIGNIFICANT OTHERS' INFLUENCE

Coaches.

Head coaches, assistant coaches, and position coaches are arguably the most noteworthy influence throughout a student-athlete's college experience (Caldwell, 1997). A coach's attitude toward academics and athletics can influence a student-athlete's performance and well-being in many ways (Wang, Callahan, & Goldfine, 2001). Coaches have a lot of influence over student-athletes as evidenced by how much, athletically, they ask of student-athletes. While some argue that collegiate coaches should exert as much if not more influence over student-athletes' academic achievements and career exploration, the contracts and incentive packages of head football coaches suggest that winning competitions is more important than graduating student-athletes (Humphrey, Yow, & Bowden, 2000). An examination of the salaries and incentive packages of Division I head football coaches indicates that only six-teen of the thirty-five highest-paid coaches had financial packages attached to student-athlete academic achievement (Fish, 2003). Twenty-seven coaches were paid salaries that exceeded $1 million, but only one coach's incentive package included financial induce-ments for academic achievement exceeding $75,000.

A coach's involvement in academic achievement is increasingly important owing to his or her influence on student-athletes both within the athletic department and across the university. Head and assistant coaches have the potential to create a positive or negative atmosphere for academic social-ization by working closely with ASCDUs. For example, student-athletes may make mental notes on their coaches' views toward academ-ics and follow their lead or meet their expec-tations on academic success. If a coach wants his or her student-athletes to pursue other identities outside athletics, then student-ath-letes are more likely to comply because they understand that the coach decides whether their one-year renewable scholarship will be renewed the following year.

Student-Athlete Peers.

The influence of student-athletes' peers on student-athletes is an important factor in the socialization process regardless of the sport, or the race or gender of the student-athlete. Because of time constraints, commonalities in their goals, and similarities in their lifestyles, student-athletes tend to interact with other student-athletes. More specifically, student-athletes often attend the same classes, partic-ipate in the same social circles, and even date one another because of shared interests. This interaction, however, seems to vary by the size of the college and the emphasis placed on its athletic program. For example, Division I student-athletes are influenced to a greater extent by student-athlete peers than those at Division III schools (Stavisky, 1998).

Peer influences can contribute to student-athletes becoming engrossed by a peer athletic subculture (Adler & Adler, 1989), which is both good and bad. More specifi-cally, student-athletes can have a positive or negative influence on each other when it comes to substance use and abuse, academic performance, athletic performance, choice of major, and post–athletic educational goals. Sometimes, however, student-athletes fail to enhance their academic identity because key players in their immediate circle may not be interested in academics (Benson, 2000). According to SCORES data, 52 per-cent of student-athletes plan to pursue a professional sports career, with 91 percent of student-athletes reporting that sports were more important than their studies (NCAA, 2011).

Student-Athletes and Nonathletes.

Student-athletes in some sports are iso-lated from nonathletes, but there is still a fair amount of interaction. Nonathletes and student-athletes interact in class, on campus, via social networks, at social gatherings, and around (before, during, and after) competi-tions. In the past, data suggest nonathletes hold negative views regarding student-athletes' academic competency (Baucom & Lantz, 2001). Negative views were related to perceived differences in academic expecta-tions of students versus student-athletes, the resources available to student-athletes, and the attention athletic success receives when compared with academic success.

Today there seems to be less negative views toward collegiate sports, but some resentment still exists between student-athletes and nonathletes. According to one SCORES survey item, 80 percent of students believe student-athletes receive special privileges and 72 percent believe student-athletes cannot compete with them in the classroom (NCAA, 2011). One concern of nonathletes about student-athletes in revenue-generating sports involves "one and done" basketball student-athletes. One and done refers to a student-athlete who attends the university for the fall semester, competes in collegiate basketball during the fall and spring semesters, and enters the National Association Basketball (NBA) draft at the end of their college basketball season.

Division I student-athletes were sampled to explore relationships between their academic performance and their interactions with fellow students (Dreher, 2008). Results suggest that lower student-athlete satisfaction in interactions with fellow students correlated with lower student-athlete academic performance. Some student-athletes, especially those from inner city and rural areas, may have negative attitudes toward students, especially those at predominately white institutions, because of their higher socioeconomic status. The reality is that nonathletes may have more supports and opportunities than student-athletes as evidenced by the fact that many student-athletes need an athletic scholarship to attend college whereas this may not be the case for most nonathletes.

The relationship between student-athletes and students can become increasingly complicated because students occupy dual roles as peers and fanatics (i.e., fans). The fan experience is described as a psychic vacation because of the need for fans to escape some of the realities of life and interact with stars (Adler & Adler, 1989). Fans include students and alumni as well as men, women, teens, and children who never attended the universities for which they cheer. Fans typically feel a sense of oneness or belongingness to the team, and tend to define themselves in terms of the team and its players (Mael & Ashforth, 1992). But as may be recalled from earlier in the chapter, most fans do not know or have close relationships with the student-athletes whom they often refer to on a first-name basis (Carodine, Almond, & Gratto, 2001).

Student-Athletes and Faculty.

Benford (2007: Sperber, 2000) points out that some faculty members believe that revenue-generating sports have exacerbated the incompatibility between collegiate athletics and academics. In fact, research suggests that faculty members hold negative attitudes toward student-athletes (Engstrom, Sedlacek, & McEwen, 1995). More specifically, faculty members, staff, and advisers held stereotypes of student-athletes as overprivileged, pampered, and whose primary motivation to attend school is to participate in sports (Fletcher, Benshoff, & Richburg, 2003). Unfortunately, student-athletes can become active participants in the perpetuation of the dumb jock stereotype by constructing attitudes and engaging in practices that conform to the collective messages student-athletes receive from their peers (Benson, 2000).

More recent research indicates that subtle reminders of negatively stereotyped identities are often sufficient to undermine the academic performance of student-athletes in the classroom (Yopyk & Prentice, 2005). The negative stigmas attached to student-athletes can detract from their academic self-concept and overall self-esteem (Sailes & Harrison, 2008). In particular, faculty members demonstrate a concern for the academic preparation of black student-athletes (Engstrom & Sedlacek, 1991; Sailes, 1993). Also, some professors behave in ways—e.g., overlooking student-athlete success or failure, lowering expectations, cutting off communication, intensifying scrutiny, and expressing negative comments—that keep student-athletes at a distance (Perlmutter, 2003). But when black male student-athletes feel respected, challenged, and supported their academic behaviors improve and they can progress toward graduation (Benson, 2000). Everyone in a student-athlete's immediate circle should keep in mind that the subtle activation of a positive self-relevant stereotype actually leads to better performance, both inside and outside of the classroom (Shih, Ambady, Richeson, Fujita, & Gray, 2002).

NEW DEVELOPMENTS: THE INFLUENCE AND USE OF SOCIAL MEDIA

Millennial student-athletes, or today's student-athletes, tend to be well versed in the use of technological innovations for communication (i.e., smart phones, social media). They are witty, quick with feedback, love all of the bells and whistles, and tend to live in the moment. Everything is about them. Student-athletes of this generation want attention and do not hesitate to record videos to upload to Facebook, Twitter, or YouTube for all to see, often without thinking about the ramifications, whether positive or negative.

Facebook.

Today, social networks and social media are a part of the fabric of American and university life. There are about one hundred twenty-three million unique users on Facebook per month. Some fail to remember that originally Facebook was only accessible to college students. According to one group of Division I student-athletes, the rationale for student-athletes' use of social networks varies. Some use social networking as a means of staying in contact with friends and family, some for communicating with other student-athletes, others for keeping abreast of developments in their sport, some for hooking up with people (i.e., sex), and others for avoiding studying (Gill, 2006). Due to athletic and academic demands, student-athletes initially utilized social networks in the athletic department computer laboratories or during study hall. Now with the advent of social networking applications on cell phones, student-athletes have greater, almost instant, access to social networks. Due to the time demands of student-athletes, meeting others is one of the leading reasons student-athletes use social networks. To increase the likelihood of making connections with others, student-athletes list their dorm room, phone, cell phone numbers, local addresses, hometown, and class schedules. Social networks are also popular because some student-athletes have celebrity status and are unlikely to attend parties and other campus social events.

Twitter.

Recently, Twitter, a social networking system based on the use of "tweets" that are 140 characters or less, provides students and student-athletes with instant access to thousands of "followers." Athletic departments may become more concerned about Twitter than Facebook because the media now follows student-athletes on "tweets" before competitions, after competitions, and during the off-season to get perspectives that they might not be able to gain through traditional outlets. Again, many of the agents discussed above follow student-athletes, providing another avenue for student-athletes to interact. At the onset of the boom in social networks, some athletic departments limited their use while others banned their use altogether by student-athletes. One of the major concerns involved student-athletes who posted inappropriate profiles, hazing rituals, slanderous statements about coaches, racism, nudity, and tweets involving substance use and abuse (Associated Press, 2006). In 2010, the NCAA opened an investigation of the football program at the University of North Carolina, Chapel Hill (UNC), based on the photos that one football student-athlete posted on Twitter. In the NCAA infraction report UNC was cited for failure to monitor social marketing. Athletic departments are now more diligent about developing social networking policies, providing education, and monitoring student-athlete and athletic department use of social media.

DEVIANCE AMONG COLLEGIATE STUDENT-ATHLETES

One negative element or by-product of collegiate sports participation is substance use and abuse. While student-athletes can arrive with addictions or develop alcohol, marijuana, caffeine, or prescription drug dependencies during their time on campus, the focus here will be on alcohol and marijuana use.

Alcohol Use.

To contextualize student-athlete substance abuse and use in a larger framework consider that a *USA TODAY* survey of one hundred nineteen schools in the FBS (Football Bowl Subdivision programs) found that nearly 54 percent allow the sale of alcohol through public concessions, in private suites, or both at one or more playing venues. In an environment where alcohol use is allowed at games and frequently used in other circles by students, it is no surprise that student-athletes use and abuse alcohol and other substances.

Alcohol can be a prominent factor in college life, and according to one report student-athletes represent more frequent and extreme examples of binge drinking (Trauma Foundation, 1998). Along with higher consumption levels, collegiate student-athletes have a tendency to experience more alcohol-related consequences, exhibit more high-risk behaviors, and engage in more sexual violence compared with their nonathletic counterparts (Leichliter et al., 1998).

Marijuana Use.

Marijuana use also is a growing reality among collegiate student-athletes. Research on student-athlete marijuana use is somewhat dated, but the latest studies suggest marijuana use among student-athletes is declining. In 2001, 27 percent of student-athletes reported they used marijuana compared with 40 percent of nonathletes (Green, Uryasz, Petr, & Bray, 2001). Recent anecdotal evidence of student-athlete marijuana use, however, seems to contradict the latest empirical evidence. In 2010 there were eighty-nine media reports of student-athlete arrests involving alleged marijuana possession or trafficking. During the same year at least four student-athletes were arrested on trafficking charges for possession of between one and ten pounds of marijuana. In addition, no less than ten professional athletes were cited for marijuana use or possession or trafficking.

Trends in collegiate and professional sports suggest marijuana use may be increasing among athletes. Also, it is important to remember that the information we have is only the tip of the iceberg. For example, each year several student-athletes are suspended because they violate team rules and these violations may be related to substance use or abuse; often the details of the suspension or removal are not provided. One explanation for any increases in student-athlete marijuana use is relaxed athletic department policies. Among the "Big Six" Division I conferences there are no conference-level policies or procedures regarding the use of marijuana by student-athletes or athletic department testing. One student-athlete explained, "Marijuana was a problem my whole time and they looked past our marijuana tests my freshman year. The people that looked at our marijuana drug tests my freshman year, it didn't matter to them because we were winning." NCAA-member institutions are responsible for setting policies related to the use and distribution of street drugs. Below is a sample of policies at Division I schools:

- (Four) strikes (positive tests) and you're out (forfeit your scholarship)
- Suspension for 10 percent of season (first positive test), 33 percent of season (second), and one year (third)
- Suspension and counseling
- Second offense results in permanent cancellation of athletic eligibility
- First positive test gets one year of testing, a second a suspension for

25 percent of season, third a one-year suspension (but remains on scholarship) and fourth nets a school dismissal

STUDENT-ATHLETE—A PROMISING COMBINATION?

Due to the intensity in criticism surrounding collegiate athletics, it can appear that there are only negative effects related to student-athlete participation. There are, however, many positive effects and outcomes associated with sports participation. Positive effects of sports participation for student-athletes include increased social interaction and support (Sellars and Dumas, 1996), the development of interpersonal skills and leadership abilities (Ryan, 1989), and increased feelings of belonging and acceptance among one's peer group (Adler & Adler, 1989). As a result of their participation in competitions, student-athletes get to travel nationally and internationally, make friends at other universities, and network with individuals who may be able to help them with a career once their eligibility expires.

Student-athletes tend to have higher GPAs in-season than out of season (Sailes & Harrison, 2008). Due to sports commitments and time constraints in-season, student-athletes typically take less demanding classes. But Rishe (2003) found that student-athletes have higher average graduation rates compared with nonathletes. While some may be surprised that student-athletes, on average, tend to have higher graduation rates compared with nonathletes, student-athletes have institutional support, mandatory study halls, and specialized academic advising not provided to other undergraduates.

Compared with male student-athletes, female student-athletes have higher graduation rates, as is the case for undergraduates overall. Contributing to the myth of the "dumb jock" stereotype is evidence pointing to the consistently lower graduation rates of athletes who play football and men's basketball (Rishe, 2003). A possible reason for greater academic success among female student-athletes compared with males is that men have had greater athletic opportunities beyond college. Consequently, female student-athletes focus more on academics whereas male student-athletes tend to focus more on professional sports opportunities beyond college.

There is clearly a lack of research on positive student-athlete outcomes, but anecdotal evidence suggests the athletic role is a positive contributor to media perceptions. The NCAA proclaims there are "over 400,000 student-athletes and almost all go professional in something other than sports" (NCAA, 2012). Former student-athletes move on to graduate school, medical school, and law school. In 2008, Florida State University safety Myron Rolle was awarded a Rhodes Scholarship (Thamel, 2008). Rolle was the first major-college football player of his generation to win what is considered the world's most prestigious postgraduate academic scholarship. Rolle became the only black and most prominent student-athlete to win the award since Bill Bradley at Princeton in 1965.

Other former student-athletes assume careers in secondary education, the human services, law enforcement, and athletics administration. Some former student-athletes become state and federal government representatives and even presidential candidates. Also, in an age where a significant number of student-athletes leave school early for professional baseball and basketball, a number of them return to complete their college degree. The number of former male and female student-athletes who return to obtain their degrees is a reminder that for some student-athletes, many who are first-generation students, earning a degree is a major positive accomplishment for their families.

SUMMARY

The goal of this chapter was to provide individuals with a greater understanding of the experiences associated with being a student-athlete at the collegiate level by exploring how their environment influences their overall development. The chapter began with the culture surrounding college sports, including the quasi-religious character of sports, to situate the lives of student-athletes in the larger social milieu of intercollegiate athletics within dual identity institutions. Next, we addressed the recruiting process, including negative recruiting practices, and factors that may influence student-athletes' decisions on where to play collegiate sports. Following this was an overview of the admissions process, including initial eligibility, before moving on to discuss preparation for and adaption to college life. This led to a discussion of ways in which student–athletes continuously balance their dual roles as both student and athlete, not an easy task. To help student-athletes adjust to their new environment—academically and athletically that is—they are provided with various institutional supports (i.e., ASCDUs, mandatory study halls, academic advising).

The next section considered influences of significant others who serve as socializing agents in the lives of student-athletes. We examined relationships between student-athletes and their coaches, as well as interactions with faculty members, students, and sports fans. We then moved beyond the immediate physical environment of student-athletes by focusing on the influence and use of social media (i.e., Facebook, Twitter) by today's millennial student-athletes. This topic led into a discussion of deviance among student-athletes at the collegiate level, particularly alcohol and marijuana use. The chapter concluded by discussing various benefits and positive outcomes (i.e., graduation rates, future career paths, opportunities to play professional sports) in the lives of student-athletes despite negative perceptions or unflattering attention in the media on what it means to be a student-athlete playing at the collegiate level.

REFERENCES

Adler, P.A., and P. Adler. (1987). Role conflict and identity salience college athletics and the academic role. *Social Science Journal* 24(4), 443–55.

Adler, P.A.,and P. Adler. (1989). The Glorified Self: The Aggrandizement and the Constriction of Self. *Sociology Quarterly* 52(4), 299–310.

Baker, W.J. (1988). *Sports in the Western world*. Urbana: University of Illinois Press.

Barnhart, T. (2003). Recruiting Becomes Increasingly Negative. *Cox News Service*. Retrieved March 17, 2004, from http://www.charleston.net/stories/012703/spo_27recruiting.shtml.

Baucom, C., and C.C. Lance. (2001). Faculty attitudes toward male Division II student-athletes. *Journal of Sport Behavior* 24(3), 265–276.

Benford, R.D. (2007). The college sports reform movement: Reframing the "edutainment" industry. *Sociology Quarterly* 48, 1–28.

Benson, K.F. (2000). Constructing academic inadequacy: African American athletes stories of schooling. *Journal of Higher Education* 71(2) 223–246.

Bowen, W.G., and S.A. Levin. (2003). *Reclaiming the game: College sports and Educational Values*. Princeton University Press: Princeton, NJ.

Broughton, E., and M. Neyer. (2001). Advising and counseling student athletes. *New Directions For Student Services* 93 (spring), 47–53.

Caldwell, P. L. (1997). *A study to determine student-athletes motivational climate influencing their athletic ad academic performance at a Midwestern University. Unpublished Dissertation.* Iowa State University.

Carye, J. (2012, March 17), "Report: Jamar Samuels ineligible due to financial benefit," Retrieved on April 1, 2012, from http://content.usatoday.com/communities/campusrivalry/post/2012/03/kansas-states-jamar-samuels-ineilgible-for-syracuse-game/1

Cooper, K. (1996). What the Basketball Recruit Wants to Know. *Coach and Athletic Director* 65, 7:24–26.

Darcey, K. (2012), "St. John's has 3 ruled ineligible for fall," Retrieved on April 18, 2012, from http://espn.go.com/new-york/ncb/story/_/id/6974420/st-john-3-players-ruled-ineligible-fall-semester

Doyle, C. A., and G. J. Gaeth (1990). Assessing the Institutional Choice Process of Student-Athletes. *Research Quarterly for Exercise and Sport* 61, 1:85–92.

Dozier, L. (2012), "The Average Salary of Football Coaches," Retrieved on February 18, 2012, from http://www.ehow.com/about_7425989_average-salary-football-coaches.html.

Dreher, D.V. (2008). *The Relationship Between Social Support and College Adjustment in Intercollegiate Athletes. Unpublished Dissertation.* The Florida State University.

Engstrom, C.M., W.E. Sedlacek, and M.K. McEwen. (1995). Faculty attitudes toward male revenue and non-revenue student-athletes. *Journal of College Student Development* 36(3), 217–227.

Engstrom, C.M., and W.E. Sedlacek. (1991). A study of prejudice toward university student-athletes. *Journal of Counseling and Development* 70, 189–193.

Feezell, T. (2009). Adding Football and the "Uses" of Athletics at NCAA Division II and III Institutions. *New Directions for Higher Education*, 148:65–72.

Feldman, B. (2007). *Meat Market: Inside the Smash-Mouth World of College Football Recruiting.* ESPN.

Fink, J.S., G.T. Trail,, and D.F. Anderson. (2002). An examination of team identification: Which motives are more salient to its existence. *International Sports Journal* 6, 195–207.

Fish, M.,(2003), "More and more college coaches are making CEO money."Retrieved on March 28, 2005, from http://www.sportsillustrated.com/basketball05/30/bkb_coaching_salaries

Fletcher, T.B., J.M. Benshoff, and M.J. Richberg. (2003). A systems approach to understanding and counseling college student-athletes, *Journal of College Counseling* 6, 34–45.

Fondren, K. M. (2010). Sport and Stigma: College Football Recruiting an Institutional Identity of Ole Miss. *Journal of Issues in Intercollegiate Athletics* 3:154–175.

Fondren, Kristi M., Duane A. Gill, and J. Steven Picou. 2011. Football, College. In Recreation, Vol. 16, of *The New Encyclopedia of Southern Culture*, edited by Charles Reagan Wilson. Chapel Hill, NC: University of North Carolina Press.

Gill, E. (2006) Social networking for student-athletes. IUPUI annual Student-Athlete Development Education Day. Indianapolis, IN.

Green G.A., F.D. Uryasz, T.A. Petr, and C.D. Bray (2001). NCAA study of substance use and abuse habits of college student-athletes. *Clinical Journal of Sport Medicine* 1, 51–56.

Greenburg, J. C. 1996. How Football Trumped Racism at Ole Miss. *The Journal of Blacks in Higher Education* 14:94.

Humphrey, J.H., D.A. Yow, and W.W. Bowden. (2007). *Stress in college athletics: Causes, consequences, and coping.* Binghamton, NY: The Haworth Half Court Press.

Klenosky, David, Thomas J. Templin, and Josh A. Troutman. 2001. Recruiting Student Athletes: A Means-End Investigation of School Choice Decision-Making. *Journal of Sport Management* 15, 2:95–106.

Knobler, M (December, 2008). Many athletes lag far behind on SAT scores. *The Atlanta Journal-Constitution* D1.

Leichliter, J.S., P.W. Meilman, C.A. Presley, and J.R. Cashin. (1998). Alcohol use and related consequences among students with varying levels of involvement in college athletics. *Journal of American College Health* 46(6), 257–262

Losing to Win. (2010). "The recruited student-athlete," Retrieved on April 14, 2012, from http://losingtowin.wfu.edu/

National Collegiate Athletic Association (2006). *NCAA Division I Manual 2006–07.* Retrieved October 23, 2006, from http://www.ncaa.

org/library/membership/division_i_manu-al/2006-07/2006-\ 07_d1_manual.pdf.

National Collegiate Athletics Association, (2010, April 20), "Estimated probability of competing in athletics beyond the high school interscholastic level," Retrieved October 1, 2010 from: http://www.ncaa.org/wps/portal/ncaahome?WCM_GLOBAL_CONTEXT=/ncaa/NCAA/Academics%20and%20Athletes/Education%20and%20Research/Probability%20of%20Competing/

National Collegiate Athletic Association (2011). *Division I Results from the NCAA GOALS Study on the Student-Athlete Experience*. FARA Annual Meeting and Symposium: San Diego, CA.

National Collegiate Athletic Association Clearinghouse (2008). *NCAA Freshman eligibility standards quick reference sheet.* NCAA Indianapolis, IN.

Nordeen, L. (2006). *The effectiveness of academic intervention programs within Division I intercollegiate athletics: An examination of race, gender, and sport type.* Unpublished Dissertation: University of Minnesota.

MacDonald, John A. 2008. Negative Recruiting the Ugly Underbelly of the Business. *The Birmingham News*. Retrieved March 26, 2010, from http://blog.al.com/bn/2008/08/nega-tive_recruiting_the_ugly_u.html.

Mael, F., and B. Ashforth. (1992). Alumni and their alma maters: A partial test of the reformulated model of organizational identification. *Journal of Organizational Behavior* 13, 103–123.

Marshall, John, 2011, "The Best Traditions in College Hoops," Retrieved on February 15, 2012, from http://rivals.yahoo.com/ncaa/basketball/news?slug=ap-picksix-traditions.

Michigan State University, (1998), "Clara Bell Smith Center," Retrieved on March 23, 2012, from http://sass.msu.edu/facilities/SmithCenter.html

Millberger, M., (2009), "13-Year-Old Gets Football Scholarship Offer," Retrieved on April 2, 2012, from http://abcnews.go.com/GMA/Weekend/seventh-grader-verbally-commits-play-football-usc/story?id=9764564

Moore, Kathy, 2011, "Division-II College Coach Salaries," Retrieved on March 30, 2012, from http://www.ehow.com/info_8724393_divisionii-college-coach-salaries.html.

Pappano, Laura, 2012, "How Big-Time Sports Ate College Life," Retrieved on January 20, 2012, from http://www.nytimes.com/2012/01/22/education/edlife/how-big-time-sports-ate-college-life.html?pagewanted=all.

Pinto, Michael, 2010, "The 50 Greatest College Football Traditions," Retrieved on February 15, 2012, from http://bleacherreport.com/articles/489238-the-50-greatest-college-football-traditions#/articles/489238-the-50-greatest-college-football-traditions/page/51.

Rishe, P. J. (2003). A Reexamination of How Athletic Success Impacts Graduation Rates: Comparing Student-Athletes to All Other Undergraduates. *American Journal of Economics and Sociology* 62, 2:407–427.

Ryan, F.J. (1989). Participation in intercollegiate athletics: outcomes. *Journal of Leadership Studies* 1(1), 91–110

Sailes, G. (1991). Black sport supremacy. *Journal of Black Studies* 2(4), 480–487.

Sailes, G. (1993). An investigation of campus stereotypes: The myth of black athletic superiority and the dumb jock stereotype. *Sociology of Sport Journal* 10(1), 88–97.

Sailes, G. and L. Harrison. (2008). Social Issues of Sports. In Leslie-Toogood, A., and E. Gill, eds. *Advising Student-Athletes: A Comprehensive Approach to Success.* Manhattan, KS: National Academic Advising Association.

Sellers, R.M., and A. Dumas. (1996). The African-American student-athlete experience. In Etzel, E.F. (ed.) et al. *Counseling college student-athletes: issues and interventions* (p. 55–76). Morgantown, W.VA, Fitness Information Technology.

Shih, M., N. Ambady, J.A. Riheson, K. Fujita, and H.M. Gray. (2002). Stereotype performance boosts: the impact of self-relevance and the manner of stereotypes activation. *Journal of Personality & Social Psychology* 83(3), 638–647.

Shulman, J.L., and W.G. Bowen. (2001). *The Game of Life: College sports and educational values.* Princeton, N.J.: Princeton University Press.

Simons, H.D., and D. Van Rheenen. (2000). Non-cognitive predictors of student-athletes' academic performance. *Journal of College Reading and Learning* 30(2), 167–181.

Sperber, M. (2000). *Beer and circus: How big-time college sports is crippling undergraduate education.* New York: Henry Holt and Company.

Suggs, W. (2003, January 17). Jock majors: Many colleges allow football players to take the easy way out. *Chronicle of Higher Education* 49(19), A33.

Thamel, P., (November 22, 2008), "Rolle Wins Rhodes Scholarship," Retrieved on May 22, 2012, from http://www.nytimes.com/2008/11/23/sports/ncaafootball/23rolle.html

Toma, J. Douglas. 1998. *Representing the University: The Uses of Intercollegiate Athletics in Enhancing Institutional Identity.* Paper Presented at the American Education Research Association Annual Meeting. San Diego, CA.

Toma, J. Douglas. 1999. The Collegiate Ideal and the Tools of External Relations: The Uses of High-Profile Intercollegiate Athletics. *New Directions for Higher Education* 105:81–90.

Trauma Foundation. (1998). *Preventing alcohol related injury and violence: Resources for action.* Trauma Foundation: San Francisco, CA.

Upton, Jodi, 2011, "Salary Analysis: NCAA Tournament Coaches Cashing In," Retrieved on March 30, 2012, from http://www.usatoday.com/sports/college/mensbasketball/2011-03-30-ncaa-coaches-salary-analysis_N.htm.

Wallace, Maxwell, 2011, "The Average Salary of a Division 3 Football Coach," Retrieved on March 30, 2012, from http://www.ehow.com/info_10043609_average-salary-division-3-football-coach.html.

Wang, J. Callahan, D., and B. Goldfine. (2001). Coaches challenges working with substitute players of a collegeiate team. *Journal of Applied research in Coaching and Athletics 16,* 110–124.

Wieberg, Steve, J. Upton, A. J. Perez, and S. Berkowitz, 2009, "College Football Coaches See Salaries Rise in Down Economy," Retrieved on March 30, 2012, from http://www.usatoday.com/sports/college/football/2009-11-09-coaches-salary-analysis_N.htm.

Women's Sports Foundation. 2008. Recruiting—Women's Sports Foundation Response to Negative Recruiting/Slander Based on Sexuality: The Foundation Position. Retrieved on March 26, 2010, from http://www.womenssportsfoundation.org/Content/Articles/Issues/Equity%20Issues/R/Recruiting%20%20Womens%20Sports%20Foundation%20

Response%20to%20Negative%20 RecruitingSlander%20Based%20on%20 Sexuality%20The%20F.aspx.

Yglesias, M. (April 4, 2011). The Case For Freshmen Ineligibility. Retrieved on April 1, 2012, from http://thinkprogress.org/ culture/2011/04/04/185907/the-case-for-freshman-ineligibility/?mobile=nc

Yopyk, D.J.A. & Prentice, D.A. (2005). Am I an athlete or a student? Identity Salience and stereotype threat in student-athletes, *Basic and Applied Social Psychology, 27*(4), 329–336.

Zimblast, A. (1999). *Unpaid professional.* Princeton, NJ: Princeton University press

INTRODUCTION

To fully understand and appreciate contemporary issues related to race[1] and ethnicity in college sport it is important to historically situate and frame our discussion within a broader discussion of the pervasive racism that has been systemic in American society since the early seventeenth century (Sage, 2000). From its inception, the United States of America (USA) has been a nation comprised of various ethnic immigrant groups. The arrival of European immigrants (particularly English colonists) during the seventeenth and eighteenth centuries led to the creation and utilization of race as a mechanism for establishing whiteness (i.e., being "white") as superior to other socially constructed racial identities and categories assigned by whites to various ethnic groups (Smedley, 1999). According to McDonald (2005), "European attempts to legitimate settlement, conquest, colonization, and slavery made skin color and phenotype meaningful while simultaneously imagining white subjectivities as superior to (especially) indigenous and African bodies" (p. 248). This exploitation and denigration first of Native Americans (i.e., via the seizure and appropriation of land) and then Africans (i.e., via the seizure and appropriation of labor) set the tone for the social and legal construction of race in the USA (Harris, 1993).

Systemic racism and white supremacy are the by-products of this social and

5

REPRESENTATION, PARTICIPATION, AND THE EXPERIENCES OF RACIAL MINORITIES IN COLLEGE SPORT

JOHN SINGER & AKILAH CARTER FRANCIQUE

legal construction of race (see Coates, 2003; Feagin, 2006, 2010; Haney Lopez, 1996). This has been reflected in the positioning of white European people at the top of the racial hierarchy (i.e., domination) and the relegation of other ethnic groups to a status beneath that of whites (i.e., subordination). Chideya (1999) expressed this point when she stated, "in the basest and most stereotypic terms, white Americans are considered 'true' Americans: black Americans are considered inferior Americans; Asian and Latinos are too often considered foreigners; and Native

---

1   Please see our "chapter definitions" text box for general insight into how we conceptualize relevant terms used throughout this chapter.

Americans are rarely thought of at all" (p. 7). Like Chideya, we acknowledge that several nonwhite immigrant groups have been negatively affected by systemic racism. In fact, it is important to note that even certain ethnic groups from Europe (e.g., Italians) faced racial discrimination before their whiteness was legally established (Omni & Winant, 1994). The "immigration experience," however, has been quite different for white ethnic groups (e.g., Italians, Irish, Germans) than it has been for nonwhite ethnic groups (Chong-Soon Lee, 1995). For example, African Americans[2] were forcibly brought in chains and enslaved for hundreds of years; as the native people to the land that would become the USA, so-called American Indians were robbed of their land, subjected to genocide at the hands of whites, and confined to reservations by the government; Latinos or people considered to be nonwhite Hispanics (e.g., Mexicans) have faced racial profiling (e.g., Arizona immigration law, SB1070) and been labeled as "illegal immigrants"; and Japanese Americans, who, unlike their German American and Italian American counterparts,

---

2   It is important to note that although the terms "African American," "black American," and "black" are used throughout this chapter, and in some cases interchangeably, they can have different meanings. For example, the term "black" typically refers to a broader array of people from the African Diaspora (e.g., the African continent, the Caribbean, North America, South America); it is a more inclusive term to describe a diverse array of people of African descent who are spread throughout the world, particularly the Western Hemisphere. The term "African American" typically refers specifically to people of African descent who were born in the USA and whose ancestral lineage is rooted in the American slave regime. The term "black American" could refer to African Americans who prefer the use of the term "black" in front of "American" or people of African descent who might not have been born in the USA but have become American citizens.

were put in internment camps during World War II. The point here is that within the racial classification system that developed in American society there has been a high value or premium placed on whiteness, where being white comes with many privileges and protections and being the racialized other (i.e., racial minority) does not (Harris, 1993; Ladson-Billings, 1998).

In this chapter we take a keen interest in the "unique and insidious heritage of injustice" (see Sage, 2000, p. 2) that black Americans have experienced and endured throughout American history. Black people are the only immigrant group to have been legally enslaved for an extended period and have segregation laws passed against them that were fully sanctioned and supported by the Supreme Court (Sage, 2000). In his book, *Systemic Racism*, Feagin (2006) discussed how Europeans and European Americans who controlled the development of the USA positioned the oppression of Africans and African Americans at the center of the new society. According to Feagin (2006), "White oppression of African Americans is archetypal because it is the original model on which whites' treatment of other non-European groups entering later into the sphere of white domination has largely been patterned" (p. xi). The construction of white identity and the ideology of racial hierarchy were intimately tied specifically to the evolution and expansion of the system of chattel slavery (Harris, 1993), which led to the creation and positioning of whiteness as being superior and blackness as inferior. In this regard, a focus on white-on-black oppression serves as an important and primary context to understand systemic racism across all major societal institutions, and how it affects various racial and ethnic minority groups in the USA (Feagin, 2006). We believe this focus on the black-white binary allows us to better analyze past, present, and future race matters in American society, higher education, and college sport.

Black Americans have made progress and achieved some gains since the Emancipation Proclamation and the Thirteenth Amendment to the Constitution "freed" them from chattel slavery in the 1860s (see Bennett, 1999, for critique of Abraham Lincoln being touted as "the great emancipator") and the Jim Crow system of overt discrimination (e.g., lynching and other racial violence, political disenfranchisement, legal segregation) legally ended as the civil rights movement was kicking into high gear. In particular, prior to the historic 1954 *Brown v. Board of Education* decision, American society, schools, and sports "were racially segregated and unequal due mostly to legalized and moralized injustices based on the social construction of race" (Hodge, Harrison, Burden, & Dixson, 2008, p. 944). Although the National Association for the Advancement of Colored People (NAACP) attacked discrimination in higher education by attempting to set enough precedence in smaller court cases to overturn the *Plessy v Ferguson* (1896) standard of "separate but equal," it was the *Brown* decision that rendered *Plessy* to be illegal and deemed racial segregation in public schools at all levels inherently unequal (Hodge et al., 2008; Taylor, 1999).

In the decades before the *Brown* decision (and even in its aftermath), the vast majority of black college students attended school and participated in athletics at historically black colleges and universities (HBCU). As a historical by-product of systemic racism, HBCU emerged primarily after the Civil War and prior to 1964 to educate and meet the special needs of black people who had been legally excluded from opportunities in the broader educational system (Thomas & Hill, 1987). The best, brightest and most talented black students (athletes) graduated from high school and attended these institutions because they had very few options outside of HBCU to attend college and participate in college sport (see Harvey, Harvey, & King, 2004). As a result, the academic and athletic programs at these institutions thrived and produced some of the most influential and prominent black women and men in various fields such as business, politics, medicine, clergy, media, entertainment, and sports. Black student attendance and sport participation at predominantly white institutions of higher education (PWIHE) (e.g., Paul Robeson playing football at Rutgers University; Jesse Owens in track and field at Ohio State University) was the exception, but certainly not the rule.

Although the *Brown* decision was met with great resistance and not readily embraced by many white decision makers in PWIHE and college sport, particularly in the South (Martin, 2010; Taylor, 1999), it did play a role in helping to create the circumstances that eventually led to the massive recruitment of talented black students (athletes) into athletic and academic programs at PWIHE. But other factors such as the growing commercialization of college sport also encouraged these PWIHE to recruit black athletes (particularly in football, basketball, and track and field) in efforts to secure the talent necessary for building highly commercialized and successful athletic programs (Sage, 2007). Events such as the 1966 men's national championship triumph of coach Don Haskin's Texas Western basketball team—which had an all-black starting lineup—over Adolph Rupp's all-white and heavily favored Kentucky squad, and University of Southern California

(USC) African American running back Sam "Bam" Cunningham's dominant performance over legendary coach Paul "Bear" Bryant's all-white Alabama squad in 1970 helped pave the way for the full-scale integration of black athletes into athletic programs at PWIHE.

Many people have heralded the desegregation of higher education and the benching of Jim Crow in college sport programs at PWIHE (see Martin, 2010, for an overview of the rise and fall of the color line in college sport) to be a breakthrough and sign of significant progress toward greater race relations and equal opportunities for black people. While this might be so, we should also analyze the desegregation of higher education in general, and the integration of college sport in particular with a critical eye. Taylor (1999) employed critical race legal scholar Derrick Bell's (1980) interest-convergence principle—which interrogates the motives behind the *Brown* decision (see Bell, 2004) and suggests that white elites will tolerate and even support the interests of racial minorities particularly when they (i.e., whites) stand to benefit the most—in his examination of the desegregation of American educational institutions. According to Taylor (1999), "several factors other than the interests of equitable education for black children may have played a seminal role, including increasing international media coverage of white racism against blacks, especially stories involving torture and lynching" (p. 187). Taylor further discussed how the U.S. Justice Department pushed hard for desegregation because it was in the national interest of the country to do so in light of its foreign policy concerns. Taylor (1999, p. 187) stated, "As the United States was attempting to position itself as the leading force against communism, continual and negative foreign reporting of

its system of racial apartheid threatened to undermine its role as a model democracy."

Bell's (1980, 2004) interest-convergence principle serves as a powerful analytic tool for making sense of the desegregation of PWIHE and the integration of black athletes into the high profile athletic programs on these campuses (i.e., football, men's and women's basketball). Furthermore, the interest-convergence principle and other critical race-based frameworks and principles (e.g., critical race theory, see Delgado, 1995; black feminist thought, see Collins, 2000; internal colonial model, see Hawkins, 2001; systemic racism theory, see Feagin, 2006; the white racial frame; see Feagin, 2010) offer explanatory power and can help us better understand some of the issues and challenges pertaining to race and ethnicity in college sport today. With this in mind, the primary purpose of this chapter is to embrace some of these critical perspectives in highlighting salient issues and challenges that racial and ethnic minority groups have been (and are) faced with as athletes, coaches, administrators, and other stakeholders in the powerful American social institution of college sport, particularly at the most highly commercialized Division I level (i.e., Football Bowl Subdivision [FBS]), where schools are governed by the National Collegiate Athletic Association (NCAA).

We frame our discussion by focusing on racial and ethnic minorities in college sport from three broad vantage points: representation, participation, and experiences. In terms of representation, we begin with a brief examination of the Native American mascot issue. As alluded to in the opening paragraph, the exploitation of Native Americans and black Americans was at the forefront of the establishment of the USA and its system of white power and privilege (see King, Leonard, & Kusz, 2007 for discussion on white power and sport). Therefore, we attempt to demonstrate how the depiction and portrayal of Native Americans as mascots for these college athletic teams might actually misrepresent the history and culture of this ethnic group. The remainder of the chapter will focus specifically on black stakeholders in college sport at PWIHE and their a) (under)*representation* in leadership and major decision-making positions, b) access to *participation* opportunities as athletes, and c) athletic, academic, and psychosocial developmental *experiences* as athletes. Our discussion of Native American mascots and primary focus on black stakeholders is not to minimize the importance of other racial and ethnic minority groups in college sport (e.g., Latinos, Asians). But it is to acknowledge that a) the (mis)representation of Native Americans as team mascots continues to be a salient issue in college sport, and b) black people are the overwhelming majority of the racial and ethnic minority population in college sport at PWIHE. When appropriate and possible, we will make reference to these other racial and ethnic minority groups as we discuss the representation, participation, and experiences of black stakeholders in college sport. We end this chapter with a brief summary and some final thoughts on the issue of race and ethnicity in college sport.

REPRESENTATION

Native American Mascots[3]

Given the purpose of higher education and the significant role colleges and universities should play in challenging students' assumptions and worldviews, and preparing them for career opportunities, leadership roles, and citizenship in an increasingly diverse world, the issue pertaining to the use of Native American mascots in college sport programs is worthy of discussion. This issue has received considerable attention over the years and several commentators have offered their perspective on it. On one side of the debate, students, fans, administrators, and other stakeholders have taken the position that there is nothing inappropriate about sport teams having Native Americans as team mascots. They have suggested that critics of the Native American mascot are being too sensitive and overexaggerating when they suggest these mascots are offensive to Native Americans. These proponents of such team mascots offer several rationales for why it is OK to have them. For example, some claim colleges and universities are actually honoring and paying homage to the cultural heritage of Native Americans by having these mascots (Eitzen & Sage, 2003). Also, some of these college and university athletic programs might be reluctant to jettison the mascot because they believe it would go against the tradition and history of the team name, and have a potentially negative effect on the

---

3   Portions of this section were adapted from Singer, J.N. (in press). *Race*. In G.B. Cunningham, and J.N. Singer, eds. *Sociology of Sport and Physical Activity (2nd ed.)*, College Station, TX: Center for Sport Management Research and Education.

identity/brand of the organization. Moreover, representatives of these institutions might even solicit the support from members of Native American tribes to justify and continue their usage of the team mascots (e.g., Florida State Seminoles claiming the university had tribal permission to use the Seminole name and logo image in an honorable way; see Staurowsky, 2007). Finally, students have also advanced the argument that other racial and ethnic groups have been used as sport team mascots (e.g., Notre Dame Fighting Irish), and these groups accept the use of their names with no problem (see Eitzen & Sage, 2003).

On the other side of the debate, critics of the usage of Native American mascots have argued that the mascot is disrespectful, and it denigrates, not celebrates, this historically marginalized racial and ethnic group in American society. As Coakley (2009) stated:

> Using stereotypes to characterize Native Americans is so common that most people don't realize they do it. When people take Native Americans images and names, claim ownership of them, and then use them for team names, mascots, and logos, sports perpetuate an ideology that trivializes and distorts the diverse histories and traditions of native cultures.

Coakley contended that by using Native American names and mascots these sport teams enable fans to express their ignorance and/or racist ideas. He further intimated that when fans and team stakeholders engage in their insensitive displays, chants, and actions at games they are misrepresenting the histories, cultural traditions, and religions of many Native American tribes and nations in the USA today. He used the example of a white European American student who paints his face, puts on a headband and a colorful shirt, carries a feather-covered spear, and rides into the football stadium on a horse named Seminole (as they have done for years at Florida State University) to further convey his point that white privilege and power is real and Native Americans continue to be subjected to various forms of "cultural identity derogation and theft" in college sport.

This race matter has become so prominent that the *Journal of Sport and Social Issues* (2004, volume 28, number 1) dedicated an entire issue to the topic, and several scholars have adopted a critical approach in analyzing the topic (e.g., Staurowsky, 2007). They suggest that proponents of having Native American team names and mascots are more concerned with their own self-interests than they are with the interests of the group that is most negatively affected by it (i.e., Native Americans). One of the major tenets of tribal critical race theory is that USA policies toward indigenous people are rooted in imperialism, white supremacy, and a desire for material gain (Brayboy, 2005). Although the NCAA has banned the display of Native American names, logos, and images on uniforms and other clothing, and the use of mascots at NCAA play-off games and championships, there are still several college and university athletic programs that remain steadfast in their commitment to the use of Native American names, logos, and mascots.

Castagno and Lee (2007) utilized critical race theory, particularly the interest-convergence principle, to demonstrate how PWIHE ultimately act in their own self-interests in how they address the issue. These scholars applied it to a university's policy that discourages, but does not prohibit, opposing teams from bringing their

American Indian mascot to the university for competition. Furthermore, the university refused to schedule competitions against opponents with an American Indian mascot unless that team is a "traditional rival or a conference member" (p. 6). Castagno and Lee (2007) believe the interest-convergence principle is demonstrated in the "traditional rival/conference member" component of the policy, insofar as

> The institution clearly recognizes and honors the interests of the Native community on campus by refusing to schedule games with some teams who have Native mascots, but the institution is even more protective of its own interests by still scheduling games with teams with whom they have long standing commitments (p. 7).

What this case study demonstrates is that racial justice for Native Americans will be pursued only to the extent that it converges with the interests, needs, desires, and expectations of the dominant racial group (see Milner, 2008). Moreover, because these leaders within higher education and college sport might have to lose something of great importance to them (e.g., loss of revenue, loss of support from alumni/fans and conference rivals) as they pursue more equitable policies and practices related to Native American mascots, many of these leaders have only been willing to go so far in addressing the interests and needs of the racialized other (i.e., Native Americans).

Under-representation of African Americans in Leadership Positions

Since the early 1990s, Dr. Richard Lapchick has published the *Racial and Gender Report Cards* (RGRC) in efforts to track the representation of racial minorities and women in the positions of athletes, coaches, and administrators (see Lapchick, Hoff, & Kaiser, 2011 for most recent report on college sport). Although African Americans have been grossly underrepresented (and continue to be) in the major leadership and decision-making positions (e.g., head coaching, upper-level administration) from the time they integrated into athletic departments at PWIHE, some progress has been made in coaching and administration opportunities for African Americans since the publication of the first report cards. For example, with the addition of six new African American head football coaches at FBS schools before the 2010 season, the overall number of African Americans in this position from 2008 increased from seven to thirteen; during the off-season in 2010 there were a record number sixteen of the eighteen total coaches of color starting the 2011 season that were African Americans (Lapchick, Hoff, & Kaiser, 2011).

Although progress has been made over the years and recent hiring trends for head football coaches has brought about optimism for some people, the numbers have fluctuated over the years and they still paint a picture that consistent and abundant opportunities for African Americans to be in these leadership and major decision-making positions continues to be an elusive quest for justice. According to the most recent report card for college sport (Lapchick, Hoff, & Kaiser, 2011), whites continue to dominate the head-coaching ranks on men's teams at the Division I, II, and III levels, respectively, holding about 90 percent of these positions, with African Americans holding roughly 4 percent to 6 percent of them. While African American men represent 21 percent of head coaches in men's basketball and 4 percent in women's basketball at the Division I level, African American women only represent 11.4 percent of head coaches in women's basketball and have no presence as head coaches in men's basketball. And while the percentages are somewhat better for African American women and men as assistant coaches in women's and men's Division I basketball programs, whites still hold more than 75 percent of the assistant-coaching positions in these basketball programs (the majority of the athletes in these sports are African Americans).

Regarding other positions of leadership the numbers are even more dismal. For example, 100 percent of conference commissioners in the eleven FBS were white men, and in all of Division I (excluding HBCU conferences) all thirty were white, with five being white women. Whites continued to hold the majority of the athletic director positions across all three divisions (at least around 90 percent), with zero African American women or other women of color holding this position at FBS schools. At the associate and assistant athletic director positions, whites still hold the majority of the positions across all three divisions, with African Americans holding 8.2, 14.4, and 5.4 percent, respectively, and Latinos and Asians holding less than 2 percent of these positions across all three levels. Finally, while women held 100 percent of the senior women's administrator (SWA) jobs, white women represented the vast majority across the three divisions (i.e., 85.1, 81.1, and 93.7 percent), with African American women representing 10.1, 15.4, and 4.2 percent of the SWA.

In many regards, the data from Lapchick and colleagues' research suggest African Americans in college sport have faced (and continue to face) occupational segregation stemming from being clustered into limited roles within the employment context. Occupational segregation "is said to exist when racial groups are distributed inconsistently across occupations or are allocated to certain positions, as compared to being equally represented in all available positions" (McDowell, Cunningham, and Singer, 2009, p. 432). This occupational segregation is similar to the widespread racial stacking (in playing positions) that African American athletes faced for years after they integrated into athletic programs at PWIHE—e.g., being denied access to the "thinking" leadership positions on the field such as quarterback or center in football, and being clustered into "skill" speed positions such as wide receiver, defensive back, and running back; see Loy & McElvouge, 1970—and to a lesser extent still face today. McDowell and colleagues' (McDowell & Cunningham, 2007; McDowell, Cunningham, & Singer, 2009) research on occupational segregation in athletic departments and administrative positions reveals that African Americans tend to be clustered into academic support positions (i.e., academic advisers and life skills coordinators). Although employees working in these positions serve an important role in helping to address the needs of college athletes, these positions are viewed within the athletic department as peripheral jobs that, in most cases, do not put African Americans on the right track to becoming senior-level administrators (e.g., athletic directors; see Suggs, 2005).

McDowell and colleagues and other scholars have provided insight into some of the complex and various factors that contribute to this occupational segregation—and, thus, under-representation of African Americans in positions of leadership. For example, some scholars have attributed this under-representation and exclusion of African Americans from heading coaching and senior-level administration positions to institutional racism (e.g., Edwards, 1985; Sage, 2007), racial stereotypes (e.g., Davis, 1995; Brown, 2002), discrimination (e.g., Anderson, 1993; Cunningham & Sagas, 2005; McDowell & Cunningham, 2007), the good ol' boys' network (e.g., Shropshire, 1996), and lack of social contacts for racial minorities (McDowell & Cunningham, 2007), among other factors. From a different point of view, McDowell, Cunningham, and Singer (2009) conducted a qualitative case study with athletic department employees at a PWIHE to understand the over-representation of African Americans in academic support positions and their under-representation in other staff and senior-level positions of leadership. They found that both supply (i.e., human capital limitations, social capital limitations, worker preferences and aspirations) and demand (i.e., products of diversity management strategies, recruiting practices, and outcomes of prejudice and discrimination) side factors helped to explain this phenomenon. To understand the under-representation of African American head coaches Cunningham (2010) created a framework that focused on the macro-level (i.e., institutionalized practices, political climate, stakeholder expectations), meso-level (i.e., prejudiced decision makers, discrimination, leadership prototypes, organizational culture of diversity), and microlevel (i.e., head-coaching expectations and intentions, occupational turnover intentions) factors and the relationship between these factors.

While the above-mentioned scholarship offers keen insights into this complex issue, African Americans and other racial minorities continue to be underrepresented in leadership positions, and our understanding of how the hiring process for selecting candidates to fill these positions continues to be limited. This explains why the Black Coaches & Administrators (BCA) has published the BCA Hiring Report Card (HRC)[4] on an annual basis since 2004, with the goal of placing the hiring process of NCAA FBS and Football Championship Subdivision (FCS) college football programs under public scrutiny and ultimately changing the way these programs act when hiring head football coaches at PWIHE. More specifically, when a school has a documented head coach opening the BCA contacts the president and athletic director (these higher education leaders serve as the hiring managers for football programs) at that institution to begin the process of evaluating their hiring process on the following five criteria: communication with the BCA and other pertinent organizations; search committee racial demographics; time frame for hiring decision; "short list" of final candidates interviewed; and adherence to affirmative action policies.

In efforts to provide a deeper examination and understanding of how the hiring process in college football might (negatively) affect African Americans and other racial minorities as they pursue head-coaching opportunities, Singer, Harrison, and Bukstein (2010) utilized critical race theory as an analytic and explanatory tool to justify and support the conception of the BCA HRC, and also apply the principles of critical race theory to the

---

4   In addition to a hiring report card for football, the BCA has also created one for women's basketball (see www.bcapsorts.com for access to these hiring report cards).

five criteria. In terms of the communication with the BCA component, these scholars discussed the importance of giving racial groups that have been historically marginalized "voice" and allowing them input into the hiring process. In a similar vein, the presence of racial minorities and whites (who are racially conscious and committed to social justice) on the search committee has potential to create a racial monitoring effect that could influence the discourse that occurs when discussing viable head-coaching candidates, as well as the actual outcome of the hiring process. The time frame component of the hiring process is important to critically analyze because it speaks to whether or not these athletic departments have shown a willingness to take time to go beyond the good ol' boys' networks of white male privilege and allow racial minorities access into these hiring networks.

The final two components involving the "short list" of candidates interviewed and adherence to affirmative action policies are particularly important to this critical examination and analysis of the hiring process at PWIHE. Singer and colleagues argued that since integration African American athletes have regularly made the "short list" for interviews to attend these schools and participate in sport (e.g., unofficial and unofficial campus visits during the recruiting process), but African American coaching candidates have not. This racial reality speaks to the value that is oftentimes placed on the black body as a physical commodity (i.e., recruitment of blacks in athlete positions to provide labor, but not in major decision-making positions). Further, it could also be argued that while several whites have attacked affirmative action as a form of racial preference for African Americans and reverse discrimination against whites in the workplace and higher education, many do not seem to have a problem adhering to affirmative

action policies when it comes to the recruitment of African American athletes. There are many cases where PWIHE allow African American athletes, particularly males, into their academic and athletic programs as "special admits" even though many of these have athletes have been considered academically un(der)prepared for college-level work (see Donnor, 2005; Downton, 2000 for examples).

From an interest-convergence perspective, this practice of intentionally and aggressively recruiting African Americans to be athletes, but not coaches (except, in many cases, as assistant coaches to help in the recruitment and mentoring of black athletes), demonstrates how PWIHE are willing to provide access and opportunity to African Americans at the entry level (i.e., as athletes) because they realize the economic benefits of doing so. As Davis (1995, p. 6) stated: "While a moral desire to end segregation may have prompted many to seek the integration of organized collegiate sport, the economic interests of others may have been of primary importance." Indeed, while some people's motives for integration could have been rooted in a sense of social justice and doing what is "right," it is important to acknowledge that many white elites who oversee the college athletics industrial complex (see Smith, 2007) were/are cognizant of the financial benefits associated with the recruitment and retention of African American athletes at PWIHE. The next section will focus on the participation of black male and female athletes at PWIHE, and the effect their presence has had on athletic programs on these campuses.

PARTICIPATION

Black Male Athletes

While African Americans have been excluded from and underrepresented in the head coaching and senior level administration positions, black males have been overrepresented in the revenue-producing sports of football and basketball in big-time college sport programs (i.e., athletic departments that have the largest budgets, highest media visibility, largest fan bases, and the most competitive football and basketball programs) at PWIHE. Today, they constitute more than half of the players in the high profile, revenue-producing Division I football and men's basketball programs (see Lapchick, Hoff, & Kaiser, 2011). According to Lapchick, Hoff, and Kaiser (2011), African American males account for 18.7 percent of athletes in all sports combined across the Division I, II, and II levels; however, when you take just the Division I level, the percentage goes up to roughly 25 percent, with about 46 percent and 61 percent of the players in football and men's basketball, respectively, being African American males. White males account for the vast majority of the remaining athletes in all sports across the three divisions and in Division I football and men's basketball. Other racial and ethnic groups (e.g., Asians, Native Americans, Latinos, mixed-raced) account for about 10 percent of the athletes in all Division I, II, and III sports.

The strong presence of black male athletes in the revenue-producing sports of football and basketball is one of the primary reasons big-time college sport has grown into the highly commercial enterprise it has become

over the past few decades. As Harris (2000, p. 37–38) stated:

> Collegiate sport in America has become a showcase of African American talent. No longer denied athletic scholarships and opportunities at major colleges and universities, African Americans dominate the record books. Statistical leaders in categories such as rushing and receiving in football, scoring and rebounding in basketball, and sprints in track and field are, almost without exception in recent years, African Americans. … Their presence is required, it seems, for teams to compete, not to mention excel, in revenue-generating intercollegiate sports.

Today, black males regularly lead their teams to the NCAA men's basketball tournament (i.e., "March Madness") and Bowl Championship Series (BCS) games in football. This kind of success on the basketball court and football playing field has helped generate revenue and great financial benefits for the NCAA, athletic conferences, and athletic departments. These financial benefits have come via ticket and merchandise sales, corporate sponsorships, television and radio contracts, appearance fees for postseason play, and monetary donations and other gifts from alumni.

Furthermore, coaches and administrators (the majority of whom are white) have been able to earn hefty salaries and compensation packages; and athletes, particularly whites, in nonrevenue sports (e.g., lacrosse, field hockey, golf, tennis) have benefitted because, in many regards, the financial success of football and men's basketball helps to underwrite and support the activities of these other athletic programs (Donner, 2005). In many respects, it could be strongly argued that the African American male football and basketball athlete has become the primary breadwinner of college sport in America today. This declaration, however, is not to suggest that the presence and labor of athletes from other racial groups have not played a role in the (commercial) success of college sport. Moreover, the presence and participation of the black male's counterpart (i.e., the black female) has also contributed to the overall growth of college sport, and is worthy of our attention.

Black Female Athletes

The participation rates of black female athletes in higher education are on the rise (Acosta & Carpenter, 2012; Lapchick et al., 2011). According to Lapchick and colleagues (2011), black female athlete participation rates at the Division I, II, and III levels are 11.6 percent, compared with 77.2 percent for their white counterparts and 18.7 percent for black male athletes. Black female athlete participation remains highly concentrated in basketball and track and field. At the Division I level specifically, black females represent 16 percent of the female athletes, while white females represent 70.6 percent. The remaining percentage make up 13.3 percent and consist of other women of color (e.g., Latino, 4.2 percent; American Indian/Alaskan Native, 0.4 percent; Asian/Pacific Islander 2.4 percent; two or more races, 1.1 percent; and other, 5.2 percent). Further, utilizing Lapchick and colleagues' (2011) analysis, black female athletes represent 51 percent and 29.1 percent of Division I basketball and track and field participants, respectively. So while scholars

indicate black female athlete participation is on the rise, what factors contribute to this increase in representation?

Some scholars credit the implementation of Title IX of the Educational Amendments of 1972 (Title IX[5], United States Department of Labor) as attributing to black female athletes' increased participation in sport (Cunningham, 2011; Smith, 2000). Smith (2000) asserted the implementation of Title IX has benefitted black women in sport by addressing the need for and implementation of sport and education programs, school-sponsored teams, and resources and scholarships. Furthermore, Cunningham (2011) suggests "women of color participating in university athletics increased 995 percent" due to Title IX and "women of color receive a percentage of scholarship monies (19.5 percent) above what might be expected based on their proportion among all female athletes (14.8 percent)" (p. 123).

Conversely, others have argued that Title IX might not have had the impact on the participation patterns of black female college athletes to the extent that others have claimed. For example, black female participation pre–Title IX was heavily concentrated in basketball, tennis, and track and field (Smith, 2000); and as indicated above, black female athlete participation at the Division I level remains highly concentrated in basketball and track and field. Thus, according to Gill (2011) "... Black female collegiate athletic participation lags behind every other identifiable ethnic category" and "in 2000, Black female student-athletes, excluding track and basketball participants, were awarded 2.7% of all Division I athletic financial aid awarded to female athletes. ..." (p. 122). So while Title IX has benefitted black females and other

---

5   See the chapter in this book on "Gender" for more insight into Title IX.

women of color (i.e., increased the number of racial minority girls and women sport participants in educational settings), black female athletes' participation and presence in athletics at PWIHE still lags behind that of white females and continues to be limited to a select few sports (i.e., basketball, track and field). This gap in opportunities (i.e., to be athletes, coaches, and administrators) between white and nonwhite females protects and maintains white privilege and power (see Rhoden, 2012). In this regard, Title IX's impact on the diversity of opportunities (i.e., in a wide range of different sports) for black women in college sport is questionable.

Today, the black male and female athlete in the highly popular and visible sports of football, men's and women's basketball, and track and field has earned a prominent place on the campuses of these PWIHE, and their presence has significantly changed the dynamics and landscape of college sport in the decades since integration. Heightened media coverage highlighting the black athlete's participation in college sports at PWIHE, however, often overshadows the details of the black athlete's daily experiences. While participation and experiences may seem synonymous, there are distinct differences and realities that challenge this notion for all college athletes in general, but black athletes in particular (Parham, 1993). Therefore, in the final section of the chapter we focus on three areas of concern regarding the experiences of black athletes in higher education: athletic exploitation, academic challenges, and psychosocial development.

EXPERIENCES

Athletic Exploitation[6]

A central tenet of critical race theory is the notion of race as property (Ladson-Billings & Tate, 1995) and some scholars have applied this tenet to the black male athlete at PWIHE (see Donnor, 2005; Singer, 2009). Ladson-Billings (1998) discussed how historically African Americans, in particular, were constructed as property in the sense that they were owned by others (i.e., white male slave owners). She also discussed that while African Americans eventually became citizens (by law), they "represent a unique form of citizen in the USA—property transformed into citizen" (p. 16). This begs the question: how might the desegregation of higher education and the integration of black males and females into athletic programs at PWIHE speak to this issue of race and property interests?

Several scholars have argued that black athletes in higher education have been exploited for their athletic prowess to the detriment of their educational interests (e.g., Benson, 2000; Brooks & Althouse, 1993; Byers & Hammer, 1995; Donnor, 2005; Edwards, 1969, 1983, 1984, 1985; Eitzen, 2003; Grant, 2003; Hawkins, 2001, 2010; Sailes, 1986; Singer, 2009; Sperber, 1990; Zimbalist, 1999). In particular, the seminal work of Dr. Harry Edwards helped set the tone and lay the foundation for other scholars who were/ are interested in the experiences of black

---

6   Polite's (2012, p. 2) definition of "exploitation," which is defined as "the unfair treatment or use of, or the practice of taking selfish or unfair advantage of, a person or situation, usually for personal gain," will be used in this section.

athletes at PWIHE. Edwards was critical in his discussions of the complicities of academic disenfranchisement, commercialization in college sport, racial discrimination, and the dual system of business capitalism dominating the notion of education; further, he discussed patterns of exploitation, lack of positive assimilation, and the valuing of participation but devaluing of education in his work (see Polite & Hawkins, 2012). In likening American sport to a plantation system, Edwards (1985) was especially critical of the white-controlled, white-dominated colleges and universities that pursue "one generation after another of academically deficient but athletically indispensable Black athletes who are perceived to have no role or legitimacy on the college campus except as sport participants" (p. 11).

In a similar vein, both Eitzen (2003) and Hawkins (2001, 2010) echoed Edward's sentiments. Eitzen (2003) compared big-time college sport programs to plantations and the athletes who serve as the primary labor force to slaves. Although he acknowledged there are differences between big-time college sport and the chattel slavery system that plagued American society in the antebellum South, Eitzen (2003) argued "the plantation/slavery metaphor is useful to understand the reality of the college sports world" (p. 122). In particular, he discussed how the NCAA preserves the plantation system by making and enforcing certain rules to protect the interests of the individual plantation owners (and severely restrict the rights of the workers, i.e., athletes); he likened the coaches who extract the labor from the workers to overseers. Further, while acknowledging that participation in athletics is voluntary and certain privileges are associated with it, athletes are still being "exploited economically,

making millions for their masters, but provided only with a subsistence wage of room, board, tuition, and books; they are controlled with restricted freedoms; they are subject to physical and mental abuse by overseers; and the master-slave relationship is accepted as legitimate" (Eitzen, 2003, p. 122).

Hawkins (2001, 2010) embraced the internal colonial model to capture the experiences of black athletes at PWIHE. This model centers race and was conceptualized based on the experiences of the black migrant labor worker in the context of slavery. Hawkins discussed how black athletes are recruited from various cities and states to these PWIHE for their athletic talent, to the neglect of their educational attainment. He likened the experiences of these athletes to that of indentured servitude, and suggested the black athlete is used primarily for the economic benefit of the NCAA and its member institutions.

Donnor (2005) used Bell's interest-convergence principle in his examination of the academic experiences of African American male football athletes to illustrate the ways through which athletic programs can deny, rather than foster, educational opportunity for African American athletes. As suggested in the introduction to this chapter, Bell's basic premise is that people in power (particularly whites) are often, in theory, supportive of laws, equity-oriented policies, and practices that do not oppress and discriminate against racial "others" as long as they (i.e., whites) do not have to alter their own ways, systems, and privileges of experiencing life. In this regard, from an interest-convergence perspective, allowing African American males into PWIHE to compete in football and basketball, and in some cases advance to the professional sport level, is not antithetical to the benefits that whites receive and the power that they continue to maintain.

Donnor (2005) utilized the legal literature to provide a deeper understanding of the educational experiences of African American male athletes in two ways: 1) by contextualizing their relationship to a PWIHE and the athletic department specifically, and 2) by presenting examples of personal and institutional practices that influence their educational opportunities. More specifically, Donnor discussed different lawsuits that were filed against PWIHE by two African American male athletes (i.e. Gregg Taylor, a football player at Wake Forest University; and Kevin Ross, a basketball player at Creighton University) and how each represented a case of educational malpractice or a breach of contract, especially given the binding agreement that exist between PWIHE and these athletes via the National Letter of Intent (NLI) that athletes sign and the athletic scholarship they receive in exchange for their participation in the athletic program.

Although both the plantiffs in the above-cited cases were unsuccessful in their lawsuits against these PWIHE, Donnor's discussion of these two cases is significant because it illuminates some larger issues related to the commodification of the black athletic body, and the devaluation of the black mind. One of the cases involved an athlete who recognized he was being exploited and attempted to take actions to combat it during his time as a student at the university. This case raises issues concerning human agency, and the role it plays in the educational experiences and outcomes of black athletes at PWIHE. An examination of the other case brings to light the issue of black male athletes' precollegiate educational experiences (i.e., K–12 schooling), and how they could negatively affect the educational experiences of these athletes once they arrive on these college campuses. In the sections below, we turn our attention to some of the academic challenges and psychosocial development issues black male and female athletes have faced at PWIHE.

Academic Challenges and Psychosocial Development

Given the exploitation of the athletic prowess of black athletes at PWIHE, issues pertaining to K-12 academic preparation (e.g., grade point average, standardized test scores, core curriculum and courses taken, "quality" of schools students attend), college educational performance (e.g., grade point average, academic persistence), educational outcomes (e.g., graduation rates, career transition), and overall personal development of black athletes at PWIHE have received considerable attention in the literature (see Adler & Adler, 1991; Anderson & South, 2007; Davis, 2007; Edwards, 1984, 1985; Hawkins, Milan, & Carter, 2007; Hodge, Harrison, Burden, & Dixson, 2008; Hyatt, 2003; Melendez, 2008; Parham, 1993; Person & Lenoir, 1997; Purdy, Eitzen, and Hufnagel, 1982; Sailes, 1998a; Sellers, Kuperminc, & Dumas, 1997; Siegel, 1994; Singer, 2009; Upthegrove, Roscigno, & Zubrinsky Charles, 1999). While a great deal of literature has focused on the cognitive (i.e., intellectual, which is typically measured via grade point average, test scores, etc.) variables related to the academic challenges and educational experiences of black student-athletes (particularly males, i.e., it has been suggested that this group lags furthest behind in terms of academic preparation for higher education; see Benson, 2000; Singer, 2009b) in the American educational system, much of the aforementioned literature has focused on some of the environmental (e.g., prevalence of racism in society and the educational system) and noncognitive (i.e., motivational) variables associated with the challenges and experiences black student-athletes face in comparison with their white counterparts.

Parham (1993) acknowledged that both nonathlete students and student-athletes face some similar developmental challenges as college students, but he argued there is a need to address the special needs of student-athletes given that they "are socialized from an early age in an environment that presents a set of challenges and demands that are in addition to and vastly different from the challenges and demands that their non-student-athlete peers have had to face" (p. 412); this often makes the struggle to resolve the "normal" developmental tasks even more difficult. In particular, Parham discussed the following additional challenges that athletes must take on: a) learning to balance academic and athletic pursuits; b) adapting to a certain degree of isolation from social and mainstream activities; c) managing success or lack thereof; d) attending to their own physical health and dealing with injury and rehabilitation; e) satisfying several different types of relationships with various groups of people (e.g., coaches, faculty members, parents, fans, peers); and f) terminating the athletic career and transitioning into other identities and endeavors.

Parham further contended that given the systemic racism that has permeated American society and its many social institutions, African American college athletes are saddled with an additional set of issues and concerns that their white counterparts do not have to contend with. According to Parham (1993, p. 419):

institutionalized discrimination based on the color of one's skin permeates our society, and it is reflected in the differential treatment that student-athletes of color receive and in the opportunities that they are afforded. Systemic biases and prejudices can be seen in virtually every component of an athletic program, from the way in which recruitment of athletes of color are carried out and handled to the ways in which academic progress (or lack thereof) is managed.

Research conducted since the 1990s provides support for Parham's contentions that institutional racism continues to have a deleterious influence on the educational experiences of African American athletes (e.g., Benson, 2000; Melendez, 2008; Singer, 2005, 2009). In the remainder of this section, we will briefly address some of the academic challenges these athletes face, with a focus on issues of identity development, negative stereotypes, and coping strategies for dealing with these challenges.

Regarding the balancing of academic and athletic roles, since the important ethnographic research of Adler and Adler (1991)—who discussed how college basketball players (the majority of whom were African Americans) gradually became detached from the academic role and engulfed into the athletic role as they moved from their freshman to senior years in college—several scholars have grappled with the tensions between the academic and athletic roles that athletes in the high-profile sports have had to navigate, and the effect this could have on the educational performance and outcomes of these athletes (see Anderson & South, 2007; Davis, 2007). For example, Benson's

(2000) research with African American football athletes at a major university revealed that the marginal academic performance of these athletes was a phenomenon created by a series of interrelated practices engaged in by many significant members of the institution (i.e., coaches, peers, faculty members, and the athletes themselves) who placed a higher premium on the athletic role. More recently, Singer's (2008) research with a group of African American male football athletes revealed that although these athletes derived certain benefits from their participation in the athletic program (i.e., scholarship, help in preparation for life challenges), the expectations and extreme time demands that coaches (in particular) placed on these athletes made it difficult to take advantage of opportunities to fully embrace the student role and engage in other educationally useful and productive activities outside of sport and play.

In efforts to address the academic and athletic divide and respond to criticisms from the public and reform-minded groups (e.g., Knight Commission, Drake Group), the NCAA has implemented measures such as the Academic Progress Rate (APR) to hold coaches more accountable for the academic performance of the athletes they recruit into their programs. Moreover, although academic support centers for athletics have been around since the late 1980s and early 1990s, many athletic departments have expanded these centers and programs in recent years in efforts to accommodate the special needs of the athlete population. Some skeptics, however, have questioned the real aim and purpose of these programs, and the effect they might actually be having on the educational experiences of black athletes at PWIHE. Spigner (1993) contended that many

academic support programs might be unwittingly supporting the sports enterprise at the expense of ensuring a meaningful education for black athletes. The title of Spigner's article, "African American student-athletes: Academic support or institutionalized racism?" suggests that institutional racism has been sustained by many of the practices in these programs, which encourage black participation in sport but little else in regard to educational activities. Many of these support programs and the personnel (e.g., advisers, learning specialists, tutors) in them have focused merely on keeping these athletes eligible (particularly those with marginal or inadequate academic preparation coming into college) and been complicit in the creation of an athletic subculture of low academic expectations (see Comeaux, 2007; Comeaux & Harrison, 2011); this, unfortunately, has the potential to cause African American athletes to focus solely or primarily on their athletic identities to the detriment of other important identities (i.e., academic, racial).

Research by Louis Harrison and colleagues (see Harrison, Harrison, & Moore, 2002; Harrison & Moore, 2007; Harrison, Sailes, Rotich, & Bimper, 2011) has revealed that African American athletes (particularly males) tend to have stronger athletic identities than their white counterparts, and that these athletes "identify more intensely with the athletic role and narrow their focus to concentrate more on athletic activities than other pursuits" (Harrison & Moore, 2007, p. 251). In many instances, the focus on sport and play during the college years creates difficult challenges for these athletes "when the fans stop cheering" (Parham, 1993) and the issue of retirement from sport and transition into another career is before them. In their study of the transition and retirement of

African American athletes from college sport participation to careers, Hawkins, Milan, and Carter (2007) found that the African American male athletes had not properly prepared for their transition from college to careers, and as a result it took these athletes one to two years to adjust to their new identity (i.e., nonathlete). These findings speak to the need to reflect upon the role stereotypes play in the issue of identity development and the retirement and career transition of African American college athletes.

Scholars have discussed the effect negative stereotypes can have on the identity and educational experiences of black athletes at PWIHE (Edwards, 1984; Hodge, Burden, Robinson, & Bennett, 2008; Hughes, Satterfield, & Giles, 2007; Sailes, 1993, 1998). The notion that black people are athletically superior but intellectually inferior to other racial groups is at the core of these negative stereotypes. Similar to the sentiments of Edwards (1984) and Sailes (1993, 1998), Hughes, Saterfield, and Giles (2007) concluded in their research that black football and basketball athletes have been "athletisized" as dumb jocks and campus entertainment, and have not been viewed as serious students. In theorizing particularly about the stereotyping of black male athletes, Hodge, Burden, Robinson, and Bennett (2008) discussed the racial, social, economical, cultural, and psychological factors that affect black male athletes' academic and athletic experiences. These authors discussed how black athletes are not only stereotyped (as being athletically superior and intellectual inferior) by members of other ethnic groups but some actually engage in self-stereotyping (see also, Hodge, Harrison, Burden, & Dixson, 2008), and the effect of internalizing these negative stereotypes can be detrimental to these athletes' self-confidence and potentially contribute to a self-fulfilling prophecy.

Steele and Aronson (1995) described this outcome of self-stereotyping as "stereotype threat," which involves "being at risk of confirming, as self-characteristic, a negative stereotype about one's group" (p. 797). The work on stereotype threat specifically hones in on a person's race, gender, and/or social class and his or her ability to be successful when taking standardized tests and in his or her overall educational attainment (see Steele, 1999; Steele & Aronson, 1995; Steele, Spencer, & Aronson, 2002). Steele and colleagues reviewed stereotype threat in numerous performance settings to include sport and athletics (e.g., golf) and found that black athletes conformed to the negative stereotypes of being intellectually inferior. Hodge and colleagues discussed how this type of self-stereotyping can have an adverse effect on the self-esteem and motivation of black athletes to pursue other developmental experiences outside of sport excellence. Given this, how should black male and female athletes cope with these (internalized) stereotypes, and the academic and developmental challenges they present?

Carter and Hawkins (2011) addressed this challenge specifically for African American female athletes attending a PWIHE. This is noteworthy given the historical (and continued) marginalization and silencing of this group of athletes at PWIHE (see Bruening, 2005; Bruening, Armstrong, & Pastore, 2005 for insight into the experiences of African American female athletes). In seeking to give voice to this group, Carter and Hawkins utilized critical race theory and black feminist thought to understand African American female college athletes' copings strategies on the campus of the PWIHE. They found that the college athletes did experience covert racism and racial microaggressions (see Solorzano, Ceja, & Yosso, 2000), which caused them to adopt an avoidance coping style. More specifically, the African American female athletes chose not to confront the issues and/or persons directly; rather these women chose to handle their issues and challenges utilizing coping strategies rooted in African American and African American female culture. Thus, the African American female college athletes coped with their racialized experiences through culturally relevant practices and traditions such as (a) prayer and church, (b) confiding with family, friends, and teammates, and (c) journaling. While, this study is specific to black female athletes, black male college athletes and other athletes of color may have similar issues (i.e., academic persistence, athletic success, interpersonal relationships) that require culturally relevant coping approaches (see Ladson-Billings, 1992, 1995) to aid in their psychosocial development.

SUMMARY AND CONCLUSION

The purpose of this chapter was to highlight and critically discuss some of the many issues and challenges that racial and ethnic minority groups have faced as stakeholders in college sport at PWIHE. In efforts to achieve this purpose, we attempted to do several things. To begin, we situated the discussion of race and ethnicity in college sport within the broader context of American history and societal race relations. In doing so, reference was made to the influence the European conquest and the American slave regime have had on the establishment of white supremacy and the subordination of "non-white" racial and ethnic groups. Moreover, we briefly discussed the history of racial segregation, and some motives (e.g., image enhancement, financial gains) behind desegregation and the eventual integration of PWIHE and their athletic programs. Given the unique and unparalleled journey of black people in American society, the focal point of the chapter was on issues pertaining to the representation, participation, and experiences of black stakeholders, particularly athletes, in college sport at PWIHE.

In terms of issues pertaining to the representation of racial and ethnic minorities in college sport, we focused on the controversial issue of Native American mascots and the potentially damaging effect the continued (mis)use of them has on the Native American community and its members. We then shifted to a discussion of the under-representation of African Americans in several occupations within college sport, particularly the major decision-making positions (e.g., athletic director, head coach). This section also involved a discussion on how African Americans tend to be segregated or stacked into peripheral positions (e.g., assistant coaches, academic advisers, life skills coordinators) that do not typically put them on track to other occupations that come with power and certain privileges. In the section on the participation patterns of African American athletes, we discussed the over-representation and high concentration of African American male and female athletes in sports such as football, basketball, and track and field, but their under-representation in most all other college sport programs at PWIHE.

In the final major section of the chapter, we attempted to provide some insight into issues pertaining to the experiences of African American athletes; a particular emphasis was placed on the athletic exploitation of this group, some of the academic challenges they face, and the effect it all has on their psychosocial development. First, we discussed how the current structure and functions within the athletics industrial complex have led to the commodification of the black athletic body (particularly the male) and devaluation of the black mind. We also highlighted some of the cognitive, noncognitive, and environmental factors that might contribute to the myriad of challenges black athletes struggle with in efforts to balance the demands of the athletic and academic roles (as well as other roles). Further, we briefly discussed the issue of identity development (particularly the salience of athletic identity of African American males) and the effect racial stereotypes could have on this development. We concluded this section and chapter with a brief discussion of some coping strategies African American athletes (particularly females) have relied on to deal with the myriad of issues and challenges before them.

We acknowledge that it was not possible in this chapter to capture in substantial detail the many complexities associated with the issue of race and ethnicity in college sport. It is, however, our hope that this chapter has at least provided a starting point from which this can be done in the future. We challenge readers to reflect on the issues presented here, and even embrace some of the critical, race-based frameworks that were used or referenced in this chapter. Moreover, readers are encouraged to fill in any gaps that we might have left. In particular, because there is a dearth of literature that focuses on the issues and experiences of African American women, we tended to focus heavily on the issues and experience of African American men. This certainly could be one limitation

of our chapter because it is our belief that African American women, particularly in the high-profile sports (e.g., basketball, track and field), might also face some of the same issues related to academics, identity development, and various stereotypes based on their race, gender, sexual orientation, and other differences. Further, other racial and ethnic minority groups might also face unique issues and challenges as athletes, coaches, and employees of athletic departments at PWIHE, and a discussion of these issues is certainly worthy of our attention.

CHAPTER DEFINITIONS

Discrimination—actions and/or policies that deny a person and/or group equal access and treatment (see Allport, 1954; Cunningham, 2011).

Ethnicity—a person's cultural affiliation often based on a shared history, values, norms, and patterns of behavior (see Coakley, 2009).

Minority—a person or group that is systemically discriminated against and disadvantaged due to historic and current experiences of subordination (see Coakley, 2009).

Prejudice—negative attitudes, either conscious or unconscious, that are directed toward persons of a particular social group (see Cunningham, 2011).

Race—a socially constructed category based on a person's biological characteristics and traits (see Coakley, 2009; Eitzen & Sage, 2003).

Racism—a belief in the inherent superiority of one racial category over all others, which can manifest in discriminatory attitudes and actions, institutional policies and practices, and organizational structures (see Coakley, 2009; Waller, 1998).

Stereotype—a generalization or belief (oftentimes negative, and in many cases, unfounded) about members of a group of people based on some identity marker (e.g., race, gender, sexual orientation, social class, etc.) (see Coakley, 2009; Hodge, Burden, Robinson, & Bennett, 2008).

Stereotype threat—the susceptibility that a negative stereotype of a person and/or group (e.g., intellectual inferiority, physical superiority) will be attributed to one's self (see Steele & Aronson, 1995).

White Supremacy—a structural (to include political, economic, and cultural) system affecting social and institutional environments in which white persons perpetuate the notion of white superiority, and thus reaffirm dominance and power of whites and the subordination of non-whites (see Stoval, 2006).

REFERENCES

Adler, P. A., and P. Adler. (1991). *Blackboards and backboards: College athletes and role engulfment.* NY: Columbia University Press.

Anderson, D. (1993). Cultural diversity on campus: A look at intercollegiate football coaches. *Journal of Sport and Social Issues* 17, 61–66.

Anderson, A., and D. South. (2007). The academic experiences of African American collegiate athletes: Implications for policy and practice. In Brooks. D.D., and R. C. Althouse, eds. *Diversity and social justice in college sports: Sport management and the student-athlete* (pp. 77–94). Morgantown, WV: Fitness Information Technology.

Bell, D. (1980). Brown vs. Board of Education and the interest-convergence principle. *Harvard Law Review* 93, 518–533.

Bell, D. (2004). *Silent covenants: Brown v. Board of Education and the unfulfilled hopes for racial reform.* New York: Oxford University Press.

Benson, K.F. (2000). Constructing academic inadequacy: African American athletes' stories of schooling. *Journal of Higher Education* 71(2), 223–246.

Brayboy, B.M.J. (2005). Toward a tribal critical race theory in education. *The Urban Review* 37(5), 425–446.

Brooks, D. & Althouse, R.. eds. (1993). *Racism in college athletics: The African American athlete's experience.* Morgantown, WV: Fitness Information Technology.

Brooks, D., and R. Althouse, eds. (2007). *Diversity and Social Justice in College Sports: Sport Management and the Student-Athlete.* Morgantown, WV: Fitness Information Technology.

Brown, G.T., (2002, October 28), "Diversity grid lock: Black coaches aim to shed hiring block," Retrieved October 29, 2002, from http://www.ncca.org/news.

Bruening, J. (2005). Gender and racial analysis in sport: Are all the women white and all the blacks men? *Quest* 57 340–359.

Bruening, J., K. Armstrong, and D. Pastore. (2005). Listening to the voices: The experiences of African American female student athletes, *Research Quarterly for Exercise and Sport* 76(1), 82–100.

Byers, W., and C. Hammer. (1995). *Unsportsmanlike conduct: Exploiting college athletes.* Ann Arbor, MI: The University of Michigan Press.

Carter, A.R., and B.J. Hawkins. (2011). Coping strategies among African American female collegiate athletes' in the predominantly white institution. In Hylton, K., A. Pilkington, P. Warmington, and S. Housee, eds. *Atlantic Crossings: International Dialogues in Critical Race Theory* (pp. 61–92). Birmingham, United Kingdom: Sociology, Anthropology, Politics (C-SAP), The Higher Education Academy Network.

Castagno, A. E., and S.J. Lee. (2007). Native mascots and ethnic fraud in higher education: Using Tribal Critical Race Theory and the interest convergence principle as an analytic tool. *Equity & Excellence in Education* 40(1), 3–13.

Chideya, F. (1999). *The color of our future*. New York: William Morrow and Company, Inc.

Chong-Soon Lee, J. (1995). Navigating the topology of race. In Crenshaw, K., N. Gotanda, G. Peller, and K. Thomas, eds. *Critical race theory: Key writings that formed the movement*, (pp.441–449), New York: The New Press.

Coakley, J. (2009). *Sports in society: Issues and controversies (10th ed.)*. Boston: McGraw-Hill.

Coates, R.D. (2003). Law and the cultural production of race and racialized systems of oppression: Early American court cases. *American Behavioral Scientists* 47(3), 320–351.

Collins, P. (2000). *Black feminist thought: Knowledge, consciousness, and the politics of empowerment, 2nd Edition*. New York: Routledge.

Comeaux, E. (2007). Student(less) athlete: Identifying the unidentified college student. *Journal for the Study of Sports and Athletes in Education* 1, 37–43.

Comeaux, E. , and C.K. Harrison. (2011). A conceptual model of academic success for student-athletes. *Educational Researcher* 40(5), 235–245.

Cunningham, G.B. (2011). *Diversity in sport organizations, 2nd edition*. Scottsdale, AZ: Holcomb, Hathaway, Publishers.

Cunningham, G.B. (2010). Understanding the under-representation of African American coaches: A multilevel perspective. *Sport Management Review* 13, 395–406.

Cunningham, G.B., and M. Sagas. (2005). Access discrimination in intercollegiate athletics. *Journal of Sport and Social Issues* 29, 148–163.

Davis, T. (2007). The persistence of unconscious racism in college sport. In Brooks, D.D. and R.C. Althouse, eds. *Diversity and Social Justice in College Sport: Sport Management and the Student-Athlete* (pp. 263–280). Morgantown, WV: Fitness Information Technology.

Davis, T. (1995). The myth of the superspade: The persistence of racism in college athletics. *Fordham Urban Law Journal* 22, 615–698.

Delgado, R. (1995). *Critical race theory: The cutting edge*. Philadelphia: Temple University Press.

Donnor, J.K. (2005). Towards an interest-convergence in education of African American football student athletes in major college sports. *Race Ethnicity and Education* Vol. 8(1), 45–67.

Downton, J. (2000, January 6). The James Brooks illiteracy scandal: Auburn university's and the Cincinnati Bengals' secret little "problem" unveiled. *Black Issues in Higher Education* 18–20.

Edwards, H. (1969). *The Revolt of the Black Athlete*. Toronto, Ontario, Canada: The Free Press.

Edwards, H. (1983). The exploitation of Black athletes. *AGB Reports* 25(6), 37–46.

Edwards, H. (1984). The black "dumb jock": An American sports tragedy. *College Board Review* 131, 8–13.

Edwards, H. (1985). Beyond symptoms: Unethical behavior in American collegiate sport and the problem of the color line. *Journal of Sport & Social Issues* 9 (3), 3–13.

Eitzen, D.S. (2003). *Fair and foul: Beyond the myths and paradoxes of sport (2nd ed.).* Lanham, MD: Rowman & Littlefield Publishers, Inc.

Eitzen, D.S, and G.H. Sage. (2003). *Sociology of North American Sport (7th ed.).* New York: McGraw Hill.

Feagin, J.R. (2006). *Systemic racism: A theory of oppression.* New York: Routledge.

Feagin, J.R. (2010). *The white racial frame: Centuries of racial framing and counter-framing.* New York: Routledge.

Gill, E. L. (2011). The Rutgers women's basketball and Don Imus controversy (RUIMUS): White privilege, new racism, and the implication for college sport management. *Journal of Sport Management* 25, 118–130.

Grant, O.B. (2003). African American collegiate football players and the dilemma of exploitation, racism and education: A socio-economic analysis of sports law. *Whittier Law Review* 24, 645–661.

Haney Lopez, I.F. (1996). *White by law: The legal construction of race.* New York: New York University Press.

Harris, C. (1993). Whiteness as property. *Harvard Law Review* 106(8), 1707–1791.

Harris, O. (2000). African American predominance in sport. In Brooks, D., and R. Althouse, eds. *Racism in college athletics: The African American athlete's experience, 2nd edition,* (pp. 37–52). Morgantown, WV: Fitness Information Technology, Inc.

Harrsion, L., C.K. Harrison, and L.N. Moore. (2002). African American racial identity and sport. *Sport, Education and Society* 7(2), 121–133.

Harrison, L., and L.N. Moore. (2007). Who am I? Racial identity, athletic identity, and the African American athlete. In Brooks, D., and R. Althouse, eds. *Diversity and Social Justice in College Sports: Sport Management and the Student Athlete,* (pp. 245–260), Morgantown, WV: Fitness Information Technology.

Harrison, L., G. Sailes, W. Roitch, and A.Y. Bimper. (2011). Living the dream or awakening from a nightmare: Race and athletic identity. *Race, Ethnicity, and Education* 14(1), 91–103.

Harvey, W.B., A.M. Harvey, and M. King. (2004). The impact of the Brown v. Board of Education decision on postsecondary participation of African Americans. *Journal of Negro Education* 73(3), 328–340.

Hawkins, B. (2001). *New plantation: The internal colonization of black student-athletes.* Winterville, GA: Sadiki.

Hawkins, B. (2010). *The new plantation: Black athletes, college sports, and predominantly white NCAA institutions.* NY: Palgrave Macmillian.

Hodge, S.R., J.W. Burden, L.E. Robinson, and R.A. Bennett. (2008). Theorizing on the stereotyping of black male student-athletes. *Journal for Student of Sports and Athletes in Education* 2(2), 203–226.

Hodge, S.R., L. Harrison, J.W. Burden, and A.D. Dixson. (2008). Brown in black and white—then and now: A question of educating or sporting African American males in America. *American Behavioral Scientist* 51(7), 928–952.

Hughes, R.L., J.W. Satterfield, and M.S. Giles. (2007). Athletisizing black male student-athletes: The social construction of race, sports, myths, and realities. *NASAP Journal* 10(1), 112–127.

Hyatt, R. (2003). Barriers to persistence among African American intercollegiate athletes: A literature review of non-cognitive variables. *College Student Journal* 37, 260–275.

King, C.R., D.J. Leonard, and K.W. Kusz. (2007). White power and sport: An introduction. *Journal of Sport & Social Issues* 31(1), 3–10.

Ladson-Billings, G. (1992). Liberatory consequences of literacy: A case of culturally relevant instruction for African American students. *The Journal of Negro Education* 61(3), 378–391.

Ladson-Billings, G. (1995). But that's just good teaching! The case for culturally relevant pedagogy. *Theory into Practice* 34 (3), 159–165.

Ladson-Billings, G. (1998). Just what is critical race theory and what's it doing in a nice field like education? *Qualitative Studies in Education* 11(1), 7–24.

Ladson-Billings, G., and W. Tate. (1995). Toward a critical race theory of education. *Teachers College Record* 97, 47–68.

Lapchick, R. (1991). *Smashing Barriers: Race and sport in the new millennium.* Lanham, MD: Madison Books.

Lapchick, R., B. Hoff, and C. Kaiser. (2011, March 3). *The 2010 Racial and gender report card: College Sport.* The Institute for Diversity and Ethics in Sport, University of Central Florida: Orlando, Florida.

Loy, J., and J. McElvouge. (1970). Racial segregation in American sport. *International Review of Sport Sociology* 5, 5–24.

Martin, C.H. (2010). *Benching Jim Crow: The rise and fall of the color line in southern college sports, 1890–1980.* Urbana, IL: University of Illionois Press.

McDonald, M.G. (2005). Mapping whiteness and sport: An introduction. *Sociology of Sport Journal* 22, 245–255.

McDowell, J., and G.B. Cunningham. (2007). The prevalence of occupational segregation in athletic administrative roles. *International Journal of Sport Management* 8, 245–262.

McDowell, J., and G.B. Cunningham. (2009). Personal, social, and organizational factors that influence black female athletic administrators' identity negotiation. *Quest* 61, 202–222.

McDowell, J., G.B. Cunningham, and J.N. Singer. (2009). The supply and demand side of occupational segregation: The case of an intercollegiate athletic department. *Journal of African American Studies* 13, 431–454.

Melendez, M.C. (2008). Black football players on a predominantly white college campus: Psychosocial and emotional realities of the black college athlete experience. *Journal of Black Psychology* 34(4), 424451.

Milner, H. R. (2008). Critical race theory and interest convergence as analytical tools in teacher education policies and practices. *Journal of Teacher Education* 59(4), 332–346.

Omni, M., and H. Winant. (1994). *Racial formation in the United States: From the 1960s to the 1990s (2nd ed.).* New York: Routledge.

Parham, W.D. (1993). The intercollegiate athlete: A 1990s profile. *The Counseling Psychologist* 21(3), 411–429.

Person, D.R., and K.M. LeNoir. (1997). Retention issues and models for African American male athletes. *New Directions for Student Services* 80, 79–91.

Polite, F.G. (2012). Introduction. In Polite, F.G., and B. Hawkins, eds. *Sport, race, activism, and social change: The impact of Dr. Harry*

Edwards' scholarship and service (pp. 1–7), San Diego, CA: Cognella.

Polite, F. G., and B. Hawkins, eds. (2012). *Sport, race, activism, and social change: The impact of Dr. Harry Edwards' scholarship and service.* San Diego, CA: Cognella.

Rhoden, W.C. (2012, June 10). Black and white women far from equal under Title IX. *The New York Times.* Retrieved from http://www.nytimes.com on June 11, 2012.

Sage, G.H. (2007). Introduction. In Brooks, D., and R. Althouse, eds. *Diversity and Social Justice in College Sports: Sport Management and the Student-Athlete*, pp. 1–17, Morgantown, WV: Fitness Information Technology.

Sage, G.H. (2000). Introduction. In Brooks, D, and R. Althouse, eds. *Racism in college athletics: The African American Athlete's Experience (2nd ed.)*, pp. 1–12, Morgantown, WV: Fitness Information Technology.

Sage, G.H. (1998). *Power and ideology in American sport (2nd ed.).* Champaign, IL: Human Kinetics.

Sailes, G. A. (1986). The exploitation of the Black athlete: Some alternative solutions. *Journal of Negro Education* 55(4), 439–442.

Sailes, G. A. (1993). An investigation of campus typecasts: The myth of black athlete superiority and the dumb jock stereotype. *Sociology of Sport Journal* 10, 88–97.

Sailes, G.A. (1998). The African American athlete: Social myths and stereotypes. In Sailes, G.A., ed. *Contemporary Themes: African Americans in Sport* (pp. 183–198). New Brusnwick, NJ: Transaction Publishers.

Shropshire, K.L. (1996). *In black and white: Race and sports in America.* New York: New York University Press.

Siegel, D. (1994). Higher education and the plight of the black male athlete. *Journal of Sport & Social Issues* 18(3), 207–223.

Singer, J.N. (2009). African American football athletes' perspectives on institutional integrity in college sport. *Research Quarterly for Exercise and Sport* 80(1), 102–116.

Singer, J.N. (2009b). Preparing African American male student-athletes for post-secondary education: Implications for educational stakeholders. In Milner, R., ed. *Diversity and Education: Teachers, Teaching, and Teacher Education* (pp. 31–50), Springfield, IL: Charles C. Thomas Publisher.

Singer, J.N. (2008). Benefits and detriments of African American male athletes' participation in a big-time college football program. *International Review for the Sociology of Sport* 43(4), 399–408.

Singer, J.N. (2005). Understanding racism through the eyes of African American male student athletes. *Race, Ethnicity and Education* 8(4), 365–386.

Singer, J.N., C.K. Harrison, and S.J. Bukstein. (2010). A critical race analysis of the hiring process for head coaches in NCAA college football. *Journal of Intercollegiate Sport* 3, 270–296.

Smedley, A. (1999). *Race in North America: Origin and evolution of a worldview (2nd Ed.).* Boulder, CO: Westview Press.

Smith, E. (2007). *Race, sport and the American dream.* Durham, NC: Carolina Academic Press.

Smith, Y. (2000). Sociohistorical influences of African American elite sportswomen. In Brooks, D., and R. Althouse, eds. *Racism in College Athletics: The African American Athlete Experience,* (2nd ed., pp. 173–197).

Morgantown, WV: Fitness Information Technology, Inc.

Solórzano, D., M. Ceja, and T. Yosso. (2000). Critical race theory, microaggressions, and campus racial climate: The experiences of African American college students. *The Journal of Negro Education* 69(1/2), 60–73.

Sperber, M. (1990) *College sports Inc.: the athletic department vs. the university*. New York: Henry Holt and Company.

Spigner, C. (1993). African American student-athletes: Academic support or institutionalized racism? *Education* 114(1), 144–150.

Staurowsky, E.J. (2007). You know, we are all Indian: Exploring white power and privilege in reactions to the NCAA Native American mascot policy. *Journal of Sport and Social Issues* 31(1), 61–76.

Steele, C. (1999). Thin ice: Stereotype threat and Black college students. *The Atlantic Online* 1–10.

Steele, C. , and J. Aronson (1995). Stereotype threat and the intellectual test performance of African Americans. *Journal of Personality and Social Psychology* 69(5), 797–811.

Steele, C. M., S.J. Spencer, and J. Aronson. (2002). Contending with group image: The psychology of stereotype and social identity threat. *Advances in Experimental Social Psychology* 34, 379–440.

Stovall, D. (2006). Forging community in race and class: Critical race theory and the quest for social justice in education. *Race, Ethnicity, and Education* 9(3), 243–259.

Suggs, W. (2005). Faces in a mostly white crowd. *The Chronicle of Higher Education* 51(31), A34.

Taylor, E. (1999). Critical race theory and interest convergence in the desegregation of higher education. In Parker, L., ed. *Race is … Race isn.'t: Critical race theory and qualitative studies in education* (pp. 181–204). Boulder, CO: Westview Press.

Thomas, G.E., and S. Hill. (1987). Black institutions in U.S. higher education: Present roles, contributions, future projections. *Journal of College Student Personnel*, 496–503.

Waller, J. (1998). *Face to face: The changing state of racism across America*. New York: Plenum Press.

Upthegrove, T.R., V.J. Roscigno, and Charles C. Zubrinsky. (1999). Big money college sports: Racial concentration, contradictory pressures, and academic performance. *Social Science Quarterly* 80(4), 718–737.

Zimbalist, A. (1999). *Unpaid professionals: Commercialism and conflict in big-time college sports*. Princeton, NJ: Princeton University Press.

I am a huge believer that sports ends up being good for kids, and especially good for girls. It gives them confidence, it gives them a sense of what it means to compete. Studies show that girls who are involved in athletics often do better in school; they are more confident in terms of dealing with boys. And, so, for those of us who grew up just as Title IX was taking off, to see the development of women's role models in sports, and for girls to know they excelled in something, there would be a spot for them in college where they weren't second-class, I think has helped to make our society more equal in general.

I think the challenge is making sure that, in terms of implementation, schools continue to take Title IX seriously ... and I think understanding that this is good, not just for a particular college, not just for the NCAA, [but that] it is good for our society; it will create stronger, more confident women. I think that is something that I just want to make sure everybody understands.

—President Barack Obama, 2012

For many children, their formative athletic experiences occur on elementary school playgrounds or in physical education (PE) classes. Playgrounds and recess cultivate the connection between education and sports informally. As they grow older, many young girls and women begin to participate on youth sports teams and high school teams, and a few make the jump from interscholastic athletics to compete at the collegiate, Olympic, and professional levels. In addition to a wide range of sports to choose from, they also have many women role models such as Candice Parker,

6

GENDER ISSUES AND CONTROVERSIES IN INTERCOLLEGIATE ATHLETICS

JACQUELINE McDOWELL & JENNIFER HOFFMAN

Abby Wambach, Jessica Mendoza, Serena and Venus Williams, Michelle Wie, Danica Patrick, and Mia Hamm.

With such accomplishments and many well-known role models, many athletes today do not know that forty years ago women did not have a lot of opportunities to participate in sports. Women athletes such as Billie

TITLE IX

No person in the United States shall on the basis of sex, be excluded from participation in, be denied the benefits of, or be subjected to discrimination under any educational program or activity receiving federal financial assistance. —June 23, 1972

Jean King, Alice Coachman, Mamie "Peanut" Johnson, and Lusia Harris were few and far between and women's school-based sport opportunities were primarily limited to track and field, volleyball, tennis, softball, and basketball. Many do not know that without President Richard Nixon signing Title IX of the Education Amendments Act into law in 1972, the landscape of women's sports would be dramatically different.

Although Title IX is an education policy, it transformed women's sports from being defined by exclusionary and marginalization practices to asserting equity for women's participation in sports and reinforcing the educational value of sports in schools and colleges. Even as Title IX has made significant improvements in women's sports, athletic opportunities remain highly differentiated by sex and gender in coeducational schools and university settings. Title IX and women's participation in college athletics underscores the tension between equality and difference in intercollegiate athletics, and highlights the gender issues and controversies in women's sports. In this chapter some of the key historical and current issues concerning women in collegiate sport are addressed. Specifically, this chapter examines Title IX and its impact on women's experiences, participation rates, and leadership roles in athletics. Additionally, the chapter concludes with a discussion of current gender issues in intercollegiate sport.

WOMEN'S INTERCOLLEGIATE SPORTS HISTORY

"We readily recognize the first woman to do anything. We all stop and salute for the pioneers, but we must continue to salute, recognize, and honor every woman who is successful," Judy *Conradt, University of Texas basketball coach (in Baker, 2008, p. 68).*

Competitive sport for women has been an integral part of college life since the 1860s when baseball games were played at Vassar College (Ballintine, n.d.). During the turn of the century intercollegiate sports began emerging as prominent extracurricular activities. Senda Berenson introduced a modified version of basketball to women students at Smith College in 1892 and the first women's intercollegiate game followed soon afterward when Stanford and the University of California at Berkeley played in front of more than seven hundred spectators in the spring of 1896 (Grundy & Shackleford, 2005). Competitive women's basketball was particularly popular at predominately white normal (i.e., teaching) schools, land-grant institutions (Radke, 2002; Radke-Moss, 2008), and historically black colleges (Grundy, 2000) during the early twentieth century.

ROLES REVERSED: WOMEN'S ATHLETICS FOOTING THE BILL

Nearly seventy-five years before Title IX legislation guaranteed women equality in university sports, some land-grant institutions fielded women's competitive teams that rivaled men's sports in terms of fan support and financial contributions from games. For example, between 1896 and 1906 Nebraska's intercollegiate women's basketball team won often and even brought in some much-needed revenue. The women's basketball team was so profitable "that the men of the campus, hard put for athletic funds, humbled themselves occasionally to the extent of borrowing from the well-filled treasury of the girls' athletic association" (Radke-Moss, 2008, p. 210).

Women's interest in organized basketball games and athletics led to the development of professional organizations, such as the National Women's Basketball Committee (which later became the Committee on

Oregon Agricultural College, currently Oregon State University, women's basketball team (1900). Women's basketball uniforms have evolved over the years from very modest long dresses to bloomers, and now being gender undifferentiated and mimicking men's styles.

Women's Athletics of the American Physical Education Association [Suggs, 2006]) and the Women's Athletics Association. These associations advocated for women participating in sports; however, despite the interest and popularity of the game, particularly in the West, there were also early limits on the game and

women's participation in competitive sports. As high numbers of women entered previously all-male institutions, questions were raised about the purpose of higher education for women. It is in this context that issues about women and gender in collegiate athletics were first suggested. Would women who were playing sports become too masculine? Would men's sports and schools themselves become too feminized?

Rather than losing their role, women's PE educators became part of a backlash in higher education in which women faculty members developed a separatist and more conservative model for women students as a strategy to sustain their role on campus. Strenuous, competitive activity for women students was discouraged at most institutions. It was replaced with a recreational athletics model highly resistive to competition with oversight dominated by women leaders in women's physical education (Hult, 1994). This philosophy emphasized moderation to curtail threats to physical and moral health that characterized many men's competitive sports (Cahn, 1994). The philosophy that limited competitive athletics for women and girls offered some shelter to the professional interests of women's physical educators in schools, appeased fears of the feminization of sports, and tempered worries over feminizing higher education. At most institutions, the concerns over women's participation in competitive sports stimulated specific differentiation between the women's and men's game and competition. Men continued in a competitive, often commercialized intercollegiate model. But despite the popularity of women's competitive basketball and other sports in the earliest years of coeducation, women's participation in intercollegiate athletics was replaced with noncompetitive sporting activities by the 1930s.

Women's physical educators from the 1920s to the 1950s had a strong professional network, a body of research, and degree-training programs that had placed graduates in high school and college women's physical education programs (Costa & Guthrie, 1994). Through the National Section on Women's Athletics (NSWA), women's physical educators asserted their exclusive jurisdiction over women's sports in educational settings (Festle, 1996). The NSWA grew out of the Women's Division of the American Physical Education Association, established in 1885. The Women's Division was a strong voice for women's physical education and was opposed to competition (Guttmann, 1991). The NSWA continued this stance and became one of the most prominent organizations for discouraging competitive women's basketball. At the college level the NWSA's influence was dramatic and swift. By the 1930s few white institutions offered women's basketball (Costa & Guthrie, 1994).

In 1953, NSWA became the National Section of Girl's and Women in Sports (NSGWS) and in 1957 was renamed the Division for Girls and Women's Sports (DGWS). By this time the stance against competition had softened a bit from the strictly anticompetitive playday to a sports day, which emphasized the "right kind" of competition for the new "sportswoman" (Festle 1996). This sportswoman was a "healthy, vibrant, graceful woman familiar with swimming or croquet … conducted toward the complete development for the individual for the place she probably will occupy in American society as a wife, mother or career woman" (Hult & Trekell, 1991, p. 12). The new sportswoman was consistent with higher education's view in the 1950s and 1960s that "collegiate instruction should somehow prepare women for female roles and foster their aspirations strictly within bounds" (Solomon, 1985, p. 191). Themes such as "A Game for Every Girl and Every Girl in a Game" reflected the participation model of women's physical education, but also the influences of John Dewey and the goals of physical education for democratic ideals (Sack & Staurowsky, 1998).

After the initial introduction of sports at the turn of the century and their popularity among women students, intercollegiate sports developed into gender-differentiated opportunities for men and women after 1930 at most colleges. For men, competitive college athletics grew in popularity among participants and spectators alike. Women's athletics became a recreational, noncompetitive activity. It was not until the 1950s and 1960s that women began to challenge the gender-differentiated restrictions on women's sport and individual athletes began to resume the competitive, intercollegiate athletics similar to the men's model.

FROM RECREATION TO COMPETITION: WOMEN'S INTERCOLLEGIATE SPORT REEMERGES

The civil rights movement brought new awareness of race and gender to the public consciousness and women's participation in sports became part of both policy discussions and institutional decisions. As women's PE organizations continued their quest to maintain control over women's intercollegiate athletic participation, the recreational model for women's athletic opportunity was beginning to be challenged. A new generation of women students and women's PE educators supported competitive intercollegiate teams. The philosophy for women's competitive sports shifted from a purely recreational stance and opposition to competition that characterized appropriate female behavior and the purpose of educating women. With these changing attitudes came a shift in the philosophy toward women's college sports, but not a change in strategy; in the late 1960s and early 1970s women leaders continued to relay a separate strategy on women's athletics leadership and governance that left women leaders vulnerable to changes in the purpose of educating women, changes in social climate, and legislative mandates on the horizon.

In response, women's physical education leaders in 1966 created the Commission on Intercollegiate Athletics for Women (CIAW) to meet the increased demand for competition among women students, but administered it in a very different way than the spectator-oriented, commercial men's college model (Carpenter & Acosta, 2001; Festle 1996). In 1967 the CIAW began sponsoring championships for women, and in 1970 the physical educators of the CIAW formed the Association for Intercollegiate Athletics for Women (AIAW) (Carpenter & Acosta, 2001; Festle, 1996). The CIAW was an organization of women physical educators, but the AIAW, while led by these women, was a national membership organization that institutions joined for women's championship events. Gone were the recreation-oriented intramural and telegraphic meets and playdays of earlier years. Women leaders of the AIAW set up competitive intercollegiate leagues, leadership, and governance at the institutional and national levels, and began to establish revenue streams with corporate sponsorship.

The AIAW, however, did not pattern the transition from recreational sport to competitive sport after men's intercollegiate athletics. Women in physical education and the AIAW advocated for a women-led alternative, with a woman-specific philosophy as opposed to the men's commercial, spectator-oriented intercollegiate model. Fears of using women's sports to serve institutional interests were especially acute and many women of the AIAW promoted an "education-based" philosophy for women's intercollegiate competition. This philosophy also contrasted with the men's spectator-oriented competition model. Women leaders were reluctant to leave the power base of the women's physical education department or combine with men's intercollegiate programs over fears that it would significantly curtail their own leadership responsibilities and opportunities. Leaders of the AIAW maintained their goal of developing an education-based philosophy and leadership model for women with a clear distinction in philosophy between women's and men's intercollegiate competition. In this women-led governance model women leaders sought to maintain control of women's college athletics. New organizational ties, both through educational networks and institutional affiliation, coupled with a commitment to fostering and cultivating leadership opportunities for women were key features of the AIAW.

TITLE IX: AN EVOLVING LAW

Title IX, also formally known as the Patsy T. Mink Equal Opportunity in Education Act, grew out of the civil rights and feminist movements of the 1960s and 1970s, which called for equal access to education, economic, political, and social opportunities. Title IX emerged from second wave feminism, and was specifically guided by liberal feminist views of formal equality. Liberal feminist thought emphasizes gender similarity and promotes advocacy to give women equal access to the same opportunities afforded to men. Liberal feminism is not against men or men's opportunity, but rather asserts that equality is achieved through social change that mandates the accommodation of women in the same structures and processes as men. Liberal feminism is also critical of differences between men and women and seeks rational treatment based on merit, rather than gender roles. Hence, Title IX with its liberal feminist underpinnings promotes equal treatment under the law in the same terms as men and addresses inequality through "legal, political, and institutional struggles for the rights of individuals to compete in the public marketplace" (Beasely, 1999, p. 51).

When Title IX was passed on June 23, 1972, it created both a policy change and a symbolic shift in the purpose of educating women. Title IX ensures women equal access to education, and has reinforced the strong ties between American sports and schooling. Title IX applies to all federally funded coeducational programs and three conditions must be present or Title IX does not apply. The conditions are: 1) education programs—Title IX only applies to elementary schools, high schools, colleges, and trade schools that offer educational programming; 2) coeducational— both men and women must attend; and 3) federally funded programs—the institution must receive federal funding, usually through student loans or federal research grants. Title IX applies to ten program areas: access to education, athletics, career education, education of pregnant and parenting students, employment, the learning environment, math and science, sexual harassment, standardized testing, and technology.

The passage of Title IX also coincided with several important events that demonstrate the complexity and controversy over changes in higher education that forced "educational institutions to make room for women to participate in college athletics" (Boutilier & San Giovanni, 1994). There were concerns about the effect of the law on revenue-producing sports, mainly football, and whether Title IX

Congresswoman Patsy Takemoto Mink was the first woman of color and the first Asian American woman elected to Congress. She is known for authoring the Title IX Amendment of the Higher Education Act.

should even apply to intercollegiate athletics. In 1975 athletic regulations were developed by the Office of Civil Rights, and in 1979 policy interpretations were established. In general, for collegiate athletic departments to be compliant with Title IX, equity must be demonstrated in three areas: equity in participation, equity in program operations, and equity in financial aid.

Equity in participation is the most well known and most contentious aspect of Title IX. This is usually measured by the "three prong" test. A school must demonstrate compliance with participation in one of the following areas:

- *Proportionality*
- *History and continuing practice of increasing opportunities*
- *Accommodation of interests and abilities*

To be in compliance with the proportionality test the number of male and female student-athletes must be substantially proportionate to their respective representation in the gender full-time undergraduate population. The Office of Civil Rights has suggested that substantial proportionality could mean exact proportionality or a 1 percent or 2 percent disparity dependent on the institution's history of proportionality. Proportionality can be a challenge for schools that have football, because football carries very large rosters and there is no gender partner with the same roster size, making it difficult for schools to achieve proportionality. As a result, some institutions cut men's programs, use roster management strategies such as padding rosters with players who do not compete, or exploit a federal loophole that allows male practice players to be counted (Thomas, 2011).

In institutions where women are underrepresented as student-athletes, the second prong requires a school to show that it has a history *and* continuing practice of expanding the underrepresented group's athletic program that is "demonstrably responsive" to the developing interests and abilities of the underrepresented gender. Finally, if schools are not in compliance with prongs one and two, they can still be in compliance with Title IX regulations if they demonstrate they are accommodating the interests and abilities

of the underrepresented gender. If there is (a) unmet interest, (b) sufficient ability to sustain a team in the sport of interest, *and* (c) a reasonable expectation of competition, the school is in noncompliance with this prong. Demonstrating that there is a lack of interest presents a challenge when there are so many women's club and recreation programs on campus that desire varsity status.

THE AIAW, WOMEN'S CHAMPIONSHIPS, AND THE NCAA

The takeover of women's leadership of women's athletics by the NCAA is marked symbolically by Title IX. NCAA leaders, under the leadership of Walter Byers, had made earlier attempts to add a women's division, but the legislation helped open the doors for the NCAA to eventually take control of women's intercollegiate athletics. Donna Lopiano, former AIAW president, even maintained, "Title IX was the first step toward the demise ... the end of the AIAW" (as quoted in Willey, 1996).

In December 1980, the NCAA voted to begin offering championships for women's athletics. This decision forced institutions to choose between membership in the AIAW or the NCAA. Grundy and Shackelford explain, "the NCAA had two things the AIAW could not hope to match: money and status" (2005, p. 179). Not only would more resources benefit women's programs across the country, but the prestige and status that men's athletics garnered was thought to be available to women only through the men's organization and not the women's. According to former University of Tennessee women's basketball coach Pat Summit, the NCAA gave "instant credibility to women's athletics." She believed that without the NCAA and its "championships in a first-class arena" women "may never have

Pat Summitt, University of Tennessee's emeritus women's basketball coach, is the winningest collegiate basketball coach in history. She began her coaching career in the 1970s, earning $250 a month, and is viewed by many people as the face of the Title IX generation.

the opportunities to make the strides that are necessary for women to have what they have today" (as cited in Grundy & Shackelford, 2005, p. 180). As the NCAA took control of women's athletics governance and championships, the AIAW ceased operation and control of women's sports in 1981.

HOW DOES YOUR SCHOOL MEASURE UP?

The Office of Postsecondary Education of the U.S. Department of Education sponsors an on-line data analysis tool that offers information provided by the EADA data. From this site you can learn about the varsity teams offered, athletically related student aid, and calculate your school's compliance with the proportionality prong. To determine a school's compliance with Title IX based on participation, calculate the proportion of women and men in the full-time undergraduate population and the student-athlete population. There should be no more than a 3 percent deviation between the proportion of women student-athletes and the full-time women's undergraduate enrollment.

Western Washington University
Number of Full-Time

Undergraduates:	12,278
Men:	5,461
Women:	6,817

Total Participants Men's and Women's Athletes: 301

Men:	135
Women:	166

	Women	Men
Under-graduates	55% (6817 ÷ 12278)	45% (5461 ÷ 12278)
Student-athletes	55% (166 ÷ 301)	45% (135 ÷ 301)
Gap	0 %	0 %

Women comprise a near equal share of undergraduates and athletes. In this case the institution complies with the proportionality standard.

Note: Data derived from EADA, 2010 report

IS TITLE IX STILL RELEVANT?

During the 2002 U.S. Open, professional tennis player Jennifer Capriati was asked what advice she would give President George Bush about changes the president should make to Title IX legislation, and in response she revealed that she did not know anything about Title IX. This comes as no surprise as a recent Gallup poll

TIMELINE 1

The Evolution of Title IX Law

1972	Title IX of the American Education Act passes in Congress.
1973	*Kellmeyer v. Florida Atlantic University* challenged the AIAW rule that banned women's athletic scholarships. The case was dismissed after a change in AIAW philosophy that allowed scholarships for women athletes.
1978	Deadline for high schools and colleges to comply with Title IX athletic requirements.
1979	Policy guidelines released for compliance with Title IX.
1984	*Grove City College v. Bell,* U.S. Supreme Court rules that Title IX compliance applies only to those programs receiving direct federal financial assistance.
1988	Civil Rights Restoration Act, U.S. Congress overrules *Grove City College v. Bell,* reinstituting Title IX to the entire institution if any educational program receives federal financial assistance through grants, student financial aid, or other federal subsidy.
1992	*Franklin v. Gwinnett County* allows the award of damages to plaintiffs if compliance with Title IX is intentionally avoided.
1993	*Favia v. Indiana University of Pennsylvania:* Institutions with financial difficulties are not excluded from Title IX.
1994	Equity in Athletics Disclosure Act (EADA) requires higher education institutions to report gender equity data. Data is publically available at: http://ope.ed.gov/athletics/
1996	*Cohen v. Brown University* upholds the 1979 regulations for Title IX compliance including the three-prong test.
2003	Commission on Opportunity in Athletics (COA) issues twenty-three recommendations on Title IX to the secretary of education.
2005	Office of Civil Rights allows the use of surveys to determine the level of interest in varsity athletics among the underrepresented gender; nonresponses indicated no interest under the survey methodology.
2005	*Jackson v. Birmingham Board of Education:* Retaliation against a person who complains about unequal treatment is a form of intentional sex discrimination under Title IX.
2005	Supreme Court dismissed a case from National Wrestling Coaches Association against the Department of Education alleging that Title IX diverts funding from men's sport to pay for women's sports.
2010	Interest surveys repealed by the Office of Civil Rights. Interest surveys no longer allowed to meet the interests and abilities for Title IX compliance.
2010	*Biediger et al v. Quinnipiac University* ruled that competitive cheerleading is not a sport for the purposes of meeting Title IX.
2010	*Mansourian et al. v. UC Davis* found that to satisfy prong two (history of program expansion of opportunities) institutions must show two steps—a history of program expansion and continuous progress toward gender equity.

revealed that 26 percent of U.S. adults have not heard much about Title IX, whereas 30 percent said they have not heard anything at all about this legislation. A mere 15 percent had heard a great deal about Title IX.

The poll also revealed that of those familiar with Title IX, the majority (61 percent) believe that the overall effect of Title IX has been mostly positive. But 47 percent said Title IX has been a major factor in the growth in women's sports, but not a main factor. Surprisingly, 30 percent believed Title IX is a minor factor or not a factor at all. Based on the poll findings, 50 percent of the U.S. population believe that Title IX regulations should stay about the same, whereas 21 percent say it should be weaker. These findings differed by sex, as more men (29 percent) than women (12 percent) wanted Title IX to be weakened.

The Gallup poll was conducted in 2003 in light of the secretary's Commission on Opportunity in Athletics impending examination of Title IX's effectiveness. The commission reaffirmed the significance of Title IX and advanced twenty-three recommendations, of which the majority recommended that the Office of Civil Rights provide further clarity and guidance pertaining to enforcement, with the commission providing a series of recommendations on ways Title IX compliance could be measured. The commission's charge ended on March 15, 2003, but a full copy of the report can be found at http://www2.ed.gov/about/bdscomm/list/athletics/report.html.

Discussion Questions:

1. Prior to reading this chapter, how much had you heard about Title IX?
2. Based on what you have heard or read about Title IX, do you believe its overall effect has been mostly positive or mostly negative?

3. How responsible do you think Title IX has been for the growth in women's sports in the last few decades? Do you believe it has been the main factor, a major factor but not the main factor, a minor factor, or not a factor at all?
4. Do you believe Title IX's regulations should be made stronger, stay about the same as they are now, or be made weaker?

Information and questions taken from Kiefer, H. (2003). What Do Americans See in Title IX's Future? Retrieved from http://www.gallup.com/poll/7663/what-americans-see-title-ixs-future.aspx?version=print

TITLE IX AND WOMEN'S INTERCOLLEGIATE SPORTS TODAY

Title IX legislation forced institutions and departments to make a determination about definitions and boundaries of participation, interests, and competition for women-students in a climate that was shifting away from separate education programs for women to mandated access and equity. Gender equity in school-sponsored sports has come to mean increased access for women students to participate in the same athletic opportunities as their peers on the men's teams. Yet the emphasis on similarity between teams raises questions about what is equity when the teams themselves are separate.

As noted by Judy Conradt, retired University of Texas basketball coach, "We haven't figured out how to be different and still be equal" (Baker, 2008, p. 68). Gaps remain between the ideals of gender equity and policy in participation and many athletic program areas such as travel allowances, athletic facilities, support services, and recruitment expenses (Cheslock, 2007). Equity has likewise not been achieved regarding the allocation of athletic scholarships for men and women. Inequities in these areas affect the quality of the athletic programs in which men and women take part and maintain women's second-class status in athletics.

Inequities in Athletic Participation Opportunities

Since the enactment of Title IX in 1972, women student-athlete participation rates in college have risen substantially—from 16,000 to about 200,000 in 2012 (Acosta & Carpenter, 2012). These increases mimic those found in interscholastic competition, as the number of girls participating in high school athletics grew from just 294,000 in 1971 to 3.2 million today (National Federation of State and High School Associations, 2011). In 1970, two years prior to Title IX, there were only 2.5 women's intercollegiate teams at most institutions. The effect of Title IX legislation was immediately evident after the 1978 mandatory compliance date when the number of women's teams more than doubled to 5.61. The number of teams has continued to increase over the years and in 2012 there was an average of 8.73 intercollegiate women's teams per institution.

Tables 7.1 and 7.2 show the growth of NCAA-member institutions from 1981–82, when the NCAA began offering women's championships, to 2011 along with the changes in selected women's team and individual sports since 1981. Growth of women's teams is due in part to institutions adding sports, but also to the addition of NCAA-member schools that already sponsor specific sports. Additional team and participation data from the NCAA participation reports can be found at NCAA.org

These gains in participation and growth of teams have not been without controversy. Title IX is often blamed for the loss of opportunity, in particular among men's individual sports. The NCAA contends that since 1989 there have been 2,748 men's teams and 1,943 women's sports dropped. During this same period, however, 3,272 men's sports have been added, particularly in indoor/outdoor track and field, tennis, cross-country, golf, swimming and diving, and rowing.

Moreover, despite these significant increases, women athletes are still underrepresented in many higher education institutions when compared with their representation in the undergraduate student population. Chart 7.1

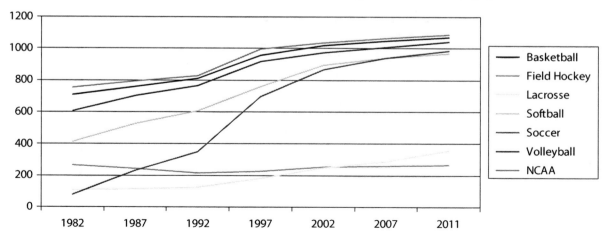

Table 7.1. Changes in Women's NCAA Team Sports

	1982	1987	1992	1997	2002	2007	2011
Basketball	705	757	810	956	1017	1050	1072
Field Hockey	268	245	213	228	252	258	264
Lacrosse	105	114	122	183	249	286	357
Softball	416	528	605	760	895	942	969
Soccer	80	230	350	694	868	941	984
Volleyball	603	701	762	915	974	1007	1039
NCAA	752	794	828	994	1036	1064	1087

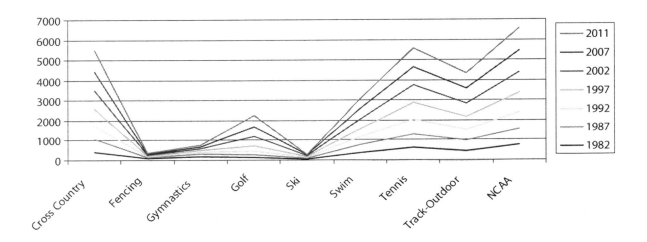

Table 7.2. Changes in Women's NCAA Individual Sports

	1982	1987	1992	1997	2002	2007	2011
Cross Country	417	633	677	834	923	967	1026
Fencing	76	55	47	43	46	45	41
Gymnastics	179	125	103	91	89	86	83
Golf	125	139	162	303	451	512	575
Ski	33	41	44	43	45	44	35
Swim	348	392	394	433	478	504	523
Tennis	610	690	723	855	898	895	921
Track-Outdoor	427	526	561	641	697	732	778
NCAA	752	794	828	994	1036	1064	1087

NJCAA soccer game between Rochester Community and Technical College and Dakota County Technical College. Soccer has grown substantially over the years. In 1977, less than three out of one hundred higher education institutions had women's soccer teams, whereas today 90 percent of four-year institutions have women's soccer teams.

reveals that in NCAA institutions women make up about 54 percent of the undergraduate population yet only 44 percent of all athletes. More gross disparities exist in NJCAA and NAIA institutions. NCAA Division I institutions tend to have more gender equity compared with Division II and III schools and other higher education institutions because of higher generated and shared revenues, which are used to support men and women's sports. It is important to know that these figures do not take into account roster management strategies, and some of the disparity in participation opportunities may be because institutions are *legally* in compliance with prong three of Title IX.

TITLE IX ABROAD

Just as intercollegiate athletics is uniquely American, Title IX is as well. With fewer professional opportunities for women around the world, American intercollegiate athletics helps all women succeed in sports. Just as athletes who crisscross the globe seeking athletic opportunities, women come to U.S. colleges and universities seeking better training, facilities, and competition. For example, the growth and interest in women's soccer has been largely attributed to the role of Title IX in creating opportunity for women athletes.

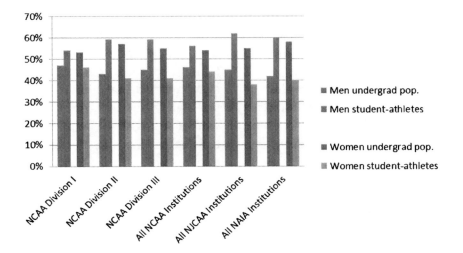

Source: 2009–10 NJCAA Participation Reports 2009–2010, EADA, 2010

Women's Soccer by the Numbers: 2011–12 National Teams—North America

	Roster	U.S. College Experience
Canada	20	18
Mexico	21	6
United States	30	30

Athletics Grant-in-aid Allocations

Prior to Title IX, the AIAW prohibited athletic scholarships, as many members of the association believed that providing scholarships would lead to "pressure recruiting," exploitation, and institutional financial burdens (Sack & Staurowsky, 1998). Moreover, AIAW leaders felt that scholarships would shift college women from competing as amateurs to being professionals. The Kellmeyer case (see Timeline) challenged the AIAW's prohibition, resulting in women starting to receive athletic grant-in-aids in 1973. Under the governance of the NCAA, women students continued to receive athletically related financial assistance, but the allocation of scholarships at many universities and colleges has not been equitable. Title IX regulations require athletic scholarship allocations to parallel student-athlete participation rates, unless there is a legal and legitimate reason for the disparity; however, in higher education institutions, grant-in-aid expenses for women's teams have historically and currently not been in proportion to the representation as student-athletes.

Recruiting and Operating Expenditures

Financial resource allocations have improved substantially over the past forty years, but gross inequities still exist. Sixty-seven percent of all operating expenses in Division I intercollegiate athletics teams are allocated to men's teams whereas only 33 percent is expended on women's teams. In Division I FBS and FCS institutions the expense budgets for athletic teams are dispersed more equally at 56 and 44 percent, respectively. At the Division II and III level the gap between expense budgets for men and women's teams mimic those of Division I institutions without football. Excluding salaries, categories that make a significant contribution to budget disparities include the substantial higher proportion of money allocated for men's teams in respect to fundraising, marketing and promoting, facility maintenance, and purchasing and maintaining equipment, uniforms, and supplies for men's teams.

LEADERSHIP POSITIONS IN WOMEN'S SPORT

The passage of Title IX in 1972 challenged the women-specific, gender-separate athletic programs and further mandated equity for women in all educational programs, including the extracurriculum. More women's teams are being fielded and more athletes are participating, and overall visibility and popularity have increased exponentially, but women-designated administrative and faculty leadership roles became rare both in role and purpose. Title IX has resulted in many positive outcomes for women in collegiate sports; however, the demise of the AIAW and Title IX legislation inadvertently resulted in a decline in the number of women occupying leadership positions in athletic administration and coaching.

Table 7.3. Disparities in Funding Men's and Women's Athletic Programs

Governing Associations	Men			Women		
	Athletic grants	Recruiting expenses	Total operating expenses	Athletic grants	Recruiting expenses	Total operating expenses
NCAA Division I	$968 mil. (54%)	68%	67%	$837 mil. (46%)	32%	33%
NCAA Division II	$241 mil. (56%)	62%	56%	$192 mil. (44%)	38%	44%
NCAA Division III	$5 mil. (51%)	63%	57%	$4 mil. (49%)	37%	43%
All NCAA Institutions	$1.2 bil. (54%)	67%	65%	$1 bil. (46%)	33%	35%
All NJCAA Institutions	$58 mil. (55%)	58%	57%	$46 mil. (44%)	42%	43%
All NAIA Institutions	$187 mil. (58%)	59%	57%	$135 mil. (42%)	41%	43%

Source: 2009–10 NCAA Gender Equity Report; EADA, 2010.

Head Coaches

As women's sports changed and became more important, popular, and paid professions in colleges, men began to pursue coaching positions on women's teams. U.S. societal ideologies typically position men as more appropriate for leadership positions; thus, men's transition into coaching and administration of women's athletics occurred with ease. Women went from holding 90 percent of head-coaching positions on women's teams in 1972 to representing 43 percent of coaches on women's teams in 2012, with the majority of women (46 percent) being employed at NCAA Division III institutions (Acosta & Carpenter, 2012). A glass wall exists in coaching as women do not have the same opportunities to coach men's teams. Before 1972, only 2 percent of men's teams, primarily individual sports such as tennis, track and field, and swimming, were coached by women and that percentage has

only risen to 3.5 percent (about 300 women) in 2012. In contrast, there are about 5,300 males compared with 3,974 female head coaches of women's teams. In women's basketball, gymnastics, volleyball, lacrosse, field hockey, and softball more women than men are coaches; however, despite being in the majority, their representation is still experiencing declines. The only two sports that have seen an increase in the number of women coaches from 1978 to 2012 are equestrian and soccer.

Early explanations for the increased percentage of men coaching women's teams proposed that the increased number of male coaches was a direct result of the substantial increase in the number of women's teams and coaches of women's teams being paid after Title IX was enacted. Prior to Title IX, women may have had more head-coaching positions because these were deemed less prestigious positions. With the average

Table 7.4. Percentage of women head coaches of women's teams

Sport	1978	1984	1988	1992	1994	2003	2006	2010	2012	Percentage Change (1978–2012)
Basketball	79.4	64.9	58.5	63.5	64.6	60.5	60.8	57	59.5	-19.9
C. Country	35.2	19.7	19.5	20.1	21.3	21.7	19.5	18.6	21.2	-14
Field Hockey	99.1	98.2	96.2	97	97	95.5	94.2	96.1	93.8	-5.3
Golf	54.6	39.7	41.3	45.7	47.1	42.9	36.8	45.8	41.6	-13
Gymnastics	69.7	59.1	53.7	52.2	41.3	41.4	43.3	50.8	51	-18.7
Lacrosse	90.7	95	95.2	95.7	93	85.7	82.5	87.5	85.1	-5.6
Soccer	29.4	26.8	23	25.8	32.9	29.4	29.9	32.5	32.2	2.8
Softball	83.5	68.6	67.2	63.7	66.7	63.8	61.3	63.8	62.1	-21.4
Swimming	53.6	33.2	26.3	28.2	28.1	26.3	25.7	24.1	26.2	-27.4
Tennis	72.9	59.7	52.2	48	48.2	36.5	33.3	28.2	29.9	-43
Track/Field	52.3	26.8	21.6	20.4	21	20	19.4	15.5	19.2	-33.1
Volleyball	86.6	75.5	71	68.7	70	59	53.5	55.7	53.3	-33.3

Source: Jana Nidiffer and Carolyn Terry Bashaw, from *Women Administrators in Higher Education: Historical and Contemporary Perspectives.* Copyright © 2001 by State University of New York Press.

number of women's sports per school growing rapidly, the labor market for coaches became tight. Coupled with prevalent gender norms of men as leaders and the increased popularity of women's sports, men became the primary labor supply. Additional explanations that have been advanced by researchers (e.g., Cunningham, Sagas, and Ashley, 2003; Kamphoff, 2010; Dixon et al., 2008; Stangl & Kane, 1991) include:

- *Homologous reproduction.* Women athletic directors tend to hire more women head coaches and male athletic directors tend to hire more men as head coaches Given that the majority of athletic departments are male-dominated, women are at a distinct disadvantage in the hiring process.

- *Work-life imbalances.* Coaching positions require extensive time commitments, with many duties performed after 5 p.m. or on weekends. Thus, difficulties in maintaining a work-life balance discourage women coaches from remaining in coaching.

- *Lower interest.* Women assistant coaches express less desire and determination to become head coaches than their male counterparts, and apply for head-coaching positions less often than men.

- *Sex discrimination.* Actual and perceived discrimination deters or prevents women assistant coaches from applying to head-coaching jobs.

- *Good ol' boys network.* A "good ol' boys" network exists that privileges men in the job search and hiring process.
- *Gender biases.* Gender biases result in women coaches being held to higher standards and qualifications than men.
- *Homophobia.* Discrimination against lesbians or fears of hiring "closet" lesbians results in a bias toward hiring males.

Moreover, in college coaching positions there is a wide salary differential between women and men head coaches and women's and men's athletic teams (see Table 7.6). Women coaches earn between forty and seventy cents for every dollar male coaches earn—figures reminiscent of the wage gap of the 1950s (The White House Project, 2009). With NCAA Division I teams, that difference can add up to more than $157,000. The average salary for head coaches of NCAA Division I men's teams in 2010 was $250,000. By contrast, the average salary for coaches of a women's team was $92,365 (EADA, 2010). More significant disparities show up in subordinate levels as the average salary for assistant coaches of men's teams was $80,930, whereas assistant coaches of women's teams had an average salary of $45,825. This equates to coaches of women's teams receiving only 36 percent of the salary budget allocated to assistant coaches. Football coaches' salaries certainly skew the figures and widen the disparity. The average head coach and assistant coach salary per Division I institution without football was $125,751 and $54,953, respectively, for men's teams and $72,695 and $41,568, respectively, for women's teams.

Much of the disparity comes from the way a coach's compensation is structured into his or her contract. All compensation (e.g., salary, cars, health benefits) received from the institution must be comparable for men and women. Many coaching contracts, however, include compensation from third parties (e.g., apparel companies or athletic associations) that are not subject to Title IX regulations (Gentry & Alexander, 2012). Differences also occur because of summer camp revenues, academic performance, and postseason competition bonuses—all of which tend to be more frequent and higher for coaches of men's teams.

Are these wage inequities between coaches of women's teams and men's teams in violation of the Equal Pay Act of 1963? The Equal Pay Act (EPA) requires that employers pay equal wages to men and women who perform jobs that require "equal skill, effort, and responsibility, and which are performed under similar working conditions." In discrimination cases that have been filed in interscholastic and intercollegiate sport, the majority of courts rule that paying coaches of men's teams higher wages than coaches of women's teams is not in violation of the law because wage differentials could be justified on the basis of experience, skill, and ability. Moreover, in the notable EPA case *Stanley v. the University of Southern California*, the court maintained men's basketball programs had greater attendance, received more media attention, produced larger donations, and raised substantially more revenue than the women's basketball program. As a result, the men's basketball coach had additional duties, such as increased public relations, promotional duties, and pressure to promote the team and win games. The court found that the responsibility for producing a large amount of revenue and the additional

Table 7.5. Head-Coaching Salaries

Collegiate Athletics Governing Associations	Women's Teams			Men's Teams		
	Women Head Coaches	Men Head Coaches	Head Coaches' Salaries	Women Head Coaches	Men Head Coaches	Head Coaches' Salaries
National Junior College Athletic Association	545	1009	$38,682	32	1591	$42,342
National Association of Intercollegiate Athletics	988	1105	$38,327	43	1403	$44,003
National Collegiate Athletic Association	3625	4911	$71,236	262	7285	$145,994

Note: Calculations for head-coach representation include information for full- and part-time head coaches. Figures for head-coach salary are reported for full-time coaches.

pressures were substantial differences in responsibilities between the two positions.

TOP SALARIES OF WOMEN'S BASKETBALL COACHES

As a consequence of Title IX, women's sports began to become more popular and the media began paying more attention to women's sports. With women collegiate basketball players such as Georgeann Wells, Candace Parker, and Brittney Griner dunking in games, women's basketball programs began regaining popularity. This increased interest has also resulted in coaches of women's teams receiving seven-figure compensations—previously unheard of in women's programs. In 2011, five coaches of women's basketball teams earned more than $1 million, compared with about thirty-one coaches of men's teams earning more than $1 million (Berkowitz & Upton, 2011).

Pat Summitt, University of Tennessee—Total Pay: $2,028,932

Geno Auriemma, University of Connecticut—Total Pay: $1,600,000
Kim Mulkey, Baylor University—Total Pay: $1,112,016
Gail Goestenkors, University of Texas—Total Pay: $1,052,500
C. Vivian Stringer, Rutgers University—Total Pay: $1,085, 500

Athletic Directors

Similar to trends in head-coaching positions, when Title IX was enacted more than 90 percent of women's intercollegiate athletics programs were administered by a woman while almost no women administered programs that included men's teams. Over the years this number has dwindled to 20.3 percent or about 215 women leading gender-combined programs. Women make up only 10.6 percent (36) of all Division I athletic directors (primarily in non-FBS and FCS institutions), 15.7 percent (46) at Division II, and 30.7 percent (133) at Division III. Furthermore, the majority of these positions are held by white women (Acosta & Carpenter, 2012).

Explanations for the decline in women athletic directors mimic those advanced for women head coaches. But in contrast to more coaching opportunities being provided, opportunities for women athletic directors have declined as separate women and men's athletic programs have become antiquated. In 1972, only 6 percent of NCAA Division I programs had combined athletic departments (Uhlir, 1987). Prior to the passage of Title IX, athletic departments generally had a male athletic director in charge of men's athletics, and a female athletic director in charge of women's athletics. After the passage of Title IX, however, athletic departments began to merge during the 1970s and 80s—most often eliminating the women's athletic director position and relegating her under the direction of the male athletic director. This trend continued into the twenty-first century, as the women's and men's athletic departments at the University of Arkansas and the University of Tennessee merged in 2008 and 2012, respectively. After these mergers, the University of Texas at Austin remains the only Division I program with separate women's and men's athletics departments.

CASE STUDY: THE TWO SHALL BECOME ONE

Separate athletic departments for men and women's athletic programs are becoming a thing of the past. After the merger of the women's and men's athletic programs at the University of Arkansas and University of Tennessee, only one Division I institution, the University of Texas, maintained separate athletic programs. The merging of athletic departments typically results in the elimination

of the women's athletic director position and her being relegated under the direction of the male athletic director. For example, at the University of Arkansas Jeff Long was hired as vice chancellor and director of intercollegiate athletics, whereas Bev Lewis, the director of the women's athletics program, was named associate vice chancellor and reported to Long. Similarly at the University of Tennessee, Joan Cronan, athletic director of the women's program, was originally named as the interim vice chancellor/director of athletics, but in June 2012 Dave Hart assumed her role and she became the senior advisor to the vice chancellor and chancellor.

A fear of merging women's and men's athletic programs is a reduction in the quality of programs, especially the women's programs. University of Arkansas EADA data from 2010–2011 and 2007–2008—the last year the institution had separate programs—reveals that the women's programs experienced an increase in women student-athletes, and subsequently a 4 percent increase in athletic-related aid. Also, the expense budget and number of assistant coaches of women's programs also increased substantially (mainly with the addition of male coaches). Parallel increases or decreases were also found for the salary of the assistant coaches, expense budgets, and recruiting budgets; however, the average salary of head coaches increased from $588,731 to $977,831 for men's coaches, while decreasing from $174,548 to $158,594 for head coaches of women's teams (of which three of nine were women). Moreover, surprisingly the revenue generated from women's sports (excluding basketball) decreased by about $430,000, whereas men's sports (excluding football and basketball) saw an increase of $260,000.

Discussion Questions

1. Should the University of Texas merge its athletic programs, or remain the lone ranger in college athletics?
2. What are some of the advantages and disadvantages of gender-combined athletic programs compared with separate programs?
3. What are some of the challenges of providing gender equity in a gender-separate athletic system?

Adapted from Gribble (2011a, b)

The Senior Woman Administrator

The senior woman administrator (SWA) role is designated for the highest-ranking woman in athletic administration among NCAA-member schools (NCAA, n.d.). First named the primary woman administrator (PWA) in 1981, the PWA was created as a strategy "inducement to gain votes" from women leaders in the AIAW for NCAA sponsorship of women's championships (Hult, 1994, p. 99). The PWA role involved women in decision making at the institutional level and conference level. The PWA also ensured the representation of women in the governance structure (Hosick, 2005a, 2005b; NCAA, 2005; Sweet & Morrison, 2006; see also Stallman, Kovalchik, Tiell, & Goff, 2006) by guaranteeing 16 percent on the NCAA Council and 18 to 24 percent on other committees to women (Hult, 1994). Through the PWA, "a token number of women entered the NCAA hierarchy" (Hult, 1994, p. 99). After the NCAA takeover of the AIAW, the PWA was assigned to the individual man or woman in the department responsible for overseeing women's athletics at each institution (Cahn, 1994; Carpenter & Acosta, 2001; Sack & Staurowsky, 1998).

Later, concerns over the potential legal issues associated with the PWA designation prompted review and clarification of it even further to a role rather than a job title or description (Copeland, 2005; Hosick, 2005a, 2005b). In 1989 the title was changed to the senior woman administrator (SWA). The SWA designation explicitly defined the role for women and clarified the responsibilities of the SWA. Today the intent of the SWA position as described by the NCAA is focused on "active involvement of female administrators as part of the athletics management team with program-wide administrative responsibilities, including decision-making at the institutional, conference, and national levels" (Sweet & Morrison, 2006, p. 8; see also Stallman et al., 2006). The NCAA makes recommendations for potential responsibilities and suggested department work by the SWA (see Table 7.4).

This role provides a pathway for women to ascend into leadership roles in the department but it also presents barriers for a critical mass of women, particularly at the Division I level. The senior woman administrator title creates a unique leadership role for women, but the SWA role has not been a very effective path for advancement. "The SWA provides a female voice at the table, many times the *only* female voice, by providing a diverse, different view—a different perspective" (emphasis added; Copeland, 2005). The SWA is an important position for Title IX oversight, but despite the NCAA suggestion for collaboration among the senior team, obligations for raising gender equity issues often fall heavily to the SWA. When combining the SWA role with compliance or academic support services, a terminal position for women is therefore created and not preparation for career advancement. Finally, the SWA is seen by many as an advocate for women in the department, a role

Table 7.4. Responsibilities and Work Suggested for the SWA at the Institutional Level

Potential Responsibilities	Suggested Department Work
Senior management team decision making Gender equity and Title IX Student-athlete advocate and educator Role model and resource Assist student-athletes with balancing athletics and academics Equity in Athletics Disclosure Act Report	Supervising sports programs Budgeting Fund-raising and development Marketing Compliance Governance Hiring, supervising, and dismissing personnel Monitoring implementation of the gender equity plan Advocating for women in the athletic department

that overshadows department responsibilities for serving the interests of all student-athletes and coaches (Hoffman, 2010).

GENDER ISSUES & CONTROVERSIES

Sexual objectification and harassment of women in sport

Today we still see encouragement for young girls and boys to be physically active. In later childhood, however, the expectations shift for girls. While it is OK for older girls to be tough and rugged within the confines of the court or field of play, off the court girls are expected to "conform as closely as possible to dominant cultural standards of beauty, behavior and grooming" (Ware, 2007, p. 10). This is especially notable in the representation of women athletes throughout the media. The representation of women student-athletes in the media is often a misrepresentation of their athletic status (Van Mullem, n.d). Women student-athletes view themselves as skilled, capable, and competitive yet they are not always portrayed as competent athletes. When women student-athletes are out of uniform, in passive poses, or in nonsporting

environments they lose more athletic credibility than their male peers. Featuring women student-athletes in posters or media guides as hyperfeminized or sexualized further reinforces them as nonathletic and passive. University athletic department media guides and other print materials as well as video content play a key role in marketing teams to the press, advertisers, sponsors, donors, and to the campus community.

The oversexualization of women in the media is not limited to college athletics or sports in general. As Deborah Rhode (2010) points out in the *Beauty Bias*, "The media's sexualized portrayals of prominent women, including everyone from athletes to politicians, also carries a cost. Overemphasis of their appearance deflects attention from their performance and reinforces sex-based double standards. That the highest-paid member of Sarah Palin's vice presidential campaign was her makeup 'artist' speaks volumes about our misplaced priorities" (p. 9). Emphasis on women as objects of sexual desire rather than their athletic skill or ability reinforces women's status as second-class citizens in college sports and suppresses interest and respect for the athletic accomplishments of women athletes (Kane, 2011).

As the commercial success of women's college athletics grows, the appropriate selection and representation of women in media content remains driven by outside interests. Portraits of women student-athletes should be based on active, athletic images of women performing in their uniform and their sporting environments. For more positive media representations of women athletes visit *"Game Face: What Does a Female Athlete Look Like"* *http://gamefaceonline.org/* or for an analysis of post–Title IX images and media representation of women athletes visit *"Playing Unfair the Media Image of the Female Athlete"* *http://www.youtube.com/watch?v=luadmO7Cugc*

Checklist for evaluating images of women athletes in the media.

- Do media guides and other images in our department reflect women as skilled, capable, and competitive athletes?
- Are women athletes pictured in their sport environment? (i.e., on the court, field, pool)
- Are women athletes in their uniform?
- Are women athletes actively participating in their sport?
- What theme does the material convey?
  a. Athletic, in action or nonathletic?
  b. Hyper-feminine or passively feminine?
  c. Sexually suggestive?
  d. Pop culture?
  e. Integrating academics or sport equipment?

Pom-Poms, Dance Teams, and Competitive Cheerleading

Cheerleading in schools and colleges raises significant questions about the role of physical activity and sports participation. Like many other aspects of school-based sports, cheerleading is a uniquely American sport phenomenon. The earliest cheerleading started with men who rallied students at college football games before the turn of the century. Women began to participate in the 1920s, but it remained a largely male-dominated activity until World War II. Since then, cheerleading has evolved into a women-dominated activity, common in high school, college, and professional sports. Today it includes sideline cheering at athletic events, competitive cheering competitions, and dance and drill teams. Despite the athletic ability needed in this activity it is not yet defined as a sport.

Before Title IX, cheerleading was the only school-sponsored physical activity in which girls could participate and represent their high school or college. Sideline pom-pom squads that performed individual jumps and maneuvers to entertain and rally the crowd characterize this traditional form. Title IX did little to call into question the legitimacy of cheerleading. Even as sporting activities have grown for women, cheerleading continues to grow among women at a similar rate. Today, estimates for competitive cheerleading include 1.5 million participants and as many as four million when other youth, middle school, and professional sideline cheering activities are included.

The contemporary image and activity of cheerleading have evolved from a form of sideline rally and entertainment to one that now includes strenuous tumbling, jumps, and tossing maneuvers. These acrobatic performances still occupy a specific place for entertaining the crowd at athletic events during time-outs, between periods, or half-time; however, these acrobatic skills and performances are also part of an organized activity where the primary goal is competition, complete with scoring, judges, and a national champion-type award structure. Like gymnastics, figure skating, or synchronized swimming, cheering teams are judged on elements that require strength, skill, and agility found only in highly athletic activities.

In 2011, twenty-one universities started a "stunt" or competitive cheer squad and competitive season. The sport of stunt came in the wake of the intercollegiate competitive cheer squads not being recognized as a sport in the Quinnipiac case. The sport, however, has not yet gained NCAA emerging sport status, in part because the two traditional cheerleading associations have not yet submitted a coordinated proposal that addresses the Title IX requirements from the Quinnipiac case. The NCAA is monitoring the development of this sport carefully. The NCAA Committee on Women's Athletics has requested the following information:

- Participation numbers
- Diversity of opportunities
- Specific injury data and risks
- Current and necessary training and certification of judges and officials
- Growth in youth sport format (scholastic or otherwise, but specific to the stunt and acrobatics and tumbling format)
- Any other relevant data

For cheerleading to garner NCAA recognition as an emerging sport, the sponsoring organization for stunt must also address competition formats, rules, and suggested NCAA rules that include competition and practice guidelines, recruiting, and financial aid regulations (Hosick, 2011).

Competitive cheer squads challenge deeply held assumptions about gender in school-sponsored sports. These teams are a space for the display of girls' and women's physical empowerment. Yet the gendering of cheerleading as a feminized domain and repositioning competition as its primary goal raises questions as to whether it is an extracurricular activity or a sport. Whether on the sideline or in competition, cheerleading does not disrupt traditionally held views about gender and sport. The strenuous skills and athleticism typically associated with sports are mediated in the context of cheerleading's feminized characteristics. Girls who participate in cheerleading possess the athletic characteristics typically associated with men's sports, but traditionally feminine characteristics dominate cheerleading. The visibility of traditional cheerleading and the traditional gender roles of "stunt" or "acro" teams further reinforces contemporary, competitive cheerleading as a marginalized, sideline activity and not an actual sport.

In 2012, the University of Maryland announced the end of its women's "acro team" or competitive cheer squad. Among the first schools to add competitive cheer as a varsity program in 2003, the elimination of this team sheds light on the difficulty of establishing any new NCAA sport, especially one long considered a school-sponsored activity or part of the overall entertainment at professional athletic events. A contemporary view of cheerleading as a women's sport illustrates the challenges of integrating competitive cheerleading into the traditional varsity sport offerings among high schools and colleges.

Quinnipiac University, Competitive Cheerleading, and Title IX

In March 2009, Quinnipiac University cut the women's volleyball team and replaced it with competitive cheerleading. These changes were challenged under Title IX, and in July 2010 a court ruled that competitive cheerleading did not meet the requirements. To qualify as a sport under Title IX, the ruling suggested that competitive cheerleading in colleges and universities must be a fully developed and organized activity characterized by: competitions against other squads in a defined season, inclusion of coaches and practices, resemble all other varsity sports at an institution in structure and operation, and be organized by a governing organization. The primary goal of the activity must be competition. Although competitive cheer meets some of the requirements, it lacks sufficient development in others. For example, the number and quality of competitions is a concern. The availability of conference, state or regional level, and national competition is limited. With no NCAA-sanctioned emerging sport or championship status, meeting the quality of competition standard remains a challenge.

"UT Cheerleaders" © Johntex, (CC BY 3.0) at http://www.commons.wikimedia.org/wiki/ File:UT_cheerleaders_San_Diego_2007-12-26.jpg.

University of Texas cheerleaders perform at the Battle of the Bands prior to the 2007 Holiday Bowl in San Diego between the University of Texas Longhorns and the Arizona State Sun Devils.

HOMOPHOBIA IN INTERCOLLEGIATE ATHLETICS

The sports domain is characterized by a masculine culture that has extreme levels of homophobia. Homophobia is neutral in that it can be exerted toward any person with homosexual orientations, but in collegiate sports it is more common for homophobic fears to be used to deter women from participating and working in sports. To be clear, a strong hegemonic masculine culture characterized by compulsory heterosexuality makes it very difficult for gay athletes, coaches, and athletic administrators to come out of the closet. Hence, under the guise of heterosexuality many compete or work without a cloud of suspicion and remain in the closet until after their careers have ended. For gay athletes and coaches who choose to publicly come out, research suggests that fears of overt intolerance and violence are more prevalent than actual negative experiences (Anderson, 2005, 2011). In contrast, heterosexuality is not commonly viewed as the norm for many women in sport. Women are prone to lesbian stereotyping simply because of their affiliation with sports, and so there is a general assumption that many women athletes, coaches, and administrators (especially single women) are lesbians or bisexual (Blinde & Taub, 1992; Griffin, 1998).

Homophobia in the intercollegiate athletics context can result in heterosexual and homosexual men and women facing prejudice, discrimination, and harassment from others—and gay and lesbian athletes are more susceptible to being ostracized by other players and have an increased fear of being benched or losing their athletic scholarships.

As a result, many gay, lesbian, and bisexual athletes choose to conceal their sexual orientations (Anderson, 2005; Blinde & Taub, 1992; Griffin, 1998).

Societal fears of homosexuality have been used as a tool in the student-athlete recruiting process as coaches suggest that a coach or players at another institution are gay or lesbians (Griffin, 1998; Kampfhoff, 2010; Thorngren, 1990; Wellman & Blinde, 1997). For heterosexual or closet homosexuals this proves to be a strong deterrent to attending that university or college so as to avoid being labeled gay or lesbian because of association. Moreover, in the hiring process many women, especially single women, are assumed to be lesbians and denied opportunities because of the suspicion. Hence, many lesbian coaches feel the need and pressure to put on a façade of heterosexuality and remain in the closet to avoid negative repercussions in the athletic department (Griffin, 1998). This fear of being labeled a lesbian does not only affect athletes and women in the coaching profession, but also discourages many single women from participating in sports and entering the coaching professions (Wellman & Blinde, 1997).

HOMOPHOBIA IN WOMEN'S INTERCOLLEGIATE SPORT

Homophobia in women's intercollegiate sport gained national attention in 2005 when Jennifer Harris, a student-athlete at Pennsylvania State University, filed a discrimination lawsuit against her former basketball coach Maureen Portland for dismissing her from the team because Harris was perceived to be a lesbian (*Harris v. Portland*, Amended Complaint, 2006; Newhall & Buzuvis, 2008). Portland had an anti-lesbian policy for her women's basketball program and used her heterosexuality and team policy to recruit players. Players were asked to spy on other players to see if they were lesbians and also instructed to exhibit a "feminine" appearance. Although the case was presented in the media as simply a "homophobia in sports" case, it is important to know that Harris likewise filed a race and sex discrimination claim. Portland had a history of recruiting a majority of white players, but dismissed a majority of African American players. She also discouraged players from wearing cornrows—a hairstyle worn predominately by African Americans. Portland's standards for appearance suggest she was reinforcing a white heterosexual femininity (Newhall & Buzuvis).

Challenging the Gender Binary: Transgender and Transsexual Student-Athletes

In the first few years after Title IX passed, attention was directed toward whether the law meant that athletic opportunity should be coeducational, such as in elementary and high school physical education classes, or if interscholastic and intercollegiate varsity athletics would remain sex and gender separated (Ware, 2007). But rather than having boys and girls compete on the same teams, over the course of a century apprehensions about the role of women in sport (Cahn, 1994) and the dissonance between masculine and feminine uses of sport and education have kept intercollegiate sports highly defined by sex and gender. Thus, men and women participate on gender-segregated teams—making coed sports much rarer in educational settings. Some individual sports, such as track or swimming, combine women's and men's athletes under a single head coach;

however, women practice and compete with and against women peers. Fencing, rifle, and skiing are the only NCAA-sponsored sports that are coed.

Title IX's legitimization of gender-segregated sports results in the marginalization of gender ambiguous and intersex students. Transgender athletes disrupt historical and current binary ideas about sex, thus increasing ambiguity about sport participation opportunities. A transgender person's gender identity or psychological identification as a male or female or gender expression does not match his or her sex at birth, whereas transsexuals are persons who have transitioned from one gender to another (Gender Spectrum, n.d). Gender transitions often involve hormone therapy and surgery, but some transsexuals choose to only change their name and gender expression. It is important to understand that transgender and transsexual people are different from intersex individuals. Individuals with intersex conditions are born with male and female reproductive chromosomes, organs, and/or genitalia, and typically do not have any confusion or ambiguity about their gender identity (Intersex Society of North America, n.d).

The collegiate environment has recently experienced an increase in the number of athletes identifying as transgender. For example, in 2002 high school student Alyn Libman transitioned (with hormones) from a female to a male prior to competing as a male on the University of California at Berkeley's club figure skating team (Marech, 2004). In 2005, Keelin (formerly Kelly) Godsey announced he is transgender. Keelin was an All-American track and field athlete on Bates College's women's team, and due to fears and potential negative repercussions of "coming out" he remained silent about his gender identity until after his junior year of competition (Jaschik, 2010). Also, in 2010 Kye (formerly Kyler Kelcian or Kay-Kay) Allums, a basketball player on George Washington University's women's team, became the first openly transgendered male to play on a Division I college sports team (Moltz, 2010). Kye is biologically female and planned to start transitioning into a male after he completed college. His decision to delay hormone treatment was primarily due to a fear of jeopardizing his athletic scholarship because testosterone is a banned substance for NCAA athletes. For unknown reasons, however, Kye chose not to compete in his senior year.

At the time of Keelin and Kye's announcements, a policy did not exist for transgender athletes competing on NCAA-sponsored athletic teams. The NCAA's stance was that athletes participate on a team based on the sex indicated on official state documents, such as a birth certificate, driver's license, or voter registration card, and if an athlete who is legally classified as a male competes on a women's team, the team must be classified as a mixed team and forfeit competing for a women's championship. Different states have different rules governing how a person's sex will be identified or changed on state documents. Thus, depending on the state where a transgender athlete resides, there are different options for competing on NCAA teams.

To address the growing concerns about sport participation opportunities and potential lawsuits that transgender athletes could file under the Equal Protection Clause of the Constitution and Title IX, in 2011 the NCAA Executive Committee followed the guidance of the *On the Team: Equal Opportunity for Transgender Athletes* report, released by the National Center for Lesbian Rights and the Women's Sport Foundation, and approved a new policy concerning the treatment of transgender student-athletes (Lawrence, 2011). The policy was enacted to allow student-athletes to participate on teams based on their gender identity, while maintaining fairness and competitive equity among sports teams. The new policy will allow transgender student-athletes to participate on college athletic teams given they remain compliant with NCAA policies on banned substances and new medical standards. Namely, a trans-male student-athlete receiving testosterone for diagnosed gender identity disorder (GID) may compete on a men's team, or if he competes on a women's team it becomes classified as a mixed team. Whereas a trans-female student-athlete taking testosterone-suppression medication for GID may compete on a men's team, but may not compete on a women's team without changing that team's status to a mixed team until she has completed one calendar year of treatment.

The gender binary system likewise affects transgender athletes' access to housing and locker rooms. In the majority of higher education institutions, residence halls, restrooms, locker rooms, etc. are designated as single sex, and transgender and transsexual students are commonly forced to choose options based on their natal sex and not gender identity or transitioned gender (Beemyn, 2005). In institutions in which transgender and transsexual students are able to receive a room assignment appropriate to their gender identity, many encounter nonsupportive or hostile roommates and still must utilize single-sex bathrooms or locker rooms. To address these challenges, many colleges and universities have started to offer gender-neutral housing and bathrooms (e.g., University of Chicago, Carleton College, Tufts University) and locker rooms (e.g., Grinnell College; Kilen & Belz, 2011).

In 2011, roughly fifty-four U.S. colleges and universities provided gender-neutral housing options. For those that do not, it has been recommended that transgender and transsexual students use facilities in accordance with their gender identity, and a private and separate changing room, shower, or restroom be provided if requested, but not required.

CHAPTER SUMMARY

This chapter has highlighted some of the key historical and current issues and controversies concerning women and gender relations in collegiate sport. Women's intercollegiate athletics flourished until the Progressive Era, but the backlash against women in higher education resulted in a very specific recreational model for women students and faculty members. Competitive sports for women students were discouraged at most institutions and moderate "gender appropriate" physical activity was emphasized. Women's competitive intercollegiate sport reemerged under the guidance of the AIAW, but women's intercollegiate competition was defined by an "education-based" philosophy as opposed to the men's commercial, spectator-oriented model.

The passage of Title IX in 1972 significantly changed the landscape of women's intercollegiate athletics. Women had increased opportunities to participate in sports, the commercial model replaced the educational model, control of women's intercollegiate athletics shifted from the AIAW to the NCAA, and separate athletic programs for men and women were combined. Title IX legislation resulted in many positive outcomes for women in sport; but even after the passage of Title IX legislation, women student-athletes, coaches, and athletic administrators continue to have inequitable representations, resources and experiences than men in intercollegiate athletics. Furthermore, since the demise of the AIAW and the passage of Title IX legislation, women's leadership positions in athletic administration and coaching positions declined.

Finally, it is important to understand that not all women and men have the same experiences, as many demographic, social, and contextual factors come into play. As noted in this chapter, women in sport are more adversely affected by homophobia and prone to stereotyping then men simply because of their involvement in the masculine domain of sport. Athletes publically identifying as transgender or intersex are marginalized because of a societal established gender binary and Title IX's legitimization of gender-segregated sports. Moreover, the intersection of a person's race, class, or religion with gender/sex can moderate her experiences in the athletic department. For example, Title IX has been largely ineffective for women of color in interscholastic sports and intercollegiate athletics because of previous segregation practices that left them out of predominately white educational institutions. Because women of color were segregated in schools during the emergence of coeducation, they lacked access to the schooling structures that promoted women's sports. This chapter acknowledges the importance of intersectionality, but the scope of the chapter has been on general women's issues and inequities. For a discussion about the representation, participation, and experiences of African American stakeholders in collegiate sport read Chapter 5.

REFERENCES

Anderson, E. (2005). *In the game: Gay athletes and the cult of masculinity*. Albany, NY: State University of New York Press.

Anderson, E. (2011). Updating the outcome: Gay athletes, straight teams, and coming out in educationally based sport teams. *Gender & Society* 25, 250–268.

Baker, C. A. (2008). *Why she plays: The world of women's basketball*. Lincoln, NE: University of Nebraska Press.

Ballintine, H. A. (n.d.). *The History of Physical Training at Vassar College* 1865–1915. Poughkeepsie, NY: Lansing & Brothers.

Beasley, C. (1999). *What is feminism? An introduction to feminist theory*. London: Sage Publications.

Beemyn, B. (2005). Making campuses more inclusive of transgender students. *Journal of Gay & Lesbian Issues in Education* 3, 77–87.

Berkowitz, S., and J. Upton. (2011, April 4) An analysis of salaries for women's college basketball coaches. *USA TODAY*. Retrieved from http://www.usatoday.com/sports/college/womensbasketball/2011-coaches-salary-database.htm

Blinde, E. M., and D.E. Taub. (1992). Women athletes as falsely accused deviants: Managing the lesbian stigma. *The Sociological Quarterly* 33, 521–533.

Boutilier, M., and L. San Giovanni. (1994). Politics, public policy, and Title IX: Some limitations of liberal feminism. *Women, Sport, and Culture*. Champaign, IL: Human Kinetics.

Boxhill, J. (1995). Title IX and gender equity. *Journal of the Philosophy of Sport* xx-xxi, 23–31.

Brown, G, (2011, November). College sports participation rates continue upward trend. *NCAA. org*. Retrieved April 20, 2012, from http:// www.ncaa.org/wps/wcm/connect/public/ncaa/ resources/latest+news/2011/november/colleg e+sports+participation+rates+continue+upwa rd+trend

Cahn, S., K. (1994). *Coming on strong: Gender and sexuality in twentieth-century women's sport.* Cambridge, MA: Harvard University Press.

Carpenter, L. J., and R.V. Acosta. (2001). Let her swim, climb mountain peaks: Self-sacrifice and success in expanding athletic programs for women. *Women Administrators in Higher Education: Historical and Contemporary Perspectives* (pp. 207–229). Albany, New York: State University of New York Press.

Cheslock, J. (2007). *Who's Playing College Sports: Money, Race and Gender.* East Meadow, NY: Women's Sports Foundation. Retrieved from http://www.womenssportsfoundation.org/ Content/Research-Reports/Money-Race-and-Gender.aspx

Copeland, J. (2005, August 15). Association takes steps to improve understanding of SWA. *NCAA News.* Retrieved October 12, 2009, from http://www.ncaa.org/wps/ncaa?key=/ncaa/ ncaa/ncaa+news/ncaa+news+online/2005/ association-wide/association+takes +steps+to+improve+understanding+ of+_swa_+-+8-15-05+ncaa+news

Cunningham, G. B., M. Sagas, and F.B. Ashley. (2003). Coaching self-efficacy, desire to head coach, and occupational turnover intent: Gender differences between NCAA assistant coaches of women's teams. *International Journal of Sport Psychology* 34, 125–137.

Dixon, M., B. Tiell, N. Lough, K. Sweeney, B. Osborne, and J. Bruening. (2008). The work/ life interface in intercollegiate athletics: An examination of policies, programs, and institutional climate. *Journal for the Study of Sports and Athletes in Education* 2, 137–160.

Fass, P. S. (1997). The female paradox: higher education for women, 1945–1963. In Goodchild, L.F., and H. S. Wechsler, eds. *The history of higher education.* (Second ed., pp. 699–723). Boston: Simon & Schuster Custom Publishing.

Festle, M. J. (1996). *Playing nice: politics and apologies in women's sports.* New York: Columbia University Press.

Gender Spectrum, (n.d.), "A Word About Words," Retrieved March 28, 2012, from http:// www.genderspectrum.org/images/stories/ Resources/Family/A_Word_About_Words.pdf.

Gentry, J. , and R. Alexander, (2012, April 2), "Pay for Women's Basketball Coaches Lags Far Behind That of Men's Coaches," Retrieved on April 15, 2012, from http://www.nytimes. com/2012/04/03/sports/ncaabasketball/ pay-for-womens-basketball-coaches-lags-far-behind-mens-coaches.html?pagewanted=all

Gr_____, (2011, December 25), "Groundwork laid for merging of UT's long-separate athletic departments," Retrieved from http://m.gov-olsxtra.com/news/2011/dec/25/groundwork-laid-for-merging-of-uts-long-separate/ on April 1, 2012.

Gribble, A., (2011, June 10), "UT merging men's, women's athletics," http://www.govolsxtra. com/news/2011/jun/09/ut-merging-mens-womens-athletics/ on April 1, 2012.

Griffin, P. (1998). *Strong women, deep closets: Lesbians and homophobia in sport.* Champaign, IL: Human Kinetics.

Griffin, P., and H. Carroll, (2010), "On the team: Equal opportunity for transgender student-athletes," Retrieved from http://www.gender-

spectrum.org/images/stories/On_The_Team.
pdf

Grundy, P. (2000). From amazons to glamazons:
The rise and fall of North Carolina women's
basketball, 1920–1960. *Journal of American
History* 87(1), 112–146.

Grundy, P., and S. Shackelford. (2005). *Shattering
the glass: The remarkable history of women's
basketball*. New York: The New Press.

Hoffman, J. L. (2011). Each generation of women
had to start anew: A historical analysis of Title
IX policy and women leaders in the extracurriculum. In Pasque, P., and S. Errington, eds.
*Empowering Women in Higher Education and
Student Affairs: Theory, Research, Narratives,
and Practice from Feminist Perspectives* (pp.
32–46). Sterling, VA: Stylus Publishing.

Hoffman, J.L. (2010). The dilemma of the senior
woman administrator role in intercollegiate
athletics. *Journal of Issues in Intercollegiate
Athletics* 3, 53–75.

Hosick, M. (2005a, August 15). SWAs perceive
lack of involvement in finance, personnel.
NCAA News. Retrieved October 12, 2009, from
http://www.ncaa.org/wps/ncaa?key=/ncaa/
ncaa/ncaa+news/ncaa+news+online/2005/
association-wide/swas+perceive+lack+o
f+involvement+in+finance%2C+personn
el+-+8-15-05+ncaa+news

Hosick, M. (2005b, August 15). Senior class:
Research raises new questions about role of
woman administrators. *NCAA News*. Retrieved
October 12, 2009, from http://www.ncaa.
org/wps/ncaa?key=/ncaa/ncaa/ncaa+news/
ncaa+news+online/2005/association-wide/
senior+class+-+8-15-05+ncaa+news

Hosick, M, (2011, August 16). NCAA committee asks for collaboration in new
sport. *NCAA.org*. Retrieved from http://
www.ncaa.org/wps/portal/!ut/p/
c4/04_SB8K8xLLM9MSSzPy8xBz9CP0os
3gjX29XJydDRwP_wGBDA08Df3Nzd-
1dXQwMDA _ 2CbEdFALxFcuk!/?WCM_
PORTLET = PC_7_2MKEBB1A0OQS10I0O7
7GEE10G3000000 _ WCM&WCM_GLOBAL_
CONTEXT = /wps/wcm/connect/public/
NCAA/Resources/Latest + News/2011/August/
NCAA+committee+asks+for +collaboration+
in+new+sport

Hult, J., and M. Trekell. (1991). *A century of
women's basketball: From frailty to the final
four*. Reston: American Alliance for Health,
Physical Education, Recreation, and Dance.

Hult, J. S. (1994). The story of women's athletics:
Manipulating a dream 1890–1985. In Costa,
D.M., and Sharon R. Guthrie, eds. *Women
and Sport: Interdisciplinary Perspectives* (pp.
83–106). Champaign, IL: Human Kinetics.

Intersex Society of North America (n.d.), "What's
the difference between being transgender or
transsexual and having an intersex condition?" Retrieved March 28, 2012, from http://
www.isna.org/faq/transgender.

Jaschik, S., (2010, October 5), "Transgender
athletes, college teams," Retrieved from http://
www.insidehighered.com/news/2010/10/05/
trans on March 29, 2012.

Kamphoff, C. (2010). Bargaining with patriarchy:
Former female coaches' experiences and their
decision to leave collegiate coaching. *Research
quarterly for exercise and sport* 81, 360–372.

Kane, M. J. (2011, July 27). Sex Sells Sex, Not
Women's Sports. *The Nation*. Retrieved from
http://www.thenation.com/article/162390/
sex-sells-sex-not-womens-sports

Kilen, M., and A. Belz, (2011), "College adds locker
rooms to gender-neutral policy," http://www.
usatoday.com/news/nation/story/2011-11-09/
gender-neutral-college/51134546/1

Lawrence, M. (2011). Transgender policy approved. *NCAA News*. Retrieved from The National Center for Lesbian Rights from http://www.ncaa.org/wps/wcm/connect/public/NCAA/Resources/Latest+News/2011/September/Trangender+policy+approved?pageDesign=print+template.

Marech, R. (2004, June 14). Olympics' transgender quandary debate rages on the fairness of new inclusion rule. *San Francisco Chronicle* A1.

Moltz, D., (2010, November 8), "Transgender Pioneer," http://www.insidehighered.com/news/2010/11/08/transgender Retrieved on March 28, 2012.

National Collegiate Athletic Association, (n.d., [a]), "Senior Woman Administrator," Retrieved from http://www.ncaa.org/wps/ncaa?key=/ncaa/NCAA/About+The+NCAA/Diversity+and+Inclusion/Gender+Equity+and+Title+IX/SWA

National Federation of State High School Association. (n.d.). 2010–11 High School Athletics Participation Survey Results. *Participation Data*. Retrieved April 20, 2012, from http://www.nfhs.org/content.aspx?id=3282

Nerad, M. (1999). *The academic kitchen: A social history of gender stratification at the University of California, Berkeley*. Albany: State University of New York Press.

Newcomber, M. (1959). *A century of higher education for American women*. New York: Harper & Brothers Publishers.

Newhall, K., and E. Buzuvis. (2006). (e)Racing Jennifer Harris: Sexuality and race, law and discourse in Harris v. Portland. *Journal of Sport and Social Issues* 32, 345–368.

Nidiffer, J. (2000). *Pioneering deans of women: More than wise and pious matrons*. New York: Teachers College Press.

Paul, J. (2001). Agents of social control: The role of physical educators as guardians of women's health, 1860-1960. In Nidiffer, J., and C.T. Bashaw. eds. *Women administrators in higher education: Historical and contemporary Perspectives* (pp. 183–206). Albany: State University of New York Press.

Radke-Moss, A. (2008). *Bright Epoch: Women and Coeducation in the American West*. Lincoln: University of Nebraska Press.

Rhode, D. L. (2010). *The beauty bias: The injustice of appearance in life and law*. New York: Oxford University Press, USA. Retrieved from http://www.oup.com/us/catalog/general/subject/Sociology/SexGender/?view=usa&ci=9780195372878

Sack, A. L., and E.J. Staruowsky. (1998). *College athletes for hire: The evolution and legacy of the NCAA's amateur myth*. Westport, Connecticut: Praeger.

Stallman, R., M. Kovalchik, B. Tiell, and A. Goff. (2006). Paper presented at Live NCAA Web Cast, Washington, DC. *Clarification of the senior woman administrator designation*.

Stangl, J. M., and M.J. Kane. (1991). Structural variables that offer explanatory power for the under-representation of women coaches since Title IX: The case of homologous reproduction. *Sociology of Sport Journal* 8, 47–60.

Suggs, W. (2006). *A place on the team: The triumph and tragedy of Title IX*. Princeton, NJ: Princeton University Press. Retrieved from http://www.amazon.com/Place-Team-Triumph-Princeton-Paperbacks/dp/0691128855/ref=sr_1_7?ie=UTF8&qid=1335336354&sr=8-7

Sweet, J., and Karen Morrison. (2006). *Current Status of the SWA within the NCAA*. Presented at the NCAA Convention, Indianapolis, IN. Retrieved from http://

www.ncaa.org/wps/ncaa?key=/ncaa/ncaa/
about+the+ncaa/diversity+and+inclusion/
gender+equity+and+title+ix/swa

Thorngren, C. M. (1990). A time to reach out—
Keeping the female coach in coaching. *Journal
of Physical Education, Recreation, and Dance*
61, 57–60.

Uhlir, G. A. (1987, July-August). Athletics and the
university: The Post-Woman's Era, *Academe*
73, 25–29.

United States Government Accountability Office.
(2007). *Intercollegiate athletics: Recent trends
in teams and participants in National Collegiate
Athletic Association sports.*

Van Mullem, H., L. Sterling, and A. Peck. (n.d.).
*Accurate representation?: Media guide images
of female college athletes competing in the
NCAA Division II.* Working Paper, Center
For Leadership In Athletics, University of
Washington. Retrieved from http://sites.

education.washington.edu/uwcla/research/
working-papers/library

Ware, S. (2007). *Title IX: A brief history with
documents.* Boston: Bedford/St. Martin's.

Wellman, S., and E. Blinde. (1997). Homophobia in
women's intercollegiate basketball. *Women in
sport & physical activity journal* 6, 63–82.

Willey, S. (1996). *The governance of women's
intercollegiate athletics: Association for
Intercollegiate Athletics for Women (AIAW),
1976–1982.* Bloomington, IN: Indiana
University Press.

Women's Sports Foundation, (2007), "Homophobia
in women's sports," Retrieved April 22,
2012, from http://www.divinecaroline.com/
22337/29668-homophobia-women-s-sports

Women's Sports Foundation, (n.d.), "Pay Inequity
in Athletics," Retrieved April 20, 2012, from
http://www.womenssportsfoundation.
org/home/research/articles-and-reports/
equity-issues/pay-inequity

As the twenty-first century collegiate athletic climate unfolds, leadership is a salient endeavor for research and practice (Kozlowski & Ilgen, 2006). In general, leaders (athletic directors and coaches) are imperative for the success of the organization because they develop a vision and align individuals with that vision through communication and inspiration (Robbins, 2003). More specifically, the quality of the coach has been shown to be the most significant influence on an athlete's experience in sport (NASPE, 2006). Given this assertion, the leaders' vital role in recruitment, selection, development, and performance makes them one of the most important human resources undertaken by an athletic department (Gardner, Shields, Bredemeier, & Bostrom, 1996; Turman, 2003; Turner & Chelladuari, 2005; Westre & Weiss, 1991).

As is the case with any written work, we had to make difficult decisions about what to include and exclude. As indicated by the subtitle of this edited text, we have selected the most prominent "issues and controversies" regarding administration and coaching in higher education. Due to the structural platform as well as the race for national recognition through winning and providing an entertainment value, we decided to focus on NCAA Division I athletics, in particular football and men's basketball since they are the most commercialized of all collegiate sports. In choosing to focus on this level, we acknowledge that these issues and controversies may not be generalizable to others. Nonetheless, since this competitive

7

COLLEGIATE COACHING AND ADMINISTRATION

BRIAN GEARITY & JANELLE WELLS

level is commonly viewed as high performing and highly desirable, a critical analysis is warranted to challenge the negative assumptions and outcomes. Thus, the content in this chapter exposes three major areas of concern within NCAA Division I athletics: a) equitable leadership representation, b) hiring processes, and c) compensation.

EQUITABLE REPRESENTATION IN LEADERSHIP POSITIONS

"The NCAA is committed to fair treatment of all student-athletes and staff and includes as part of its core values: *An inclusive culture that fosters equitable participation for student-athletes and career opportunities for coaches and administrators from diverse backgrounds,"* from NCAA Gender Equity Planning Best Practices.

While women, ethnic, and racial minorities, herein collectively referred to as underrepresented individuals, have advanced in the professional sector, typically they earn less and obtain lower-status positions (U.S. Bureau of Labor Statistics, 2009). In 2009, under-represented employees earned 25 percent less than White men and represented 36 percent of higher management (EEOC, 2009; U.S. Bureau of Labor Statistics, 2009). Despite the above quote from an official NCAA publication, collegiate athletics is no exception to inequality in leadership positions (Acosta & Carpenter, 2012; Lapchick, 2011).

Historically, leadership positions in collegiate athletics have been a segregated landscape dominated by White, Protestant, heterosexual, able-bodied, middle- to upper-class men (Fink, Pastore, & Riemer, 2001; Lapchick, 2011). When focusing on athletic administration and head coaches, under-represented groups have lacked visibility in high-powered leadership positions. For example, only nineteen under-represented individuals (excluding separate women's athletic departments) were Division I athletic directors and twenty-eight were Division I head coaches in the Football Bowl Subdivision (FBS) at Predominantly White Institutions (PWI) during the 2010 athletic season (Lapchick, 2011).

The success of the few under-represented individuals to leadership positions defies the norm of their place in higher education. .Some casually dismiss this social issue, arguing that women and other under-represented individuals are just not interested in or "cut out for" leadership positions. Then again, many previously used the same argument to prevent equality legislation (i.e., Title IX, Civil Rights Act of 1964). Indeed, this faulty logic crumbles as evidenced by the rapid increase in women's participation in sports and the ascension of minority coaches (Acosta & Carpenter, 2012; Lapchick, 2011).

As depicted in Table 1, under-represented individuals account for 45 percent of senior athletic administrators, yet only 18 percent of athletic directors at the Division I level (Irick, 2010). In terms of head coaches, specifically basketball, under-represented individuals account for 27.2 percent at the Division I level (see all collegiate sport head coaches in Table

Table 1. 2009-2010 Division I Percentages of Athletics Administrative Staffs Excluding Historically Black Institutions

Position	White		Black		Other Minority		Total	
	Men	Women	Men	Women	Men	Women	Men	Women
Director of Athletics	82.0	7.6	6.0	0.6	3.5	0.3	91.5	8.5
Associate Director of Athletics	62.3	25.2	5.5	3.0	2.2	1.8	70.0	30.0
Assistant Director of Athletics	63.7	23.8	6.4	2.5	1.9	1.8	71.9	28.1
Senior Woman Administrator	0.6	84.2	0.0	9.6	0.0	5.5	0.6	99.4

Source: National Collegiate Athletic Association. Copyright © 2011 by the National Collegiate Athletic Association.

Table 2. 2009–2010 Division I Percentages of Head Coaches

Sport	Men's Teams						Women's Teams					
	White		Black		Other Minority		White		Black		Other Minority	
	Men	Women	Men	Women	Men	Women	Men	Women	Men	Women	Men	Women
Baseball	90.1	0.0	5.1	0.0	4.8	0.0	N/A	N/A	N/A	N/A	N/A	N/A
Basketball	72.8	0.0	26.0	0.0	1.2	0.0	28.7	50.4	5.1	14.6	0.3	0.9
Bowling	N/A	N/A	N/A	N/A	N/A	N/A	25.8	16.1	32.3	25.8	0.0	0.0
Cross-Country	75.6	6.5	13.4	2.0	2.6	0.0	66.3	11.7	11.7	7.2	2.4	0.6
Fencing	75.0	10.0	0.0	0.0	15.0	0.0	65.2	17.4	0.0	4.3	13.0	0.0
Field Hockey	N/A	N/A	N/A	N/A	N/A	N/A	11.5	76.9	0.0	1.3	0.0	10.3
Football	83.7	0.0	14.2	0.0	2.1	0.0	N/A	N/A	N/A	N/A	N/A	N/A
Golf	92.4	1.0	5.2	0.0	1.0	0.3	38.2	53.7	4.1	0.0	0.4	3.7
Gymnastics	87.5	0.0	6.3	0.0	6.3	0.0	48.5	45.5	3.0	0.0	1.5	1.5
Ice hockey	98.3	0.0	0.0	0.0	1.7	0.0	69.4	25.0	0.0	0.0	2.8	2.8
Lacrosse	98.3	0.0	1.7	0.0	0.0	0.0	11.2	86.5	0.0	2.2	0.0	0.0
Rifle	95.0	5.0	0.0	0.0	0.0	0.0	80.0	20.0	0.0	0.0	0.0	0.0
Rowing	96.6	0.0	0.0	0.0	3.4	0.0	54.9	40.7	1.1	0.0	2.2	1.1
Skiing	100.0	0.0	0.0	0.0	0.0	0.0	86.7	13.3	0.0	0.0	0.0	0.0
Soccer	86.9	0.0	4.5	0.0	8.6	0.0	56.2	28.3	4.4	1.6	7.9	1.6
Softball	N/A	N/A	N/A	N/A	N/A	N/A	30.2	58.9	2.1	4.2	1.1	3.5
Swimming	91.7	4.9	1.4	0.0	2.1	0.0	78.3	15.8	1.5	0.0	3.0	1.5
Tennis	83.8	2.3	6.9	0.0	6.5	0.4	53.3	28.6	7.6	1.3	6.7	2.5
Track, indoor	69.8	3.5	20.4	3.5	2.7	0.0	61.9	9.8	14.7	10.7	2.6	0.3
Track, outdoor	70.6	4.4	19.9	2.6	2.6	0.0	61.7	9.9	15.0	10.2	2.9	0.3
Volleyball	87.0	0.0	8.7	0.0	4.3	0.0	42.7	37.1	1.9	8.1	8.1	2.2
Water Polo	87.0	0.0	0.0	0.0	13.0	0.0	71.9	15.6	0.0	0.0	12.5	0.0
Wrestling	92.7	0.0	4.9	0.0	2.4	0.0	N/A	N/A	N/A	N/A	N/A	N/A
Other	92.3	5.1	0.0	0.0	2.6	0.0	56.4	34.5	0.0	5.5	3.6	0.0

Source: National Collegiate Athletic Association. Copyright © 2011 by the National Collegiate Athletic Association.

2; Irick). While there has been an increase in under-represented individuals over the past fifteen years (Irick), the percentages are not equal to total population counts in the United State. (60 percent; U.S. Census Bureau, 2011). Nor are these percentages equitable considering that the viable hiring pool (i.e., senior athletic administrators for athletic directors or student-athletes for coaches) is well represented with under-represented individuals (36 percent student-athletes; Everhart & Chelladurai, 1998; 45 percent senior athletic administrators: Irick; Zgonc, 2010). While we may not expect the front offices to replicate the on-field percentages no matter how comparisons are made, the gap between under-represented individuals and current leaders should not be as widespread (Shropshire, 1996).

WHY THE LACK OF WOMEN COLLEGIATE ATHLETIC LEADERS?

"You would think after all these years, and all the Title IX opportunities, that there would be more women coaching," Digit Murphy, former Brown head women's hockey coach, winningest coach in Division I women's hockey (Borzi, 2012).

When focusing on all athletic institutional leadership positions (e.g., university president, athletic director, or academic officers), the lowest representation of women is found at the athletic director position (Sander, 2011a). According to Acosta and Carpenter (2012), during the 2010–2011 athletic season, 10.6 percent of NCAA Division I athletic directors and 20 percent of head coaches were women. The percentage of athletic directors diminishes to 4.9 percent when selecting only Division I FBS institutions (Lapchick, 2011).

More than forty years after the enactment of Title IX, society may (mis)perceive that the inequity women face in athletics has subsided. From a participation view, women have reached historically high rates (9,274 collegiate teams), yet this achievement may be overshadowed by the loss of women in leadership positions (Acosta & Carpenter, 2012; Lopiano, 2005; Whisenant, Pedersen, & Obenour, 2002). Within collegiate athletic administration, Acosta and Carpenter (2012) noted an average of 1.41 women for every 3.94 positions, and this disparity grows when focusing on the NCAA Division I level where on average there are 1.78 women for every 5.98 administrators.

In terms of coaching, while the overall number of women coaches employed and paid in a college setting is higher than ever, the percentage of women coaches has dramatically declined (Acosta & Carpenter, 2012). In 1972 nine out of ten collegiate coaches for women's teams were women. By 2012, that ratio had plummeted to just less than one out of two. Expressed as a percentage, the shift went from about 90 percent in 1972 to under 50 percent in 2012. Clearly, some drastic changes occurred to create this vast inequality. The issue of gender inequity is not limited to institutions of higher education in America. At the university or elite level, for example, men comprise 80 percent of all coaches in Canada, 75 percent in the UK, and 80 percent in the United States (Reade, Rodgers & Norman, 2009).

These compelling statistics have contributed to the need to theorize and study women collegiate athletic leaders. Numerous topics and theoretical approaches—e.g., hegemonic masculinity (Norman, 2010; Whisenant et al., 2002), homologous reproduction (Stangl & Kane, 1991), homophobic and sexist exclusion (Cahn, 1994; Coakley, 2009), leader and gender role stereotypes (Burton, Barr, Fink, & Bruening, 2009; Embry, Padgett, & Caldwell, 2008; Grappendorf, Pent, Burton, & Henderson, 2008; Kellerman & Rhode, 2007), biased networks and evaluations (Kellerman & Rhode, 2007), rate of career advancement and satisfaction (Whisenant et al., 2002; Sagas & Cunningham, 2004), combination of athletics (Grappendorf & Lough, 2006; Sagas & Cunningham, 2004), and work-family life balance (Inglis, Danylcuk, & Pastore, 2000)—have all contributed to the scholarly literature on the lack of women athletic leaders. Relative to men, women also receive fewer promotions (e.g., Knoppers, Meyer, Ewing, &Forrest, 1991; Whisenant, 2003), greater negative athletic work experiences (Inglis et al., 2000), and systematic denial to leadership positions (Clausen & Lehr, 2002; Lough & Grappendorf, 2007).

Reviews of research (Kilty, 2006; Knoppers, 1992) have categorized the litany of potential barriers for women coaches at three levels: individual (e.g., lack of assertiveness, low human capital), structural (e.g., economics, legislation), and social relations (e.g., hegemony, homophobia). An argument at the individual level would state women lack the necessary skills or traits to be effective coaches, and thereby justifiably lose opportunities to better, male coaches. For example, some may believe that coaching requires a certain personality profile that women simply lack. Another individual argument could hypothesize that women do not enter or leave coaching to have a family. One would speculate that women were naturally more concerned with being a mother than a coach and would voluntarily withdraw from coaching. While women coaches would obviously face the difficulty of managing their pregnancy with the demands of coaching, this individual argument fails to account for the thousands, if not millions, of women in other careers who do this on a daily basis. The logic here is that women could not possibly balance pregnancy, child-rearing, and their job. Does this also suggest men are somehow immune to these issues or uninterested in child-rearing? Contrary to popular belief, empirical evidence exists demonstrating that men and women share some similar beliefs regarding work-family balance. In a study of two-year college coaches, Pastore (1992) determined men and women cited family constraints at similar levels.

A structural argument would point out repeated cultural patterns such as the lack of resources for women's teams and women athletic leaders. Compared with men, women's sports have always been severely under-resourced. Title IX was supposed to be a significant step in equity, but perhaps its passing led to an unintended, negative effect. Passed in 1972, Title IX states:

> No person in the United States shall, on the basis of sex, be excluded from participation in, be denied the benefits of, or be subjected to discrimination under any program or activity receiving Federal financial assistance.

Faced with the legal requirement to offer sports to women, universities had to decide whether to cut (men's) sports or add women's teams. Most decided on the latter. Title IX thus

Figure 8.1. 2010 NCAA champion University of Connecticut women's basketball head coach, Geno Auriemma, (far left) and former student-athletes, Maya Moore and Tina Charles, present President Barack Obama with a team jersey at the White House.

helped to create more opportunities for women to participate in a greater number and variety of sports, but it also created more opportunities for men to coach (see Figure 8.1) and administer women's teams. As athletic departments "took in" women's teams, more coaching and athletic director positions went to men. This step helped to create the structural problem of men in positions of greater power.

Before Title IX women's sports were largely governed for and by women. Since women were not provided equal rights they organized their own governing body, the Association for Intercollegiate Athletics for Woman (AIAW). The mission of this organization was similar to that of the male-dominated NCAA, but it differed in important ways (Wu, 1999). The AIAW sought to integrate athletics into the entire university experience. The spirit of the AIAW was guided by amateur ideals, not the commercialization and win-at-all-costs ethos favored by the NCAA. Universities sponsored by the AIAW implemented rules and adapted practices to meet these aims such as scholarship bans and preventing off-campus recruiting. Eventually, the NCAA was able to draw in AIAW members with its incentives to participate in their women's championship games. The AIAW closed its doors in 1983 as more members left for the NCAA. Although the NCAA had no interest in expanding women's sports before Title IX, male administrators likely saw this as an opportunity to increase their power and revenues.

Lastly, a social relations view would look at how gender and opportunities are influenced by relations of power and dominant norms. For example, a recent report demonstrates

a positive relationship between coaches and administrators who are men (Acosta & Carpenter, 2012). That is, universities that employ a man as the top administrator tend to hire more men as coaches. The opposite also holds true. That is, university athletic departments led by women employ more women coaches. Also of interest here would be the continued stereotyping of women coaches (and athletes) as lesbians or "butch," thus promoting a highly sensitive issue. Negative stereotyping through homophobia hurts women coaches as it becomes unattractive for parents to send their children off to play for this coach, athletes themselves may not want a LGBT coach, and university administrators could circumvent this issue by hiring a man (Mullins, 2008). Ultimately, the effect continues to marginalize women coaches.

ATHLETIC DIRECTOR: WOMEN WITH EXCEPTIONAL QUALIFICATIONS NEED ONLY APPLY

Women ascending to the position of athletic director overcome many barriers. To reach this achievement, women in particular had exceptional support and qualifications. Unlike many of their contemporary male peers, 85 percent of women athletic directors had been former collegiate athletes and 89 percent had been former coaches (Grappendorf, Lough, & Griffin, 2004; Teel, 2005;). The current North Carolina State athletic director, Deborah Yow, followed the coaching career path to her current position. Yow began her career as a high school basketball coach and transitioned into the collegiate ranks in 1976. With coaching stints at the University of Kentucky, Oral Roberts University, and the University of Florida, Yow made the switch to administration. Prior to Yow's first athletic director appointment at St. Louis University in 1989, she served as an athletic administrator at Florida and UNC Greensboro. After five years at St. Louis, Yow became the athletic director at the University of Maryland, and served in this capacity for sixteen years before returning to her native state of North Carolina. During her career, Yow served on numerous committees and wrote several scholarly articles and books. Yow's relentless efforts and accomplishments were recognized as an inductee into the North Carolina Sports Hall of Fame.

Women collegiate athletic leaders leave the workplace for a variety of reasons such as a conflict of values and a perceived lack of opportunity for advancement (Kamphoff, 2010). Researchers and sport stakeholders are interested in the experiences of successful women leaders in order to increase opportunities, reduce discrimination, and transform women's sports. Because of the popular belief that women are not as effective leaders as men, women often experience a hostile environment. In order to enter, persist, and succeed many women leaders have to be "superwomen." Research shows women coaches often experience a need to continuously prove themselves to overcome the burden of doubt (Norman, 2010).

Women athletic leaders employ a variety of strategies to help manage the workplace. For example, women coaches perceive a need to appear to be nonthreatening to their male peers. If women are perceived as a threat to male domination in coaching or the existing patriarchy, women may face negative repercussions. One strategy women use to manage gender relations is to ask top male coaches for advice (Norman, 2010). Secretly, women were not earnestly interested in the men's advice. Rather, the women saw this as an opportunity to stroke the egos of their male counterparts, which would help them pass as unthreatening.

Due to homophobia and heterosexism (the belief that only heterosexuality is normal), women athletic leaders often employ various sexuality management strategies. For example, some choose to "come out" while others hide their sexuality. Still, some coaches employ an ambiguous approach to sexuality by being open, but not out (Iannotta & Kane, 2002). These strategies have varying degrees of efficacy at the micro or day-to-day level for individuals or at the macro level to affect larger numbers of people or social movements.

To continue to further the advancement of women athletic leaders, women have identified several strategies they believe would help them enter and endure the workplace. These include greater coaching opportunities, mentoring, professional development, organizations to administer sports for women, competitive salaries, women role models, and workplace support (i.e., day care, ability to take children on road; Kamphoff, 2010; Kilty, 2006; Norman, 2008).

WHY THE LACK OF ETHNIC AND RACIAL MINORITY SPORT LEADERS?

"I don't know if it [race] will ever be a nonissue. But 25 years from now, I hope there are some other barriers broken down—a couple of national titles won by African-American head coaches," Jon Embree, Colorado head football coach (Miller, 2012).

Numerous factors have contributed to the struggle facing ethnic and racial minorities to enter and advance in leadership positions. A minority is "a socially identified population that suffers disadvantages due to systematic discrimination and has a strong sense of social togetherness based on shared experiences of past and current discrimination" (Coakley, 2009, p. 276). While race and ethnicity are often used synonymously, race has more socially constructed meanings and the latter is based on cultural traditions. For the purpose of this section, ethnic and racial minorities refer to historically marginalized

and 16 percent by a minority head coach (Lapchick, 2011).

Currently, one of the most significant issues regarding ethnicity, race, and coaching is the under-representation of minority coaches. In 2010, African Americans accounted for 45.8 percent of all Division I football players, while whites made up 45.1 percent (Lapchick, Hoff, & Kaiser, 2011). In the same year, African Americans accounted for an even greater percentage

"The Bench" © Shane Adams, (CC BY 2.0) at http://www.flickr.com/photos/ishane/2037631504.

Figure 8.2. From the looks of the Kansas basketball bench, the majority of student-athletes is opposite of the majority of the coaching staff.

groups of people that have experienced disadvantages and discrimination due to shared experiences and qualities. Regarding ethnicity and race, equality in collegiate athletic participation has risen (Zgonc, 2010); however, this growth has been overshadowed by the stagnant representation of minorities in leadership positions (Lapchick, 2011; Irick, 2010). Of all FBS institutions during the 2010 athletic season, only 11.8 percent were led by an ethnic or racial minority athletic director

of all men's basketball players (60.9 percent), while whites made up 30.5 percent. Although minorities are well represented in these highly visible sports, notably absent are minority coaches (see Figure 8.2). During this time there were only twenty-eight ethnic minority head football coaches in Division I. Across all NCAA divisions, minority coaches, in particular African American coaches, are not well represented (see Table 3), especially considering African

Table 3. 2009–2010 Percentages of Head Coaches by Race by Sex by Division

	D-I	D-II	D-III
White Head Coaches of Men's Teams	89.3%	89.2%	92.3%
African American Head Coaches of Men's Teams	6.6%	4.8%	3.7%
White Head Coaches of Women's Teams	87.7%	89.5%	91.9%
African American Head Coaches of Women's Teams	7.2%	4.8%	3.9%

Table 4. 2009–2010 Percentages of Assistant Coaches by Race by Sex by Division

	D-I	D-II	D-III
White Assistant Coaches of Men's Teams	76.8%	79.5%	87.3%
African American Assistant Coaches of Men's Teams	18.1%	13.3%	8.1%
White Assistant Coaches of Women's Teams	78.8%	81.8%	88.9%
African American Assistant Coaches of Women's Teams	14.2%	9.7%	5.9%

American athletes comprise nearly half of all football players and more than half of all men's basketball players.

Division I men's basketball had the most diversity among head coaches throughout all sports. In 2008–2009, 21 percent of all men's basketball head coaches were African American. All other sports such as softball, baseball, and soccer have a lower representation from minority groups. The under-representation of minorities is not confined to men's teams. Table 3 depicts a significant difference favoring the representation of white head coaches of women's teams.

The difference in representation of assistant coaches by race is less, but still considerable. Table 4 shows the percentage of assistant coaches by race and sex of team across all NCAA divisions. While White assistant coaches of men's and women's teams still decidedly outnumber African American, the difference is not as severe as the head coach position.

CUNNINGHAM'S MODEL OF UNDER-REPRESENTATION OF RACIAL MINORITIES IN COACHING POSITIONS

Under-represented leaders have subtly, yet assuredly, experienced discrimination during the hiring process and on the job (Acosta & Carpenter, 2012; Lopiano, 2001; Messner, 2002). According to Fink and her colleagues (2001), individuals who differentiate from the Protestant, White, heterosexual, able-bodied majority may face discriminatory practices. Greenhaus, Parasuraman, and Wormley (1990) have categorized discrimination into two forms: access and treatment. Discrimination may occur prior to one's entrance into a workplace (e.g., access discrimination) or after one's hiring by an organization (e.g., treatment discrimination; Greenhaus et al., 1990). Cunningham's (2007) model of under-represented racial minorities in coaching positions draws upon the role access discrimination and treatment discrimination play in athletic leadership positions. Although Cunningham (2007) focused on coaching positions, it appears likely racial minorities in other athletic leadership positions experienced similar forms of discrimination. Therefore, for the purposes of this section we apply Cunningham's (2007) model and other research to athletic leaders in general.

ACCESS DISCRIMINATION

When an individual of a specific social category is limited to entering a profession it is known as access discrimination (Greenhaus et al., 1990; Terborg & Ilgen, 1975). Cunningham (2007) identified four ways (i.e., racial bias, historical precedent, donor/alumni expectations, and social network) racial minorities experience access treatment. Racial bias is either overt (i.e., intentional) or subtle racism. For example, ethnic and racial minorities may receive lower starting salaries or fail to be recruited (Terborg & Ilgen, 1975). Even after obtaining exceptional qualifications through professional athletics or the business sector (Farrell, 1999; Naughton, 1998), ethnic and racial minorities have been known to "work the ranch, but they cannot run it" (Burdman, 2002, p. 24). Historical precedent refers to the history of minorities being passed over for leadership positions. Since athletic leaders have normally always been White, hiring a minority would be considered outside the norm and thus a historical precedent.

HIRE ME: I'M OVER QUALIFIED AND A MINORITY

Let's look at the current head football coach at the University of Louisville, Charlie Strong, as an example of overcoming racial bias and historical precedent. Strong, an African-American man, was repeatedly passed over for head-coaching positions in spite of impressive accomplishments, including: twenty-seven years as a coach, the first African-American defensive coordinator in the SEC (in 1999 for South Carolina), and helpintoguide Florida's defense to two national championships in 2006 and 2008. Another factor probably working against Strong was his marriage to awWhite woman. Strong's appointment at Louisville may demonstrate overcoming the racial bias and historical precedent of being an African-American man and an interracial marriage.

Within the world of collegiate sports, donors and alumni are thought to influence, if not outright dictate, decision making (Myles, 2005). If donors give millions of dollars they may also want to have a say in who gets hired and who does not. For example, donor John Burton demanded the University of Connecticut return his $3 million "gift" because he was not consulted when a new head football coach was hired (Sander, 2011b). If universities take a donor's money they may also be inclined to look the other way should the donor harbor any biases towards minorities. Interestingly, in a 2006 ESPN article on the most powerful boosters in collegiate sport, of the ten names listed all were White and nine were men (Fish, 2006).

Also, the influence of social networks has hindered ethnic and racial minorities' advancement to leadership positions. Naughton (1998) revealed ethnic and racial minorities have less exposure to the affluent social network associated with athletic leaders. Myles (2005) and anecdotal evidence suggests many athletic directors or hiring committees have a particular coach in mind should an opening occur. As one assistant athletic director at a big-time university told the author (Brian), "You don't fire a head coach without having the next coach already on board." In some cases this practice results in coaches being hired in extremely short time frames such as one or two days, thus limiting the possibility of a fairer search process.

TREATMENT DISCRIMINATION

Treatment discrimination occurs when a member of a subgroup receives fewer resources, rewards, or opportunities within a job (Greenhaus et al., 1990). This unfair treatment stems from their social category, rather than their work performance. Cunningham's (2007) model identifies that treatment discrimination and limited advanced opportunities leds to greater occupational turnover, which leads to a limited pool of racial minority applicants and ultimately causes an under-representation of racial minority athletic leaders.

African-American coaches report experiencing discrimination on staffs led by White head coaches (Cunningham & Sagas, 2005; Hamilton, 1997). Cunningham and Sagas (2005) revealed White head coaches hired more White assistant coaches, and vice versa for their African-American counterparts. Furthermore, the results of Cunningham and Sagas' (2005) study indicated a significantly higher proportion of potential African-American assistant coaches (48 percent), than the proportion currently holding the position (33 percent). Hamilton's (1997) study of professional basketball players' salaries determined differences in salary distribution by race. At the higher end

of salary distribution, African American's received lower premiums than Whites, while at the lower end of the distribution, African American's received higher premiums than Whites. Each of these studies is an example of treatment discrimination in athletics.

While access and treatment discrimination may aid in the explanation of under-represented leaders in coaching and administration, discriminate hiring or promoting practices, political constraints, societal attitudes, stereotypes, and harmful ideologies have also limited career opportunities (Abney & Richey, 1991; Coakley, 2009; Teel, 2005). Myles (2005) and Moore (2002) also assent discrimination combined with positional segregation, tokenism, cultural deprivation, and a lack of mentors have hindered the advancement under-represented leaders.

HIRING PROCESS

"History has proven that hiring is about relationships" (Floyd Keith, Executive Director of the Black Coaches Association (Lapchick, Jackson, & Lilly, 2010).

To reduce access and treatment discrimination, it is important for athletic organizations to conduct due diligence early in the hiring process. Organizations participate in a hiring process when they recruit and select qualified individuals for positions. Chelladurai (2006) describes hiring as "the process of selecting a person from the pool of qualified applicants gathered during the recruiting process" (p.170). In collegiate athletics the recruiting process may include a multitude of factors such as professional society advertisements, job fairs, referrals, or headhunters. The lack of visibility and representation of these outlets causes

Table 5. 2011 Top Ten Highest Paid Athletic Directors

Rank	School Name	AD Name	Conference	Annualized Salary
1	Vanderbilt	David Williams, II*	SEC	$2,560,505
2	Florida	Jeremy Foley	SEC	$1,545,250
3	Louisville	Tom Jurich	Big East	$1,422,204
4	Texas	DeLoss Dodd	Big 12	$1,093,391
5	Ohio State	Gene Smith	Big 10	$1,074,546
6	Wisconsin	Barry Alvarez	Big 10	$1,000,000
7	Oklahoma	Joe Castiglione	Big 12	$975,000
8	Notre Dame	Jack Swarbrick	Independent	$932,232
9	Tennessee	Dave Hart Jr.	SEC	$750,000
10	LSU	Joe Alleva	SEC	$725,000

* Vice chancellor for university affairs and athletics

Source: *USA Today* (Steve Berkowitz and Jodi Upton of USA TODAY, and Robert Lattinville and Caitlin Ahearn of Stinson Morrison Hecker).

Note: Top 10 AD salaries complied from open record database.

under-represented individuals to suffer systematic discrimination throughout the recruitment and selection process (Shrosphire, 1996).

The hiring process in sport is complicated by the organizational fit and individual knowledge, skills, and abilities (Chelladurai, 2006; Mathis & Jackson, 2006). While the job announcement references the individual job fit, it may not address the individual organization fit, which includes values, attitudes, and culture (Chelladurai, 2006). Schein (1985) contends "organizations tend to find attractive those candidates who resemble present members in style, assumptions, values, and beliefs" (p. 235), which welcomes hiring managers to consider the use of other resources such as references and interviews, allowing personal judgments and biases to enter the hiring process. Chelladurai (2006) cautions decision makers—e.g. search committees

members, presidents, chancellors, administrators, as well as the outspoken influence of financial donors and alumni, on this subjective portion of the hiring process because of personal biases.

Singer, Harrison, and Bukstein (2010) also argue this subjectivity does not allow equal access in the hiring network. Historically private networks such as the "good ol' boys' network" have controlled the hierarchical structure of athletics. In the sport context, th "good ol' boys'"refers to a social network controlled by White males who inhibit the access of under-represented individuals to positions that historically have been held by White males (Myles, 2005; Shropshire, 1996). Since the majority of hiring decision makers (i.e., athletic directors, university presidents) that hire athletic administrators and coaches are White males (Lapchick, 2011), the power of these informal structures has probably limited the progression of under-represented individuals (Mainiero, 1986).

Michael and Yukl (1993) demonstrate the importance of networking through a managers' success rate. Therefore, under-represented individuals must make constructive efforts to expand their social network. Diversity initiative—(i.e., Black Coaches Association [BCA], NCAA Leadership Institute, and the NCAA Pathway Program) on the national level may assist with this expansion. Despite recent and optimistic hires, a need exists to continuously scrutinize hiring practices to reduce discrimination and highlight the progression of under-represented individuals to leadership positions.

COMPENSATION

"The hell with gold. I want to buy futures in coaches' contracts," Sheldon Steinbach, Higher Education lawyer (Brady, Upton, & Berkowitz, 2011).

Another serious issue in collegiate athletics is the illustrious compensation packages administrators and coaches receive. For example, the University of Alabama's head football coach, Nick Saban, recently received a contract extension through 2019 guaranteeing him an average of $5.62 million per year (Nick, 2012). The University of Mississippi, in a desperate attempt to win more SEC contests, will pay new head football coach Hugh Freeze a reported $100,000 bonus for each conference victory (Hugh, 2012). As most athletic departments lose money, often millions, the calls for fiscal responsibility have become louder. Coaches' exorbitant salaries appear to be more indicative of the entertainment industry rather than publically funded and tax-exempt educational institutions.

Since many universities charge all students a fee to support athletics, many question who really benefits from this arrangement. Adding complexity to the issue of compensation is the inequity in pay between men's and women's teams, and differences among men and women coaches.

Recently, administrators' salaries have been on a rise, pushing the market-bearing rates. For example, in 2007, following three national championships, University of Florida's Athletic Director, Jeremy Foley, became the highest paid athletic director in the nation. With notable hires under his leadership, such as head men's basketball coach Billy Donovan, and former head football coah, Urban Meyer, who now resides as the head football coach at Ohio State University (OSU), Foley agreed to an eleven-year contract worth up to $1.2 million annually. Five years after this ceiling breaker several athletic directors now earn more than $1 million in compensation. As depicted in Table 5, note that the top ten highest paid Division I FBS athletic directors are males.

RECENT CONTROVERSY SPOTLIGHT

Scapegoat: The coach or the athletic director

Five years following the historical hire of the first African American athletic director at the University of Central Florida, UCF Athletic Director Keith Tribble resigned his post during the 2011 athletic season amid an NCAA investigation of recruiting practices. As the athletic director Tribble garnered national attention by growing the athletic department and overseeing $150 million in athletic facility upgrades, building a new football stadium, and positioning UCF for conference realignment. Regardless of these highlights, Tribble's departure became overshadowed by the NCAA's investigation. According to Auerbach's *USA TODAY* (2011) report, Tribble "violated principles of ethical conduct when he knowingly (a) attempted to provide an improper inducement to the mother of a prospective student-athlete and (b) provided false and misleading information to the institution and enforcement staff" (p. 1).

Athletic directors are not always the scapegoat for an athletic department, as was the case at Ohio State University in 2011. Longtime coach and ten-year OSU veteran Jim Tressel "resigned" in May, while OSU Athletic Director Gene Smith retained his position. Per Tressel's contract and NCAA compliance rules, he was to notify the athletic compliance department of potential violations, and he failed to do after being informed of several football student-athletes' NCAA infractions. These two examples display the need for integrity as the NCAA and universities try to protect their image and the so-called amateurism status of their student-athletes.

As noted earlier, women coaches on average make less than their men counterparts, even when they coach the same sport (e.g., basketball, tennis, or golf). Also, coaches of men's teams tend to earn more than those who coach women's teams. That is, a coach, regardless of sex, of a men's team would likely receive a higher salary than coaching a similar women's team. Table 6 illustrates the trend of lower pay for women's teams within the same sport.

The gap in coaching compensation for the same sport seems to be a clear indicator of inequality. This income gap suggests several universities may not be in compliance with

federal equal employment opportunity laws under Title VII of the Civil Rights Act of 1964. If coaches are doing equal work, it would be unlawful for universities to compensate them differently. Differential pay is lawful, however, if it is based on: "(i) a seniority system; (ii) a merit system; (iii) a system that measures earnings by quantity or quality of production; (iv) a differential based on any other factor other than sex" (USEEOC). While this legal issue will continue to be played out in the courts, what else does this say about equality and democracy within the purportedly sacred institution of higher education? Has higher education "sold its soul" for profit?

The income gap may also result in women athletes receiving a lower-quality coach. If higher salaries are offered for coaching men's teams, then there probably will be a greater number of qualified applicants for these positions. Also, research in sports coaching demonstrates that a coach's years of experience and the strength of the coach-athlete relationship are key determinants in the quality of an athlete's overall experience

Table 6. 2010 FBS head coaches' median compensation of a sample of sports by gender.

	Men	Women
Baseball/Softball	$189,000	$115,000
Gymnastics	$100,000	$108,000
Ice Hockey	$332,000	$152,000
Soccer	$123,000	$112,000
Tennis	$104,000	$83,000
Track	$76,000	$79,000
Volleyball	$134,000	$129,000

Note: Data retrieved from the Equity in Athletics Data Analysis.

(NASPE, 2006). If coaches are unable to gain experience or there is frequent turnover, then coaches may be less effective.

THE ONE PERCENT: HIGHEST-PAID COACHES

"We've long gone past anything that's reasonable. If you put too much value on a program, it starts to swallow the university. It starts to guide the moral compass. Soon, a coach is going to make $10 million a year. There's just no stopping it," David Ridpath, Ohio University sports-management professor and member of the reform-oriented Drake Group (Arace, 2012).

Collegiate coaches, particularly winning coaches, have long reaped great financial benefits. For example, in the late 1800s and early 1900s it was not uncommon for crew and football coaches to earn more coaching part time than professors working full time (Smith, 1988). The interest in coaches' salaries and benefits has become one of the most highly publicized and hotly contested issues, in large part because of its rapid growth and exorbitance. *USA TODAY's* publications on coaching salaries annually garner much attention. Precise determinations of a coach's total compensation is challenging because funds may come from multiple sources (e.g., university, sponsors, or bonuses), and private universities are not legally required to provide this information.

Understanding compensation requires an analysis of institutional and noninstitutional factors. Institutional compensation includes—and may not be limited to—a base salary that is guaranteed by the university or its affiliates (i.e., foundation), memberships, expense accounts, housing and spouse/family allowance,

appearances, as well as bonuses for on-field and off-the-field performance goals (e.g., postseason appearances, number of wins, accolades, academic performance, or attendance sales). Noninstitutional compensation is income received from a source other than the institution. This type of compensation may include endorsement contracts or separate booster organizations. Together, these two categories of compensation provide a lucrative "package" for administrators and coaches.

As of 2012, the average salary of a NCAA FBS head football coach was $1.5 million (Berkowitz & Upton, 2012). At large, high-revenue universities it is commonplace for coaches to make $2 million to $3 million per year. For example, in 2011 Mack Brown, the head football coach at the University of Texas at Austin, made $5.19 million a year, Nick Saban at Alabama made $4.68 million, and Bob Stoops at Oklahoma took in $4.075 million. Even at universities with smaller revenues and lower enrollments, coaches are handsomely compensated, such as Boise State's Chris Petersen who made $1.53 million and June Jones at Southern Methodist who pulled in $1.7 million. Clearly, universities are willing to pay millions to win.

The immense salaries are not exclusive to football. The highest paid head men's basketball coach in 2011 was Louisville's Rick Pitino, who pulled in nearly $8 million (Berkowitz & Upton, 2012). Other coaches also fared well. Duke's Mike Krzyzewski made nearly $4.2 million, and Kentucky's John Calipari was paid just over $4.75 million. As for coaches at smaller, lower-revenue generating schools, Mark Few at Gonzaga made a mere $900,000 and George Mason's Jim Larranga earned a paltry $700,000.

Although not equal to their male counterparts, women's basketball coaches also receive top dollar. For example, in 2011 Pat Summitt, the longtime head coach at Tennessee, made more than $2 million, while rival Geno Auriemma (see Figure 8.1) at Connecticut received $1.6 million from the institution alone, not including noninstitutional compensation from sponsors such as Nike (Berkowitz & Upton, 2012). Many of the head women's basketball coaches who have consistently made the NCAA tournament earned more than $500,000.

While much attention has been given to the highest salaries, many more collegiate coaches do not earn nearly as much. For example, the 2010 median salary of FCS head coaches for men's programs varied dramatically across sports. For example: rifle, $6,000; skiing, $57,000; tennis, $29,000; soccer, $80,000; baseball, $83,000; and lacrosse, $115,000. The 2010 median salary of FCS assistant coaches for the same sports also varied: rifle (no assistants reported); skiing, $16,000; tennis (no assistants reported); soccer, $43,000; baseball, $60,000; and lacrosse, $76,000 (Fulks, 2011).

Salary ranges can greatly vary as some nonrevenue sports such as baseball or softball have head coaches making between $100,000 to $1 million (Fulks, 2011; Haurwitz, 2008). In general, coaches' salaries rise in relation to the athletic department's revenues and competitive level. That is, since both University of Texas Austin and Ohio State University generate a tremendous amount of revenue they also tend to be on the highest end for all coaches' salaries. Coaches' salaries also demonstrate a downward trend as competitive level decreases. That is, coaches at the FCS (Division I without football), Division II, and Division III earn much less than their FBS peers.

Assistant coaches and support staff (e.g., athletic trainers, operations directors,

strength and conditioning coaches,) salaries can also wildly vary. For example, when Lane Kiffin was hired in 2010 as the head football coach for the University of Tennessee he hired his father, Monte Kiffin, as the defensive coordinator for $1 million. It is now not uncommon for football offensive and defensive coordinators to make well into the six-figure range. Many Division I strength and conditioning coaches also now earn more than $150,000 (Forde, 2010). Still, assistant coaches for lower-revenue generating sports may earn as little as $25,000 to $40,000. With much research and commentary focusing on higher-end salaries, one might incorrectly assume that all collegiate coaches are multimillionaires.

Naturally, there are multiple ways to interpret coaches' salaries. Among the multiple reactions, the most common may range from jealousy to bewilderment to anger. Some may believe that big-time collegiate athletics and their accompanying big-time salaries are a distraction from the university's central mission and that people (coaches) are being heavily rewarded but do little to advance the mission of the university. The question of collegiate athletics' educational value could be raised: "Why does an institution of higher learning overwhelmingly support athletics, particularly at the expense of other, possibly more aligned, educational endeavors?" While coaches have long been paid on par with university faculty members and administrators, the highest paid coaching salaries are now often ten to one hundred times more than the average salary of a university professor, or even the president. Have sport coaches and staff suddenly become much more valuable in today's society?

Another reading would acknowledge that the increase in salaries has less to do with coaches per se and more to do with the overall economics of collegiate sport. As collegiate athletics has turned into a billion-dollar industry, those who have benefitted the most are arguably its leaders. As the history of collegiate sport informs us, university athletic departments and their supporters are willing to pay the price for coaches whom they believe will deliver victory.

Fueling the controversy and disdain for high coaching salaries are significant financial losses. Despite the hoopla surrounding billion-dollar television contracts and millions of people attending games, nearly all athletic programs—at all levels—lose money (i.e., in the red). Although educational institutions are classified as a "nonprofit" and should technically not be making money, most athletic department expenses significantly exceed revenue. Pinpointing revenues and expenses is made difficult since universities do not share a standard reporting procedure. For example, some universities count donations made to the athletic department or its foundation as revenue. According to the NCAA's 2008 revenue report, only twenty-five FBS programs showed a profit or net revenue. In addition, only eighteen programs reported a profit for all years from 2004–2008. Athletic programs would lose significantly more if not for the nearly $800 million in student fees and university subsidies "propping up athletic programs" (Gilum, Upton, & Berkowitz, 2010). Many university faculty groups and other advocacy groups have denounced the increased expenses, especially as students continue to shoulder the burden of rising tuition and room and board costs.

Lastly, the rise in coaching salaries and the accompanying expectation to win have been blamed for contributing to moral violations. The most recent case of this could be the sexual abuse allegations at Penn State. Numerous football coaches and administrators (academic and athletic) could have been influenced to cover-up the allegations at Penn State in an effort to protect their hefty salaries and maintain the university's image. With recent major scandals rocking multiple big-time universities such as Miami, North Carolina, and OSU, that coaches will break the rules to win and profit no longer seems mere speculation, but rather overwhelmingly evident. Among other likely, but less publicized, moral violations would be physical or verbal abuse of players, lying to athletes regarding choice of academic major, and the use of coercion to obtain any number of questionable ends.

DIVERSITY INITIATIVES

On a national level the NCAA has recently been more active in establishing initiatives to promote diversification. In 2001 the NCAA Leadership Institute for Ethnic Minority Males was created (NCAA, 2011a). As noted, the original intent was to increase diversity, yet it excluded ethnic and racial minority women. Consequently, the first NCAA Leadership Institute for Ethnic Minority Males and Females was held in 2006.

The purpose of the NCAA Leadership Institute for Ethnic Minority Males and Females is to provide leadership training to ethnic and racial minorities in athletic administration (NCAA, 2011a). Candidates must apply to attend the NCAA Leadership Institute, and then be selected by the NCAA Minority Opportunities and Interest Committee (MOIC) to participate in a week-long workshop led by respected leaders from all sectors of higher education (NCAA,

2011a.). The extensive leadership training prepares under-represented individuals for athletic administrative positions at any level (e.g., conference, institutional, and national; NCAA, 2011a.).

In 2007 the NCAA continued to create opportunities for under-represented leaders by implementing the NCAA Pathway Program. Formerly known as the Fellows Leadership Development Program, the NCAA Pathway Program provides services to senior athletic administrators with the intention to become an athletic director (NCAA, 2011b). These initiatives are instrumental to the NCAA's commitment to diversity and evolving organizational behavior (Schneider & Allison, 2000). Since the inception of the institute, ethnic and racial representation at the Division I senior athletic administration and athletic director positions have seen a rise of 8 percent and 2 percent, respectively (Irick, 2010).

In addition to the NCAA, the BCA has initiated awareness for the advancement of under-represented individuals. The BCA annually publishes a black coaches and administrators hiring "report card" that includes the following four measures: communication between the university and the BCA, composition of the search committee, time frame, and final candidates. The decision to include the time frame or duration of the search assumes that an increased search time would allow more qualified (minority) coaches to apply and interview. The more recent practice of hiring a "coach-in-waiting" has interesting implications for discrimination and the efficacy of hiring practices. The BCA and others also support a proposal called the "Robinson Rule," named after former long-time Grambling State head football coach and African-American Eddie Robinson. Similar to the NFL's "Rooney Rule" that requires

consideration of minority candidates for leadership positions at the expense of heavy fines and sanctions, the Robinson Rule would expect universities to do the same.

COACH PREPARATION AND EDUCATION: THE NEXT BIG ISSUE?

There are several reasons why the education and preparation of collegiate coaches may be the next big issue and controversy (Gearity & Denison, in press). Indeed, how many of the issues and controversies throughout this text could be addressed, if not wholly resolved, by having highly qualified coaches? Evidence is mounting of coaches' moral failings, blatant disregard for NCAA rules, and negative testimony from collegiate athletes. Most professions would think their system dysfunctional if their primary recourse to manage its human resources (i.e., coaches) was through disciplinary actions (i.e., suspension, termination). Would it not be more useful to rigorously prepare and then regulate coaches through education and policy? For far too long the sole criterion of effective coaching has been a winning percentage.

Let's take a look at two recent statements made by collegiate coaches as examples of a need for greater knowledge and preparation. In light of the allegations of abuse at Penn State, former head football coach Joseph Paterno stated, "This is a tragedy. It is one of the great sorrows of my life. With the benefit of hindsight, I wish I had done more" (Press, 2011, para. 11). Although not as severe, the current men's basketball coach at Iowa made these comments regarding Jarrod Uthoff, a player on the team who had requested permission to transfer: "I don't know how to deal with transfers like some guys who do it a heck of a lot more often" (Ryan, 2012, para. 5). A highly trained educator should easily be able to handle these simple events (e.g., child abuse and transfer). Taken at face value, these statements speak to a coach's lack of preparation and critical reflection.

Can we educate coaches? England and Canada are making national efforts to improve the rigors and requirements to coach at all levels. By extension, the scholarly research and literature on the science of coaching is rapidly expanding. Sport and physical cultural studies scholars in the United States are adding to this body of knowledge. The National Council for Accreditation of Coaching Education already has accredited a small group of universities and organizations. The National Association for Sport and Physical Education is on its second edition of national standards for quality coaches. Still, collegiate coaches do not currently need to graduate from one of these programs prior to obtaining full-time employment.

It is often taken for granted that coaches need extensive knowledge and training to facilitate athletic performance and to make good, moral decisions. Furthermore, recognizing the social and moral issues of coaching is paramount to the relationship between athletics and higher education. Coach education is thus a reasonable course of action to help provide coaches with the knowledge and critical thinking skills necessary for such a complex job. It is only a matter of time, perhaps a long time however, before this knowledge makes its way to influence policy and public opinion.

CONCLUSION

Since athletic leaders are imperative for the success of the organization, it is important to make ethical and educated hiring decisions. These leaders will not only create a vision for the student-athletes and staff (Robbins, 2003), but their decisions affect entire communities. The content in this chapter focused on three major issues and controversies within NCAA Division I athletics: a) equitable leadership representation, b) hiring processes, and c) compensation.

While men, especially White men, have dominated athletics (Anderson, 2009), time is needed to change the landscape. According to Coakley's (2001) decade-old statement, "job equality in most sport organizations will not come until today's twenty-year-olds are grandparents" (p. 219). Once these ideologies evolve, biases and norms can also change and allow under-represented individuals equal representation in leadership positions.

One institution currently resisting the win-at-all-cost mentality is Northwestern University (NU). After missing the NCAA men's basketball postseason tournament for twelve seasons, NU Athletic Director Dr. Jim Phillips chose to stay true to the school's principles and extended head coach Bill Carmody's contract (Haugh, 2012). Will NU's uncharacteristic move start a revolution, or will we continue down the path of economic gain and ethical loss?

WEBSITE RESOURCES

http://www2.indystar.com/NCAA_financial_reports/ A public database of athletic department financial statements.

http://www.usatoday.com/sports/graphics/basketball_contracts/flash.htm A 2006 compensation database of NCAA tournament men's basketball coaching contracts.

http://ope.ed.gov/athletics/EADA The Equity and Athletic Data Analysis provides custom reports for public inquiry in relation to equity in athletic data.

REFERENCES

Abney, R., and D.L. Richey. (1991). Barriers encountered by Black female athletic administrators and coaches. *Journal of Physical Education, Recreation, and Dance* 62(6), 19–21.

Acosta, R. V., and L.J. Carpenter. (2012). *Women in intercollegiate sport: A longitudinal, national study, thirty-five year update—1977–2012.* Unpublished manuscript. Available for downloading at www.acostacarpenter.org

Anderson, E. D. (2009). The maintenance of masculinity among the stakeholders of sport. *Sport Management Review* 12, 3–14.

Auerbach, N. (2011, November 9). Keith Tribble resigns amid UCF's NCAA investigation. *USA TODAY.* Retrieved from http://content.usatoday.com/communities/campusrivalry/post/2011/11/keith-tribble-resigns-amid-ucfs-ncaa-investigation/1#.T3kRcSO5J_8

Berkowitz, S., and J. Upton. (2012). *USA TODAY college football coach salary database, 2006–2011.* Retrieved February 7, 2012, from http://www.usatoday.com/sports/college/football/story/2011-11-17/cover-college-football-coaches-salaries-rise/51242232/1

Borzi, P.,(2012), "Number of women coaching in college hockey dwindling," Retrieved March 26, 2012, from http://www.nytimes.com/2012/03/18/sports/in-college-hockey-female-coaches-often-skate-away-from-demands-of-the-job.html?_r=1&pagewanted=all

Burdman, P. (2002). Old problem, new solution? Can programs such as the NCAA's leadership institute for ethnic minority males boost the numbers of Black head coaches, athletic directors? *Black Issues in Higher Education* 19(4), 24–28.

Burton, L., C.A. Barr, J. S. Fink, and J.E. Bruening. (2009). Think athletic director, think masculine? Examination of the gender typing of managerial subroles within athletic administration positions. *Sex Roles* 61, 416–426.

Brady, E., J. Upton, and S. Berkowitz, (2011), "Salaries for college football coaches back on rise," Retrieved March 22, 2012, from http://www.usatoday.com/sports/college/football/story/2011-11-17/cover-college-football-coaches-salaries-rise/51242232/1

Cahn, S. K. (1994). *Coming on strong: Gender and sexuality in twentieth century women's sport.* New York, NY: Free Press.

Chelladurai, P. (2006). *Human resource management in sport and recreation (2nd ed.).* Champaign, IL: Human Kinetics.

Clausen, C. L., and C. Lehr. (2002). Decision-making authority of senior woman administrators. *International Journal of Sport Management* 3(3), 215–228.

Coakley, J. (2001). *Sports in society: Issues and controversies (7th ed.).* Boston, MA: McGraw Hill.

Coakley, J. (2009). *Sports in society: Issues and controversies (10th ed.)*. Boston, MA: McGraw Hill.

Cunningham, G. B. (2007). *Diversity in sport organizations*. Scottsdale, AZ: Holcomb Hathaway.

Cunningham, G. B., and M. Sagas. (2005). Access discrimination in intercollegiate athletics. *Journal of Sport and Social Issues* 29, 148–163.

Embry, A., M.Y. Padgett, and C.B. Caldwell. (2008). Can leaders step outside the box? An examination of leadership and gender role stereotypes. *Journal of Leadership and Organizational Studies* 15, 30–45.

Equal Employment Opportunity Commission, (2009), "The U.S. Equal Employment Opportunity Commission: 2009 Job Patterns for Minorities and Women in Private Industry (EEO-1)," Retrieved January 17, 2012, from http://www.eeoc.gov/federal/reports/index.cfm.

Everhart, C. B., and P. Chelladurai. (1998). Gender differences in preferences for coaching as an occupation: The role of self-efficacy, valence, and perceived barriers. *Research Quarterly for Exercise and Sport* 69, 188–200.

Farrell, C. S. (1999). Black coaches convention focuses on job-hunting strategies: Collegiate athletic directors, sensitized to concerns, participate in interview clinics. *Black Issues in Higher Education* 14, 25–28.

Fink, J. S., D.L. Pastore, and H.A. Riemer. (2001). Do differences make a difference? Managing diversity in Division IA intercollegiate athletics. *Journal of Sport Management* 15, 10–50.

Fish, M., (2006), "Most powerful boosters," Retrieved March 26, 2006, from http://sports.espn.go.com/ncf/news/story?id=2285986

Forde, P., (2010), "Strength coaches doing heavy lifting," Retrieved February 8, 2012, from http://sports.espn.go.com/ncf/columns/story?columnist=forde_pat&id=5310210

Fulks, D. L. (2011). *2004–10 revenues and expenses: NCAA division I intercollegiate athletics programs report*. Indianapolis, IN: The National Collegiate Athletic Association.

Gardner, D. E., D.L.L. Shields, B.J.L.Bredemeier, and A. Bostrom. (1996). The relationship between perceived coaching behaviors and team cohesion among baseball and softball players. *Sport Psychologist* 10, 367–381.

Gearity, B. T. and J. Denison, (in press). Coach-educator as stranger. *Cultural Studies, Critical Methodologies*.

Gillum, J., J. Upton, and S. Berkowitz, (2010). "Amid funding crisis, college athletics soak up subsidies, fees," Retrieved February 8, 2012, from http://www.usatoday.com/sports/college/2010-01-13-ncaa-athletics-funding-analysis_N.htm

Grappendorf, H., and N. Lough. (2006). An endangered species: Characteristics and perspectives from female NCAA Division I athletic directors of both separate and merged athletic departments. *The Sport Management and Related Topics Journal* 2(2), 6–20.

Grappendorf, H., Pent, A., Burton, L., and A. Henderson. (2008). Gender role Stereotyping: A qualitative analysis of senior woman administrators' perceptions regarding financial decision making. *Journal of Issues in Intercollegiate Athletics* 1, 26–45.

Greenhaus, J. H., S. Parasuraman, and W. M. Wormley. (1990). Effects of race on organizational experiences, job performance, evaluations, and career outcomes. *Academy of Management Journal,* 33, 64–86.

Hamilton, P. (1997). Taking advantage of the Internet in sport. *Sport Coach* 20(1), 24–26.

Haugh, D. (2012, March 24). In keeping Carmody, NU did wrong thing for right reason. *Chicago Tribune*. Retrieved from http://articles.chicagotribune.com/2012-03-24/sports/ct-spt-0325-haugh-northwestern-basketball--20120325_1_northwestern-athletic-director-jim-phillips-shaka-smart

Haurwitz, R., (2008), "Garrido to make a million—someday—under new salary package," Retrieved February 8, 2012, from http://www.statesman.com/blogs/content/shared-gen/blogs/austin/longhorns/entries/2008/11/13/garrido_to_make.html

"Hugh Freeze gets bonus for sec wins,"(2012), Retrieved March 26, 2012, from http://espn.go.com/college-football/story/_/id/7434101/mississippi-hugh-freeze-earns-100k-sec-win

Iannotta, J. G., and M.J. Kane. (2002). Sexual stories as resistance narratives in women's sports: Reconceptualizing identity performance. *Sociology of Sport Journal* 19, 347–369.

Inglis, S., K.E. Danylchuk, and D.L. Pastore. (2000). Multiple realities of women's work experiences in coaching and athletic management. *Women in Sport and Physical Activity Journal* 9(2), 1–14.

Irick, E. (2010). *2009–2010 NCAA race and gender demographics*. Indianapolis, IN: The National Collegiate Athletic Association.

Kamphoff, C. S. (2010). Bargaining with patriarchy: Former female coaches' experiences and their decision to leave collegiate coaching. *Research Quarterly for Exercise and Sport* 81(3), 360–372.

Kellerman, B., and D.L. Rhode. (2007). *Women and leadership: The state of play and strategies for change*. San Francisco: Jossey Bass.

Kilty, K. (2006). Women in coaching. *The Sport Psychologist* 20, 222–234.

Knoppers, A., B. B. Meyer, M. Ewing, and L. Forrest. (1991). Opportunity and work behavior in college coaching. *Journal of Sport and Social Issues* 15, 1–20.

Knoppers, A. (1992). Explaining male dominance and sex segregation in coaching: Three approaches. *Quest* 44, 210–227.

Kozlowski, S. W. J., and D.R. Ilgen. (2006). Enhancing the effectiveness of work groups and teams. *Psychological Science in the Public Interest* 7, 77–124

Lapchick, R., (2011), "The 2010 racial and gender report car: College sport," Retrieved February 3, 2012, from http://web.bus.ucf.edu/sportbusiness/?page=1445

Lapchick, R., B. Hoff, and C. Kaiser. (2011). The 2010 Racial and Gender Report Card: College Sport. *The Institute for Diversity and Ethics in Sport (TIDES) at the University of Central Florida.*

Lapchick, R., S. Jackson, and A, Lilly. (2010). *Building positive change: The black coaches and administrators hiring report card for NCAA FBS and FCS football head coaching positions (2010–11)*: University of Central Florida: The Institute for Diversity and Ethics in Sport (TIDES).

Lopiano, D., (2001), "Recruiting, retention and advancement of women in athletics," Retrieved April 23, 2012, from http://www.womenssportsfoundation.org/cgibin/iowa/issues/coach/article.html?record=878

Lough, N., and H. Grappendorf. (2007). Senior woman administrator's perspectives on professional advancement. *International Journal of Sport Management* 8, 193–209.

Mainiero, L. A. (1986). Coping with powerlessness: The relationship of gender and job dependency to empowerment-strategy usage. *Administrative Science Quarterly* 31, 633–653.

Mathis, R. L., and J. H. Jackson. (2006). *Human resource management (11th ed.)*. Mason, OH: South-Western.

Messner, M. A. (2002). *Taking the field: Women, men, and sports*. Minneapolis, MN: University of Minnesota Press.

Michael, J., and G. Yukl. (1993). Managerial level and subunit function as determinants of networking behavior in organizations. *Group and Organization Management* 18, 328–351.

Miller, T., (2012), "Coaches see progress in hiring," Retrieved March 26, 2012, from http://espn.go.com/college-football/story/_/id/7623932/opportunities-black-coaches-rise-college-football

Moore, D. (2002). An exploratory analysis of power, opportunity and proportion as related to the careers of women in leadership positions within intercollegiate athletics. *Dissertation Abstracts International* 63, 2364.

Mullins, A. (2008). The UK coaching system is failing women coaches: A commentary. *International Journal of Sports Science & Coaching* 3(4), 465–467.

Myles, L. R. (2005). *The absence of color in athletic administration at Division I institutions.* (Unpublished doctoral dissertation). University of Pittsburgh, Pittsburgh, PA.

Naughton, J. (1998). Black athletic directors remain a rarity in NCAA's Division I. *Chronicle of Higher Education* 44(43), A29–A31.

National Association for Sport and Physical Education. (2006). *Quality coaches, quality sports: National standards for sport coaches.* Reston, VA.

NCAA, (n.d.), "Gender equity planning: Best practices," Retrieved April 19, 2012, from https://nfca.org/web_docs/convention/11/speakers/milutinovich/GE_Best_Practices.pdf

NCAA, (2011a), "NCAA leadership institute for ethnic minority males and females," Retrieved January 15, 2012, from http://www.ncaa.org/wps/portal/ncaahome?WCM_GLOBAL_CONTEXT=/ncaa/NCAA/Academics+and+Athletes/Student-Athlete+Affairs/Leadership+Institute+Index

NCAA, (2011b), "NCAA Pathway programs," Retrieved January 15, 2012, from http://www.ncaa.org/wps/portal/ncaahome?WCM_GLOBAL_CONTEXT=/ncaa/ncaa/academics+and+athletes/student-athlete+affairs/pathway+index

"Nick Saban gets raise, extension," (2012), Retrieved March 27, 2012, from http://espn.go.com/college-football/story/_/id/7740227/alabama-crimson-tide-grant-coach-nick-saban-raise-2-year-extension

Norman, L. (2008). The UK coaching system is failing women coaches. *International Journal of Sports Science & Coaching* 3(4), 447–464.

Norman, L. (2010). Bearing the burden of doubt: Female coaches' experiences of gender relations. *Research Quarterly for Exercise and Sport* 81(4), 506–517.

Pastore, D. L. (1992). Two-year college coaches of women's teams: Gender differences in coaching career selections. *Journal of Sport Management* 6, 179–190.

Press, A., (2011, November 9, 2011), "Paterno says he should have done more, breaks down telling players he will retire," Retrieved from http://thetimes-tribune.com/paterno-says-he-should-have-done-more-breaks-down-telling-players-he-will-retire-1.1230071#axzz1n7a1jegG

Reade, I., W. Rodgers, and L. Norman. (2009). The under-representation of women in coaching: A comparison of male and female Canadian coaches at low and high levels of coaching. *International Journal of Sports Science & Coaching* 4(4), 505–520.

Robbins, S. P. (2003). *Organizational Behavior.* Prentice-Hall, Saddle River, NJ.

Ryan, B., (2012, April 19), "Transcript of Bo Ryan interview with ESPN's 'Mike and Mike,'" Retrieved from http://thegazette. com/2012/04/19/transcript-of-bo-ryan-interview-with-espns-mike-and-mike/

Sagas, M., and G.B. Cunningham. (2004). Does having the "right stuff" matter? Gender differences in the determinants of career success among intercollegiate athletic administrators. *Sex Roles* 50, 411–421.

Sander, L. (2011a). In the game, but rarely No. 1. *Chronicle of Higher Education* 57(26), A1–A15.

Sander, L., (2011b), "Pickens says UConn should have listened to angry donor," Retrieved March 26, 2012, from http://chronicle.com/ blogs/players/pickens-says-uconn-should-have-listened-to-angry-donor/28068

Schein, E. H. (1985). *Organizational culture and leadership. A dynamic view.* San Francisco, CA: Jossey-Bass.

Schneider, I. E., and M.T. Allison. (2000). The journey toward diversity. In Allison, M.T., and I. E. Schneider, eds. *Diversity and the recreation profession: Organizational perspectives* (pp. 281–285). State College, PA: Venture Publishing, Inc.

Singer, J., C.K. Harrison, and S.J. Bukstein. (2010). A critical race analysis of the hiring process for head coaches in NCAA college football. *Journal of Intercollegiate Sport* 3, 270–296.

Shropshire, K. L. (1996). *In black and white: Race and sports in America.* New York: New York University Press.

Stangl, J. M., and M.J. Kane. (1991). Structural variables that offer explanatory power for the under-representation of women coaches since Title IX: The case of homologous reproduction. *Sociology of Sport Journal* 8, 47–60.

Teel, K. (2005). *A study of the female athletic directors at NCAA Division I and Division II institutions.* (Unpublished doctoral dissertation). Baylor University, Waco, TX.

Terborg, J. R., and D.R. Ilgen. (1975). A theoretical approach to sex discrimination in traditionally masculine occupations. *Organizational Behavior and Human Performance* 13, 352–376.

Turman, P. D. (2003). Coaches and cohesion: The impact of coaching techniques on team cohesion in the small group sport setting. *Journal of Sport Behavior* 26, 86–104.

Turner, B., and P. Chelladurai. (2005). Organization and occupational commitment, intention to leave, and perceived performance of intercollegiate coaches. *Journal of Sport Management* 19, 193–211.

U.S. Bureau of Labor Statistics, (2009), "Employment & earnings (Data File)," Retrieved January 17, 2012, from http://www. bls.gov/cps/demographics.htm#race

U.S. Census Bureau, (2011), "Resident population by sex, race, and Hispanic-origin status: 2000 to 20009 (Data File)," Retrieved January 14, 2012, from http://www.census.gov/compendia/ statab/cats/population.html

U.S. Equal Employment Opportunity Commission (n.d.), "The equal pay act of 1963," Retrieved

April 24, 2012, from http://www1.eeoc.gov// laws/statutes/epa.cfm?renderforprint=1

Westre, K. R., and M.R. Weiss. (1991). The relationship between perceived coaching behaviors and group cohesion in high school football teams. *The Sport Psychologist* 5, 41–54.

Whisenant, W. A. (2003). How women have fared as interscholastic athletic administrators since the passage of Title IX. *Sex Roles* 49(3/4), 179–184.

Whisenant, W. A., P.M. Pedersen, and B.L. Obenour,. (2002). Success and gender: Determining the rate of advancement for intercollegiate athletic directors. *Sex Roles* 47, 485–491.

Wu, Y. (1999). *Kellmeyer: The lawsuit that ruined women's control of intercollegiate athletics for women?* Paper presented at the Proceedings of the twenty-seventh NASSH conference.

Zgonc, E. (2010). *1999–2000 – 2008–2009 NCAA student-athlete ethnicity report*. Indianapolis, IN: The National Collegiate Athletic Association.

8

INTRODUCTION

Collegiate sport has had a distinct cultural impact on the institution of higher education in the United States (Southall & Nagel, 2009). But some are beginning to question whether this has benefited higher education. Tales of student-athletes, coaches, and programs involved in less than ethical actions have become increasingly common, leading some in American culture to argue that sport, in general, may have a negative influence upon impressionable younger generations. Indeed, some even speculate that corruption and deviant behavior is the norm, rather than the exception, in college sport (Prevenas, 2011). Recent cases such as Ohio State football players exchanging memorabilia for payment, free tattoos, and other impermissible gifts (McGee, 2011), or allegations that University of Miami (Fl) football players (from 2002–2010) received cash payments, gifts, access to a booster's yacht, and prostitutes (Robinson, 2011) are used to support this view. Furthermore, college sport has been criticized for being insulated from the campus community or larger society. In 2011, allegations of child molestation surfaced at Penn State involving Jerry Sandusky, a former defensive coordinator for the school. A public outcry ensued as the media discovered that the alleged behavior may had been taking place for years without intervention.

Those defending the virtues of organized sport are hard-pressed to explain much of the negative behavior in college sport. Indeed,

CRIME, DEVIANCE, AND VIOLENCE IN INTERCOLLEGIATE ATHLETICS

MARK VERMILLION, CHRIS MESSER & KRISTA BRIDGMAN

Prevenas (2011) asks the question: With so much corruption in college football, how can there still be so many fans? Many attribute these behaviors to greed or bad choices made by rogue individuals such as athletes, boosters, coaches, or other stakeholders. But a look at recent research examining NCAA major infractions involving misconduct, such as cheating or impermissible benefits to student-athletes, shows that individual and organizational forms of misconduct have been consistently occurring within collegiate sport for decades (Vermillion & Messer, 2011). These findings suggest a more systemic problem than just a few bad apples, and that crime and deviance in collegiate athletics can't be explained adequately without examining critical contributing social factors. Therefore, the purpose of this chapter is to:

- Differentiate between deviant, criminal, and violent behaviors within college sport.
- Expose students to explanations of sport deviance by examining criminological and sociology of deviance theories to better explain incidences and patterns of deviant or violent behavior in college sport.
- Identify and analyze social problems within collegiate sport, such as gambling or hazing.
- Provide information regarding deviance and violence among not only athletes, but also coaches and spectators.

Finally, something to consider: Plato said knowledge was the intersection of truth and belief. That is, developing knowledge is a combination of evidence and personal views. It is crucial to ask all questions—and, of more importance, to find all potential answers. As a result, the search for explanation requires individuals to not only set aside preconceived notions and personal biases, but also to examine the social fabric surrounding our concepts of deviant behavior in college sport. C. Wright Mills (1959) coined the phrase *sociological imagination* to bridge the connection between our personal experiences and the larger historical and social forces that actually help shape and mold those experiences. Tapping into our sociological imaginations will greatly affect our examination of deviance, crime, and violence in collegiate sport. To begin, it is necessary to distinguish between these concepts and briefly examine their respective roles in intercollegiate athletics.

DEVIANCE

Woods (2011) defines deviant as "an adjective that means departing from or deviating especially from an accepted norm" (p. 318). Deviance consists of any ideas, actions, or characteristics that cross toleration limits in a society, culture, or group (Coakley, 2009). Deviance is a social construction, meaning social groups help "create" what behaviors, attitudes, and identities will be evaluated and treated as deviant. Deviance is therefore relative, varying from group to group and across social settings. For instance, in the context of collegiate sport, male fans routinely go shirtless and cover their body in paint with symbols that represent their school pride. This behavior is perceived as "normal" by others at sporting events. In any other context, however, such as the worksite or classroom, such behavior could result in formal or informal punishment. Therefore, as Durkheim (1933) noted, the existence of deviance helps establish acceptable social boundaries, which vary across social contexts.

To better understand the relative properties of deviance, we need to examine the unique role of norms in shaping what deviance looks like in society; that is, deviance can only occur when there are established norms to violate. Hughes and Kroehler (2008) define norms as the social prescriptions and proscriptions in daily life. They organize our actions and thoughts, and tell us what behaviors, ideas, and conditions are acceptable and unacceptable in certain situations. College sport, for example, is comprised of many norms operating in a variety of situations and arenas. Some of these

norms can be described as formal—those codified into laws, bylaws, rules, and written expectations—or informal, the "unwritten" rules in society (Coakley, 2009).

The consequences for violating formal norms result in official, more punitive responses. In college baseball, for example, intentionally throwing at a batter will result in expulsion and suspension from future games. Formal deviance, or the violation of formal norms, is especially exemplified through NCAA infractions, such as when the University of Connecticut men's basketball coach, Jim Calhoun, was sanctioned for promoting an atmosphere of noncompliance (McGee, 2011). There are also a plethora of informal norms in collegiate athletics. For example, it is expected in soccer that only the team captain should argue a call with the referee. Other players are expected to let their captains argue for them. The violation of informal norms produces nonofficial reactions and responses. For instance, Cyphers and Fagen (2011) discussed a process known as "negative recruiting" in women's collegiate athletics. By alluding to heterosexuality within their collegiate sport programs, potential homosexual recruits may understand the team climate before they decide on attending that school for athletics. Therefore, a formal policy of heterosexuality in intercollegiate programs does not exist, but some may have certain expectations that are advanced more informally and subtly.

CRIME

The discussion above highlighted a number of examples of behaviors that violate society's expectations, but these actions don't run contrary to any legal statutes. Indeed, not all deviance is criminal, just as not all crimes are deviant behaviors (Siegel, 2011). According to Hughes and Kroehler (2008) crime is the result of violating formalized and codified statutes that must be enforced by some legal entity. For instance, if an athletic program is caught cheating by the NCAA, a bylaw is broken, but NOT a law. When we discuss criminal wrongdoing within athletics, we are usually discussing individuals—athletes, coaches, managers, athletic administrators, or fans—that have violated a law. But we can also focus on organizations, such as athletic departments, that may have broken applicable statutes or laws. Epstein (2009) categorizes crime in sport by the following: crimes against the person, such as assault; against property, such as counterfeiting merchandise or tickets; against public health, safety, and welfare, such as disorderly conduct; and against government, such as illegal gambling.

VIOLENCE

Violence within college sport, like violence in society at large, is a learned process involving formal and informal interactions across generations (Eitzen & Sage, 2009). Violence is conceptually different from deviance and crime. Specifically, Coakley (2009) defines violence as "excessive physical force, which causes or

"Loyola MD at Saint Louis" © Baccaga, (CC BY-SA 3.0) at http://www.commons.wikimedia.org/wiki/File:Loyola_MD_at_Saint_Louis_NCAA_Tournament.jpg.

has the potential to cause harm or destruction" (p. 196). But of more importance, actions that normally represent violent behavior are not necessarily considered deviant within U.S. college sport. For example, tackling is a vital component of football, but the behavior would be considered violence in a marital dispute. Even so, some types of tackles are seen as excessive and therefore violent *and* deviant. As illustrated later, violence is a mainstay in collegiate athletics. In fact, Lumpkin, Stoll, and Beller (2003) assert that violence in college sport has increased over the years. They point to a couple factors that have produced this outcome, notably: 1) games have become more organized and the stakes for winning have increased, and 2) intercollegiate sport has become increasingly intertwined with both big business and entertainment. We will also show that violence is related to many off-the-field factors, such as status and media coverage.

The concepts of deviance, crime, and violence are interrelated. Indeed, certain actions or ideas may be defined as deviant, violent, and criminal, regardless of the sport situation (Blackshaw & Crabbie, 2004). For instance, the allegations of child molestation or sexual assault that were recently reported involving Penn State University and Syracuse University serve as examples of violent, criminal, and deviant actions within both society and sport. But

for purposes here, it is important to highlight the important, unique features that distinguish these concepts and to examine factors that produce them in collegiate athletics.

TOWARD EXPLANATIONS OF DEVIANCE IN COLLEGE SPORT

Coakley (2009) noted how examining deviance within sport is difficult because many behaviors considered "normal" in college sport may actually be labeled as deviant in society. For example, fan behavior at college sporting events is drastically different compared with audiences at other events, such as art showings, keynote speeches at college graduation ceremonies, or during political rallies.

Making matters even more difficult, there has been a historical reluctance among social scientists to integrate a "sociology of deviance" framework to better understand the institution of sport (Atkinson & Young, 2008). As a result, scant research exists to help us understand the social forces that underlie the production of deviance in the context of intercollegiate athletics. Popular media coverage of sport, however, appears very concerned with sport deviance, especially while covering college athletics. Therefore, it would seem that a more comprehensive, rigorous explanation of collegiate sport deviance is needed. It is important to note that sport deviance cannot be explained or described by one theory because of the diverse nature of collegiate sport deviance (Atkinson & Young, 2008). Thus, we draw from several theoretical insights in the sociology of deviance and criminology, illustrating how they can contribute in different ways to a more comprehensive understanding of deviance in college sport.

SOCIAL THEORIES OF SPORT DEVIANCE

Ritzer (2010) defines social theory not merely as a systematic, scientifically oriented set of interrelated tenets that aid in predicting social life, but as a host of theories examining socially relevant topics that have sustained their saliency over time. Using this dynamic view of theory to explain certain events, actions, or ideas affords scholars, students, and those interested in sport the opportunity to understand deviance in intercollegiate athletics from a variety of viewpoints. We organize our discussion of college sport deviance using sociology of deviance theories—often folded into criminology—to better expand our understanding of sport deviance. While these theories were developed to explain deviant behavior in general, we believe they can also provide a unique lens through which to interpret college sport deviance. Siegel (2011) organizes these sociological theories of deviance into three categories: (a) social structural; (b) social process; and (c) social reaction.

Social Structural Theories

Social structural theories emphasize the systemic, society-rooted ways in which deviance is created. These perspectives point to factors such as economic disparities, poverty, and unemployment as the underlying causes of deviance in society. Two theories considered as social structural are social disorganization and anomie theory.

Social disorganization theory was initially formulated in the early 1900s to explain the discrepancy in crime between inner cities and other areas. Shaw and McKay (1942) emphasized the role of urbanization, immigration, and industrialization in producing higher rates of crime in inner cities. Specifically, they argued these processes help produce "social disorganization," or an inability of communities in flux to effectively respond to social problems. Shaw and McKay noted that inner cities were characterized by transitional neighborhoods, poverty, unemployment, and the inadequate functioning of social institutions such as education and government. These characteristics, they contended, caused higher rates of crime as residents perceive fewer opportunities and are less attached to their communities.

In fact, a disproportionate number of college athletes come from these very areas. This could be due to the emphasis placed on sport participation in a youth's early years in some of these areas. Success in sport may be viewed as a "way out" from the lack of other opportunities in socially disorganized areas. Indeed, Hartmann (2000) notes that popular ideology views sport as a progressive "way out of the ghetto," providing disadvantaged groups with opportunities for success. Scholars, however, have criticized this opinion by arguing that sport primarily reproduces and reinforces inequality, where minorities reap less rewards when earning equal accomplishments. Moreover, the success stories of inner-city athletes may deflect attention away from the larger, more persistent socioeconomic problems experienced by the larger community. Eitzen and Sage (2009) examined the related myth that sport is a positive tool for social mobility because it provides access to education or professional sport opportunities. Their research, however, does not provide much support for the idea that sport serves as a social mobility escalator (Eitzen & Sage, 2009).

Anomie theory, advanced by Robert Merton (1968), attributes crime and deviance to a disconnect between pursuing conventional goals and achieving them through socially sanctioned means. Merton focused on the predominant goal of financial success and the legitimate means through which success is typically achieved (e.g., education and employment), and contended that much crime and deviance emerges as a result of blocked opportunities for certain groups to pursue goals conventionally. But the theory can certainly be extended to analyze crime and deviance in intercollegiate athletics. A common, conventional goal among most college athletes and their respective programs is winning. To pursue this goal, a variety of means are used, including recruiting the best athletes, practicing, and devising a better game plan. Other goals must also be simultaneously reached, including staying academically eligible, which must be pursued using other means. At times, a dilemma occurs between the goals that athletes and their programs pursue and the means available to attain them. Accordingly, athletes and programs can respond by deviating from conventional standards. For instance, a coach or booster may offer impermissible benefits to gain a recruiting advantage over other teams, as was the case in the mid-1980s when Southern Methodist University's football program received "the death penalty" as punishment for repeatedly paying players with cash, cars, and other gifts. As summarized in the ESPN documentary *Pony Excess,* the SMU football program believed it was untouchable, did not have to play by the same rules as everyone else, and had a payroll of football players that it had to meet.

Social Process Theories

A second category of sociological theories emphasizes the social process, or the learning and interaction processes involved in causing criminal or deviant behavior. Three relevant perspectives include differential association, drift, and social bond theory. Differential association theory was initially developed by Edwin Sutherland (1947), who believed that just as individuals are socialized into learning popular slang, they learn criminal behavior as well. Differential association theory maintains that learning is more likely to occur in small, informal group contexts such as peer groups, families, and teams. This interaction provides the opportunity for individuals to internalize the values and beliefs of others depending, in part, on how important the relationship, how often they interact, and how long the relationship has lasted. For example, in late 2011 the Bethany College men's golf team came under scrutiny when nude photos of the team circulated on the Internet. The team captain claimed the photo was part of a team-building activity that was very similar to other photos taken by the UCLA golf team in 2004 (Halley, 2011). To explain why the entire team might participate in such an event, differential association theory would suggest that each golf player's interaction with his team led to the internalization of group norms and behavior. In sport, it is not uncommon for teams to adopt rituals and practices that are perceived to foster group cohesion. Moreover, it is clear that this behavior was influenced by another golf team, highlighting the role of learning in producing deviant behavior.

Drift theory is an extension of differential association theory and emphasizes the rationalization process used by individuals when committing crimes. Sykes and Matza (1957) identified five common "techniques of neutralization," or excuses and justifications commonly used by criminals or deviants to rationalize their behavior. These techniques are also prominent in cases of crime and deviance in sport. First, people may *deny responsibility*, or claim their behavior is beyond their personal control due to a variety of factors (e.g., living in poverty, being raised in an abusive home). Second, individuals can engage in the *denial of injury* by asserting the offense in question didn't harm anyone. A third technique involves the *denial of victim*, or declaring the alleged victim wasn't a victim after all, that he or she "had it coming." Fourth, one may *condemn the condemners* by diverting attention away from themselves and casting their accusers as hypocrites. Finally, criminals and deviants often *appeal to higher loyalties* and portray their actions as necessary for a larger, more important cause (e.g., stealing to help feed one's family). See Figure 1 on the next page.

Social bond theory accentuates the factors that operate and work together to prevent people from engaging in criminal and deviant behavior. Hirschi (1969) identified four key components to the social bond, or the connection that exists between individuals and society. The first part of the social bond is *attachment*, or the degree to which individuals empathize with others, such as how teammates become closely bonded through off-season workouts. Second, *commitment* refers to the time and energy one invests in pursuing conventional goals. For instance, those who have worked hard to obtain a successful job are viewed as less likely to commit crime, in part because they don't want to jeopardize what they had worked hard to achieve. If an athlete is ascending through the ranks of his or her sport's collegiate elite, that athlete would theoretically be less likely to risk not only their career, but also any professional opportunities that may soon emerge. The third component to Hirschi's social bond is *involvement*, which represents the degree to which individuals participate in conventional, socially sanctioned activities. In other words, the more time spent on after-school clubs, sporting activities, work, etc. the less time one has to engage in illegitimate behavior. Lastly, *belief* represents the degree to which one accepts and shares a conventional value and belief system. For example, Doherty and Danylchuk's (1996) seminal work regarding leadership within intercollegiate athletics identified the transformational leader as someone who could get employees, coaches, and/or athletes to believe in the mission of both the athletic teams and the overall athletic department. As individuals set aside their individualistic pursuits in favor of more "team" or group-oriented objectives, the group's cohesion increases (Carron, Hausenblas, & Eys, 2005).

Figure 1. Examples of Techniques of Neutralization in Intercollegiate Athletics (Sykes & Matza, 1957)

Neutralizing Technique	Example
Denial of responsibility	2010: After scoring a touchdown to take a 41–16 lead, Wisconsin attempted a two-point conversion against Minnesota. Although there are no rules against running up the score, going for two late in a game is viewed by many as bad sportsmanship. Head coach Brett Bielema denied responsibility, stating that a predetermined game plan called for the action: "You know what? If we're playing and somebody is going to go for two against me because they're up 25, that's what they should do, that's what the card says" (Lindsey, 2010, n.p.). http://bleacherreport.com/articles/487378-was-wisconsin-coach-bielema-wrong-for-running-up-the-score-on-the-gophers
Denial of injury	2008: Paul Donahoe, a former wrestler at the University of Nebraska, was kicked off the squad along with teammate Kenny Jordan after separate nude images of the men surfaced on a pornographic website targeting gay men. Donahoe admitted to being paid for the images, but denied injury by explaining, "I didn't hurt anyone, and I didn't do anything illegal … I mean, it's not illegal to get naked and take pictures" (Lavigne, 2009, n.p.). http://sports.espn.go.com/espn/otl/news/story?id=4242983
Denial of victim	2011: A fight broke out among players during a men's basketball game featuring Xavier and Cincinnati. Xavier's Tu Holloway defended the violence by stating that his team had been "disrespected" and therefore the fight was warranted: "We got disrespected a little bit before the game, guys calling us out. We're a tougher team. We're grown men over here. We've got a whole bunch of gangsters in the locker room—not thugs, but tough guys on the court. And we went out there and zipped them up at the end of the game" (Katz, 2011, n.p.). http://espn.go.com/mens-college-basketball/story/_/id/7339184/cincinnati-bearcats-coach-embarrassed-brawl-xavier-musketeers
Condemnation of condemners	1987: Brian Bosworth was suspended from participation in the Orange Bowl after testing positive for anabolic steroids. Bosworth declared the NCAA a hypocritical organization that had allowed players to use steroids for decades only to suddenly impose drug rules that were retroactively enforced. He stated that he was being punished for "what's in my system from a year ago. The NCAA drug law didn't come into effect until August, so you tell me who is at fault" (Neff, 1987, n.p.). http://sportsillustrated.cnn.com/vault/article/magazine/MAG1126827/2/index.htm
Appeal to higher loyalties	2011: Jim Tressel met with NCAA investigators to explain his reasons for not reporting NCAA violations. Players had exchanged memorabilia for free tattoos from a parlor owner under FBI investigation. Tressel explained that he was more concerned about his players: "I just emblazoned in my mind, 'Oh my God. There's a homicide. There's drug trafficking. There's possession of criminal tools. This is a bad situation. This is frightening.' And, you know, it—I was scared, quite frankly" (*ESPN*, n.d., n.p.). http://search.espn.go.com/jim-tressel-and-ohio-state/

Hirschi noted that when any of these parts are weakened, criminal or deviant behavior is more likely to occur than if each component remains strong. Holistic development within collegiate athletics, which includes a focus on developing the physical, social, emotional, and academic aspects of student athletes, could be informed by ideas similar to Hirschi's regarding deviance. For example, the NAIA's (National Association of Intercollegiate Athletics) "Champions of Character" program is based upon the five core values of integrity, respect, responsibility, sportsmanship, and servant leadership ("Champions of Character core values," n.d.), which mirror many of the same sentiments regarding deviant behavior that Hirschi posited. The program revolves around the idea that if student-athletes embody the aforementioned core values, they will be more likely to adhere to the commonly held values promoted by the NAIA and extend a positive force on campus or in their community.

Hirschi's (1969) notion of *attachment* (based upon empathy or the "golden rule") is closely aligned with the NAIA's idea of "responsibility," which focuses on the individual's bonding to their team and the team's welfare (oftentimes ahead of their own personal achievements or gain). *Commitment* is very similar to the program's notion of "integrity." Specifically, integrity is defined as "positive internal traits that guide behavior" ("Champions of Character core values," n.d., n.p.). These traits that guide athletes' behaviors imply the

individual athlete's internalization of commonly held societal values. *Involvement* in conventional activities is related to not only participation in college sports, but also the conscious decision to participate on the NAIA level, as compared with other levels, such as the varying divisions of the NCAA (FBS, FCS, Division I [formerly Division IAAA], Division II, and Division III) or the NJCAA (National Junior College Athletic Association). Finally, *belief* involves the acceptance of conventional

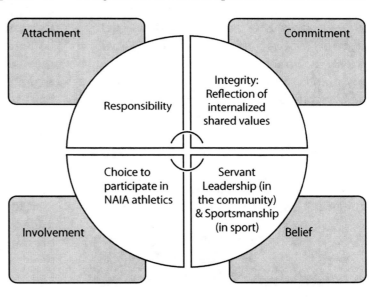

Figure 2. The outside quadrants represent components of Hirchi's (1969) social bond: attachment, commitment, involvement, and belief. The inner circle represents core values from the NAIA's "Champions of Character" program.

values, and the categories of "servant leadership" and "sportsmanship" relate to beliefs in both sport (sportsmanship) and the community (servant leadership). See Figure 2.

Social Reaction Theories

A third set of theories are called social reaction perspectives, because they emphasize the societal response to crime and deviance more than the act itself. Two theoretical mainstays are labeling and radical theory. Labeling theory stresses that no act is inherently criminal or deviant, but that the behavior is labeled as such only if it is judged or evaluated accordingly (Thio, Calhoun & Conyers, 2012). For instance, most people contend that homicide is morally reprehensible; however, in certain situations such as wartime or protecting one's family during a break-in, homicides are generally viewed as justifiable. Intercollegiate athletics provides a very visible outlet for understanding the dynamics of labeling. Consider the case of male cheerleading: in her study of Division I male cheerleaders, Bemiller (2005) highlighted the difficulties experienced by men who participate in a female-dominated sport. The male cheerleaders who participated in the study

expressed a heightened awareness of their own stigmatization and developed a number of strategies to defend their participation, such as emphasizing the need for physical prowess in cheerleading.

Labeling theories also inform us of the consequences and power of labels, which are differentially applied according to certain statuses in society. For instance, in 2009 Elizabeth Lambert, a New Mexico's women's soccer player, was suspended after pulling an opposing player down by her ponytail, in addition to a series of other excessive behaviors throughout the game. The situation received headline news across the nation, arguably because the player was female. It's hard to imagine the same scenario in men's soccer would receive such widespread media attention and public analysis. Nevertheless, the negative publicity surrounding Lambert caused her image to be at the very least temporarily tarnished.

Radical theory assumes that class conflict underpins crime in society. A key contributing theorist is Quinney (1977), who examined two types of crime: crimes of accommodation and resistance, and crimes of domination and repression. The former are crimes that society has historically paid most attention to because they cause the most fear among its members. These are street-oriented crimes such as robbery, larceny, and murder. Quinney characterizes these as crimes of accommodation because the acts are often committed as a means of accommodating, or adjusting, to an economic and political system that has disadvantaged the working-class, the same class that disproportionately commits these crimes. It could be argued that many athletes who receive extra benefits do so because they perceive the standard set of benefits to be minimal compared with their individual worth. For instance, in 2011 the Auburn football program came under attack when reports surfaced that the father of quarterback Cam Newton had previously attempted to sell his son's commitment to Mississippi State in exchange for nearly $200,000. On the other hand, the elite ruling class is more likely to commit acts of domination and repression, such as white-collar crime, as a means to maintain their superior position in society. Regarding intercollegiate football and economic elitism, in 2011 the Bowl Champion Series reported a 22 percent increase in revenue paid out among the five BCS games from 2010. Specifically, the five football games generated more than $174 million ("2011 timeline: The year in review," 2011). For radical theorists, this type of profit system only exacerbates already existing inequity. While revenues continue to soar, the athletes who are largely responsible for producing those profits in the first place remain unpaid. Moreover, in 2011 Fiesta Bowl chief John Junker and chief operating officer Natalie Wisneski pleaded guilty for their roles in a fraudulent campaign-contribution scheme, illustrating the ever-strengthening nexus between politics, college sport, and money.

PRAXIS AND THEORY INTEGRATION

Karl Marx (with Engels) (1998 [1845]) advocated for the notion of *praxis*, which speaks

of translating theoretical understandings into action. MacIver (1942) also noted the occurrence of one incident must precede the occurrence of another incident. Figure 3.

Consequently, the "result" that we are able to observe is preceded by another phenomenon, which may not always be readily visible. To accurately identify, explain, and hopefully ameliorate collegiate sport deviance, we need to critically understand all influences present in a situation defined as

Figure 3. Using MacIver's (1942) notion of antecedent of incident, the above figure illustrates graphically the simplistic chain of events regarding how one college athlete could punch another athlete after their game.

deviant. The aforementioned theories allow us the opportunity to examine the underlying social dynamics.

Within college sport, incidences of deviant or violent behavior are exceedingly complex. Having an array of theories to use when examining collegiate sport deviance allows for greater flexibility and increased levels of critical thinking. Consider the following scenario involving the University of Oregon–Boise State University football game: In 2009, the University of Oregon played Boise State University in a nationally televised football game. It was a midweek game that was to kick off the NCAA's sportsmanship initiative to promote fair play and extol the virtues of modern collegiate athletics. After Oregon lost the game, 19–8, both teams went through the obligatory ritual of shaking hands. Then, Oregon's running back, LaGarrette Blount, punched Boise State linebacker Byron Hout after he was seen visibly taunting Oregon players, including Blount ("School: Blount's actions 'reprehensible,'" 2009). Hout's punishment was handled internally by Boise State athletics, and Blount was suspended by coach Chip Kelly for most of the season ("Punch earns Oregon's Blount a season-long suspension," 2009). The scene was particularly egregious in light of the fact that the punch and skirmish occurred not only on national television, but during the NCAA's sportsmanship weekend.

"LeGarrette Blount" © Alex McDougall, (CC BY-SA 3.0) at http://commons. wikimedia.org/wiki/File:LeGarrette_Blount_2009-09.03.jpg.

It is very easy to blame this action on a single person at a single moment. We know, however, that a considerable amount of deviant or violent behavior cannot be solely attributed to a person's rational choice to engage in an abnormal or reprehensible act (See Shoemaker [2009] for a discussion on the limitations of rational choice theories). The aforementioned theories provide us with differing lenses to view various forms of sport deviance or violence and the environmental factors that produce them. Now that we have developed a theoretical background, our next charge is to apply the theoretical understandings and tools we have—much like Marx's idea of *praxis*—to explain or describe how sport deviance manifests itself within our collegiate sporting landscape.

COLLEGIATE ATHLETES AND DEVIANCE

Discussions centering on athletes and deviance or violence can be analyzed from a variety of differing viewpoints. For our analysis, we will focus on two major categories of deviance and violence: 1) on-field, and 2) off-field. Keep in mind that deviance is a social construction; therefore, the actions, thoughts, and activities we discuss as examples of on-field and off-field deviance are presented here as deviance because society, or a significant portion of society, has labeled them accordingly. Violence within collegiate sport can be understood in a variety of ways. Violence, remember, is a highly variegated concept with numerous meanings. As previously mentioned, violence relates to the "use of excessive physical force, which causes or has obvious potential to cause harm or destruction" (Coakley, 2009, p. 196). Also, because of the violent nature of many collegiate sports, violence does not necessarily relate exclusively to illegal or immoral behaviors. As with certain forms of deviant behavior, some forms of sport violence are actually entirely normalized and expected.

Research addressing sport violence has revealed that aggression is a key component to understanding violent behaviors in sport. Berkowitz (1993) noted aggression involves *both* inflicting physical harm on another person and the expectation that accomplishing this is reasonably high. Cox (2007) further elaborated on two distinctions of aggression, namely hostile aggression and instrumental aggression. Hostile aggression involves having an overall goal to harm more so than succeed in the contest. An example of hostile aggression occurred when a Wichita

State University baseball player intentionally threw at an opposing batter in the on-deck circle, shattering some of his facial bones (Doxsie, 2009). While both the pitching coach and the player were reprimanded, this action exemplifies hostile aggression because it was not only outside the norm, but also was done to harm or injure the player as compared with winning the game.

With instrumental aggression, the component of harm is not the primary goal, but the means to achieve another goal, such as winning, glory, or fame. Consider the following hypothetical example from college rugby: a player's violent hit on an opposing player in order to dislodge the ball from his or her grasp.

It is a violent action, but the goal of the hit was not necessarily to hurt the offensive player, as it was done in the flow of the game. These types of plays, in a variety of collegiate sports, are not necessarily outside the rules of the games. Consequently, to better distinguish between types of on-field deviance or violence we need to understand how types of deviant behavior compare to not only the rules of the games, but also the normative expectations of risk within each contest.

On-Field Deviance and Violence

Deviant or violent behavior within collegiate sport is oftentimes covered and highlighted by media outlets. These behaviors or actions, however, are not always considered as deviant, referring to what Coakley (2009) calls the relativist approach to studying sport deviance. Specifically, he noted the situational definitions of sport deviance vary based upon time, space, and place. Within collegiate rugby, for example, routine tackles or hits by players would be well outside the rules in other sports. Each sport (and the NCAA), however, develops rules to govern competition within contests. For example, during the 2011–12 college football season, the NCAA instituted a new rule that stated if an athlete begins taunting opponents or excessively celebrating (such as jumping into the end zone) before scoring a touchdown, the penalty would wipe out the score (Johnson, 2011). This systematic and formalized response from the NCAA is one way of controlling on-field deviant behavior by athletes. Since violence is one common form of deviant behavior, understanding how violence is related to sport experience and how to categorize on-field violence are important steps that should be taken to further examine collegiate sport deviance.

Dunning (1999) identifies the role of emotion, especially enjoyment, within sport participation and consumption. Indeed, a great number of people enjoy consuming the atmosphere of collegiate athletics, such as the specific traditions, pregame and postgame celebrations (such as tailgating or parades), and the sporting contests themselves. Dunning (1999), however, highlighted arguments that convincingly document the increase in sports violence in general. Moreover, if sport consumption is enjoyable, then we must identify the link between American culture and the consumption of sport violence in college sports. To better understand sport violence, we need a way to distinguish between types of violence within college sports.

Smith (1981) developed a set of four categories for separating and understanding on-field violence. These categories are brutal body contact, borderline violence, quasi-criminal violence, and criminal violence. Brutal body contact refers to the common physical practices within a game, match, or competition. This type of activity in society is often seen as deviant, but because of the violent nature of many college sports, the violence is normalized, resulting in athletes, coaches, and fans accepting these physical practices as being part of the normal game. As one Clemson University football coach said about losing to Georgia Tech, "In a nutshell, we just physically got whipped" (Hood, 2011, ¶6). This quote, which was echoed by both coaches and players alike, illustrates

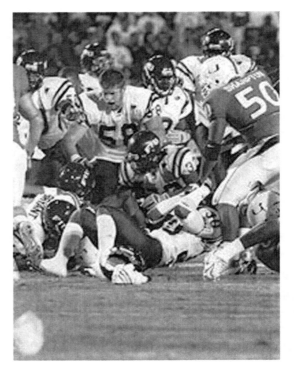

Source: AP Photo / Wilfredo Lee. Copyright © by Associated Press.

the accepted and basic physicality expected within college football. Borderline violence, while accepted by coaches, athletes, and fans, involves actions outside of the rules of the game. These actions, however, are often used within the context of competition. An example of borderline violence might include a hard foul in basketball, used as a way of "protecting the paint" or slowing down an opposing team's momentum. The commonality of these first two types of on-field violence involves the acceptance of violence by most involved parties (e.g., athletes, coaches, fans, advertisers, etc.).

Quasi-criminal violence involves actions that not only violate expectations and rules of the game, but can also violate governing laws. Examples of quasi-criminal violence include severe unnecessary roughness penalties in football (often resulting in player ejections), flagrant fouls committed with the intent to inflict harm in basketball, certain types of "cross-checks" or other illegal hits in sports such as ice hockey or lacrosse, and even large-scale fights between teams or multiple opposing players. The brawl between the University of Miami (FL) and Florida International University is another example of quasi-criminal violence. In 2006 the two schools engaged in a bench-clearing fight that resulted in the suspension of thirty-one players from both schools. Multiple players were seen punching and kicking their opponents, with one player even swinging his helmet as a weapon ("Miami, FIU have 31 suspended for role in brawl," 2006).

Finally, criminal violence involves actions that are clearly outside the realm of sports and escalate to the point that local law officials might intercede and/or prosecute these violent behaviors as criminal acts. While Coakley (2009) noted these types of actions are relatively rare, they do include those assaults after or during the contest that seem to be premeditated. Epstein (2009), when discussing how criminal law can be synthesized within sport studies, identified a variety of crimes against persons that would be related to the criminal violence category. Epstein's (2009) list of crimes against persons includes assaults, battery, hazing, manslaughter, mobbing, reckless homicide, and reckless endangerment. An example of criminal violence within college sports could include the incident after the University of Nebraska–Missouri University football game. A local Columbia, MO, television station caught on video a Nebraska football player punching a Missouri fan as he ran onto the field after a Missouri win (Olson, 2003). While charges were not filed by the local police, the incident serves as an example of criminal violence within college sport.

Another important way to examine participation and consumption of on-field sport violence is through gender experiences. Lawler (2002) identified the relationship of gender and violent sports. Specifically, she noted how women's participation in violent sports, such as martial arts, hockey, or rugby, is not a passing novelty but represents a true cultural shift in how girls and women are consuming and participating in sport. Although violence is a normal part of many sports in American culture, Lawler (2002) noted how females' consumption of violent sport is deviant in that it violates gender stereotypes in our culture. Specifically, she stated:

> When I was 27 years old, I hit a man
> hard enough to break his ribs. I did a
> lot of soul-searching afterwards.
> I decided I liked it.

> Like most women my age—like most women, period—I was trained to be a nice girl growing up. I spent most of my life following the litany of things nice girls do—and the things nice girls don't do (Lawler, 2002, p. xv).

Gatz, Messner, and Ball-Rokeach (2002) noted the paradoxical question surrounding sport: does sport cause or cure violence? This question can be examined in part by focusing on female sport participation. Sport scholars noted the rigidity of gender ideologies within sport. As these ideologies have changed in society, it can be posited that sport is serving as an arena whereby females can challenge previously held stereotypes of how to act, behave, and what sports to participate within. Indeed, Lawler (2002) noted how many of the women she interviewed looked forward to the physicality of their chosen sport and relished the opportunity to understand not only how their body reacted to that contact, but also how that physical sport became tied to their self-image. Therefore, sport does not necessarily cause nor cure violence; the increase of female participation in violent sport may perhaps just be a reflection of changing gender roles and ideologies.

As sport continues to experience the shift in women's roles within physicality-based or violent sport, the collegiate sporting landscape today has responded by sponsoring nineteen women's sports. Indeed, in the forty years since the passage of Title IX, there are more females participating in collegiate athletics than at any other time in American history (Acosta & Carpenter, 2012). Since many of the collegiate sports consumed in American culture have a modicum of violence, one would not be surprised to see an increase in the number of women participating in violent sports.

On-field deviance or violence in collegiate athletics is not only extensively covered by a variety of media outlets, but is also the subject of much debate within fan message or discussion boards or in the popular sport press. Although one may posit that this on-field deviance/violence is detrimental to the public perception of college sports, the increasing scrutiny of off-field deviance and violence by collegiate student-athletes has helped expand the discussion of what constitutes acceptable and unacceptable behavior or ideas among collegiate student-athletes in general, especially in regard to off-field behaviors.

Off-Field Deviance and Violence

The high-profile nature of intercollegiate athletics has led to increased public scrutiny for college athletes, particularly involving off-field violence. This phenomenon is especially salient when examining incidences of domestic or family violence. For many years, popular press reports have covered the many examples of off-field violence involving collegiate athletes. Recent examples include the death of Yeardley Love, the University of Virginia student-athlete killed by a former male student-athlete (Ng, 2012), or the woman raped by an Arizona State University football player, which resulted in an $850,000 civil lawsuit and landmark changes in women's safety issues among the state's largest schools (Munson, 2009). Other high-profile examples of student-athletes involved in domestic violence include:

- University of Florida wide receiver Chris Raney was arrested and charged with aggravated stalking (Zagier, 2011).
- University of Oregon running back La Michael James (a Heisman Trophy finalist in 2010) was arrested on suspicion of strangulation, assault, and menacing (Zagier, 2011).
- Former team captain and University of Missouri football player Derrick Washington pleaded guilty to domestic assault while currently in prison for a separate incident of felony deviate sexual assault ("Ex-Mizzou football captain pleads to assault," 2012).
- University of Florida tight end A.C. Leonard was arrested on suspicion of domestic battery ("UF freshman arrested on domestic battery charge," 2012).

It is common to explain such deviant acts with individualistic explanations, such as the perpetrator was a "bad seed" or the victims put themselves in a bad situation. These views can be understood by "rational choice" or "reasoning" theories, which highlight the individual's personal decision making; individuals choose to engage or not to engage in specific behaviors. These explanations, however, are too atomistic and do not take into account the complex social dynamics (Shoemaker, 2009) of intercollegiate athletics.

There are many social factors that relate to violence and student-athletes. One possible factor focuses on disposition. Specifically, does an individual athlete have a disposition to violence, or can team dynamics influence acts of violence? Collichio (2000) examined one hundred fifty-three male student-athletes and the issue of violence against women. They concluded male athletes were

more supportive of and more likely to exhibit behaviors associated with violence against women. Also, male athletes participating in contact sports seem to have a greater behavioral disposition to violence against women as compared with both nonathletes and male athletes in non-contact sports. One major finding, however, was that the team environment played a greater role in determining violence against women as compared with individual (e.g., psychological) dispositions of athletes (Collichio, 2000).

The organizational context also influences how student-athletes and nonathletes perceive violence against women. Specifically, hiding alleged incidents helps to alter or save public images, which are very important in college sports. Recently, two University of Iowa football players were accused of assaulting a female student-athlete on campus. Regarding this incident, Rood (2008) noted many universities often benefit from hiding or concealing incidences, and "... athletes often benefit from their efforts to quietly resolve alleged crimes, and victims don't" (p. 4). As a result, many of these acts go unpunished or lightly punished, which may influence student-athletes' perceptions of such acts. The heinous crimes allegedly committed at Penn State by former defensive coordinator Jerry Sandusky also serve as an example of how administrators see tangible benefits from quietly resolving such public acts of deviance. The university's handling of the Sandusky allegations has continued to come under scrutiny along with the roles played (or not played) by not only the football program and athletic department, but also of university officials and the school's board of trustees (Erdley, 2012).

Finally, awareness, identification of the issue, and continued research serve as the collective focus for the NCAA regarding how to better understand violence. The NCAA held a panel to discuss domestic violence and determined how student-athletes, academic institutions, and the NCAA can collectively better address the issue ("Experts discuss domestic violence and student-athletes," 2011). While no specific plans are currently in place, NCAA President Mark Emmert indicated the NCAA has some outreach systems available and will continue to monitor the issue ("Experts discuss domestic violence and student athletes," 2011).

Criminal Arrests and Convictions

There has long been a real concern regarding student-athletes and "... the dual mission of keeping intercollegiate sports clean while generating millions of dollars each year as income for colleges" (Byers, 1995, p. 5). Intercollegiate athletics was intended to be for amateur students engaging in athletic contests. As early as 1929, however, the Carnegie Foundation for the Advancement of Teaching issued a report demanding colleges and universities regain control of the games, questioning the assumption of amateurism and intercollegiate athletics (Savage, Bentley, McGovern, & Smiley, 1929). A concern for student-athletes and criminal conduct was a logical outgrowth of this worry, and has captivated society's interest ever since as evidenced in journalistic accounts of criminal behavior and student-athletes.

More recently, Dohrmann and Benedict (2011) researched and wrote a special report for *Sports Illustrated* where they looked at the criminal backgrounds of Division I FBS (Football Bowl Subdivision) players in the top 25 poll rankings. After researching more than 7,000 background checks on nearly 3,000 collegiate football players, they found more than 200 of these athletes had criminal backgrounds or police records. Of the 277 criminal incidents discovered:

- 38 percent involved drug and alcohol offenses
- 27 percent involved nuisance crimes (disorderly conduct, criminal mischief, resisting arrest)
- 20 percent involved violent crimes (domestic violence, assault and battery, sex crimes)
- Nearly 15 percent involved property crimes (burglary, shoplifting)

At the time the data was gathered, only one program in the top twenty-five had zero players on the roster with a police record. That school, Texas Christian University, was just recently involved in a seven-month drug-sting operation resulting in the arrests of four football players (Watson, 2012). Nearly 25 percent of the poll's top twenty-five schools had more than ten players on their teams with police records, and one program (Pittsburgh) had more than twenty players with police records (Dorhmann and Benedict, 2011).

Similarly, the highly publicized Duke Lacrosse sexual scandal, which involved male student-athletes and allegations of raping and sexually assaulting an exotic dancer, revealed that fifteen of the team's forty-seven players (32 percent) had police records for drunken or disorderly conduct. These statistics were known to the school's administrators prior to the high-profile incident, which occurred a year later (Tapper & Taylor, 2006). In the oft-cited study regarding male student-athletes and sexual assault on college campuses, however, Crosset, Benedict, and McDonald (1995) concluded that while male student-athletes are over-represented in sexual assault reports in campus police records, the differences were not significantly different when compared with the general male student population of those universities.

Rood (2008) noted how some colleges or universities try to keep their student-athletes' criminal activities out of the public eye. Indeed, Crosset (1999) echoed the importance of institutional silence and how it can perpetuate such behaviors. According to sociologist Harry Edwards, student-athletes enjoy an elevated status in both society and on campus, which may contribute to their behavior (Tapper & Taylor, 2006). In addition to status, what else can explain society's fascination with student-athlete criminal behavior?

To address this question, we can rely upon the works of Foucault and Bentham. Michel Foucault (1977) noted how modern society's surveillance, which is further exacerbated by modern technologies such as social media, provides a glimpse into the personal lives of individuals. Because student-athletes—in certain sports—are highly publicized from an early age, they begin to develop a celebrity status. Legions of fans consume these athletes' on-field/court exploits, or follow their personal lives via Facebook and Twitter. Echoing the notion of surveillance, Jeremy Bentham's eighteenth century version of the perfect prison, known as *panopticon*, is predicated upon constant observation (Bosovic 1995). Specifically, the threat of someone watching inmates at all times forces them to alter their behaviors. As a result, individuals who do not conform to behavior expectations are publically identified as criminals or deviants. Student-athletes are highly visible both on campuses and in larger society. Because their on-field/court lives are so highly consumed,

it is not surprising that their off-field failures are as equally covered.

If society still holds to the notion that sport participation helps integrate the individual into society (see Fejgin 1994 for a review of the developmental hypothesis), then those participating in sport should exemplify the positive values cherished in American culture, such as hard work, character, and sportsmanship. Student-athletes who fail to adhere to social expectations are highlighted and used as examples of what NOT to do, exemplifying not only Emile Durkheim's (1933) positive function of deviance, but also Foucault's (1977) vision of public punishment and control over certain groups of people.

NONATHLETES AND DEVIANCE

As cited earlier, fans may also engage in a variety of deviant behaviors. The amount of time, money, and dedication a spirited fan will devote to his or her team is astounding. Perhaps a business professional by day, the same individual may become a painted face, screaming fan by the evening. The question remains, why are we so attracted to identify with a team and to what extent can conventional fan behavior cross the line into

deviant fan behavior? According to Tajifel and Turner (1979), people have a need to belong to groups. A fan's social identity is the individual's self-concept or self-esteem resulting from a seeming membership of social groups (Hogg & Vaughan, 2002). As in competition, this social group, or identification with a collegiate team, presents an "us versus them" disposition. The fan feels he or she has an existence with the team, similar to that of a stakeholder, and is therefore entitled to communicate judgment about the team's functions whether practical or unrealistic.

Wakefield and Wann (2006) investigated the degree of identification a person has with his or her team; that is, the degree to which the fan feels a psychological connection with the team. If the team wins, does the fan now self-identify as a winner? Does the converse apply? Although a mainstream fan is well controlled during a competition, there are highly identified fans who demonstrate abnormal or socially unacceptable behaviors during or after games. These fans go out of their way to ensure their viewpoint is considered when communicating the sporting environment, sometimes escalating into verbal or even physical assaults. Included among these abnormal, inappropriate behaviors are rioting fans, as illustrated in 2003 after the University of Minnesota men's hockey team won the Frozen Four.

Seifried (2011) illustrates how deviant fan behavior has extended itself beyond the playing field and infiltrated cyberspace. Increasingly, fans have turned to blogs and the like to voice their pleasure or displeasure with their favorite team's performance; however, some of this behavior has translated into cyber bullying, where the fan can remain hidden behind a computer screen, and where the risk associated with personal confrontations and counterattacks is reduced. This sovereignty fosters a platform for an overly identified fan to engage in controversial—and often emotionally violent—behavior. Therefore, just as athletes may engage in over-conformity, so can fans.

SOCIAL PROBLEMS WITHIN COLLEGIATE ATHLETICS

Both scholarly research and journalistic accounts have identified a wide variety of social problems within college athletics. Many of these incidences are not necessarily criminal, but do violate the expectations that society has for collegiate athletics. Three types of social problems that have been discussed, identified, or examined within college athletics: gambling, organizational deviance, and hazing.

Gambling and College Sport

There have been many attempts to control or curb gambling's relationship with college sports throughout American history. While sport has long dealt with the specter of gambling, college sports have been protected by legislation designed to keep the integrity of the institution intact. Specifically, the Illegal Internet Gambling Enforcement Act (IIGEA) was an attempt to regulate online gaming, an industry whose value has been estimated at more than $10 billion per year (Ahrens, 2006). The Professional and Amateur Sports Protection Act (PASPA), however, was legislation specifically aimed at controlling sport and gambling activities, and was designed to further complement and strengthen previous legislative attempts (Vermillion,

Stoldt, Bass, 2009). It has been estimated that more than $380 billion a year is wagered illegally on sports in the United States every year ("American Gaming Association," n.d.). Because of the prevalence of both illegal sport gambling and the high-profile nature of college sport, the NCAA formally articulated its stance regarding the relationship of illegal gambling activities and other illegal enterprises, such as organized crime ("College sports betting—NCAA official statement," 2009). As a result of such linkages, the NCAA has pledged to keep educating student-athletes and monitoring illegal gambling enterprises.

There have been a number of high-profile examples of illegal gambling activities involving student-athletes. For example, in 1996 Boston College's football team was involved in perhaps the biggest gambling scandal in NCAA history. Thirteen players, the head coach, and the athletic director were fired ("Boston College continues to sort out mess from gambling scandal," 1997). Furthering the NCAA's concerns, Engwall, Hunter, and

Steinberg (2004) concluded college students were twice as likely to engage in gambling compared with the general population. More alarming, student-athletes were more likely to gamble than nonathletes. While student-athletes are educated against the dangers of gambling and gambling-related activities, it is feared that organized, illegal gambling groups could prey upon in-debt student-athletes and persuade them to begin shaving points or throwing games, thereby ruining the integrity of college sports (Woods, 2011). For example, the University of San Diego men's basketball team was recently under investigation by both the NCAA and federal authorities for an alleged gambling ring involving the team's all-time leading scorer, a former assistant coach, and another former player ("FBI investigating point shaving scandal," 2011).

While many notable gambling scandals involve high-profile sports such as basketball or football, the NCAA's latest report on student-athletes and gambling lists collegiate golf as the sport with the highest incidences of gambling ("Results from the 2008 NCAA study on collegiate wagering," 2009). To combat illegal gambling in collegiate sports, the NCAA has developed relationships with gaming officials in Las Vegas and is in consultation with other organizations, such as professional leagues, to develop proactive measures to limit illegal wagering or gambling on college sports ("NCAA: Point shaving threatens college sports," 2011). With the continued growth of college sports, one can presume that a variety of groups—including the NCAA and other watchdog groups—will continue to monitor gambling associations involving student-athletes, coaches, athletic departments, and NCAA competitions and championships.

Organizational Deviance

Crime and deviance is not only committed at the individual level. Indeed, organizations have also served as perpetrators and have violated the expectations of workers, consumers, and societies at large. This section examines the concept of organizational deviance, some of the key factors associated with producing it, and how these factors may play out in intercollegiate athletics.

Organizational deviance has been defined as "an event, activity, or circumstance, occurring in and/or produced by a formal organization, that deviates from both formal design goals and normative standards or expectations, either in the fact of its occurrence or in its consequences, and produces a suboptimal outcome" (Vaughan, 1999, p. 273). Most important, the concept of organizational deviance points to the notion that organizations can be viewed as a collective unit and that deviance can be attributed to the organization itself, rather than the individual members that comprise the group. For example, a common accusation against the NCAA is that the organization fails to provide a genuine balance between the academic and athletic experience for many student-athletes, which is central to the NCAA's mission. This complaint has been raised throughout the NCAA's history, while the individuals who comprise it have been routinely replaced, suggesting the organization's structures, processes, and features can be blamed if a true balance between academics and athletics is not experienced by student-athletes. Therefore, it is necessary to examine some of these features that can produce organizational deviance.

First, there are structural characteristics of organizations that can lead to deviant behavior. Much of this can be attributed to the size and complexity of large organizations. At times, information does not flow uniformly throughout large organizations, a process called "structural secrecy." Consider a large room of people where the person in the front is given a message, he or she must privately tell the next person, that person tells the next, until the message makes its way to the back of the room. Understandably, the message probably won't stay exactly the same by the time the last person receives it, particularly if the message is lengthy and detailed.

An example of structural secrecy is the alleged sexual abuse case at Penn State involving Jerry Sandusky and the flow of communication during the reporting of the abuse. According to Sara Ganim (2011), Mike McQueary, then a graduate student, was the first person affiliated with the Penn State program to witness the sexual abuse. McQueary reportedly told his father, and together the next day they reported the incident to the head coach, Joe Paterno. While the precise information relayed to Paterno is not known, there is, according to Ganim (2011), ample evidence the details became less explicit and implicating as the narrative made its way through the necessary chain of command. This can in part be contributed to the tendency for "bad" news to be unwelcome at the top of organizations.

A second feature of organizations that can produce deviant behavior is goal displacement. At times, certain goals trump all others, leading to the ends justifying the means. Organizational goals can include maximizing profits, meeting deadlines, reaching more clientele, winning games, and so on. Another goal can simply involve surviving. In 2011, a reporter for *The New York Times* uncovered a long tradition of deception among a variety of women's programs to appear compliant with Title IX, which prohibits sex discrimination in federally financed education programs. Thomas (2011) noted that as women's enrollment into universities has grown precipitously over the years, athletic programs have struggled to maintain a proportional number of female athletes. For many programs, the result has been deception. According to Thomas, the University of South Florida's cross-country roster included numerous women who had never competed in a race, some of whom were unaware they were even included on the team roster. In their women's basketball programs, Texas A&M and Duke reported male practice players as female participants. And at Cornell, fifteen of

the thirty-four fencers on the women's team were male.

Hazing

In 2006, Northwestern University suspended its women's soccer team after pictures were posted on the Internet of a hazing incident. The pictures showed several players wearing only T-shirts and underwear, with many of them covered in marker. A few pictures showed players kissing each other or providing lap dances to males. Still other pictures showed women blindfolded with their hands tied together. Hazing is a growing concern within intercollegiate athletics, and has been defined as:

> Any activity expected of someone joining a group that humiliates, degrades, abuses or endangers, regardless of the person's willingness to participate. This does not include activities such as rookies carrying the balls, team parties with community games, or going out with your teammates, unless an atmosphere of humiliation, degradation, abuse or danger arises (Hoover, 1998, p.8).

Only recently have sociologists attempted to tackle and interpret the forces behind hazing. As Coakley (2009) notes, hazing is a form of deviant overconformity, where players seek to achieve team unity through ritualistic behavior. New team members are socialized to adopt team value systems, and enduring humiliating or degrading experiences at the hands of team leaders helps solidify dedication, loyalty, and conformity to the team. Moreover, silence is expected among participants and nonparticipants.

Players, whether hazees or hazers, often feel immense pressure to maintain and perpetuate hazing rituals. As Waldron, Lynn and Krane (2011) note, resistance can lead to ostracism. In their interviews of athletes who had experienced hazing, the researchers found that hazing is often presented as a positive, bonding experience, but a number of negative physical and emotional consequences often result. They suggest that only changing social norms through proactive administrators, coaches, and team leaders will help counteract hazing experiences. This is particularly important as hazing experiences have become increasingly public, which only serves to intensify the emotional injuries that may already scar a student-athlete.

SUMMARY

The institution of intercollegiate athletics is exceedingly complex. Examining definitions and incidences of criminal, deviant, or violent behavior is crucial for better understanding intercollegiate sport. A better understanding of sport deviance helps to contain future occurrences of deviant behavior in intercollegiate sport. Deviant behavior was differentiated from criminality and violence to better identify sport deviance. As discussed, deviant behavior within intercollegiate athletics takes many forms, including more than criminal arrests, and involves a variety of groups associated with college sports, such as participants, coaches, fans, and other consumers.

Since sport deviance is so complex we proposed using a variety of criminological frameworks for examining separate facets of intercollegiate athletics. Using Siegel's (2011) proposed frameworks, the theories were divided into three categories: social structural, social process, and social reaction. The reviewed theories are not grand theories nor do they attempt to explain all forms of sport deviance, but they can explain specific forms of deviant behavior associated with intercollegiate athletics.

Finally, it would be a clear omission if we did not examine popular social problems associated with intercollegiate athletics. Whether arrest records, domestic violence involving student-athletes, incidences of hazing, or gambling on college sport, these social problems force both society and the governance structure of intercollegiate athletics to understand not only the prevalence of such issues, but also how social science can contribute to ameliorating (or containing) such issues. Organizational deviance in college athletics, for example, illustrates the complexity and sensitivity of these types of social problems in collegiate athletics. The amount of time, labor, and resources that must be devoted to addressing these concerns are important issues for students, student-athletes, coaches, fans, collegiate administrators, and sport consumers to consider while moving forward.

REFERENCES

2011 timeline: The year in review. (2011, December 19–25). *Street & Smith's Sports Business Journal.* Retrieved from http://www.sportsbusinessdaily.com/Journal/Issues/2011/12/19/Year-End/Timeline.aspx?hl=2012%20bowl%20revenues&sc=0

Acosta, V. R., and L.J. Carpenter, (2012), "Women in intercollegiate sport: A longitudinal, national study thirty-five year update," Retrieved from http://www.acostacarpenter.org/

Ahrens, F. (2006, May 25). Bill to ban gambling gets 4th chance. *The Washington Post.* Retrieved from http://www.highbeam.com/doc/1P2-131849.html

"American Gaming Association," (n.d.), Retrieved from http://www.americangaming.org/about-aga

Atkinson, M., and K. Young. (2008). *Deviance and social control in sport.* Champaign, IL: Human Kinetics.

Bemiller, M. (2005). Men who cheer. *Sociological Focus* 38, 205–222.

Berkowitz, L. (1993). *Aggression: its causes, consequences, and control.* Philadelphia, PA: Temple University Press.

Blackshaw, T., and T. Crabbie. (2004). *New perspectives on sport and 'deviance:' Consumption, performativity and social control.* London, UK and New York, NY: Rutledge Taylor and Francis Group.

Bosovic, M. (1995). *The panopticon writings.* London, Verso.

Boston College continues to sort out mess from gambling scandal. (1997, July 25). *Las Vegas Review-Journal.* Retrieved from http://www.reviewjournal.com/lvrj_home/1997/Jul-25-Fri-1997/sports/5778474.html

Byers, W., and C. Hammer. (1995). *Unsportsmanlike conduct: Exploiting college athletes.* Ann Arbor, MI: The University of Michigan Press.

Carron, A. V., H.A. Hausenblas, and M.A. Eys. (2005). *Group dynamics in sport (3rd ed.).* Morgantown, WV: Fitness Information Technology.

"Champions of character core values."(n.d.), Retrieved from http://www.championsofcharacter.org/page/corevalues.php

Coakley, J. (2009). *Sports in society: Issues and controversies (10th ed.).* Boston, MA: McGraw Hill.

College sports betting—NCAA official statement (2009). *NCAA.org.* Retrieved from http://www.ncaa.org/wps/wcm/myconnect/ncaa/NCAA/Media + and + Events / Press + Room/ Current+Issues/ Sports + Wagering?pageDesign = Printer + Friendly + General + Content + Layout

Collichio, G. S. (2000). *Peer group support and propensity for violence against women: A study of male intercollegiate athletes.* (Unpublished thesis). State University of New York, Brockport. Brockport, NY.

Cox, R. H. (2007). *Sport psychology: Concepts and applications (6th ed.).* Boston, MA: McGraw Hill.

Crossett, T. W. (1999). Male athletes' violence against women: A critical assessment of the athletic affiliation, violence against women debate. *Quest* 51, 244–257.

Crossett, T. W., J.R. Benedict, and M.A. McDonald. (1995). Male student-athletes reported for sexual assault: A survey of campus police departments and judicial affairs offices. *Journal of Sport & Social Issues* 19, 2, p. 126–140.

Cyphers, L., and K. Fagan. (2011, January 26). On homophobia and recruiting. *ESPN The Magazine*. Retrieved from http://m.espn.go.com/wireless/story?storyId=6060641&wjb

Doherty, A. J., and K.E. Danylchuk. (1996). Transformational and transactional leadership in interuniversity athletics management. *Journal of Sport Management* 10, 292–309.

Dohrmann, G., and J. Benedict. (2011, March 7). Rap sheets, recruits and repercussions. *Sports Illustrated* pp. 31–39.

Doxsie, D. (2009, April 28). Valley bean ball incident—10 years later. *Pantagraph.com*. Retrieved from http://www.pantagraph.com/sports/college/valley-bean-ball-incident-years-later/article_f73d2e4c-d1cd-5714-9b11-3085f55184da.html

Dunning, E. (1999). *Sport matters: Sociological studies of sports, violence, and civilization*. London, UK and New York, NY: Rutledge Taylor and Francis Group.

Durkheim, E. (1933). *The division of labor in society*, translated by G. Simpson. NY: The Free Press.

Eitzen, D. S., and G.H. Sage. (2009). *Sociology of North American sport (8th ed.)*. Boulder, CO and London, UK: Paradigm Publishers.

Engwall, D., R. Hunter, and M. Steinberg. (2004). Gambling and other risk behaviors on university campuses. *Journal of American College Health* 52, 6, 245–256.

Epstein, A. (2009). Incorporating the criminal law into sports studies. *Sport Management and Related Topics (SMART) Journal* 12, 3. Retrieved January 19, 2012, from http://www.thesportjournal.org/article/incorporating-criminal-law-sport-studies

Erdley, D. (2012, January 19). Penn State trustees blindsided by Sandusky presentment. *Pittsburgh Tribune-Review*. Retrieved from http://www.pittsburghlive.com/x/pittsburghtrib/news/breaking/s_777455.html

ESPN, (n.d.), "Exclusive Jim Tressel NCAA interview audio," Retrieved from http://search.espn.go.com/jim-tressel-and-ohio-state/

Ex-Mizzou football captain pleads to assault. (2012, February 14). *USA TODAY*, n.p. Retrieved from http://www.usatoday.com/sports/college/football/story/2012-02-14/missouri-running-back-derrick-washington-pleads-guilty-to-assault/53098016/1

Experts discuss domestic violence and student-athletes. (2011, January 13). *NCAA News* p. 4.

FBI investigating point-shaving scandal. (2011, April 13). *ESPN*. Retrieved from http://sports.espn.go.com/ncb/news/story?id=6339867

Fejgin, N. (1994). Participation in high school competitive sports: A subversion of school mission or contribution to academic goals? *Sociology of Sport Journal* 11, 3, 211–230.

Foucault, M. (1977). *Discipline & punish: The birth of a prison* (A. Sheridan, trans). New York, NY: Vintage Books.

Ganim, S. (2011, November 11). Who knew what about Jerry Sandusky? There were many missed chances to investigate as early as 1995. *The Patriot-News*. Retrieved from http://blog.pennlive.com

Gatz, M., M.A. Messner, and S. J. Ball-Rokeach. (2002). *Paradoxes of youth and sport*. Albany, NY: State University of New York Press.

Halley, J. (2011, September 1). Racy photo gets Bethany golf team in trouble. *USA TODAY*. Retrieved from http://content.usatoday.com/communities/campusrivalry/post/2011/08/racy-photo-getscollege-golf-team-in-trouble/1

Hartmann, D. (2000). Rethinking the relationships between sport and race in American culture:

Golden ghettos and contested terrain. *Sociology of Sport Journal* 17, 229–253.

Hirschi, T. (1969). *Causes of delinquency*. Berkeley, CA: University of California Press.

Hit 'em hard, hit 'em often—good off-field advice for college athletes? (2011, March 15). *News Wise*. Retrieved from http://newswise.com/articles/hit-em-hard-hit-em-often-good-off-field-advice-for-college-athletes

Hogg, M.A. . and G.M. Vaughan. (2002). *Social Psychology (3rd ed.)* London: Prentice Hall.

Hood, D. (2011, October 30). Steele says defense got physically whipped. *Tigernet.com*. Retrieved from http://www.tigernet.com/view/story.do?id=10086

Hoover, N.C., (1999), "National survey: Initiation rites and athletics for NCAA sports teams," Retrieved from http://www.alfred.edu/sports_hazing/docs/hazing.pdf

Hughes, M., and C. Kroehler,. (2008). *Sociology: The core (9*th *ed.)* Boston, MA: McGraw Hill.

Johnson, G. (2011, February 10). Football rules committee recommends restrictions on blocking. *NCAA.org*.Retrievedfrom http://www.ncaa.org/wps/portal/!ut/p/c4/04_SB8K8xLLM9MSSzPy8xBz9CP0os3gjX29XJydDRwP _ wGBDA08Df3Nzd1dXQwMDA_2CbEdFALxFcuk!/?WCM_PORTLET = PC_7_2MKEBB1A0OQS10I0O77GEE10G3000000_WCM&WCM _ GLOBAL_CONTEXT = /wps/wcm/connect/public/NCAA/Resources/Latest + News/2011/February/Football + Rules + Committee + recommends + restrictions + on + blocking

Katz, A. (2011, December 11). Penalties pending after Cincinnati brawl. *ESPN.com*. Retrieved from http://sports.espn.go.com/espn/otl/news/story?id=4242983

Lavigne, P. (2009, June 14). Naked in Nebraska: A wrestler's story. *ESPN: Outside the lines*. Retrieved from http://sports.espn.go.com/espn/otl/news/story?id=4242983

Lawler, J. (2002). *Punch! Why women participate in violent sports*. Terra Haute, IN: Wish publishing.

Lindsey, Kevin. (2010, October 10). Was Wisconsin coach Bielema wrong for running up the score on the Gophers? *Bleacher Report*. Retrieved from http://bleacherreport.com/articles/487378-was-wisconsin-coach-bielema-wrong-for-running-up-the-score-on-the-gophers

Lumpkin, A., K.S. Stoll, and M.J. Beller. (2003). *Sports Ethics: Applications for fair play (3rd ed.)* Boston, MA: McGraw Hill.

MacIver, R. M. (1942). *Social Causation*. N Y: Ginn and Company.

Marx, K. and F. Engels. (1998[1845]). *The German ideology: Including theses on Feuerbach and introduction to the critique of political economy*. Amherst, NY: Prometheus Books.

Merton, R. (1968). *Social theory and social structure*. NY: The Free Press.

McGee, R. (2011, May 30). The most scandalous year ever in college sports. *ESPN The Magazine*, pp. 52–58.

Miami, FIU have 31 suspended for role in brawl. (2006, October 16). *ESPN.com*. Retrieved from http://sports.espn.go.com/espn/wire?section=ncf&id=2627453

Mills, C.W. (1959). *The sociological imagination*. London: Oxford University Press.

Munson, L. (2009, January 30). Landmark settlement in ASU rape case. *ESPN.com*. Retrieved from http://sports.espn.go.com/espn/otl/news/story?id=3871666

NCAA: Point shaving threatens college sports. (2011, April 11). *NCAA* Retrieved from http://www.ncaa.org/wps/portal/!ut/p/c4/04_SB8K8xLLM9MSSzPy8xBz9CP0os3gjX29XJydDRwP_wGBDA08Df3Nzd1dXQwMD A_2CbEdFALxFcuk!/ ?WCM_PORTLET = PC_7_2MKEBB1A0OQS10I0O77GEE10G3000000_WCM&WCM_GLOBAL_CONTEXT = /wps/wcm/connect/public/ncaa/resources/latest + news/2011/april/ncaa + point + shaving + threatens + college + sports

Neff, C. (1987, January 5). Bosworth faces the music. *Sports Illustrated*. Retrieved from http://sports.espn.go.com/espn/otl/news/story?id=4242983

Ng, C. (2012, February 6). UVA lacrosse murder trial: George Huguely pleads not guilty. *ABC News*. Retrieved from http://abcnews.go.com/US/uva-lacrosse-murder-trial-george-huguely-pleads-guilty/story?id=15522445

Olson, E. (2003, October 14). Nebraska player allegedly assaults Missouri fan. *Southeast Missourian*. Retrieved from http://www.semissourian.com/story/122139.html

Prevanas, N. (2011, August 22). Open court: Corruption becoming norm in college sports. *Green Valley News*. Retrieved from http://www.gvnews.com/sports/open-court-corruption-becoming-norm-in-college-sports/article_8bc78b0a-cd03-11e0-a188-001cc4c03286.html

Punch earns Oregon's Blount a season-long suspension. (2009, September 4). *USA TODAY.com*. Retrieved from http://www.usatoday.com/sports/college/football/pac10/2009-09-04-oregon-blount-suspension_N.htm

Quinney, R. (1977) *Class, state, and crime*. NY: David McKay.

"Results from the 2008 NCAA study on collegiate wagering," (2009, November 13), Retrieved from http://www.ncaa.org/wps/wcm/myconnect/5a30d30040962f3190739a7e5b626114/Results_2008_NCAA_Study_Collegiate_Wagering.pdf?MOD=AJPERES&CACHEID=5a30d30040962f3190739a7e5b626114

Ritzer, G. (2010). *Sociological theory (8th ed)*. Boston, MA: McGraw-Hill.

Robinson, C. (2011, August 16). Renegade Miami football booster spells out illicit benefits to players. *Yahoo! Sports*. Retrieved from http://sports.yahoo.com/investigations/news?slug=crrenegade_miami_booster_details_illicit_benefits_081611

Rood, L. (2008, August 31). College athletes and criminal charges: Some work to keep allegations quiet. *The Des Moines Register*. Retrieved from http://www.desmoinesregister.com/article/20080831/NEWS10/808310335/College-athletes-criminal-charges-Some-work-keep-allegations-quiet

Savage, H. J., H.W. Bentley, J. T. McGovern, and D.F. Smiley. (1929). American college athletics bulletin number twenty-three. *The Carnegie Foundation for the Advancement of Teaching*. NY. Retrieved from http://www.carnegiefoundation.org/publications/american-college-athletics-bulletin-number-twenty-three

School: Blount's actions 'reprehensible'. (2009, September 4). *ESPN.com*. Retrieved from http://sports.espn.go.com/ncf/news/story?id=4445891

Seifried, C.S. (2011). Sport facilities as a broadcast studio for extensibility? Geographic information systems-based diagrams of a high- and low-identified fan. *Journal of Sport Management*. Human Kinetics, Inc.

Shaw, C., and H. McKay. (1942). *Juvenile delinquency in urban areas*. Chicago, IL: University of Chicago Press.

Shoemaker, D. (2009). *Theories of delinquency: An examination of explanations of delinquent behavior (6th ed.)* NY: Oxford University Press.

Siegel, L. J. (2011). *Criminology (11th ed)*. Belmont, CA: Wadsworth.

Smith, M. D. (1981). Sports violence: A definition. *Arena Review* 5, 1, 2–8.

Southall, R. M., and M.S. Nagel. (2009). Using the theory of institutional logics to examine big-time college sport. In Smith, E., ed. *Sociology of sport and social theory* (pp. 67–80). Champaign, IL: Human Kinetics.

Sutherland, E. (1947). *Principles of Criminology (4th ed.)*. Philadelphia, PA: J.B. Lippincott.

Sykes, G. and D. Matza. (1957). Techniques of neutralization: A theory of delinquency. *American Sociological Review* 22, 664–670.

Tajfel, H., and J.C. Turner. (1979). An integrative theory of intergroup conflict. In Austin, W.G., and S. Worche, eds. *The Social Psychology of Intergroup Relations* (pp. 33–47). Monterery, CA: Brooks-Cole.

Tapper, J., and A. Taylor. (2006, April 18). Is jock culture a training ground for crime? *ABC News*. Retrieved from http://abcnews.go.com/WNT/Story?id=1857059&page=2

Thio, A., T. Calhoun, and A. Conyers. (2012). *Deviance today*. Boston, MA: Pearson.

Thomas, K. (2011, April 25). College teams, relying on deception, undermine gender equity. *The New York Times*. Retrieved from http://www.nytimes.com/2011/04/26/sports/26titleix.html

UF freshman arrested on domestic battery charge. (2012, February 16). *Rivals.com*. Retrieved from http://rivals.yahoo.com/ncaa/football/news?slug=ap-gators-playerarrested

Vaughan, D. (1999). The dark side of organizations: Mistake, misconduct, and disaster. *Annual Review of Sociology* 25, 271–305.

Vermillion, M., and C. Messer. (2011). The NCAA: An enforcement agency involved in the production of organizational deviance. *Journal of Contemporary Athletics* 5, 55–75.

Vermillion, M., G.C. Stoldt, and J. Bass. (2009). Social problems in Major League Baseball: Revisiting and expanding Talamini's analysis twenty years later. *Journal of Sport Administration and Supervision* 1,1, 23–38.

Wakefield, K.L., and D.L. Wann. (2006). An examination of dysfunctional sport fans: Method of classification and relationships with problem behaviors. *Journal of Leisure Research* 38, 168–186.

Waldron, J. J., Q. Lynn, and V. Krane. (2011). Duct tape, icy hot & paddles: Narratives of initiation onto US male sport teams. *Sport, Education and Society* 16, 111–125.

Watson, G. (2012, February 15). Tanner Brock and three other players arrested in TCU drug bust. *Yahoo! Sports*. Retrieved from http://sports.yahoo.com/blogs/ncaaf-dr-saturday/tanner-brock-three-other-players-arrested-tcu-drug-175545577.html

Woods, R. B. (2011). *Social issues in sport (2nd ed.)* Champaign, IL: Human Kinetics.

Zagier, A. S. (2012, February 14). Ex-Mizzou football captain pleads to assault. *Rivals.com*. Retrieved from http://rivals.yahoo.com/ncaa/football/news?slug=ap-missouri-washington

Insanity is doing the same thing over and over again and expecting a different result.

Albert Einstein

Those who cannot remember the past are condemned to repeat it.

George Santayana

INTRODUCTION

Pay-for-Play Debate

In 2012 college sport faced what many considered to be a seminal "pay-for-play" decision. The National Collegiate Athletic Association (NCAA) Board of Directors proposed allowing Division I athletic departments the flexibility of adding a $2,000 stipend to an athletic grant-in-aid (e.g., athletic scholarship) in order to provide athletes with awards closer to the full cost of attendance. During the override period numerous athletic departments objected, claiming such stipends would bankrupt them. In addition, some critics objected to the stipends as clearly antithetical to the concept of amateurism as embodied in the NCAA's collegiate model.

Amid the contentious pro and con debate surrounding this issue, the NCAA's position was crystallized in the March 30, 2011, issue of *USA TODAY*: "The NCAA's new president is adamant that, on his watch, there'll be no straying from college athletics' most time-honored tenet: 'It's grossly unacceptable and inappropriate to pay players ... converting them from students to employees'" (Wieberg, 2011, para.1).

In the many subsequent editorials and commentaries, however, there was no mention that

9

COLLEGE SPORT REFORM

RICHARD SOUTHALL

pay-for-play was actually not a new concept, but part of college sport's culture dating as far back as the days just after World War II.

In 1945 Wake Forest University's football team compiled a 5–3–1 (3–1–1 Southern Conference) record. At season's end Wake Forest was one of three teams considered for the inaugural Gator Bowl, to be held in Jacksonville, FL. Since it was a new bowl game, Gator Bowl officials were leery of extending a bid and being publicly rejected by a team. Therefore, prior to their "official" bid, they sought to determine each team's level of interest. As part of its decision-making process, Wake Forest officials polled their players.

According to Dr. Herb Appenzeller (a well-known sport risk-management expert and a member of the 1945 Wake Forest football team), since playing in the Gator Bowl would involve several additional weeks of practice and a long trip during the holidays, the initial vote was 33–1 against accepting a bid to play in the game (North Carolina Sports Hall of Fame, n.d.). As Appenzeller said, "We were tired and wanted to go home for Christmas break. The only guy who voted to play in the bowl game was from Florida" (Personal Communication, March 3, 2012).

While the players' preference was clear, a group of Wake Forest boosters had other ideas, believing many benefits would be derived from "their" team playing in the bowl game. While the players' vote was based on their aversion to more work (i.e., practices), the boosters saw an opportunity for good publicity for the university, an excuse for a winter Florida vacation for boosters/alumni and their families and friends, and a chance to enjoy one more football game. The boosters thought the players—not seeing the big picture—had made a shortsighted decision. The boosters asked to meet with the players so they could "encourage" them to reconsider their decision.

The next day a team meeting was held and the players were told if they would accept a bid, each player would receive $100. After a short closed-door meeting, the players voted again; the vote was 34–0 to accept a bid, if one was extended (Personal Communication, March 3, 2012).

An interesting footnote to this pay-for-play episode is that one week later—after the university had already accepted the Gator Bowl bid—the Wake Forest starters reconsidered their decision. The players were not uncomfortable turning their backs on amateurism and getting paid; they simply felt starters should be paid more than non-starters. The team reopened negotiations, demanding a $50 increase in starters' salaries. The boosters, recognizing their tenable position, quickly agreed to the players' demand (Personal Communication, March 3, 2012).

On January 1, 1946, Wake Forest played in the inaugural Gator Bowl, beating South Carolina 26–14 (Gator Bowl Association, n.d.). The Demon Deacons finished nineteenth in the final AP Poll (SR/College Football, n.d.). The game's "official" team payout, which went directly to each university, was $20,000. Newspaper accounts did not mention the "unofficial" payments to the Wake Forest players. Appenzeller does not know whether South Carolina players also received bowl-game salaries (Personal Communication, March 3, 2012).

Once More Unto the Breach

From June 2010 to March 2012, the University of North Carolina at Chapel Hill endured a very public investigation into what media accounts described as "... one of the widest-ranging scandals in recent college football history" (Curtis, 2011, para. 1). The subsequent NCAA public infractions report levied "... charges of academic fraud, unethical dealings between assistant coaches and NFL player agents and failure to monitor players' off-field activities" (Curtis, 2011, para. 2).

Long regarded as an athletic department that followed NCAA policies and did things the right way—the "Carolina Way"—the NCAA investigation and subsequent infractions report had a profound effect on UNC Athletic Association staff members, boosters, as well as UNC alumni, faculty members, and students. The penalties were the first ever imposed on the university's football program. UNC had not been involved in an athletics scandal for more than fifty years. Its iconic former men's basketball coach, Dean Smith, and former university-system president, William Friday, were both known for their strict—almost maniacal, some said—adherence to NCAA rules. Friday, cofounder of the Knight Commission on Intercollegiate Athletics, was viewed as a leading proponent of reform in big-time college sport (Maisel, 2012).

The current UNC chancellor, Holden Thorp, expressed the university's angst: "Obviously, this has been a painful, difficult experience. .We don't like to have this kind of attention brought to any part of the university, especially one as visible as the athletics program" (Maisel, 2012, para. 12). UNC's former athletic director, Dick Baddour, expressed the belief UNC would recover from the scandal, stressing there still was "… a 'Carolina way' of doing things, and reminded the media that Smith took over the Tar Heel basketball program when his boss, Frank McGuire, resigned after the NCAA put his program on probation. That turned out pretty well" (Maisel, 2012, para. 13).

UNC trustee Chair Wade Hargrove sounded a familiar refrain: "'Lessons have been learned. This university (and the) board of trustees are committed to ensuring past mistakes are not repeated,' Board Chairman Wade Hargrove said. 'We can do better. We will do better.'" (Hartness, 2011, para. 2).

Such statements conceded mistakes had been made, but indictments of big-time college sport were largely absent. "'Winning and winning within the rules are not mutually exclusive,' Hargrove said." (Hartness, 2011, para. 13).

In fact, UNC Chancellor Holden Thorp clearly identified intercollegiate athletics as being part of UNC's mission. "Public universities have to succeed in both academics and athletics" (Hartness, 2011, para. 12). In addition, Thorp noted the university's reliance on football to fund its broad-based athletic program. "'We can't succeed in athletics unless we have a competitive football program,' Thorp said, noting that football revenue is important to the university's financial structure" (Hartness, 2011, para. 12). Consistently, all accounts noted the scandal resulted from the actions of rogue individuals unwilling to abide by NCAA rules. University and athletic department administrators vowed to redouble efforts to comply with NCAA "legislation."

On Friday, February 17, 2012, approximately one hundred twenty UNC faculty members released "A statement of principles for Athletics at UNC." Media accounts described the statement as a call for "… academic integrity to take priority at the university over athletic success" (Moore, 2012, para. 1). The group's press release insisted the pursuit of athletic excellence must rest on a foundation of "academic integrity" and should always reflect the following three principles:

1. **Institutional Openness.** The university should confront openly the many conflicts created by its commitment to winning in the athletic arena. The university must commit itself to honest, open, regular conversation about the divergent imperatives, and competing values, that drive athletic and academic success. All data needed to understand the athletics department, and to address the issues raised by its operations, should be readily available.

2. **Educational Responsibility.** The university should commit itself to providing a rigorous and meaningful education to every student. All students should be integrated fully into the life of the campus, and they should be well prepared for life after college. All students—those who participate in sports and those who do not—should be permitted and encouraged to take full advantage of the rich menu of educational opportunities available at UNC.

3. Mission Consistency. Athletics must be integrated into the common enterprise of the university. Faculty committees and administration must be empowered to oversee athletics and ensure that it supports and remains in alignment with the university's core missions. In times of hardship, the university must consistently work to preserve these core missions, even if such preservation comes at the expense of athletic success (University of North Carolina at Chapel Hill, 2012, para. 13–16).

Responding to the statement, UNC's athletic director, Larry "Bubba" Cunningham, expressed support for the principles, noting "… [T]he athletic department already follows the faculty group's three 'core principles' " (Niss, 2012, para. 2). UNC alumni and fans posted a wide range of reactions to the statement and subsequent news reports and commentaries. Reactions ranged from the analytical:

> Unfortunately, colleges and universities are money making (sic) businesses (sic) which must market their schools in multi-dimensional ways to attract their best applicants. A school must have the whole package: a great academic reputation and a great social/entertainment reputation. It looks like the professor is trying to put the university in the proper place in the continuum (sic) which has a monastery on one end and a three-ring circus on the other. Good luck. (UNC General Alumni Association, 2012, para. 6),

to less than supportive:

> I think the faculty should pay more attention to teaching students and less attention to athletics (UNC General Alumni Association, 2012, para. 1),

to outright hostile:

> Is it possible that we have any faculty that could read this self-serving pile of crap and recognize how stupid it makes them look? Do they truly not realize that the only issues of true significance in the whole "football" scandal were those arising on the academic side of the University?
> … Instead they go public with drivel like this, making me and many other alumni and North Carolina taxpayers wonder just what are we really getting for our hard-earned tax dollars down in Chapel Hill. It would be humorous if it weren't so sad (UNC General Alumni Association, 2012, para. 2).

One of the faculty statement's authors expressed surprise at the backlash from college sport fans, noting most responses centered on one of three basic questions: (a) Why don't these professors mind their own business? (b) What do they know about the life of the college athlete? and (c) Why do faculty hate athletes so much? (Smith, 2012).

In the weeks following the statement's release, UNC was thrust into the national spotlight as a reminder of the need for college-sport reform. Local and national media, including the *News & Observer*, *Chronicle of Higher Education*, and *The New York Times*, as well as a plethora of websites and blogs covered the unfolding events. On February 28, 2012, UNC hosted a panel discussion, "Big-Time College Sports: What

Needs to Change." According to DeCock (2012):

> A standing-room only crowd at the Sonja Hayes Stone Center Theater on the UNC campus, one that included UNC athletic director Bubba Cunningham as well as a number of other senior athletic administrators, gathered to hear the insights of former UNC president Bill Friday, Duke professor Charles Clotfelter and civil-rights historian Taylor Branch, a visiting professor at UNC (para. 2).

DeCock (2012) summarized the panelists' positions:

- Friday wants stiffer penalties for rule-breakers and more of the TV money generated by athletics to go to academics, injured athletes and former athletes seeking to obtain a degree.
- Branch is concerned with the hypocrisy of "imposed" amateurism at the college level while the NCAA [National Collegiate Athletic Association] and universities make millions through athletics.
- Clotfelter thinks any meaningful change will have to begin by challenging trustees and other university governing bodies that have become invested in the status quo.

Commenting on the possibility of such panels leading to meaningful college sport reform, DeCock (2012) was not optimistic:

> It's going to take more than academic hand-wringing to really fix what's wrong: government intervention, in the form of a reassessment of the NCAA's tax-exempt non-profit status, and the threat of revolution, in the form of a viable alternative governing body created by current NCAA members willing to break away on their own.
>
> "If you want reform, don't look first at ESPN [Entertainment and Sports Programming Network]," Clotfelter said. "Go to the boards of trustees at our universities and ask them what they want from athletics" (paras. 11–12).

UNC, it seemed, was the new ground zero for discussions involving college sport reform. On the heels of the statement and the Friday/Branch/Clotfelter panel, Joe Nocera, *New York Times* op-ed columnist, traveled to Chapel Hill on March 14, 2012, for a program billed as "Big-Time Sports and the University: A Conversation with Joe Nocera of the *New York Times*." Flyers advertising the event highlighted several possible topics:

- Is it time to kill the N.C.A.A.?
- Should college athletes collect salaries?
- Should Universities sponsor semi-pro teams?
- Does corporate money threaten the University's mission?

Throughout his talk, and consistent with many of his columns, Nocera's primary theme was the lack of "due process" afforded NCAA athletes.

In an ironic turn of fate, the week before Nocera had visited Chapel Hill the University of Kentucky men's basketball coach, John

Calipari, considered by many the personification of big-time college basketball ills, publicly criticized college sport's inherent hypocrisy and declared the NCAA's eminent extinction:

> They're not going to be around long. The NCAA will not. Before I retire from coaching, they will no longer oversee college athletics. ... The NCAA Tournament, for example. It's more about the selection committee getting on TV, everybody getting their tickets on the aisle, down low, all the parties they go to, the traveling. But we don't take the parents of the participants. But they take their kids and their families.
>
> The decisions they make on the $2,000 (expense allowance for student-athletes) ... It's a stipend. It's not salary. It's not "pay-for-play." It's a stipend. It's expenses. And then schools vote against it. All this stuff piles up to where people are going to say, "Enough's enough" (DeCourcy, 2012, paras. 63–64).

Amid the tumultuous discourse, some UNC faculty members believed real reform might occur: "... there's an energy here that feels palpable" (Personal communication, 2012).

Increasingly, the off-the-field college sport landscape seemed replete with calls for reform or outright revolution. The calls came not only from sportswriters and columnists (Nocera, Frank Deford, Jason Whitlock et al.) and such well-known authors as Taylor Branch (Branch's *The Shame of College Sports* was published October 2011 in *The Atlantic*), but also from union leaders (National Football League Players Association Executive Director DeMaurice Smith), educators (including U.S. Secretary of Education Arnie Duncan), plaintiff attorneys (the NCAA was, as is often the case, a defendant in several lawsuits), university faculty members (UNC's group, The Drake Group, Coalition on Intercollegiate Athletics), and a wide range of reform-minded organizations (Reform the NCAA, National College Players Association, Knight Commission on Intercollegiate Athletics). Even college football players (Deunta Williams, Troy Reddick), coaches (Steve Spurrier, John Shoop), and university athletic administrators (most notably East Carolina University's Terry Holland) were increasingly offering opinions. Even the "Godfather" of amateur basketball, Sonny Vaccaro (former Nike, Adidas, and Reebok marketing executive)—to whom " ... The multibillion-dollar industry that college athletics is today can in many ways be traced" (Rice, 2011, para. 2)—was part of the conversation: "What I wanted was to spread a message about how young kids were misused in the system of the NCAA" (Rice, 2011, para. 12).

As spring 2012 turned to summer, it seemed as if the NCAA's "Collegiate Model of Intercollegiate Athletics," long under attack by critics, might undergo fundamental change. But as postings on message boards attested, many fans cared little for fundamental change within college sport; their concerns revolved around whether their team would qualify for a Bowl Championship Series (BCS) bowl game, be selected for the NCAA's March Madness basketball tournament, or avoid NCAA sanctions from the latest "impermissible benefits" scandal. Despite such benign neglect, it seemed plausible reform could give way to revolution.

The turmoil of 2012 reflected many of the same fundamental questions that have long been part of the college sport reform debate.

Rather than offering a chronology of college sport reforms, this chapter first offers a theoretical framework (institutional logics theory) through which to examine that reform. In addition, this chapter defines and deconstructs *amateurism* and, specifically, the NCAA's *Collegiate Model of Athletics*. The chapter then concludes with an expanded articulation of Sack's (2009) three distinct models of college sport reform.

Using Institutional Logics Theory to Examine College Sport Reform

For the past one hundred fifty years, the "state" of big-time college sport reform has been a tug-of-war between notions of commercialism, education, amateurism, and professionalism. Recurring scandals have inevitably led to calls for reform. Those enmeshed in college sport seek reform while still seeking to protect their model, while academicians lament the enterprise's corrosive effect on the pursuit of knowledge and clamor for reform. This dichotomous landscape of protectionism criticism reflects different philosophical assumptions and disagreements over facts.

Within individual organizations such fundamental values are often referred to as an organization's "culture." Similarly, on an institutional level what may originate as informal rules or policies often evolve into taken for granted daily assumptions or norms, reflective of an institution's goals and future expectations (Thornton & Ocasio, 2008). These prescriptions eventually become taken for granted facts or logics (Southall, Nagel, Amis, & Southall, 2008). Such institutional logics do more than just establish institutional commonalities; they offer a sense of order, history, and legitimacy (Thornton & Ocasio, 2008). Institutional logics become entrenched

within an institution's day-to-day activities and become commonplace expectations for institutional members.

These institutional social schemes become "articles of faith" from which policies, procedures, and bylaws "logically" arise. Since each institution's logics possess their own social identity, when institutions evolve or merge with other institutions conflicts between logics may arise. As a result, struggles for dominance may result in the diminishing legitimacy of what are viewed as inferior logics (Meyer and Hammerschmid, 2006).

It should be noted, however, that institutions may coexist within a field, their logics not in conflict. Also, institutional logics are not static sets of rules, but may evolve over time. Within the shared institutional field of higher education and intercollegiate athletics, contestation or conflict among these competing logics is reflected in the continual cycles of scandal and reform.

In fact, prior to 1948 (See Table 1—College Sport Reform, 1855–2012.), the NCAA did not exert a regulatory role within college sport. The "Sanity Code" is a logical outcome of the conflict between increasingly commercialized college sport logics and the logics associated with amateurism and students engaged in intercollegiate athletics as an avocation.

For a variety of reasons, it may be advantageous for institutional members to proclaim they subscribe to one set of logics within a shared institutional field, while actually operating in accordance with other conflicting logics. As the result of several historic "tipping points" (See Table 1) arising from a search for additional revenue streams to sustain big-time college-sport's growth, commercial institutional logics became operationally dominant. Simultaneously, universities recognized the need to maintain college sport's institutional legitimacy within the institution field of higher education. Providing such legitimacy it is necessary to construct a ceremonial façade, which consists of official rhetoric espousing educational values not apparent in the operational business practices of institutional actors (e.g., NCAA-member institutions, as well as coaches and corporate partners). Such brand management allows actors to operate within a set of commercial logics that justify increased revenue opportunities while simultaneously placing college athletes within an institutional field dominated by educational logics. Strategic placement of public service educational announcements within highly professionalized and commercialized college sport broadcasts (e.g., NCAA men's and women's basketball tournament and BCS bowl games) is an example of this practice (Southall et al., 2008; Southall and Nagel, 2008; Southall, Southall, & Dwyer, 2009).

Although the NCAA was originally a discussion-based body, it evolved into an umbrella institution. The NCAA has become synonymous with its "Collegiate Model of Athletics" that emphasizes a balance between academic and athletic pursuits. Since its members are educational institutions, referring to educational logics when referring to the collegiate model makes perfect sense to external observers.

The next section provides a detailed analysis of the NCAA Collegiate Model of Athletics. An understanding of the model provides a basis for the subsequent discussions of competing models of college sport reform.

Amateurism and the Collegiate Model of Athletics

Merriam-Webster Dictionary (2012) defines reform as "… amendment of what is defective, vicious, corrupt, or depraved; to amend or improve by change of form or removal of faults or abuses; to put an end to (an evil) by enforcing or introducing a better method or course of action." Inherent in the definition is an ideal, non-evil method or course of action, or a model of behavior to which we should aspire. As a result, any discussion of college sport reform presupposes an ideal form of college sport, one to which everyone associated with college sport agrees and aspires. Succinctly, the purpose of reform is to achieve and sustain a college sport ideal.

For many people associated with college sport since its inception, *amateurism* has been an integral component of idealized college sport. It is also important to remember, as Sack and Staurowsky (1998) noted, being a sporting amateur involves participation in sport as a leisure activity. For "amateur" athletes, sport is supposedly freely pursued in one's leisure or unobligated time. "Amateur sport, as the term has been defined historically and as it is currently defined in the NCAA Manual, is an 'avocation,' meaning that it is a form of leisure activity" (Sack & Staurowsky, 1998, p. 4). From this perspective the fundamental distinction between college and professional sport is that college sport is connected to education and the athletes are not paid.

NCAA documents clearly reveal the NCAA has long recognized the importance of aligning college sport with amateurism, especially in light of big-time college sport's increased commercialism:

> Critical for the future of intercollegiate athletics will likely be a better

understood definition of amateurism that isolates the principle to the way in which student-athletes are viewed without imposing its avocational nature on revenue-producing opportunities. This is largely a Division I issue because of the ability of institutions in that division to better capitalize interest in their sports. To that end, the work of the Division I Amateurism Cabinet will be an important plat-form (sic) for addressing this challenge (National Collegiate Athletic Association, 2010a, para. 3).

Such alignment has practical business advantages as well, since "[t]he principle of amateurism has served intercollegiate athletics well in litigation where courts have held that the NCAA is permitted a certain degree of discretion in its efforts to preserve the concept" (National Collegiate Athletic Association, 2010a, para. 2).

The NCAA's effort to develop a formalized Collegiate Model of Athletics was the brainchild of the late NCAA President Myles Brand, a philosopher who made contributions to the philosophy of action, and was keenly aware of the power of language in forming perceptions. Just as had former NCAA Executive Director Walter Byer, who created the term "student-athlete," Brand sought to engender spontaneous consent and support for a modified definition of amateurism in college sport through the propagation and acceptance of the Collegiate Model of Athletics as a "term of art" (National Collegiate Athletic Association, 2010c, para. 1). He intended the Collegiate Model of Athletics "… as a surrogate for—but not a replacement for—the concept of amateurism to the degree it was too

frequently used as a descriptor for intercollegiate athletics" (National Collegiate Athletic Association, 2010c, para. 1). Brand intended to clearly demarcate "… college sports from The Professional Model of Athletics. As he described it, he wanted the term (created in 2003) to change the way people talked about intercollegiate athletics" (National Collegiate Athletic Association, 2010c, para. 1).

To achieve such demarcation, two basic principles must be consistently highlighted: "(1) Those who participate in college sports are students, and (2) intercollegiate athletics is embedded in the values and mission of higher education" (National Collegiate Athletic Association, 2010c, para 2). According to NCAA documents, in all comparisons between the two models, a professional athlete must be negatively characterized as a member of "… a work force, a commodity that can be traded from team to team" (National Collegiate Athletic Association, 2010c, para. 2). Meanwhile, to protect the collegiate model, it must be emphasized college athletes are students engaged in a mere avocation. In addition, when describing the professional model, the ultimate goal must be seen to be revenue generation through entertainment. Conversely, though generating revenue is necessary for the support of athletic programs, such activities should be de-emphasized. In this portrayal the collegiate model's goal "… is to acquire an education, including learning the value of hard work and team work, self-sacrifice and self-discipline, resilience and persistence, and the pursuit of excellence" (National Collegiate Athletic Association, 2010c, para. 2).

Ultimately, professional sport is framed as a mercenary activity, in which a community and its fans are held hostage by a professional franchise:

In the professional model, the team is connected to a community only so long as the community supports the franchise through the building and maintenance of facilities and the purchase of tickets. In the collegiate model, the team is enduringly connected to a community through the sponsoring college or university (National Collegiate Athletic Association, 2010c, para. 2).

For college sport advocates, the Collegiate Model of Athletics is a worthwhile university ancillary; therefore, protecting this model is a vital function of the NCAA and its president:

Protecting the collegiate model is nearly by definition the primary focus of the office of the NCAA president. As the voice and face of intercollegiate athletics, the president must continually reinforce the concept and steadily build the context for the relationship of intercollegiate athletics to higher education (National Collegiate Athletic Association, 2010c, para. 1).

In order to protect the collegiate model of athletics, throughout the first two decades of the twenty-first century the NCAA engaged in "… an aggressive public and media relations agenda that addresse[d] critics when" in the NCAA's view "… they inaccurately characterize[d] college sports" (National Collegiate Athletic Association, 2010c, para. 4). The NCAA's agenda included utilizing emerging new-media platforms (e.g., Twitter, blogs, and social media) to protect the collegiate model and provide an alternative to what the NCAA's national staff described as "…

the doggerel of cynics" (National Collegiate Athletic Association, 2010c, para. 4).

Clashing Models of College Sport Reform

While twenty-first century reformers continued to offer thoughtful reform proposals, their positions remained firmly grounded in three twentieth century reform models. The basic elements of these models: 1) college sport is incompatible with universities' intellectual pursuits; 2) intercollegiate athletics benefits the vast majority of college athletes (four hundred thousand of whom will go pro in something other than sports) and is consistent with modern universities' focus on entrepreneurial academic capitalism; and 3) to provide educational and athletic opportunities for nonrevenue sports, big-time college sport exploits a labor force of NCAA Football Bowl Subdivision (FBS) football and men's basketball players.

Since its inception, intercollegiate athletics proponents have described it as a uniquely American enterprise and highlighted its academic, educational, and participatory elements. Conversely, most college sport reformers have noted big-time college sport's overtly commercial, corporate, or spectator-driven facets. Almost universally, reformers assume "… commercialism and professionalism are incompatible with traditional academic values" (Sack, 2009, p. 77). Calls for reform reflect "… an inherent tension between the intellectual independence of the academy and the use of corporate dollars to support any aspect of higher education" (National Collegiate Athletic Association, 2010b, para. 2). Tensions between the idealized collegiate model and big-time college sport's reality reveal themselves in three clashing reform models: (a) intellectual elitism, (b) academic or jock capitalism, and (c) athletes' rights (Sack, 2009; Southall & Nagel, 2010).

In addition, most reformers focus on two NCAA Division I sports, FBS football and men's basketball (and, to a lesser extent, women's basketball, baseball, and hockey). For the most part, reform discussions bypass Division I "Olympic" nonrevenue sports, or athletic programs in NCAA Division II and Division III. They also, most often, refer to intercollegiate athletics as organized and conducted in the Ivy League and Division III as approximating the college sport ideal. A solid grasp of these theoretical models can provide a mechanism for understanding the historic arc of college sport reform.

Intellectual Elitism

Intellectual elitists decry commercialized big-time college sport's negative influence on higher education's academic integrity. Intellectual elitists are determined to "... defend academic integrity in the face of the burgeoning college sport industry" (The Drake Group, n.d.). Some noteworthy reformers who would most likely be viewed as intellectual elitists include William Dowling; John Gerdy; The Drake Group (TDG) founder Jon Ericson; Frank Splitt; and William Friday, cofounder of the Knight Commission on Intercollegiate Athletics. These reformers contend rampant commercialism and television and corporate sponsors' search for profits have led to a loss of academic integrity in higher education. Sack summarized this position's primary criticisms of commercialized college sport:

> To win games and keep the revenue flowing, universities recruit athletes with embarrassingly low academic credentials, and keep them eligible by turning a blind eye to cheating or by steering them into courses with little academic substance (Sack, 2009, p. 78).

According to this model, universities pursue revenue and waive normal enrollment standards, *cluster* athletes in specific majors or courses, and construct multimillion-dollar athletic-academic support facilities. Such outcomes reflect an inherent conflict between highly commercialized college sport and universities' intellectual activities.

Intellectual elitists are highly critical of "athletic scholarships" or what the NCAA terms "grant-in-aids." Awarding financial aid based on athletic performance invariably attracts athletes whose priority is athletics rather than traditional academics. In addition, athletic grant-in-aids give coaches inordinate control over athletes, subverting a chance for a meaningful student-professor relationship. Succinctly, intellectual elitists see one purpose of a university: "... not to create athletes, but well-educated citizens" (Sack, 2009, p. 78). Intellectual elitists, especially those who are professors at large research-intensive universities (many of which also sponsor big-time college football and men's basketball), bemoan not only highly commercialized college sport, but also rampant academic capitalism.

Academic/Jock Capitalism

Not surprisingly, intellectual elitists are sometimes criticized as being out of touch with reality, ensconced in the "ivory towers" on predominately white universities. For academic capitalists, big-time college sport is culturally significant. While research and teaching are two important university functions, a third seems to be providing students, faculty members, alumni, trustees, and other university stakeholders with top-flight football and men's basketball programs. Such programs are widely popular and serve an important role as the "front porch of the university," a tie that binds colleges to various communities.

Academic capitalism emphasizes a university's fiscal bottom line. Southall and Nagel (2010) took academic capitalism's major tenets and developed a college sport specific model: "jock capitalism." For jock capitalists, as long as commercialism and revenue generation associated with big-time college sport is done tastefully, it is consistent with the collegiate model.

Adhering to modern-day market capitalism, jock capitalists apply "market economic theory" to big-time athletic department business functions and reject commercialism as incompatible with intercollegiate athletics and higher education in general. The NCAA notes "[c]ommercialism has been a part of intercollegiate athletics from its earliest beginning" (National Collegiate Athletic Association, 2010b, para. 1). Universities that sponsor big-time sports programs are well aware of the enterprise's inherent costs and recognize the need to generate revenue sufficient to support broad-based athletic departments. For university stakeholders, benefits that accrue to a university from participating in big-time college sport simply outweigh costs. Revenue sports, in addition to providing "educational benefits" for their athletes, are business ventures that must generate revenue for the rest of the athletic department in order to provide athletic and academic opportunities for non-revenue sport athletes.

Not surprisingly, jock capitalist reform efforts seek to protect "amateurism" or the collegiate model while not inhibiting big-time college sport's business practices. This was clearly articulated in Brand's 2006 State of the Association address:

> Our mission is to ensure that intercollegiate athletics participation is an integral part of the higher-education experience. ... Using 'business' and 'college sports' in the same sentence is not the same as labeling college sports as a business. It is not. College sports exhibits business aspects only when it comes to revenues—the enterprise is nonprofit on the expenditure side. ... [W]e will be inflexible in our devotion to principles and in our commitment to higher education (Brand, 2006, para. 2, 10, 16, emphasis in original).

Jock capitalists believe engaging in big-time commercialized college sport is necessary to achieve "good" educational goals for the vast majority of college athletes. Jock capitalists see no inherent conflict between commercial and educational institutional logics. This belief—to which institutional members are inflexibly committed—situates legitimate reform efforts as those that occur within the existing institutional structure. Since college athletes are not employees, but students, jock capitalists view commercialism as consistent with the collegiate model. Consequently, highly commercialized college sport activities that mimic those of professional sport in all ways except for player compensation are acceptable since they help achieve educational goals.

Jock capitalism's institutional logics allow for revenue sports to operate as business ventures that generate revenue for the rest of the athletic department—in order to provide athletic and academic opportunities for the four hundred thousand student-athletes "who will be going pro in something other than sports." Therefore, maximizing football and men's basketball revenue streams is both necessary and desirable.

Jock capitalist reform efforts focus on ensuring NCAA and member athletic department academic outcomes are met. Within this model, ensuring athletes graduate equates with maintaining academic integrity. Notable academic reform efforts consistent with this model are the result of the NCAA's Academic Performance Program (APP), which includes the Academic Progress Rate (APR) and the Graduation Success Rate (GSR) (National Collegiate Athletic Association, 2012a). Since the introduction of the APP the NCAA has reported increased graduation rates for college athletes (National Collegiate Athletic Association, 2012a).

Athletes' Rights

Athletes' rights advocates recognize big-time college sport is deeply embedded within the cultural fabric of universities and U.S. society; however, they view athletic grant-in-aids as employment contracts, not educational gifts. They contend terms such as "student-athlete" and "amateurism" are primarily tools used to defend the business of college sport and achieve *hegemony* within college sport's institutional field.

Gramsci defined hegemony as "... the 'spontaneous' consent given by the great masses of the population to the general direction imposed on social life by the dominant fundamental group [*hegemon*]" (Gramsci, 1971, p. 12). The institution of college sport maintains its hegemony through the use of language, persuasion, and subtle and not so subtle coercion by members of the "athletic-industrial complex" (Smith, 2009). The NCAA is the most visible organization within the college sport field, but it is not the only institutional entity. The institute of college sport is an increasingly sophisticated and complex corporate web.

Within this institutional setting, when jock capitalists argue that amateurism defines the participants, but not the enterprise, athletes' rights advocates see this as a formula for exploitation (Sack, 2009). Within a higher education setting, athletes' rights advocates argue that revenue-sport athletes "... deserve the same educational opportunities as any other students; as workers, they deserve the same rights as any other employees (McCormick & McCormick, 2008).

Within an increasingly unstable institutional field, one of the NCAA's functions is to maintain a semblance of order and stability, and allow for institutional stakeholders to engage in the business of college sport. Athletes' rights advocates criticize the NCAA and university presidents' jock capitalist belief that "... there should be more, not less, [commercialism] as long as it stays within the framework of amateurism and promotes the accomplishments of the athletes and their teams" (Smith, 2009b, p. 28). They support their view of the NCAA as the institution's "shell corporation" by referring to a statement by Tim McGhee, executive director of corporate sponsorship at AT&T (NCAA Corporate Champion): "I see an NCAA that is more responsive to corporate partners and how we market our products and services" (Smith, 2009b, p. 28).

Athletes' rights advocates contend the NCAA, through its access to traditional new-media platforms and developed educational metrics (e.g., APR and GSR), has sought control of the dialogue surrounding the college sport industry for its university members and their dominant corporate partners. Both groups prefer to be seen as separate from each other. Media partners (e.g., Turner Sports, CBS, ESPN, and Fox) and the plethora of corporate entities that populate the college sport business landscape (e.g., BCS, IMG, Learfield, CLC et al.) prefer to be seen as merely supporting college sport. They prefer fans think of college sport as amateur and nonprofit, not as a multibillion-dollar industry.

Protecting the Collegiate Model

The most visible personification of the institution of college sport and the individual most responsible for perpetuating college sport hegemony is the NCAA president. Consequently, the NCAA president's single most important duty is to protect the collegiate model. This duty is clearly outlined in NCAA documents:

> Protecting the collegiate model is nearly by definition the primary focus of the office of the NCAA president. As the voice and face of intercollegiate athletics, the president must continually reinforce the concept and steadily build the context for the relationship of intercollegiate athletics to higher education. It will be critical to begin re-establishing through messaging with the use of various communication platforms the concept of the collegiate model.

It is also critical to understand that the term serves as a template for behavior by those engaged in college sports. The consistent use of the term—with the steady drumbeat of what it means—can be an effective constraint on practices that threaten to estrange intercollegiate athletics from higher education or from those firmly held perceptions that endear college sports to the American public (National Collegiate Athletic Association, 2010c, para. 3).

In response to criticism by athletes' rights advocates and in order to protect the collegiate model, in 2010 the NCAA launched an "… aggressive public and media relations agenda that addresse[d] critics when they inaccurately characterize college sports" (National Collegiate Athletic Association, 2010c, para. 4). As part of a strategy to address both intellectual elitists and athletes' rights advocates, the organization fully engaged "… emerging platforms for social interaction (blogs, Twitter, other social networks) … to provide an alternative to the doggerel of cynics" (National Collegiate Athletic Association, 2010c, para. 4).

The campaign sought to draw attention to improvements in graduation rates and the NCAA's forceful response to academic scandals.

The NCAA identifies clear distinctions between the collegiate and professional models of athletics. From this perspective, professional sports' sole purpose is profitable entertainment. Contrarily, the collegiate model's primary purpose is to enhance the educational development of students who participate in intercollegiate athletics.

Company Towns: An Emerging Concept in College Sport Reform

Aware the individuals most directly responsible for generating billions of dollars in college sport revenue—the athletes themselves—are being treated in a manner many deem unfair and exploitative, but also recognizing especially provocative labels may also stir sensitivities that distract from the core issues at stake—the fair treatment of the athletes—Weiler and Southall (2012) describe revenue-sport athletes as existing within college sport "company towns." They propose this metaphor provides a more accurate depiction of football and men's basketball players' circumstances, while also highlighting a long tradition of injustice in the American workplace to which, somewhat incredibly, a particular class of individuals is still subject in 2012.

In practice, big-time college sport programs fall somewhere on the spectrum between two extremes—*educational utopia* and *exploitation*. While neither pole perfectly encapsulates the experience of athletes in revenue-generating college sports, the company-town existence of turn-of-the-twentieth-century workers and twenty-first century big-time revenue-sport college athletes are analogous:

- Athletes' housing and socialization patterns often reflect segregated existences, in which they are physically, culturally, and socially isolated from the rest of the campus community, much as residents in company towns lived in relative isolation.
- Athletic department staff and coaches very carefully monitor and scrutinize athletes' behavior (especially revenue-sport players), much more so than is the case for the general student body. The recent flap over whether college athletes have a right to use social media, a right that every other student possesses, is but one example.
- While the NCAA insists it does not "pay" college athletes, an athletic grant-in-aid is a tightly controlled form of payment, akin to "scrip." While consistently described as not being "pay," jock capitalists continually refer to a "full-ride" scholarship's extremely high monetary value in order to play up its worth. But for the large percentage of athletes in revenue sports who do not graduate, the "value" of a scholarship is particularly degraded (College Sport Research Institute, 2010, 2011). Indeed, an athletic grant-in-aid denies players access to a market-recognized medium of exchange (i.e., cash). As such, college athletes are like company town employees who could only use their payment to redeem goods at company-owned stores (often at very inflated prices). Such "nonpayment" has the effect of preventing athletes the freedom to market their services within a functioning market economy.
- Particularly in football, by far the most lucrative college sport property, players face endemic health problems. In recent years research on football players' head trauma and its potential long-term negative health effects has cast a pall over the sport. As a result, while the extensive health services provided to the athletes may appear to be generous, they can also be viewed as capital expenditures to protect universities' investments in the labor-force engine that drives the collegiate model.
- Mirroring historic hostility to union organization or worker advocacy efforts among capitalists and many state legislators, calls for meaningful, independent representation of athletes have been repeatedly

rebuffed by the NCAA and legislatures. The mismatch in power, resources, and leverage between the NCAA and its corporate partners on the one hand (backed by the tolerance of state and federal law for their position), and that of unorganized workers/athletes is especially striking.

- The NCAA justifies its stance toward athletes via systematic paternalism. It treats the athletes well, providing them with room and board, health benefits, and educational opportunities (the more benevolent company towns invested significantly in educational opportunities for the workers and their families); it affords them opportunities otherwise unavailable to the athletes or other students; it provides for their futures; it cloisters the athletes in a secure and congenial setting that maximizes their productivity and ostensibly potential for future growth and development.

This paternalistic college sport perspective, which refers to athletic departments' beneficence, is precisely the argument used by company town industrialists to defend their monopolistic practices.

Unlike indentured servants or slaves, but similar to company town workers, college athletes are "free" labor. They are not compelled to participate in college sport. Also, involvement in intercollegiate athletics is not a right, but a privilege. According to accepted notions of what is meant by freedom, the fact minority college athletes might have disproportionately fewer alternatives for improving their circumstances does not change this fact.

Company towns were often the creation of larger economic entities, such as U.S. Steel, which maintained a number of such towns. Likewise, the NCAA sits in a particular relationship to member institutions that bear immediate responsibility for the practices described above.

Revenue-sport athletes are not necessarily physically separated from the rest of the student body, but their rights and privileges differ from those of all other students, including athletes in other sports. Transfer rules and the right to turn professional (golfers and tennis players can do this without restriction, for instance) all mark them as separate from other students. Their freedom of movement is more restricted, a condition of the terms of their "payment." The fact that they sign away lifetime rights to their likenesses is illustrative of this "special treatment" and suggests they live in a "company town" whose boundaries might be invisible, or nonphysical, but nevertheless clearly differentiate them from all other students on campus.

A "Modest" Radical Reform Proposal

The history of college sport reform suggests institutional change proceeds at a pace somewhat less than glacial. Seemingly moderate reform proposals, such as multiyear grant-in-aids or minimal cost of living increases, reveal college presidents, faculty athletic representatives, university athletic administrators, coaches, and even college athletes consistently resist change. While conceding reform may be morally and practically justified, they cling to the status quo.

Such reactions demonstrate the institution of college sport and those members who occupy the field may be ill equipped to discover or develop real solutions to big-time college sport's issues. Viewing the world through the institution's logics, these stakeholders may be unable or unwilling to spontaneously withdraw their spontaneous assent. They're trapped within big-time college sport's hegemony.

Recognizing eighteenth century definitions of amateurism may be offensive to some, defenders of the collegiate model freely concede that free-market forces (e.g., television, corporate sponsorship, BCS, coaches' salaries, rampant professionalism in certain sports, etc.) exist, but claim such forces are probably beyond their control and may actually benefit the four hundred thousand student-athletes "who will go pro in something other than sports."

But since the fictitious collegiate model does not reflect today's big-time NCAA Division I college football and men's basketball athletics-as-entertainment juggernaut, any reforms developed to protect the collegiate model are most likely doomed. The collegiate model, if it ever existed, died long ago. For a variety of reasons, substantive change will not come from the NCAA, university presidents, Congress, or state legislatures.

Nevertheless, just as *Brown v. Topeka Board of Education* overturned *Plessy v. Ferguson* and ended segregation in public education, a current class-action lawsuit (*O'Bannon v. NCAA*), or a yet-to-be-filed case, may be the catalyst for substantive change. If the court finds the NCAA's collegiate model violates the Sherman Act, college sport may be forced to create a new model, incorporating aspects of the international Olympic system, in which professional and amateur athletes coexist.

If the NCAA would be deemed a monopoly and ordered to restructure, current NCAA Football Bowl Subdivision (FBS) and men's Division I basketball players might also be recognized as employees (an accepted reality for many scholars), while other college athletes would retain their "amateur" status.

Undoubtedly, this would require major legal and economic changes to the current collegiate model. College sport—as it has developed over the past one hundred fifty years—would cease to exist, but such reformation would not mean the end of Western civilization. Significant market changes would result, but other industries (e.g., telecommunications, air transportation, and petroleum) compelled to transition from monopolistic to free-market economies have survived and even thrived.

A post–collegiate model world could include two non-NCAA college football and men's basketball organizations whose member teams would play their games in existing college facilities and still provide entertainment for alumni, students, and fans. Players could be members of a players' association that would negotiate employment conditions. Not wanting to adopt this clearly professionalized model, some universities might choose to de-emphasize big-time college sport and revert to a model more clearly aligned with many elements of the collegiate model.

Within this new institutional field college football and men's basketball players would be employees. As a result, it would be necessary to sort out (perhaps in court) how Title IX does or does not apply. There also would be significant tax and workers' compensation implications, and college coaches' and administrators' markets would be affected. Similar to many athletic departments today, big-time college football and basketball programs might be structured as separate corporate entities associated with (or sponsored by) university communities, but operated as for profit or not-for-profit entities. Athletes' rights advocates would most likely contend fans would retain their emotional attachments to these teams, but player exploitation would be greatly diminished.

If such reform occurred, the institution of college sport would be fundamentally altered. Universities, however, could still provide non-entertainment athletic opportunities for students in nonrevenue sports. The NCAA (just as it does currently) could provide governance for these sports, or existing national governing bodies (NGBs) could step in and provide organizational structure. Within this new reality the scale and scope of "Olympic" sports would be scaled back, allowing these students to concentrate on their educational experiences—surely a welcome development.

A Proposed Structure

In such a hybrid model, college football and men's basketball players could sign multi-year contracts for a maximum of five years (one "in-active" season would be allowed). Programs could provide players with room and board—an easily budgeted fixed cost. A negotiated salary structure could involve a minimum salary scale for first-year players, with annual salary increases. As would be expected, starters would make more than nonstarters.

A proposed multilevel salary structure might look something like this:

- Level 4: fourth-year starter
- Level 3: third–year starter
- Level 2: second-year starter
- Level 1: first-year starter

To incentivize performance, players could receive end-of-season bonuses based on a team's final conference standing (each conference would set its bonus amounts based upon a specific revenue source. Just as within the current collegiate model, coaching salaries would vary based on market forces.

Players could, if their association thought it important, negotiate educational benefits be included in every contract. Being interested in these individuals' education, universities could offer a variety of educational benefits including three semesters of full tuition, and books and fees "vouchers" for each season a player is on a team's roster. A player could choose to redeem all or some of the vouchers while playing or just retain the credits and attend school full time after completing his playing career. A player would be free to attend school full time and complete his bachelor's and/or master's degrees during his college sport career. A team could, if it desired, incentivize being a full-time student while playing. Such a voucher program would recognize the value of a college education, but remove the current system's inherent hypocrisy, reflected in the need to resort to hyphenated words, such as "student-athlete" when referring to players.

Lifetime health insurance might be a negotiated benefit. Premiums would increase for players who have exhausted their eligibility, but lifetime coverage should be a negotiated benefit. Premiums could be based on players' post–career income levels and players could opt out of the program, but players should have unfettered access to health insurance.

In addition to negotiated salaries, players could also receive a percentage of royalties from products utilizing their names and likenesses, based upon an agreed-upon calculus. Players would be able to negotiate endorsements deals similarly to those for coaches within the collegiate model.

Without a doubt, these proposals are not consistent with the NCAA's current collegiate model. But it is an honest and honorable proposal. Adopting this "radical" reform proposal would allow universities to return to their core educational mission.

SUMMARY

Reform has been synonymous with college sport from its inception. An examination of the historical record reveals competing philosophies or institutional logics. Those involved in college sport—administrators, faculty members, fans, coaches, and players—view intercollegiate athletics through their unique lens. In the second decade of the twenty-first century, U.S. college sport once again finds itself enmeshed in a cycle of reform. The NCAA contends things are getting better, while critics complain intercollegiate athletics is at an all-time low. Prospects for substantive change seem elusive, but stakeholders continue to discuss reform.

Meanwhile, the games go on … spring turns to summer … March Madness concludes … spring practice continues … recruiting never stops … message boards circulate rumors … players declare for the draft … final exams … reform proposals wind through the NCAA legislative process … columnists chronicle the latest scandal … reform is in the air.

REFERENCES

Brand, M. (2006, January 7). 2006 State of the association address. *NCAA.org. Online.* Retrieved from http://www.ncaa.org/wps/wcm/myconnect/public/ncaa/about+the+ncaa/who+we+are/myles+brand+legacy/legacy+of+leadership/2006+ncaa+state+of+the+association

Byers, W., and C. Hammer. (1995). *Unsportsmanlike conduct: Exploiting college athletes.* Ann Arbor, MI: The University of Michigan Press.

College Sport Research Institute, (2010), "Adjusted graduation gap report: NCAA Division I football," Retrieved from http://exss.unc.edu/research-and-laboratories/college-sport-research-institute/research/

College Sport Research Institute, (2010), "Adjusted graduation gap: NCAA men's and women's basketball," Retrieved from http://exss.unc.edu/research-and-laboratories/college-sport-research-institute/research/

College Sport Research Institute, (2011), "Adjusted graduation gap: NCAA Division I football," Retrieved from http://exss.unc.edu/research-and-laboratories/college-sport-research-institute/research/

Curtis, D. (2011, June 22). North Carolina football violations outlined in NCAA notice. *Sporting News.* Retrieved from http://aol.sportingnews.com/ncaa-football/feed/2010-08/unc-investigation/story/north-carolina-football-facing-several-serious-ncaa-violations#ixzz1qB5rzJdM

DeCock, L. (2012, February 28). Panel explores NCAA reform. *newsobserver.com.* Retrieved from http://blogs.newsobserver.com/accnow/panel-explores-ncaa-reform

DeCourcy, M. (2012, March 5). Kentucky coach John Calipari: "I've got the best job in basketball." *Sporting News.* Retrieved from http://aol.sportingnews.com/ncaa-basketball/story/2012-03-05/kentucky-coach-john-calipari-ive-got-maybe-the-best-job-in-basketball#ixzz1oO5tPwTT

Gator Bowl Association, (n.d.), "History of the Gator Bowl," Retrieved from http://www.gatorbowl.com/?page_id=606

Gramsci, A. (1971). The Intellectuals. In *Selections from the Prison Notebooks*. Hoare, Q., and and G. N. Smith, eds., (p. 3–23). New York: International Publishers.

Hartness, E. (2011, September 22). UNC chairman: "Lessons learned" in football scandal. *Wralsportsfan.com*. Retrieved from http://www.wralsportsfan.com/unc/story/10168341

Maisel, I. (2012, March 12). Scandal stains UNC's reputation. *ESPN.com*. Retrieved from http://espn.go.com/college-football/story/_/id/7678094/butch-davis-era-sets-north-carolina-tar-heels-back

McCormick, A. C., and R.A. McCormick. (2008). The emperor's new clothes: Lifting the NCAA's veil of amateurism. *San Diego Law Review* 45, 495–545.

Meyer, R.E., and G. Hammerschmid. (2006). Changing Institutional Logics and Executive Identities: A Managerial Challenge to Public Administration in Austria. *American Behavioral Scientist* 49, 1000–1014.

Moore, H. (2012, February 17). UNC faculty make stand for academics over athletics. *TWEAN Newschannel of Raleigh*. Retrieved from http://triangle.news14.com/content/top_stories/653948/unc-faculty-make-stand-for-academics-over-athletics

National Collegiate Athletic Association. (2010a). Amateurism. *President's Briefing Document*. Retrieved from http://fs.ncaa.org/Docs/newmedia/2010/Emmert/Part5/amateurism.html

National Collegiate Athletic Association. (2010b), Commercialism. *President's Briefing Document*. Retrieved from http://fs.ncaa.org/Docs/newmedia/2010/Emmert/Part5/commercialism.html

National Collegiate Athletic Association. (2010c). Protecting the Collegiate Model. *President's Briefing Document*. Retrieved from http://fs.ncaa.org/Docs/newmedia/2010/Emmert/Part5/protecting.html

National Collegiate Athletic Association, (2012), "Academic information about colleges," Retrieved from http://www.ncaa.org/wps/wcm/connect/public/ncaa/academics/how+academic+reform+is+measured

Niss, S. (2012, February 27). UNC athletic director responds to faculty statement on athletics and academics. *dailytarheel.com*. Retrieved from http://www.dailytarheel.com/index.php/article/2012/02/faculty_athletics_0224

North Carolina Sports Hall of Fame, (n.d.), "Herb Appenzeller—2010," Retrieved from http://www.ncshof.org/inductees_detail.php?i_recid=290

Rice, L. (2011, April 4). At HLS symposium, the "godfather of grassroots basketball" decries exploitation of college athletes. *Harvard Law School*. Retrieved from http://www.law.harvard.edu/news/spotlight/student-pursuits/sonny-vaccaro-sports-law-symposium.html

Sack, A. (2009). Clashing models of commercial sport in higher education: Implications for reform and scholarly research. *Journal of Issues in Intercollegiate Athletics* 3, 76–92. Retrieved from http://csri-jiia.org/documents/puclications/research_articles/2009/JIIA_2009_6_Clashing%20Models%20of%20Commercial%20Sport.pdf

Sack, A. L., and E. J. Staurowsky. (1998). *College athletes for hire: The evolution and legacy of the NCAA's amateur myth*. Westport, CT: Praeger Publishers.

Smith, E. (2009a). *Race, sport and the American dream*. Chapel Hill, NC: Carolina Academic Press.

Smith. M. (2009b, September 21-27). The right man at the right time: NCAA's Brand brought academic reform, a respect for need to generate revenue. *Street & Smith's SportsBusiness Journal* 12(21), 1, 28–29.

Smith, J. (2012, February 28). Student comes before "athlete." —Article. *Newsobserver.com*. Retrieved from http://www.newsobserver.com/2012/02/28/1889227/student-comes-before-athlete.html

Southall, R. M., and M.S. Nagel. (2008). A case-study analysis of NCAA division I women's basketball tournament broadcasts: Educational or commercial activity? *International Journal of Sport Communication* 1, 516–533.

Southall, R. M., M.S. Nagel, J. Amis, J., and C. Southall. (2008). A method to March Madness: Institutional logics and the 2006 National Collegiate Athletic Association Division I men's basketball tournament. *Journal of Sport Management* 22(6), 677–700.

Southall, R. M.,and M. S. Nagel. (2009, December 17). Big-time college sports contested terrain: Jock capitalism, educational values, and social good. *Human Kinetics Sport Management News*. Retrieved from http://www.humankinetics.com/hkarticles/hk-articles/big-time-college-sports-contested-terrain-jock-capitalism-educational-values-and-social-good?associate=5167

Southall, R. M., C. Southall, and B. Dwyer. (2009). 2009 bowl championship series telecasts: Expression of big-time college-sports commercial institutional logics. *Journal of Issues in Intercollegiate Athletics* 2, 150–176.

Retrieved from http://csri-jiia.org/documents/puclications/research_articles/2009/JIIA_2009_9_BCS_Institutional_Logics.pdf

SR/College Football, (n.d.), "1945 Wake Forest Demon Deacons schedule and results," Retrieved from http://www.sports-reference.com/cfb/schools/wake-forest/1945-schedule.html

The Drake Group, (n.d.), "Home," Retrieved from http://www.thedrakegroup.org/index.html

Thornton, P. H., and W. Ocasio. (2008). Institutional logics. In Greenwood, R., C. Oliver, R. Suddaby, and K. Sahlin-Andersson, eds. *The Sage Handbook of Organizational Institutionalism* (p. 99–127). Thousand Oaks, CA: Sage Publications.

UNC General Alumni Association, (2012, February 21), "Letters from readers … Faculty members seek unity between academics, athletics," Retrieved from http://alumni.unc.edu/article.aspx?sid=8746

University of North Carolina at Chapel Hill. (2012, February 17). Faculty group issues statement on athletic principles. *uncnews.unc.edu*. Retrieved from http://uncnews.unc.edu/content/view/5103/68/Wieberg, S. (2011, March 29). NCAA president: Time to discuss players getting sliver of revenue pie. *USA TODAY*. Retrieved from http://www.usatoday.com/sports/college/mensbasketball/2011-03-29-ncaa-pay-for-play-final-four_N.htm

Weiler, J., and R.M. Southall. (2012). *Sold my soul to the company store: College athletic departments as "company towns."* Manuscript in preparation.

Table 1. College Sport Reform, 1855–2012

Year	Organization	Document/Action
1855	Harvard University	Harvard crew agrees to not permit graduate students to compete in regattas.
1871	Harvard University	Harvard faculty limits baseball games to Saturdays and holidays.
1881	Princeton University	Faculty Committee on Athletics policies regarding absences from campus.
1882	Harvard Athletics Committee	Prohibits competition against professionals and regulates hiring of coaches.
1883	Harvard Athletics Committee	*Harvard Athletics Committee Resolutions*
1889	Intercollegiate Football Association	Special convention to discuss amateurism and eligibility issues.
1898	Brown University	*Brown Conference Report*
1906	IAAUS (NCAA)	*Proceedings of the First Annual Convention*
1916	NCAA	NCAA Constitution defines amateurism.
1922	NCAA	9- or 10-Point Code approved—No power to enforce code.
1929	Carnegie Foundation	*American College Athletics*
1931	Carnegie Foundation	*The Study of Athletics in American Universities and Colleges*
1934	NCAA	Creates Eligibility Committee—No enforcement powers.
1935	University of North Carolina at Chapel Hill	President Frank Graham outlines plan for college sport reform: No athletic scholarships or recruiting.
1935	National Association of State Universities	Graham Plan adopted.
1935	Southeastern Conference	Votes to "openly" offer athletic scholarships that exceed expenses in lieu of "under the table" payments.
1941	NCAA Institutions	Majority of presidents indicate NCAA should be given legislative and enforcement powers.
1946–1948	NCAA & Conferences	*Principles for the Conduct of Intercollegiate Athletics (Sanity Code)*
1949	University of Virginia	Resolves not to conform to the "Sanity Code."
1950	NCAA	Motion to expel the seven "Sanity Code" violators fails to garner two-thirds vote (111–93). Code dies.
1951	NCAA	Eliminates controls over financial aid to athletes and NCAA enforcement powers.
1951	NCAA	Votes to enforce national television contract provisions.
1951	CCNY and West Point	Point-shaving and academic cheating scandals.
1951	NCAA	Walter Byers becomes first NCAA executive director.

Year	Organization	Document/Action
1952	NCAA Council	12-Point Reform Package
1952	ACE	Creates Special Committee on Athletic Policy.
1952	Ivy League	Bans postseason, bowl games, spring practice, and athlete subsidization.
1952	NCAA Council	Sanctions University of Kentucky with one-year "death penalty." As a result, members boycott Kentucky and it is banned from NCAA basketball tournament.
1953	Conference of Conferences	Plans developed for investigative and enforcement cooperation between conferences and NCAA.
1954	Ivy League	Ivy Agreement institutes "freshmen" ineligibility and three years of eligibility, bans athletic scholarships, and mandates "progress" toward degree.
1956	NCAA	Allows "full-ride" athletic scholarships.
1957	NCAA	"Full-ride" scholarships include tuition and fees, room and board, and $15 "incidental" stipend.
1965	NCAA	1.6 freshmen GPA grant-in-aid and eligibility requirement.
1966	Division for Girls and Women's Sports	Commission on Intercollegiate Athletics for Women (CIAW) formed.
1968	NCAA	Subdivides membership status into "College" and "University" divisions.
1968	NCAA	Freshmen eligibility allowed for all sports except football and basketball.
1972	CIAW	Renamed Association for Intercollegiate Athletics for Women (AIAW).
1972	NCAA	Freshmen eligibility instituted for football and basketball.
1972	U.S. Congress	Title IX of Education Amendments Act passed.
1973	NCAA Special Convention	Membership realigned into three self-determined "divisions"—I, II, and III (except in football, which has classification requirements).
1973	NCAA	One-year scholarship (grant-in-aid) adopted by show of hands following no debate.
1973	NCAA	1.6 GPA repealed—replaced by 2.0 high school GPA
1974	ACE	*An Inquiry into the Need for and Feasibility of a National Study of Intercollegiate Athletics*
1974	US Congress	Buckley Amendment (FERPA) becomes law.
1975–1977	Various NCAA members	Discussion leads to formation of College Football Association (CFA), which promotes Division I football and works to increase TV revenue.

Year	Organization	Document/Action
1975	NCAA Special Convention	Enactment of various "cost-containment" measures: squad size and grant-in-aid limits.
1977	ACE	Establishes Commission on Athletics—Possible athletic proposals published in *Educational Record*.
1978	NCAA	Division I subdivided into Division IA and IAA.
1981	NCAA	Adopts governance plan including women's athletic programs.
1981	CARE	Center for Athletes' Rights and Education (CARE)—*Athletes' Bill of Rights* drafted.
1981	NCAA	First women's championships are held.
1982	UNC, Harvard, and ACE	Lobby NCAA to reinstitute first-year ineligibility.
1983	NCAA	*Select Committee on Athletics Problems and Concerns in Higher Education*
1983	NCAA	Adoption of Proposition 48.
1983	ACE	Proposes formation of Board of Presidents that would have power to veto NCAA "proposals."
1983	NCAA	Creates "advisory" Presidents Commission to help "reform" college sport.
1984	U.S. Supreme Court	*NCAA v. Board of Regents.* NCAA TV policy found to be a violation of Sherman Antitrust Act.
1987	NCAA	Delivers "death penalty" to Southern Methodist University football program.
1987	NCAA	Rejects Presidents Commission proposal to reduce football and basketball grant-in-aids.
1989	NCAA	Passes Proposition 42.
1989	Knight Foundation	Creation of Commission on Intercollegiate Athletics
1990	AAUP	*The Role of Faculty in the Governance of College Athletics*
1991	AAUP	*Statement on Intercollegiate Athletics*
1991	Knight Commission	*Keeping Faith with the Student-Athlete: A New Model for Intercollegiate Athletics*
1991	U.S. Congress	Hearing held on National College Athletics Accountability Act.
1991	U.S. Congress	House subcommittee hearings raise issues related to standardized tests, which have been the basis for Propositions 48 and 42.
1991	NCAA	Restricted-earning coaches' category proposal enacted.
1991	Rex Lee Commission	*Rex Lee Commission Report* makes eleven recommendations regarding NCAA enforcement, including: open meetings, neutral judges, and preliminary notice of impending investigations.

Year	Organization	Document/Action
1992	NCAA	Adoption of Proposition 16 (sliding scale).
1992	Knight Commission	*A Solid Start: A Report on Reform of Intercollegiate Athletics*
1993	Knight Commission	*A New Century: Intercollegiate Athletics in the United States*
1994	U.S. Congress	*Equity in Athletics Disclosure Act*
1996	NCAA	Division I approves (115–0) new "Board of Directors" and "Management Council" structure. Institutional voting abolished; faculty representation reduced.
1996	NCAA	Proposition 16 modifies Proposition 48: Core courses and sliding scale for HS GPA and standardized test scores.
1999	NCAA	Reacting to *Cureton v. NCAA,* the NCAA changes Proposition 16 eligibility rules.
1999	NCAA	Reacting to *Law v. NCAA,* the NCAA settles restricted-earning coaches' case for $54.5 million.
1999	NACAR	Holds conference calling for faculty to reform college sport. Renames itself The Drake Group.
2000	Pac 10 Conference Faculty Senates	Pass resolutions supporting college sport reform.
2000	COIA	National faculty-senate organization—Coalition on Intercollegiate Athletics (COIA)—formed.
2001	CAC/NCPA	College Athletes Coalition formed. Later renamed the National College Players Association.
2001	Knight Commission	*A Call to Action: Reconnecting College Sports and Higher Education.*
2002	NCAA	Division I increases its minimum progress-toward-degree and GPA requirements.
2003	NCAA	NCAA President Myles Brand articulates "The Collegiate Model" at National Symposium on Athletics Reform.
2003	AAUP	*The Faculty Role in the Reform of Intercollegiate Athletics*
2003	COIA	*A Framework for Comprehensive Athletics Reform*
2003	COIA	Announces a national network of faculty leaders from fifty universities in six conferences.
2003	The Drake Group	*Reclaiming Academic Primacy in Higher Education*
2004	NCAA	Myles Brand expands the concept of the collegiate model during *State of the Association Address.*
2004	PCAR	Presidential Coalition for Athletics Reform meets. Purpose is to reform the Bowl Championship Series (BCS).

Year	Organization	Document/Action
2004	COIA	*Campus Athletics Governance, the Faculty Role*
2004	The Drake Group	*The Faculty-Driven Movement to Reform Big-Time College Sports*
2004	Knight Commission	*Challenging the Myth: A Review of the Links among College Athletic Success, Student Quality, and Donations*
2004	NCAA	Adopts Academic Performance Program (APP), which includes Academic Progress Rate (APR) and Graduation Success Rate (GSR) metrics
2005	NCAA	Division I board passes proposals to penalize teams with low graduation rates by imposing loss of scholarships.
2005	NCAA	Fifty-member Presidential Task Force formed. Examines rapid increase in expenses in Division I (arms race).
2005	COIA	*Academic Integrity in Intercollegiate Athletics: Principles, Rules, and Best Practices*
2005	COIA/NCAA	*A Report to the NCAA Presidential Task Force*
2005	NCAA	Committee on Academic Performance (CAP) revises APR to allow athletes who "depart for professional opportunities" to count as a "1-for-1" instead of a "1-for-2."
2005	NCAA	*Presidential Task Force on Future of Division I Intercollegiate Athletics Report*
2006	U.S. Congress	*Letter to NCAA President Myles Brand*
2006	NCAA	*Reply to October 2, 2006, Letter of the Honorable William Thomas*
2006	The Drake Group	*A Commentary on NCAA President Myles Brand's November 13, 2006, Reply to the Honorable William Thomas's Letter of October 2, 2006*
2007	COIA	*Framing the Future: Reforming Intercollegiate Athletics*
2007	College Sport Research Institute	College Sport Research Institute (CSRI) founded at the University of Memphis.
2007	Knight Commission	Faculty summit on intercollegiate athletics held.
2007	Knight Commission	*Faculty Perceptions of Intercollegiate Athletics: A National Study of Faculty at NCAA D-I FBS Institutions*
2008	NCAA/FARA	NCAA Faculty Athletics Representative Association survey reveals members report "lack of power over athletics" and a membership that is "too white and too male."
2008	CSRI	Inaugural CSRI Scholarly Conference on College Sport.
2008	NCAA	First-year eligibility requirements adjusted: Sliding scale (high school GPA and SAT/ACT scores) and sixteen core high school courses.

Year	Organization	Document/Action
2008	NCAA	NCAA CAP policies regarding transfers adjusted.
2008	CSRI	CSRI relocates to the University of North Carolina at Chapel Hill.
2008	NCAA	Coaches' APR created.
2009	NCAA	Inaugural Scholarly Colloquium on Intercollegiate Athletics held at NCAA Convention.
2009	Knight Commission	*Quantitative and Qualitative Research with Football Bowl Subdivision University Presidents on the Costs and Financing of Intercollegiate Athletics*
2009	U.S. courts	*O'Bannon v. NCAA* filed in the U.S. District Court Northern District of California.
2009	NCAA	Fifth anniversary of APR and GSR.
2010	Knight Commission	*Restoring the Balance: Dollars, Values, and the Future of College Sports*
2010	CSRI	Inaugural Adjusted Graduation Gap (AGG) Report released.
2011	U.S. courts	*O'Bannon v. NCAA* certified as a class-action lawsuit.
2011	NCAA	Presidential Retreat (fifty-four D-I presidents) held.
2012	NCAA	Multiyear scholarships "allowed" in Division I.
2012	NCAA	NCAA Division I Board of Directors affirms support for $2,000 additional stipend. NCAA working group directed to develop recommendations for implementation.
2012	UNC faculty	*Statement of Principles for Athletics at UNC*
2012	NCAA	*University Of North Carolina, Chapel Hill Public Infractions Report*
2012	CSRI	5th Annual CSRI Conference on College Sport.
2012	COIA	*Report to the Membership*

Adapted and expanded from (Benford, 2007; Smith, 2011)

IAAUS, Intercollegiate Athletic Association of the United States; NCAA, National Collegiate Athletics Association; ACE, American Council on Education; AAUP, American Association of University Professors.

ONE HUNDRED YEARS AND COUNTING: RESOURCES FOR GAINING AN UNDERSTANDING OF COLLEGE SPORT REFORM

Over the past one hundred-plus years, college sport has been continually reformed. As has been outlined in this chapter, reform efforts can be grouped according to alignment with various models of college sport reform. For anyone interested in exploring the history of college sport reform, the following list of books, reports, and articles provides a place to begin the journey. The list is not exhaustive and any omitted contributions simply reflect the limitations of my bookshelf. I hope this list is helpful to you in your exploration. Part of any journey is its uniqueness.

RESOURCES

Benford, R. D. (2007). The college sports reform movement: Reframing the "edutainment" industry. *The Sociological Quarterly* 48, 1–28.

Bowen, W. G., and S.A. Levin. (2003). *Reclaiming the game: College sports and educational values*. Princeton, NJ: Princeton University Press.

Branch, T. (2011, October). The shame of college sports. *The Atlantic*. Retrieved from http://www.theatlantic.com/magazine/archive/2011/10/the-shame-of-college-sports/8643

Branch, T. (2012). *The cartel: Inside the rise and imminent fall of the NCAA*. San Francisco: Byliner.

Byers, W., and C. Hammer. (1995). *Unsportsmanlike conduct: Exploiting college athletes*. Ann Arbor, MI: the University of Michigan Press.

Chu, D. (1989). *The character of American higher education & intercollegiate sport*. Albany, NY: State University of New York Press.

Clotfelter, C. T. (2011). *Big-time sports in the American universities*. New York: Cambridge University Press.

Duderstadt, J. J. (2003). *Intercollegiate athletics and the American university: A university president's perspective*. Ann Arbor, MI: The University of Michigan Press.

Dunnavant, K. (2004). *The fifty-year seduction: How television manipulated college football, from the birth of the modern NCAA to the creation of the BCS*. NY: St. Martin's Press.

Falla, J. (1981). *NCAA: The voice of college sports*. Mission, KS: National Collegiate Athletic Association.

Feinstein, J. (2000). *The last amateurs: Playing for glory and honor in division I college basketball*. Boston, MA: Little, Brown.

Fleisher, A. A., B.L. Goff, and R.D. Tollison. (1992). *The national collegiate athletic association: A study in cartel behavior*. Chicago: The University of Chicago Press.

Gerdy, J. R. (2006). *Air ball: American education's failed experiment with elite athletics*. Oxford, MS: University Press of Mississippi.

Hawkins, B. (2010). *The new plantation: Black athletes, college sport, and predominately white NCAA institutions*. New York: Palgrave Macmillan

Hutchins, R. M. (1938, December 3). Gate receipts and glory. *Saturday Evening Post*.

Sack, A. L. (2008). *Counterfeit Amateurs: An athlete's journey through the sixties to the age of academic capitalism*. University Park, PA: The Pennsylvania University Press.

Sack, A. L., and E.J. Staurowsky. (1998). *College athletes for hire: The evolution and legacy of the NCAA's amateur myth.* Westport, CT: Praeger Publishers.

Shulman, J. L., and W.G. Bowen. (2001). *The game of life: College sports and educational values.* Princeton, NJ: Princeton University Press.

Smith, R. A. (1988). *Sports & freedom: The rise of big-time college athletics.* New York: Oxford University Press.

Smith, R. A. (2011). *Pay for play: A history of big-time college athletic reform.* Urbana, IL: University of Illinois Press.

Sperber, M. (1990). *College sports inc.: The athletic department v. the university.* New York: Henry Holt and Company, Inc.

Sperber, M. (2000). *Beer and circus: How big-time college sports is crippling undergraduate education.* New York: Henry Holt and Company.

St. John, W. (2004). *Rammer jammer yellow hammer: A journey into the heart of fan mania.* New York: Crown Publishers.

Telander, R. (1996). *The hundred yard lie: The corruption of college football and what we can do to stop it.* Chicago: University of Illinois Press.

Thelin, J. R. (1994). *Games colleges play: Scandal and reform in intercollegiate athletics.* London: The Johns Hopkins University Press.

Toma, J. D. (2003). *Football U: Spectator sports in the life of the university.* Ann Arbor, MI: The University of Michigan Press.

Yaeger, D. (1991). *Undue process: The NCAA's injustice for all.* Champaign, IL: Sagamore Publishing Inc.

Yost, M. (2010). *Varsity green: A behind the scenes look at culture and corruption in college athletics.* Palo Alto, CA: Stanford University Press.

Zimbalist, A. (1999). *Unpaid professionals: Commercialism and conflict in big-time college sports.* Princeton, NJ: Princeton University Press.

Author Bios

Gary Sailes is an Associate Professor in the Department of Kinesiology at Indiana University. His scholarly interest is Critical Race Theory in American Sport. As a consultant, he has led two Congressional hearings on college sports abuses and lectures to the NCAA and college athletic departments on student athlete, coach and staff professional development.

Bobbi Knapp is an Assistant Professor in the Department of Kinesiology, with a cross appointment in Women, Gender and Sexuality Studies, at Southern Illinois University in Carbondale. Her research focuses on issues of gender within the sporting realm, such as the exploration of issues regarding women's experiences in football. She is also the co-founder of WIN for Southern Illinois, a not for profit organization whose mission is to educate and empower girls and women through sport.

B. David Ridpath is an Associate Professor and the Khan Nandola Professor of Sport Administration at Ohio University in the Department of Sports Administration and College of Business. He has several years of practical experience in the sports industry and teaches classes in marketing, sponsorship, risk management, sports law, and issues in intercollegiate athletics.

Christian Gilde is an Assistant Professor of Business in the Business and Technology Department at the University of Montana Western. His scholarly interests include marketing, consumer behavior, sport sociology and management and he serves as a reviewer for journals such as the *Journal of Consumer Behaviour* and the *Southwest Teaching and Learning Journal*.

Michael Malec is Associate Professor in the Department of Sociology at Boston College. He is a Past-President of the North American Society for the Sociology of Sport and former Editor of *The Journal of Sport and Social Issues*.

Emmett Gill is an Assistant Professor in Residence in the Department of Athletics at North Carolina Central University. He is the National Coordinator of the Student-Athletes Human Rights Project.

Kristi McLeod Fondren is an Assistant Professor in the Department of Sociology and Anthropology at Marshall University. Her research interests in sports revolve around the

257

process of recruiting and the student-athlete experience, as well as how institutional identities intersect with the recruiting process.

John N. Singer is an Associate Professor of Sport Management in the Department of Health and Kinesiology at Texas A&M University. His research focuses primarily on critical race issues in sport contexts.

Akilah R. Carter-Francique is an Assistant Professor in the Department of Health and Kinesiology at Texas A&M University. Her scholarship focuses on critical investigations with people of color and women in the sport and physical activity context. Through these investigations she works to provide culturally relevant solutions promoting social justice and empowerment (see Sista to Sista™ at www.sistatosista.org).

Jacqueline McDowell is an Assistant Professor in the Department of Recreation, Sport and Tourism at the University of Illinois at Urbana-Champaign. Her research focuses on diversity and inclusion issues in sport and recreation with a particular focus on workplace and participation identity issues and structural, social and psychological constraints and facilitators.

Jennifer Lee Hoffman is an Assistant Professor in the Center for Leadership in Athletics at the University of Washington. Her research examines the relationship between intercollegiate athletics and higher education. She has published work on the tensions between market and educational interests, equity in athletics and education, and leadership in intercollegiate athletics.

Brian T. Gearity is an Assistant Professor in the School of Human Performance and Recreation at the University of Southern Mississippi. His research focuses on psychosocial aspects of quality coaching and coach education. He also specializes in qualitative research methods and is currently conducting an ethnographic study of coaching high school football.

Janelle E. Wells is an Assistant Professor in the Department of Sport Management at Florida State University. She researches leadership strategies and development in the field of sport. Specifically, she has examined leadership behaviors and career development of underrepresented individuals in collegiate athletics.

Mark Vermillion is an Associate Professor in the Department of Sport Management at Wichita State University. His research and teaching focuses on the sociocultural and psychological foundations of sport with a special emphasis on understanding crime and deviant behavior in sport. He has worked with student-athletes and sport practitioners regarding diverse topics, such as student development, organizational leadership strategies, and sport-specific consumer research projects.

Chris M. Messer is an Associate Professor in the Department of Sociology at Colorado State University-Pueblo. He has authored several articles and a book from his research in the areas of Organizational Deviance, Social Movements and the Sociology of Sport.

Krista Bridgmon is an Associate Professor in the Department of Psychology at Colorado State University Pueblo and a Licensed Psychologist. Her research interests and publications include topics in higher education stress and coping, doctoral student attrition and educational psychology.

Richard M. Southall is an Associate Professor in the Department of Sport and Entertainment Management at the University of South Carolina and Director of the College Sport Research Institute (CSRI). He examines college athlete graduation rates, as well as legal, ethical and institutional issues within the college-sport industry, having spent the past 12 years investigating and deconstructing the NCAA's Collegiate Model of Athletics.

CPSIA information can be obtained at www.ICGtesting.com
Printed in the USA
LVOW09s2029100915

453700LV00001B/1/P